American Cabinetmakers

ALSO BY WILLIAM C. KETCHUM, JR.

Early Potters and Potteries of New York State (1970, 1987)

The Pottery and Porcelain Collectors Handbook (1971)

American Basketry and Woodenware (1974)

A Treasury of American Bottles (1975)

Hooked Rugs (1976)

The Catalogue of American Antiques (1977, 1980, 1984, 1990)

The Family Treasury of Antiques (1978)

The Catalogue of American Collectibles (1979, 1984, 1990)

Collecting American Craft Antiques (1980)

Auction (1980)

Western Memorabilia (1980)

Toys and Games (Smithsonian Illustrated Library of Antiques) (1981)

Furniture, Vol. II (Smithsonian Illustrated Library of Antiques) (1981)

The Catalogue of World Antiques (1981)

Boxes (Smithsonian Illustrated Library of Antiques) (1982)

Chests, Cupboards, Desks, and Other Pieces (1982)

Pottery and Porcelain (1983)

American Folk Art of the Twentieth Century (1983)

Collecting Bottles for Fun and Profit (1985)

Collecting Toys for Fun and Profit (1985)

Collecting Sporting Memorabilia for Fun and Profit (1985)

Collecting the 40's and 50's for Fun and Profit (1985)

All American Folk Art and Crafts (1986)

American Country Pottery (1987)

Holiday Ornaments and Antiques (1990)

American Redware (1990)

How to Make a Living in Antiques (1990)

Country Wreaths and Baskets (1991)

American Stoneware (1991)

Collecting the West (1993)

Western Memorabilia (1993)

American Pottery and Porcelain (1994)

American Cabinetmakers

MARKED AMERICAN FURNITURE, 1640–1940

WILLIAM C. KETCHUM, JR., WITH
THE MUSEUM OF AMERICAN FOLK ART

CROWN PUBLISHERS, INC.
NEW YORK

Published by Crown Publishers, Inc., 201 East 50th Street, New York, New York 10022. Member of the Crown Publishing Group.

Random House, Inc. New York, Toronto, London, Sydney, Auckland

CROWN is a trademark of Crown Publishers, Inc.

Manufactured in the United States of America

Design by Kay Schuckhart

Library of Congress Cataloging-in-Publication Data
Ketchum, William C., 1931
    American cabinetmakers : marked American furniture 1640–1940 /
William C. Ketchum, Jr., with the Museum of American Folk Art—1st ed.
    Includes bibliographical references and index.
    1. Furniture—United States—Marks.   I. Museum of American Folk
Art.   II. Title.
NK2405.K48   1995
749.213'0278—dc20   94-40639
                                                                CIP

ISBN 0-517-59562-1

10   9   8   7   6   5   4   3   2   1

First Edition

CONTENTS

When the Museum of American Folk Art was organized in 1961, its founders contemplated the development of a comprehensive library on all aspects of the American folk arts, to support exhibition planning, research, and publications at the institution. During the Museum's early years, its library began to take shape under the volunteer direction of Millia Davenport Harkavy, well known as an expert on American costume. It was not until the early 1980s, however—when the Museum received a gift of the collection of books, catalogs, and pamphlets assembled by the pioneering scholar Jean Lipman and her late husband, Howard—that efforts to create a comprehensive library were undertaken. It fell to Edith Croft Wise, the Museum's very gifted librarian from 1983 until her retirement in 1992, to create a true resource for the study of folk art. As the Museum's assistant director during that period, I had the privilege of working closely with Mrs. Wise in these efforts. My predecessor as director of the Museum, Dr. Robert Bishop, took a deeply encouraging interest in the library and eventually donated a portion of his own collection to enhance its holdings.

In 1990 he asked me whether I thought the Museum's library would be a fitting repository for the photographs, clippings, and notes on labeled furniture that he had begun to compile with Katherine B. Hagler almost two decades before. As noted in the Introduction to this book, Dr. Bishop had intended this material to be the basis of a reference work on the subject. After assuming the directorship of the Museum of American Folk Art in 1977, however, he turned his attention to other projects, and the book he hoped to publish was never undertaken, although many other works sprang forth from his prolific pen.

The materials that Robert Bishop had assembled for the book were concerned principally with "high style" furniture rather than the folk arts, but I suggested to him that the Museum's library would be an excellent place for them to be housed, because they would find regular use by researchers and students in the Museum's Folk Art Institute. Since the Museum's educational programs, including the library, were dedicated to an understanding of all aspects of American folk art in the broader context of American history, culture, and the decorative arts, these files would serve an important role in bridging the gap between "folk" and "fine." Soon after, Dr. Bishop arranged for his research materials to be delivered to the Museum, where expert volunteers Eugene P. Sheehy and Rita G. Keckeissen organized them.

Robert Bishop died in 1991, leaving a profound legacy in the Museum to which he devoted such dedication and creative energy. In discussing his contributions to the Museum with William C. Ketchum, Jr., a distinguished author in the field of American folk and decorative arts and an instructor at the Museum's Folk Art Institute, I mentioned Dr. Bishop's file of research materials on labeled furniture. After reviewing this material, Mr. Ketchum accepted my invitation to undertake the project originally envisioned by Dr. Bishop. I am delighted not only that this valuable book has been published by Crown in association with the Museum library, but that Robert Bishop's hopes for the material that he placed in the Museum's care are now fully realized. With the assistance of a number of students (Joan Bloom, Jennifer Brody, William Brooks, Suzanne Demish, Dodie Dohoney, Juliette V. Ibelli, Linda Moore, Joan

Pearlman, and Patricia Wells) in the Museum's Folk Art Institute, William Ketchum substantially augmented the materials assembled by Dr. Bishop and Katherine Hagler, and has produced an exceptionally useful reference work. I am deeply grateful to him for accepting my challenge and to Crown Publishers for recognizing the importance of this project. The Museum has earned a national reputation for the quality of its exhibitions and educational projects; I am pleased that this splendid reference work will focus attention on its library.

—GERARD C. WERTKIN

Every book has a story behind it, and this one is no exception. *American Cabinetmakers* was to have been Robert Bishop's retirement project, a retirement that, sadly, he was not able to realize. In the 1970s, as museum editor and consulting curator of furniture at Greenfield Village and Henry Ford Museum, Bob Bishop recognized the great need for a user-friendly reference book, similar to Laughlin's *Pewter in America* or the Kovels' *Dictionary of Marks: Pottery and Porcelain,* that would allow collectors, dealers, and museum personnel to identify the surprisingly large number of marked pieces of American furniture that still survive.

In association with another member of the museum staff, Katherine B. Hagler, Associate Curator of Furniture, he began the project that proceeded rapidly for several years. Some 800 turners and cabinetmakers were documented, and a substantial number of illustrations were acquired from the Henry Ford Museum and other cooperating institutions. However, Dr. Bishop's acceptance of the directorship of the Museum of American Folk Art and Mrs. Hagler's death effectively brought an end to the project. Little new material was added to the files after 1978.

It was always, though, Bob's intention that the book be finished. I recall him referring to it at dinner during the 1980s as "one of many retirement projects." Accordingly, when, following Bob's death in 1991, his successor as museum director, Gerard C. Wertkin, asked me to complete the project, I was delighted to undertake the task.

It has proven a formidable one. Well assisted in research by students in the museum's Folk Art Institute, I have been able to double the number of known makers of marked or labeled furniture. Moreover, chiefly through the unstinting cooperation of America's two great antique furniture dealerships, Bernard and S. Dean Levy, Inc., and Israel Sack, Inc., we have been able to acquire many previously unpublished images of marked furniture.

That more than 1,500 turners and cabinetmakers marked their products in some way— by label, stamp, brand, stencil, or inscription in ink, pencil, paint, or chalk—will come as a surprise to many in the field. None of the standard references, such as Ethel Hall Bjerkoe's *The Cabinetmakers of America,* has hinted at such numbers. However, over the past twenty years a large number of specialized books in the field have been written, and when these are combined with the endless stream of highly specific articles on American furniture makers published monthly in *The Magazine Antiques* as well as other periodicals, the material available for research increases greatly.

Indeed, without limits the field becomes overly large. However, Robert Bishop, early on, established guidelines for the book; and we have adhered to these. Because it deals with men who

Banner of the New York City Chairmakers' Society, which was carried by members during parades and important civic events. Chair- and cabinetmakers were among the most important early-American artisans. Courtesy, the Hitchcock Chair Company, Riverton, Conn.

worked in wood, it excludes cast iron, wire, wicker or rattan, and other alien materials. Because it deals with furniture makers, those who produced clocks or musical instruments such as pianos are not included unless they are known to have made cases as well as contents. Because *maker* is the operative term, those who sold rather than made mirrors and frames are not included, even though this distinction has proven difficult since many looking glass manufacturers also imported wares. One may argue with these limitations, but they have served well to define the scope of the book.

It should also be noted that the marks have not been edited. Each has been included exactly as set down by the maker, with Old English *f*'s for *s*'s, with misspelling and odd grammar. And, where two versions or printings of a mark or label are known, the differences are recognized.

However, in keeping with the book's purpose, to serve as a reference for makers' marks, only a brief outline of each turner's or cabinetmaker's history is included. Those desiring more detailed information (where available) should refer to the books and periodicals cited at the end of each entry. In line with Robert Bishop's dislike for pedantic footnoting, these have been kept as simple and direct as possible.

American Cabinetmakers

Manufacturers' marks on furniture, like those on silver, pewter, and other objects, served to identify the maker and to encourage potential customers to buy other work from his hand. The advantage of such identification (assuming one is producing a quality product) is obvious, yet it was not until the late eighteenth century that makers' marks began to appear on American furniture. A strong Puritan ethical opposition to such self-promotion had much to do with this. Indeed, among certain religious groups, such as the Shakers, strictures against signature pieces were so strong that only a tiny portion of the known work can be so identified.

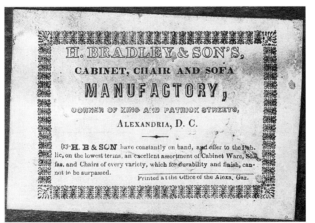

Among the general business public, however, the custom of marking furniture, as well as other manufactured products, became general after 1800. These marks took several forms. A name, or rarely, initials might be simply scratched into the raw wood, often in an inconspicuous place, such as a drawer bottom or inside the back of a cupboard. The signature might be written in one of several media—pencil (perhaps the most popular), ink, paint, white chalk, or red joiner's chalk. The date of manufacture and even location might be added. Such documentation is extremely valuable, both historically and financially.

A marked piece may serve to identify other unmarked pieces that show similar techniques of design and construction. Moreover, within the antiques world, it is well recognized that a piece bearing the signature of a known American cabinetmaker can be worth three to five times what an unmarked piece of similar quality and form would bring.

Another early method of marking furniture was with a metal hand stamp, which could be used to hammer a name or initials into the soft wood. If heated, such a stamp would produce a singed burned mark referred to as a brand. Impressed marks and brands were particularly popular with Windsor chair makers, who found that the pine bottoms of their chairs were well suited to receive such marks. Most, though not all, of these manufacturers spelled out at least their last names. However, there were a small number of craftsmen—such as Job Allen, who used the logo *JAA,* and Robert Rhea, who was content with nothing more than an *R*—who used only initials. While Appendix A lists initials associated with known cabinetmakers, there are undoubtedly others whose marks have not been identified. Appendix B lists currently unidentified initials.

The problem of identification of such initial marks is compounded by the fact that many early owners of American furniture also stamped or branded their possessions, both to deter theft and to make identification possible in case of major city fires, during which the furnishings of numerous houses might be carried into the streets and mixed together in the desperate attempt to avoid the flames.

The next step in marking was the introduction of labels. Some of these were nothing more than a piece of paper on which the name and address of the cabinetmaker were written in ink. Others were printed and contained specific information not only as to the name and location of the craftsman but also as to the types of furniture he made. Finally, there were the most expensive, engraved labels, such as those used by Joseph Meeks & Sons of New York City, which were illustrated with examples of furniture made by the cabinetmaker or even a representation of his factory or warerooms.

Labels are extremely important in the identification and dating of northeastern furniture. However, they rarely are found in the South, not because they were not used but rather because a combination of heat, damp, and insects has led to their destruction.

After 1825 stenciled marks became popular, especially among the growing number of midwestern furniture factories. A sheet metal or cardboard stencil and an ink pad or paintbrush could quickly and inexpensively identify a maker. Those who wanted something a bit more lavish might employ a stamped brass label or even, in rare cases, a porcelain plaque.

In some cases, as with the work of Gustav Stickley, one is likely to find a combination of marks. His pieces often bore both an impressed stamp and a paper label. Other craftsmen, particularly chairmakers, might in a fit of enthusiasm mark a piece several times or in several places. The variations are endless.

One thing is certain, though. Anyone interested in American furniture should examine pieces closely for marks. They are often in obscure locations and hard to read, but once located they document the piece and related examples and greatly enhance its value.

✺A✺

ABBOT, DANIEL

Two birdcage Windsor side chairs owned by the Society for the Preservation of New England Antiquities bear beneath the seat the stamped mark

D. ABBOT & CO.

Daniel Abbot (also spelled Abbott) was a chair-maker working on Middle Street in New-buryport, Massachusetts, c. 1809–1815. In partnership with Benjamin McAllstar before June 6, 1809, on that date he established the firm D. Abbot & Co., which is thought to have remained active until around 1815. Ref.: Fales, *Essex County Furniture.*

ABBOTT, JOSEPH

A small Empire mahogany desk and book-case or secretary sold at auction in August 1994 is signed and dated

Joseph Abbott/S. Andover/June 5, 1847

It is attributed to a cabinetmaker of that name working in South Andover, Massachusetts, c. 1830–1850. Ref.: *Bee,* August 12, 1994.

Small mahogany Empire desk and bookcase or secretary signed by the South Andover, Massachusetts, cabinetmaker Joseph Abbott and dated June 5, 1847. Courtesy, Bider's Auction Gallery.

ABERNATHY BROTHERS

A mirrored dresser in the Victorian Renais-sance Revival style is in a private New Mexico collection. The back has been ink-stamped

ABERNATHY BROS. MAKERS/ LEAVENWORTH, KAN.

and the piece dates c. 1870–1900. Nothing is currently known of the manufacturers. Ref.: Lonn Taylor and Dessa Bokides, *New Mexican Furniture, 1640–1900* (Santa Fe: Museum of New Mexico Press, 1987).

ACKERMAN, GEORGE

A large, two-door kas of paneled construc-tion in the collection of the Ohio

Historical Society is inscribed

> Made by George Ackerman, William Knemmule, Otto Seitz and Jacob Ackerman, March 27, 1896, Zoar, Ohio

George Ackerman and his fellow craftsmen were members of the Zoar sect, active at Zoar, Ohio, c. 1817–1898. Ref.: *Zoar Furniture, 1817–1898: A Preliminary Study* (New Philadelphia, Ohio: Tuscarawas County Historical Society, 1978).

ACKERMAN, JACOB

See George Ackerman.

ACKLEY, JOHN BREINTNALL

Located on Front Street in Philadelphia as early as 1790, John Breintnall Ackley was a prolific maker of Windsor chairs in many forms until about 1805, when he became a druggist and apothecary. A rare set of four bow-back Windsors with upholstered seats bear his partial printed paper label:

> ALL KINDS OF/Windsor Chairs and Settees/ made and sold . . . painted/any color by/ John B. Ackley/ North Front St. Philadelphia/ 1796

More common is Ackley's impressed stamp:

> I.B.ACKLEY

which has been found on bamboo-turned bow-back Windsor side and armchairs, a comb-back writing-arm Windsor, a birdcage Windsor armchair, a Windsor high chair, and an unusual pair of Gothic ladder-back Windsor armchairs now at the Independence National Historical Park in Philadelphia. Refs.: Bjerkoe; Fairbanks and Bates; Santore II.

ACKLEY, MASSEY

The impressed mark

> M. ACKLEY

on a Windsor side chair in the Winterthur collection is thought to be that of Massey Ackley,

Bamboo-turned comb-back writing-arm Windsor chair, c. 1796–1805, with the label and brand of the Philadelphia chairmaker John B. Ackley (working c. 1790–1805). Courtesy, Bernard and S. Dean Levy, Inc., New York.

Detail of the partial label and impressed brand, I.B.ACKLEY, of the Philadelphia Windsor chair maker John B. Ackley. Courtesy, Bernard and S. Dean Levy, Inc., New York.

son of John B. Ackley (see previous entry), active in Philadelphia c. 1800–1815.

ADAMS, ⸺

A Federal cylinder-top desk with French feet, c. 1800–1815, offered at auction in 1991 bears a partial label inscribed

Adams. . . . Stonington, Ct.

Nothing further is known.

⸻

Chippendale mahogany slant-top desk with ogee bracket feet signed by Moses Adams (1759–1795), a Beverly, Massachusetts, cabinetmaker, working c. 1785–1795. Courtesy, Israel Sack, Inc., New York.

ADAMS, JOSEPH

A Windsor continuous-arm chair impressed

J. ADAMS

which was illustrated in *Antiques* for October 1968, is possibly by Joseph Adams, who worked on Center Street in Boston, c. 1789–1790. Ref.: Bjerkoe.

ADAMS, LEMUEL

See Kneeland & Adams.

ADAMS, MOSES

Born in Ipswich, Massachusetts, in 1759, the cabinetmaker Moses Adams worked in Beverly, Massachusetts, until his death in 1795. A Chippendale mahogany slant-front

Detail of the incised signature—M. Adams, 1791—of Moses Adams, which appears on the back-board of the Chippendale mahogany slant-top desk. Courtesy, Israel Sack, Inc., New York.

desk from his hand bears on its backboard the incised signature

M. Adams, 1791

Ref.: Bjerkoe.

ADAMS, NEHEMIAH

Although numerous pieces of Federal furniture have been ascribed to Nehemiah Adams (1769–1840) of Salem, Massachusetts, he is best known for the spectacular Gentleman's secretary, c. 1795–1798, now at Winterthur, which was discovered in Cape Town, South Africa. It bears two printed paper labels with a feather border, each reading,

Nehemiah Adams/Cabinet-Maker/Newbury Street/(near the Common)/SALEM/Maffachufetts.

Adams, in partnership with several other Salem cabinetmakers, was active in the so-called venture trade, owning sailing vessels and regularly shipping furniture to such exotic locales as Mauritius and Cape Town. He also was something of an affliction to his community. In his diary the Reverend William Bentley, comment-ing on fires that had burned down two shops occupied by Adams, described the cabinetmaker as "guilty of many acts of carelessness so as to be a terror to the neighbors." Refs.: Bjerkoe; Montgomery; *Antiques,* December 1933.

ADAMS, STEPHEN

A Sheraton mahogany butler's secretary, illustrated in *American Collector* for June 1937 and inscribed

Stephen Adams, 1810

is attributed to Stephen Adams, who was born in Lexington, Massachusetts, in 1798 and was working in Haverhill, either Massachusetts or New Hampshire, c. 1810–1812.

ADAMS & TODD

A Sheraton card table now at Historic Deerfield bears the fragmentary printed paper label of Samuel Adams and William Todd, partners in the cabinetmaking business on Cambridge Street, Boston, from 1798 until Todd's death in 1800. Although Adams was active as early as 1796 and as late as 1809, this appears to be his only labeled piece. Refs.: Hewitt, Kane, and Ward; *Antiques,* April 1962.

ADRIAN, FRANZ

One of the few known Mennonite cabinet-makers, Franz Adrian was born in 1836 in southern Russia. He migrated to Kansas after the Civil War, settling at the Hoffnungsau Mennonite community near Buhler, where he died in 1910. Among the pieces he made for family and friends is a decorated corner cabinet bearing the painted inscription

FRANZ 1879 ADRIAN

Ref.: Reinhild K. Janzen and John M. Janzen, *Mennonite Furniture: A Migrant Tradition, 1766–1910* (Intercourse, Pa.: Good Books, 1991).

ALBRECHT, CHARLES

A Hepplewhite piano, advertised in *Antiques* for March 1959, bears the inlaid mark

CHARLES ALBRECHT/MAKER/
Philadelphia

Albrecht, active in Philadelphia c. 1789–1824, was a joiner by training, so, unlike most pianomakers, he may have produced both case and works. Ref.: Hornor.

ALEXANDER, RICHARD

The little-known Philadelphia craftsman Richard Alexander (working c. 1815–1820) is remembered for a single piece, a Federal tall case clock for which he made the mahogany case. It bears the printed paper label **RICHARD ALEXANDER/CABINET AND CHAIR MAKER/No.92,/SOUTH-**

Federal mahogany tall clock case bearing the label of the Philadelphia cabinetmaker Richard Alexander (working c. 1815–1820). The label is dated 1818. Courtesy, Bernard and S. Dean Levy, Inc., New York.

Stenciled mark of the cabinetmaker J. P. Allen as it appears on an Empire bureau.

Courtesy, Jacqueline and Frank Donegan.

THIRD STREET, (opp . . . St. Paul's Church)/PHILADELPHIA/WHERE ORDERS WILL BE THANKFULLY RECEIVED, AND/PUNCTUALLY COMPLIED WITH./(1818)

Ref.: *Antiques,* September 1964.

ALEXANDER, WILLIAM

The cabinetmaker William Alexander is listed in Pittsburgh business directories from 1837 through 1844, although his shop was actually located in the suburb of Sharpsburg, Pennsylvania. He is known for a heavily carved Empire sideboard in mahogany, which is stamped in several places

Wm ALEXANDER

Ref.: *Antiques,* May 1983.

ALEXANDER, WILLIAM

See Stone & Alexander.

ALLEN, ABNER

Three signed pieces are attributed to Abner Allen (1776–1855), a Shaker craftsman and member of the Enfield, Connecticut, community. These are a pine cupboard and case of drawers, inscribed in pencil

March 18th 1830 GFM Made by
Abner Allen

a lift-top desk on stand, pencil-signed on the bottom,

This made bye/Abner Allen in the/Year of his age/66 & 10 mos./1842

and a small chest of drawers, again signed in pencil, this time on the back

May 16, 1849. Abner Allen. A.E. age 66

The seeming discrepancy in Allen's age evident in the latter two inscriptions is probably explained by a 2 being transcribed as a 9 or vice versa. Ref.: Rieman and Burks.

ALLEN, AMOS DENISON

Amos Denison Allen (1774–1855), chair- and cabinetmaker, was apprenticed to the well-known Windsor chair maker Ebenezer Tracy (see his entry), whose daughter he married in 1796, the same year he opened a shop in Windham, north of Norwich, Connecticut. Allen was extremely active in the field, employing at times a dozen apprentices and journeymen. His order book, owned by the Connecticut Historical Society and covering the years 1796–1803, indicates that he produced a wide variety of furniture, including clock cases, tables, bedsteads, desks, secretaries, and sideboards. Of all these, however, only a single Chippendale cherry chest of drawers bearing the impressed mark

A. D. ALLEN

is known. However, this mark appears on dozens of Allen's Windsor chairs, including bow-back and fan-back side chairs as well as continuous-arm, sack-back, and comb-back armchairs. All bear a distinct resemblance to

Decorated c. 1815–1820 Federal fancy chair bearing the rare mark of the Windham, Connecticut, turners Amos D. Allen and Frederick Tracy.

Courtesy, James E. Elliott, Antiques.

Windsors made by his teacher. Refs.: *Connecticut Furniture: Seventeenth and Eighteenth Centuries* (Hartford: Wadsworth Atheneum, 1967); *Antiques,* August 1956.

ALLEN, JOB A.

Although few examples of his work are known, the chairmaker Job A. Allen of White Creek, Washington County, New York, is credited with two different marks. A rod-

Empire mahogany bureau with mirror, c. 1830–1850, bearing the stenciled mark J.P. ALLEN/MANUFACTURER/Manchester, MASS. Courtesy, Jacqueline and Frank Donegan.

back Windsor bears the stamped impression

J. A. ALLEN

while an unusual bamboo-turned rod-back rocker with comb is stamped

JAA

Both date c. 1800–1820. Ref.: *Antiques,* May 1981.

ALLEN, J. P.

J. P. Allen, active in Manchester, Massachusetts, c. 1830–1850, is known for a pair of carved Empire card tables and a desk and bookcase that incorporates both Empire and Victorian characteristics. All are stenciled

J.P. ALLEN/MANUFACTURER/
Manchester, MASS.

Ref.: Williams and Harsh.

ALLEN, J. T., & CO.

A Victorian Renaissance Revival rocking cradle on stand at the Shelburne Museum, Shelburne, Vermont, is stenciled

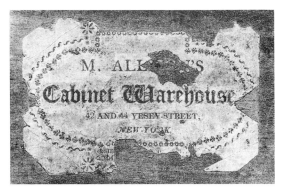

Detail of label of Michael Allison, appearing on a c. 1808–1815 Federal mahogany library table. The label and the piece may be dated by reference to the Manhattan directory, which places Allison at 42 and 44 Vesey Street during this period. Courtesy, Bernard and S. Dean Levy, Inc., New York.

D.Cox's—Pat. Feb. 1867/ Manufactured by/J. T. Allen & Co./167 Canal Street/ N.Y. The Allen firm was active c. 1865–1875, making a variety of inexpensive household furnishings.

ALLEN, JOSEPH

A Philadelphia-style Chippendale walnut secretary-bookcase offered at Sotheby's, January 31–February 3, 1979, bears the name **Joseph Allen** on a drawer bottom. The maker is thought to be the Joseph Allen recorded in the Philadelphia tax records of 1783 as a "joyner." Ref.: Bjerkoe.

ALLEN, OLIVER

Oliver Allen of Norwich, Connecticut, is known for a single marked piece, a massive Empire walnut bureau bearing a label imprinted **Furniture/Oliver Allen/Offers for sale (a few rods North of the Norwich/Bank, Shetucket Street) an extensive assort-/ment of Cabinets and Chairs: furniture of the best materials and war'nted workman-ship./LOOKING GLASSES/Gilt and Mahogany Frames/N.B. All orders thank-fully received and punctually/attended to/NORWICH, CONN.** Although he was regarded by Bjerkoe as a cabinetmaker, there seems to be no evidence that Allen was such. His label reads like that of a furniture wholesaler or retailer. By appearance the bureau would date c. 1830–1840. Refs.: Bjerkoe; *Antiques,* November 1931.

Sheraton mahogany sofa, c. 1808–1815, bearing the stenciled mark of Michael Allison. Stenciled makers' marks from this period are rare. Courtesy, Israel Sack, Inc., New York.

Detail of stenciled mark of Michael Allison on the Sheraton mahogany sofa. Allison was working at this location during the period 1808–1815. Courtesy, Israel Sack, Inc., New York.

ALLEN & BRO.

An Elizabethan Revival adjustable arm-chair in a private collection bears a brass label embossed
TRADEMARK/ALLEN & BRO./OXFORD ARM CHAIR/1209 CHESTNUT ST PHILADA PA/REGISTERED PATENT
as well as cast in the brass adjusting ratchet
ALLEN & BRO. PHILADELPHIA PA./PAT: FEB. 6.94
and is a product of William Jr. and Joseph Allen, who took over their father's manufactory (established c. 1835) in 1847. Once one of Philadelphia's largest makers of Victorian furnishings, the firm continued under family management until 1902. Ref.: *Antiques,* May 1974.

ALLEN & TRACY

A decorated Federal fancy chair, c. 1815–1820, offered for sale in the fall of 1994, was branded on the rear seat rail
ALLEN & TRACY/WINDHAM
The Windham, Connecticut, craftsmen Amos

D. Allen and Frederick Tracy (active c. 1803–1818) were in partnership in 1818, at which time they accepted an apprentice. Ref.: Undated 1994 letter from James E. Elliott.

ALLISON, MICHAEL

Michael Allison (1773–1855), working c. 1800–1847, was one of New York City's most prolific cabinetmakers as well as the one who produced the largest variety of marks and labels, most of which can be associated with changes in building numbers on Vesey Street, where he maintained his shop. Marks listed here are coordinated with the dates he appears at a given address in the Manhattan directories:
1800–1802
34 and 42 Vesey Street
(No marked examples are known.)
1804–1805
40 Vesey Street
(No marked examples are known.)
1806–1807
40 & 42 Vesey Street
A printed paper label:
M. Allison/42 Vesey-Street/Near The Bear Market/New York
A printed paper label:
M.ALLISON,/CABINET MAKER/42/VESEY-STREET,/ NEAR THE BEAR MARKET, NEW YORK,/Who has a general assortment of warranted ready made/Furniture on hand.
A printed paper label:
M.ALLISON/CABINET MAKER,/NO.42, VESEY-STREET,/(NEAR THE BEAR MARKET)/NEW YORK/Who has a general assortment of warranted/ready made Furniture on hand.
1808–1815
42 and 44 Vesey Street

Stenciled:

M.ALLISON/Cabinet Maker,/42 & 44 Vesey Street,/Near Bear Market/ NEW YORK

A printed paper label:

M. ALLISON'S/Cabinet Warehouse/42 AND 44 VESEY-STREET,/NEW-YORK/ & sm . . . . . 1816–1847 46 and 48 Vesey Street

A printed paper label:

M. ALLISON'S/Cabinet and Upholstery Furniture Warehouse/No. 46 & 48 Vesey Street/Furniture of various kinds warranted. Sold/on liberal terms. All orders thankfully/received and punctually executed/New York May 1817

A printed paper label with wording identical to this but dated simply "May" and headed by an engraving of a brick Federal-style building bearing a sign reading, "M. ALLISON'S CABINET WAREHOUSE."

A printed paper label:

M.ALLISON,/AT HIS/CABINET AND UPHOLSTERER/WAREHOUSE,/(No. 46 & 48)/VESSEY-STREET, NEW-YORK, HAS CONSTANTLY ON HAND, AND FOR SALE,/A GENERAL ASSORTMENT OF/FASHIONABLE CABINET FURNITURE,/WARRANTED GOOD./ *February, 1819*

A printed paper label:

M.ALLISON,/CABINET-MAKER, No. 46 & 48 Vesey-Street,/Grateful to his friends and the public for/past favors, relying on the superior quality of/his work for fashion and durability, takes this/method to inform them that he has constantly/ on hand, and constantly making/CABINET FURNITURE, SOFAS, MA-/HOGANY and ROSE WOOD CHAIRS,/ Of all descriptions, faithfully made of the/best

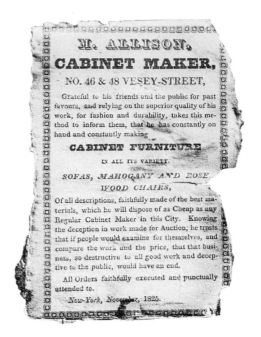

Detail of the printed paper label used by Michael Allison during the period 1825–1847. At this time Allison's address was 46 and 48 Vesey Street, Manhattan. Courtesy, Peter Hill, Washington, D.C.

materials, which he sells as cheap as any regular Cabinet-Maker in this city. Knowing/the deception in work made for Auction he/trusts that if people would examine for them-/selves, and compare the work and the price, that/that business so destructive to all good work, a/ deceptive to the public, would have an end./ *All orders faithfully executed, and punctu-/ally attended to.*/NEW YORK. October, 1823

A printed paper label:

M.ALLISON,/CABINET MAKER,/NO.46 & 48 VESEY-STREET,/Grateful to his friends and the public for past/favors, and relying upon the superior quality of his/work, for fashion and durability, takes this me-/thod to inform them, that he has constantly on/ hand and constantly mak-ing/ CABINET FURNITURE/IN ALL ITS VARIETY/SOFAS, MAHOGANY AND ROSE WOOD CHAIRS,/Of all descrip-tions, faithfully made of the best ma-/terials, which he will dispose of as Cheap as any/ Regular Cabinet Maker in this City. Knowing/the deception in work made for Auction, he trusts/that if people would examine for themselves, and/compare the work and the price, that that busi-/ness, so destructive to all good work and decep-/tive to the public, would have an end./All Orders faithfully executed and punctually attended to./New-York, November,1825. Refs.: Montgomery; Scherer.

Detail of the label of Richard Allison. His shop at 58 Vesey Street was a short dis-tance from that of his brother, Michael. Courtesy, Bernard and S. Dean Levy, Inc., New York.

ALLISON, RICHARD

Richard Allison (1780–1825), brother of the well-known Michael Allison (see previous entry), never attained his sibling's success. Although he made similar Federal fur-niture and had his shop but a few doors away from Michael, Richard worked at his trade only from 1806 to 1814, spending his remain-ing years as a grocer. Only a half dozen marked pieces are known, five of which are labeled

A GENERAL ASSORTMENT OF/ WARRANTED/Cabinet Furniture,/MADE AND SOLD BY/RICHARD ALLISON/ NO. 58 VESEY-STREET/NEW/YORK.
A sixth piece, a Federal butler's desk, is inscribed on a drawer bottom
Made by R. Allison N. York/Cost $67/
July 1810
Ref.: *Antiques,* May 1973.

Federal mahogany library table, labeled by the New York City cabinetmaker Michael Allison (1773–1855), active c. 1800–1847. The label is one Allison used from 1808 through 1815. Courtesy, Bernard and S. Dean Levy, Inc., New York.

ALLWINE, LAWRENCE

Lawrence Allwine, one of the more inventive Windsor makers, was active at 99 South Front Street in Philadelphia, c. 1786–1800. Before 1810 he was living near Zanesville, Ohio, where he both made chairs and ran a tavern. All known examples from his hand are branded

L. ALWINE/PHILADa

These include plain-seat and upholstered fanback chairs and a rod-back settee that some believe was made in Ohio despite its Philadelphia stamp. Allwine patented a quick-drying paint for his chairs that others attempted to copy, leading him to complain in print,

"Some malicious persons in the city calling themselves Windsor chair-makers, who have endeavoured in vain to imitate my painting and patent colours, and of course failed therein, having their chairs returned on account of the paint sullying and sticking to the clothes of the person who sat on them, reported that they were my paints and not good. I therefore call on any of them or either of them, to prove the same, or to produce a piece of painting equal in goodness to mine, and I will engage to have painting done in a superior stile, much cheaper and more durable than can be done by any other person on the continent."

Federal mahogany chest of drawers bearing the label of the New York City cabinetmaker Richard Allison (1780–1825). Richard Allison, brother of the better-known Michael Allison, was active only from 1806 until 1814. Courtesy, Bernard and S. Dean Levy, Inc., New York.

Clearly, Philadelphia was too small a place for a person of such talent! Refs.: Hornor; Santore II.

ALLYN, CHARLES, JR.

A miniature Federal chest of drawers owned by the Connecticut Historical Society is attributed to Charles Allyn, Jr., of Windsor, Connecticut. It is inscribed in pencil

Charles Allyn Windsor Feb 25 1808

Allyn (b. 1787) is believed to have been an apprentice to the cabinetmaker Aaron Colton of Hartford. Ref.: *Antiques,* May 1986.

ALLYN, STEPHEN B.

A braced bow-back Windsor side chair in the collection of the Connecticut Historical Society is branded

ALLYN

and is credited to Stephen B. Allyn (1774–1822) of Norwich, Connecticut.

Allyn's advertisements in the *Chelsea Courier* indicate that he was in partnership c. 1797–1803 with one Daniel Huntington III as cabinet- and chairmakers. Thereafter, until 1812, he worked alone in the Chelsea section of Norwich. Ref.: *Connecticut Chairs in the Collection of the Connecticut Historical Society* (Hartford: Connecticut Historical Society, 1956), *Bulletin of the Connecticut Historical Society,* Vol. 32, No. 4.

ALVORD, WILLIAM

See John Meads.

ALWAYS, JAMES

The Windsor chair maker James Always worked c. 1786–1815 at 40 James Street, New York City. The few surviving examples of his work consist of comb-back and continuous-arm chairs stamped

I. ALWAYS

Refs.: Santore II; *Antiques,* May 1981.

ALWAYS & HAMTON

During one year, 1792, the Windsor chair maker James Always (see previous entry) was in partnership with Abraham Hamton (Hampton), presumably at the 40 James Street address in Manhattan. This relationship produced several marked pieces, including a settee and a continuous-arm chair, both branded

I. ALWAYS/I. HAMTON

Ref.: Santore II.

Late Victorian oak dental cabinet in the Eastlake mode, dating c. 1880–1910 and bearing the label of the American Cabinet Co., Two Rivers, Wisconsin. It is typical of mass-produced household furnishings of the period. Private collection.

AMERICAN CABINET COMPANY

A large oak dental cabinet with beveled glass mirror in the splash back in a private collection bears the printed label

THE AMERICAN CABINET CO.
TWO RIVERS, WIS. U.S.A.

The piece dates c. 1880–1910 and is related in style to oak household furnishings of the period. Nothing is presently known of the manufacturer.

Detail of the printed paper label of the American Cabinet Co., affixed to the Victorian oak dental cabinet. Private collection.

AMERICAN CHAIR COMPANY

See Thomas Warren.

AMORY, JOHN

A Federal Pembroke table, c. 1790–1810, with a Newport, Rhode Island, history bears the signature

John Amory

This is probably an owner's name. Ref.: *MAD,* August 1977.

ANDERSON, _____

A set of four c. 1800 upholstered New York Federal side chairs at the Albany Institute of History and Art are branded

ANDERSON

a mark sometimes associated with the Manhattan cabinetmaker Elbert Anderson. However, because several other cabinetmakers named Anderson were working in New York City at the same time, this attribution is far from certain. Ref.: *Antiques,* May 1974.

ANDERSON, ELBERT, SR.

The cabinetmaker Elbert Anderson, Sr., worked at 5 Maiden Lane in Manhattan from 1786 until 1796. Three identifiable pieces from this period are known: a Federal sideboard, a card table, and a portion of a dining table, all bearing paper labels reading,

Elbert Anderson/Makes all kinds of/ CABINET WARE/on the most Modern & Approved/Methods & on the most reasonable terms/No.5 Maiden Lane/ NEW YORK.

These labels are embellished with engravings of a Federal clock case, serpentine sideboard, slant-top desk, and chair. From 1796 to 1800 Anderson had a shop on Duane Street, and from 1799 to 1803 he was in partnership with a son, Elbert Jr. However, no marked pieces reflecting either the address change or the partnership are known. Refs.: Hinckley; *Antiques,* May 1974.

ANDERSON, JAMES

An unusual rent table, with octagonal top, several drawers, and a shaped pillar base combining Empire and Victorian characteristics is signed in pencil on a drawer bottom

James Anderson Maker/
Hamilton Co./Harrison Ohio/1857

Ref.: *Made in Ohio.*

ANNESLEY & CO.

An Empire pier table in mahogany, cherry, and marble at the New York State Museum in Albany, New York, is branded

ANNESLEY & CO./ALBANY, N.Y.

Partners in the firm were Richard L. Annesley and James H. Vint, active 1885–1945. Although made c. 1890, the table faithfully reflects the Empire taste of an earlier period. Ref.: Scherer.

APPLETON, NATHANIEL

A Federal short sideboard, mahogany with carved and reeded stiles, which was advertised in *Antiques* for November 1983, bears the signature

Nathaniel Appleton

This is believed to be the Nathaniel Appleton who was working in Salem, Massachusetts, c. 1800–1815 and who, until 1806, was in partnership with one Ives. His shop was at the corner of Derby and Handy streets. Ref.: Bjerkoe.

APPLETON, WILLIAM

Although he was in business in Salem, Massachusetts, from at least 1794 until around his death in 1822, William Appleton (b. 1765) is known for only two pieces of marked furniture, both in the Federal style: a desk and bookcase and a tambour desk (both at Winterthur), both labeled

William Appleton,/CABINET-
MAKER,/Corner of Charter and Liberty
Streets/Salem, Massachusetts {last line
uncertain}

Both pieces may be dated 1795–1804, because it was only during this period that Appleton's shop was at the corner of Charter and Liberty streets. Refs.: Montgomery; *Antiques,* October 1965, April 1966.

ASH, GILBERT

One of the earliest identified makers of American Chippendale furniture, Gilbert Ash (1717–1785) of Manhattan is known for two heavily carved side chairs. The first, at the Albany Institute of History and Art, is inscribed in pencil

Made by Gilbert Ash in wall-Street at/
Newyork

while the second, at Winterthur, bears the inscription, also in pencil

Made by Gilbert Ash in wall Street/
R . . . nie . . . Sold . . . at new york

During his long career (he was listed as a free-man joiner in 1748 and advertised frequently in Manhattan newspapers during the 1750s and '60s), Ash produced a variety of furnishings for important clients, including Sir William Johnson and members of the Van Rensselaer family. Refs.: Bjerkoe; Downs; *Antiques,* February 1983.

ASH, THOMAS AND WILLIAM

Although there has been confusion as to the identity of the New York City Windsor chair makers Thomas and William Ash (working c. 1785–1794), it seems likely that both were sons of Gilbert Ash (see previous entry). They have left behind a fair number of chairs (including upholstered braced bow-backs) bearing the printed paper label

Thomas and William Ash,/Windfor Chair Makers,/No. 17, John-ftreet, New-York

There is also a much larger but fragmentary label that has been deciphered to bear the names of Thomas and William and a John Street address. A complete example has not been found. Finally, a sample chair with each leg turned in different style is labeled

Thomas and William Ash, No.27 John St., New York, Where Windsor settees and Garden Chairs are made in the Neatest Manner

The style of both chairs and labels would date them to the eighteenth century, and the proprietors are listed at 17 John Street in a 1785 business directory. At some point Thomas left the business, and upon William's death in 1815 it passed to his son, also named Thomas, who made both Windsors and "fancy chairs." Refs.: Bjerkoe; Santore II; *Bee,* November 6, 1981.

ASHTON, THOMAS

Thomas Ashton was a maker of Windsor chairs active in Philadelphia, c. 1805–1815. Among known examples of his work are step-down rod-back side chairs branded

THs ASHTON

Refs.: Bivins; Santore II.

ASTENS, THOMAS

A carved neoclassical mahogany tilt-top table, c. 1820–1830, bears a printed paper label that reads

THOMAS ASTENS/ Cabinet and Warehouse/20 Beaver Street./All orders executed in a prompt and fashionable manner.

and a similar piece but with fixed marble top and label dated 1822 is described in *The Magazine Antiques,* March 1935. Astens worked at 20 Beaver Street in 1822, moving to 8 Vestry Street the following year. Previously, he had been at 12 Beaver Street, from 1818 through 1821. Ref.: Bjerkoe.

ATWOOD, T.

T. Atwood (c. 1785–1865) was a chairmaker active in Worcester, Massachusetts, as early as 1808. By 1819 he had a chair factory in New Bedford, New Hampshire, and was selling "flag bottomed, Fancy & Common" chairs in Nashua, New Hampshire, in 1832. After 1840 he was in New York State. His products are stamped

T. ATWOOD

Ref.: Santore II.

AUSTIN, D. B.

An unusual late-eighteenth-century braced comb-back continuous-arm chair inscribed on the underside of the seat in punchwork **Made by D.B. Austin for his cousin Daisy Olive Berry** may be the work of the same craftsman whose die stamp,

D. AUSTIN

appears on the seat rail of a Chippendale ribbon-back side chair of the same period. This man is thought to be a member of the Austin family of cabinetmakers active in Charlestown and Salem, Massachusetts. Refs.: Bishop; *Antiques,* November 1965.

AVERY, J. COFFIN

A c.1800–1820 New Hampshire Federal bowfront chest of drawers bearing the signature (twice)

J. Coffin Avery

is attributed to a cabinetmaker by that name active in Sandwich, New Hampshire. Ref.: *Antiques.*

AXSON, WILLIAM, JR.

A massive Chippendale mahogany chest on chest (at the Charleston Museum), gouge-marked on the bottom with a conjoined

WA

is attributed to William Axson, Jr. (1739–1800), a cabinetmaker working in Charleston, South Carolina, during the period 1765–1780. Ref.: *Antiques,* January 1985.

B

BABIN, A.

A walnut and cypresswood Louisiana armoire bearing the painted signature

A. Babin

and dated 1803, which was found near Donaldson, Louisiana, is attributed to Babin. Nothing further is known. Ref.: *Antiques,* May 1983.

BACHMAN, JACOB

A Federal mahogany and cherry slant-front desk inscribed on the bottom

Jacob Bachman

is attributed to a cabinetmaker by that name active c. 1790–1800 in Northampton County, Pennsylvania. Ref.: Beatrice B. Garvan, *The Pennsylvania German Collection* (Philadelphia: Philadelphia Museum of Art, 1982).

BACON, H.

A braced bow-back armchair and several matching side chairs stamped beneath their seats

H. BACON

have been attributed to a New England chairmaker of that name working c. 1780–1810. However, this may also be an owner's mark. Ref.: Fairbanks and Bates.

BADLAM, STEPHEN

T he Revolutionary War veteran Stephen Badlam (1751–1815) worked from 1777 until his death on the present River Street in Dorchester Lower Mills, Massachusetts. He was a prolific cabinetmaker, whose stamp

S. BADLAM

appears not only on Federal card and dining tables, side and upholstered lolling chairs, and mirrors but also on such unlikely pieces as a cradle and a serving tray. Refs.: Bjerkoe; Comstock, *American Furniture*: Fairbanks and Bates; Montgomery.

BADLAM, STEPHEN, JR.

S on of the well-known Dorchester cabinetmaker Stephen Badlam (see previous entry), Stephen Badlam, Jr. (1779–1847), never attained his father's prominence. He is known only for a Federal bowfront dressing box with mirror (dressing glass) at Winterthur, which bears the partial label

Stephen Badlam, jun./42 CORNHILL/ BOSTON/A constant supply of fashionable/LOOKING-GLASSES/

. . . Wholesale & Retail

Although there is no direct evidence that Badlam made this piece, it is likely, because he may be presumed to have been trained by his father, a known maker of looking glasses. Badlam Jr. does not appear to have had a long independent career. He is listed at the Cornhill address only in 1820, and by 1827 he was jailer for the City of Boston. Refs.: Bjerkoe; Montgomery.

BAILEY, CONSTANT

Constant Bailey of Newport, Rhode Island, is known for a William and Mary walnut

chest of drawers, now in a private collection, which is inscribed in ink

Maid By Constant Bailey/Shop Joyner in Newport/Rhod Island

That Bailey was active around 1750 is known from the fact that in that year he entered into a venture contract for shipping furniture to North Carolina. Refs.: Bivins; *Old Time New England Furniture* (Boston: Society for the Preservation of New England Antiquities, 1987).

BAILEY, J.

A Hepplewhite linen press inscribed on the back

Made by J. Bailey/Flemington, N.J. 1803

was advertised in *Antiques* for January 1979, and a seemingly identical example of the same form but inscribed simply

I. BAILEY/Flemington, N.J., 1807

was offered in a Christie's sale, November 5–6, 1985. Nothing further seems to be known of this elusive New Jersey cabinetmaker.

BAILEY, JONATHAN

A late Federal butler's desk in the collection of the Ohio Historical Society at Glendower in Lebanon, Warren County, Ohio, is signed

Jonathan Bailey/Lebanon/January 12, 1832 and is attributed to Jonathan Bailcy, a Haverhill, Massachusetts, craftsman who was listed in the Warren County census for 1830. By

Carved Federal mahogany lolling chair, c. 1785–1795, bearing the stamp of the cabinetmaker Stephen Badlam. Courtesy, Bernard and S. Dean Levy, Inc., New York.

Detail of impressed mark, S. BADLAM, of Stephen Badlam on the hood of the child's cradle. It is rare for such pieces to be marked. Courtesy, Israel Sack, Inc., New York.

1840 he was in Cincinnati, where he worked into the 1860s. Ref.: *Made in Ohio.*

BAILEY, PHINEAS

A Federal tall case clock bearing a label with the handwritten notation

P. Bailey,/Chelsea, Vermont./1817

is attributed to Phineas Bailey, who is recorded as owning a clock shop in Chelsea, c. 1810–1817. Because a similar case containing works of another clockmaker is known, there is reason to believe that Bailey made the case rather than simply the works. Ref.: *Antiques,* August 1981.

Country Chippendale pine-hooded cradle bearing the impressed mark of Stephen Badlam (1751–1815), a cabinet- and chair-maker who worked at Dorchester Lower Mills, Massachusetts, c. 1777–1815. Courtesy, Israel Sack, Inc., New York.

BAILEY, THOMAS

A Federal mahogany and bird's-eye maple chest of drawers with French feet is signed in two places

Thomas Bailey 1808

and is attributed to the cabinetmaker of that name who worked in Newburyport, Massachusetts, during the first decade of the nineteenth century. Ref.: *Antiques,* January 1979.

BAKER, BENJAMIN

A lthough Benjamin Baker (1737–1822) worked in Newport, Rhode Island, for some thirty years (c. 1760–1790), little is known of his life or production. A Chippendale mahogany high chest of drawers or highboy from his hand bears the chalk signature

Benjamin Baker

and the same name appears on a Chippendale clock case now in the collection at Sturbridge Village. Refs.: Cooper; Heckscher.

BAKER, DANIEL

The little-known Windsor chair maker Daniel Baker (1780–1858) was active in Trenton, New Jersey, c. 1800–1814. Among his products is a rod-back birdcage Windsor with medallion, which is branded beneath the seat

D. BAKER

It is in the collection of the New Jersey State Museum. Ref.: *Furniture and Furnishings from the Collection of the New Jersey State Museum* (Trenton: New Jersey State Museum, 1970).

BAKER, JOHN

A Federal mahogany demilune card table offered at Sotheby's June 30–July 1, 1983, bears the ink inscriptions

J. Baker, 1794

and

J.B.

These are thought to mark the hand of John

Ink signature of John Baker on the 1794 card table. Courtesy, Bernard and S. Dean Levy, Inc., New York.

Baker, an Ipswich, Massachusetts, cabinetmaker active c. 1760–1795. Ref.: *American Collector,* September 1937.

BALCH, ISRAEL, JR.

Israel Balch, Jr. (d. 1809), of Mansfield, Connecticut, is known for a single marked piece, a magnificent bamboo-turned settee, branded three times under the seat

I. BALCH. Jr

Refs.: Santore II; *Antiques,* September 1988.

BAMFORD, JOSEPH

A Federal tiger maple tall chest with French feet, dating c. 1800–1810, bears the signature

Hepplewhite mahogany card table signed on the back in ink J B/ J. Baker 1794 for the Ipswich, Massachusetts, cabinetmaker John Baker, active c. 1760–1795. Courtesy, Bernard and S. Dean Levy, Inc., New York.

Jos. Bamford

which may be that of the maker or an owner. Ref.: *Antiques,* March 1984.

BANCROFT, JONATHAN

Jonathan Bancroft (d. 1860), best remembered as superintendent of the Corey furniture works in Portland, Maine, operated independently, c. 1830–1836, turning out saber-leg mahogany Empire side chairs stamped on the rear seat rail

J. BANCROFT

Ref.: *Antiques,* May 1982.

BANCROFT, TIMOTHY W. AND CHARLES P.

The brothers Charles P. and Timothy W. Bancroft owned a company that made Empire furniture in Worcester, Massachusetts, c. 1839–1841. Their printed paper label,

T.W. & C.P. Bancroft/Worcester, Mass, 1841

is found on heavy mahogany pillar and scroll furniture. Ref.: *Antiques,* October 1979.

BANDO, L.

A child's walnut side chair in the Victorian Renaissance Revival style, which is at the Smithsonian Institution, is inscribed in pencil,

Victorian Renaissance Revival walnut child's side chair with penciled inscription by the New York City cabinetmaker L. Bando, an employee of Alexander Roux & Company. Courtesy, the Smithsonian Institution.

Made by L. Bando/July 18/1888/ Roux & CO./2 E 20

It is thought that Bando was a cabinetmaker employed by the New York City firm of Alexander Roux & Company (see Alexander Roux).

BARBER, F.

A Victorian swivel chair in oak with caned seat and back is stenciled

Pat'd April 25 1871 by F. Barber

Because many patent holders sold or leased their rights to manufacturers, this chair, which has an Ohio history, may well have been made by someone other than Barber.

BARJON, DUTREUIL, JR.

The free black cabinetmaker Dutreuil Barjon, Jr., is listed in the New Orleans directories from 1822 until 1858. He is known for an armoire (at Bocage Restoration) in mahogany veneer with an oval stencil reading,

**D. BARJOHN Jr/CABINET MAKER/
No. 279 Royal St./NEW ORLEANS**

Because Barjon was at 279 Royal only during the years 1830–1841, the piece may be dated to that period. Ref.: *Antiques,* June 1977.

BARNARD, SAMUEL

Although he was born and died in Watertown, Massachusetts, Samuel Barnard (1776–1856) spent his working life in Salem, where he participated in the West Indies trade and was listed as a cabinetmaker as early as 1802. The only identified piece from his hand is a Federal D-top mahogany and bird's-eye maple card table impressed

S.B

which is in a private collection. Refs.: Hewitt, Kane, and Ward; *Antiques,* May 1982.

BARNES, A.

A Sheraton mahogany two-drawer stand, c. 1810–1820, offered at auction in November 1994 was signed

A. Barnes/New Haven, CT

It is not known if this is an owner's or a maker's mark.

BARNES, L.

A Federal side chair with cane seat, elaborately carved openwork back, and painted musical motifs on the crest rail bears the brand of

L-BARNES

who was working in Portsmouth, New Hampshire, c. 1810–1820. It is in the collections of Greenfield Village and the Henry Ford Museum.

BARNET, SAMPSON

The earliest known Delaware Windsor chairs were made by Sampson Barnet of Wilmington (active c. 1776–1795). Among the examples bearing his brand,

S. BARNET

are fan-back side and armchairs and sack-back armchairs. Several may be seen at the Historical Society of Delaware. Refs.: *Plain and Ornamental; Antiques,* May 1985.

BARNS & HAZLER

A Windsor braced-back continuous-arm chair advertised in *Antiques* for February 1931 bears the extremely rare printed paper label

**Barns & Hazler/Windfor Chair
Makers/from Philadelphia/No. 93
Golden Hill/New-York**

Nothing further is known of this partnership, although on form the chair would date c. 1790–1810.

BARNUM, S. W.

A c. 1800–1820 grain-painted washstand in the country Sheraton manner, which was included in the 1972 exhibition *American*

Federal inlaid mahogany lift-top Bible box on stand, c. 1790–1810, bearing the brand of Theodore Barrell. He may have been either a cabinetmaker or an owner of the piece.

Courtesy, Israel Sack, Inc., New York.

Furniture in the Western Reserve, is signed

S. W. Barnum

It is thought to be an Ohio piece, but nothing is known of the maker.

BARRELL, THEODORE

An unusual Federal inlaid mahogany lift-top Bible box on stand with turned and reeded legs is branded in several places

THEODORE/BARRELL

The piece would appear to date c. 1790–1810.

The name could be that of either a cabinet-maker or an owner.

BARRETT, ANDREW

A privately owned sewing table is inscribed in pencil

Made by Andrew Barrett Feb 1881

Barrett (c. 1836–1917) was a member of the Shaker sect, associated with the Mount Lebanon, New York, community. He is thought to have added a gallery to an earlier table to convert it for sewing purposes. Ref.: Rieman and Burks.

BARRETT, NATHAN

A late Federal New England mahogany desk and bookcase or secretary, advertised in *MAD,* February 1980, was signed on a drawer back

NATHAN BARRETT

This is most likely an owner's name.

Detail of the interior of the Federal Bible box on stand, showing the impressed mark THEODORE/BARRELL.

Courtesy, Israel Sack, Inc., New York.

BARRY, JOSEPH B.

The Irish-born cabinetmaker Joseph B. Barry (1757–1838) established a shop in Philadelphia in 1794 that remained open until 1844, turning out a variety of furnishings in the latest taste. Barry's first location was at 148 South Third Street, as reflected in his engraved label from the c. 1798–1804 period, which is illustrated with a "Lady's Drefsing Commode" flanked on each side by a pier table, beneath which appear the words

Joseph B. Barry,/CABINET MAKER & UPHOLSTERER/FROM LONDON/No. 148 South Third Street/PHILADELPHIA

below which are a sideboard with knife cases flanked by two chairs, then the phrase

Orders for the West Indies or elsewhere Executed in the neatest manner

and/Attended to with the Strictest punctuality.

In 1804 Barry's address became 132 South Second Street, and he took this opportunity to alter his label. The phrase "FROM LONDON" was removed, the address was changed to "No. 132 South Second Street," and an American eagle was added to the elaborate metalwork atop the illustrated sideboard. No examples of this label are known, but its evolution is obvious from the appearance of the Joseph B. Barry & Son label described in the next entry.

Two known signed pieces by Barry are a Classical mahogany sideboard in a private collection, inscribed in pencil

J.B. Barry 1813

and a tall case clock, also privately owned, signed in chalk

J. Barry

Refs.: Bjerkoe; Cooper; *Antiques,* January 1975.

Classical mahogany sideboard attributed to the Philadelphia cabinetmaker Joseph B. Barry (1757–1838), active on South Second Street from 1804 to 1810.

Courtesy, Ginsburg & Levy, New York.

BARRY, JOSEPH B., & SON

In 1810 Joseph B. Barry (see previous entry) took his son Joseph into partnership, a relationship that continued at least until 1822. In confirmation of this event, the 1804 label described in the previous entry was crudely altered by squeezing in the phrase "& Son" to the right of the larger "Joseph B. Barry" and adding *S* to the words "CABINET MAKER & UPHOLSTERER." A large classical figure was also engraved at each side of the text. These stopgap labels were employed despite the fact that the address was not accurate; Barry had been listed since 1805 at No. 134 rather than 132 South Second Street. At some point this was corrected by production of a newly designed label, which, while retaining the original furniture illustrations (but dropping the classical figure on the right), reworked the proprietors' names to read,

Jos.h B. Barry & Son,/CABINET MAKERS & UPHOLSTERERS:/No. 134 South Second Street/PHILADELPHIA

The text at the foot of the label remained unchanged.

Joseph Jr. vanished from the Philadelphia directory during the period 1822–1829, and when he returned appears to have been working alone at a different address through 1841. Ref.: *Antiques,* March 1954.

BARRY, JOSEPH & COMPANY

A pair of Classical mahogany armchairs branded

J. BARRY & CO.

on the front seat rails reflect the fact that Philadelphia directories for the period 1830–1833 list the cabinetmaking firm of Joseph Barry and Company at 129 Walnut Street. The "CO." may have been Joseph Jr. or another partner. Ref.: *Antiques,* May 1994.

BARTELS, WILLIAM H.

A late-nineteenth-century Victorian sewing hassock in the collection of the Illinois State Museum is signed

W.H. Bartels/May 1883

William H. Bartels, an Illinois cabinetmaker active c. 1880–1895, also made an ornate fireplace surround signed

Bartels./ 93

which is in the same collection. Ref.: Correspondence, Illinois State Museum, May 11, 1973.

BARTLETT, LEVI

A Federal card table in a private collection bears the printed paper label of Levi Bartlett (1784–1864):

Mahogany, Cherry, and/Birch furniture, of all/kinds, and of the latest/fashions, manufactured/by LEVI BARTLETT,/opposite Gale's Tavern,/Concord, N.H.

Bartlett, born in Salisbury, was first associated with the cabinetmaker Hubbard C. Gale of Concord (see his entry). After Gale's death in 1805, Bartlett took over the shop, running it and a second works in Salisbury until 1809, when he sold out and moved to Boston, where he became a merchant. Only two labeled pieces by Bartlett are known. Refs.: *Antiques,* May 1979, May 1982.

BASSETT, STEPHEN

A sophisticated Federal inlaid mahogany bowfront chest of drawers, c. 1790–1800, bearing the inscription

Made by Stephen Bassett for daughter Rebecca toward wedding outfit

is the only present evidence of the existence of a Massachusetts cabinetmaker of that name.

BATCHELLOR, OLIVER

Oliver Batchellor (1791–1816) of New Ipswich, New Hampshire, had an all-too-brief career, leaving behind only a well-made Sheraton mahogany card table inscribed in chalk

Oliver Batchellor/Cabinetmaker

Refs.: Currier; *Antiques,* July 1968.

BAUDOUINE, CHARLES A.

One of the most successful nineteenth-century cabinetmakers, Charles Baudouine (1808–1895) of New York City produced much Rococo and Renaissance Revival furniture. He was in business on Pearl Street as early as 1828, moving c. 1839 to Broadway, where he had several addresses before retiring around 1856. While at 333 Broadway during the 1840s, he employed the stencil

Charles Baudouine/333 Broadway/ New York

Federal inlaid mahogany bowfront chest of drawers, c. 1790–1800, signed "Made by Stephen Bassett for daughter Rebecca toward wedding outfit." Bassett was a Massachusetts cabinetmaker.

Courtesy, Israel Sack, Inc., New York.

Detail of stenciled mark of the New York City cabinetmaker Charles A. Baudouine (1808–1895). He was at 335 Broadway c. 1849–1854. Courtesy, Munson-Williams-Proctor Institute, Utica, N.Y.

By 1852 the address was 335 Broadway and the stencil read,

FROM/C.A. BAUDOUINE/ 335/BROADWAY/ NEW-YORK

During this period he also employed a label illustrated with an engraving of his factory and

**Detail of the ink signatures of Moses Bayley and Joshua Morss on the Queen Anne
high chest of drawers or highboy.** Courtesy, Israel Sack, Inc., New York.

his showroom that read,

BAUDOUINE'S/Fashionable Furniture &
Upholstery/ESTABLISHMENT/
335 BROADWAY/NEW-YORK/
Keeps constantly on hand the/Largest
Assortment of Elegant Furniture/to be
Found in the United States.

Only a single copy of this label is known. Refs.:
Fairbanks and Bates; *Antiques,* May 1981, September 1981.

BAYCOCK, A. J.

A Federal Pembroke table c. 1810–1820 offered
at Christie's January 23, 1988, is inscribed in
pencil

This table was made in Brookfield,
Madison County, New York. By A.J.
Baycock and moved to Jefferson County
into the Village of Champion in
May the 31st 1825.

Nothing more is known of Baycock, and the
inscription is more likely that of an owner than
that of the cabinetmaker.

BAYLEY, MOSES, AND JOSHUA MORSS

A c. 1748–1749 Queen Anne curly maple
high chest of drawers or highboy bears the
signatures of a pair of obscure Massachusetts
cabinetmakers. It is inscribed in ink

Made by Mofses Bayley Newbury/
February AD 1748/9

and in pencil

Made by/Joshua Morss/Jan 1748/9

Although Moses Bayley is listed as a cabinetmaker and house joiner by Bjerkoe, the birth
date she gives, 1744, either is wrong or refers
to another Moses, possibly a son. Nothing is
known of Joshua Morss. Refs.: Bjerkoes;
Antiques, May 1979.

BEAKES, WILLIAM, JR.

A William and Mary walnut chest of drawers signed

William Beakes 1711

is attributed to the cabinetmaker William

Beakes, Jr., who was apprenticed to William Till of Philadelphia in 1694. Refs.: Fairbanks and Bates; *Antiques,* October 1989.

BEAL, SAMUEL

Samuel Beal, a Boston cabinetmaker and furniture warehouse owner, advertised in the *Daily Evening Transcript* for July 24, 1830, a wide variety of furniture, including chairs, tables, couches, bureaus, and washstands. Among the pieces from his hand is a center table in the Victorian Neo-Grec mode, which is inscribed

S. Beal

Ref.: Fairbanks and Bates.

BEALE, JOSEPH

The Philadelphia cabinetmaker Joseph Beale (active at 261 High Street, 1797–1807) is known for at least two signed pieces of Federal furniture, a mahogany and satinwood secretary desk pencil-signed on a drawer bottom

J. Beale

and a lyre-base worktable upon which the same name is branded. Refs.: *Antiques,* April 1961, June 1985, May 1991.

BEALL, GUSTAVUS

Gustavus Beall, who described himself as a cabinetmaker "from New-York," had a

Queen Anne curly maple high chest of drawers or highboy, c. 1748–1749, signed by the Newbury, Massachusetts, cabinetmakers Moses Bayley and Joshua Morss. Courtesy, Israel Sack, Inc., New York.

shop and wareroom on High Street in Georgetown, District of Columbia, from at least 1811 until he sold out in 1819. A partial label on a late Federal breakfast table in the manner of Duncan Phyfe can be deciphered as follows:

Cabinet Ware-House/GUSTAVUS BEALL/ Having taken the Stand lately occupied by WORTHING/TON & BE . . . in High Street, George Town, respectfully/informs his Friends and the Public in general that he has comm/enced the above business, and solicits their patronage/Having received a large supply of the best

Signed Federal mahogany and satinwood secretary-desk by the Philadelphia cabinet-maker Joseph Beale, who worked at 261 High Street, c. 1797–1807. Courtesy, Bernard and S. Dean Levy, New York.

materials from New-York, and employed good and faithful workmen trusts/that by his application and industry he shall not be altogether/unworthy of attention/ . . . . His furniture shall be made in a new way, supe/rior in elegance. . . .
Ref.: *Antiques,* May 1975.

BEALS, LEWIS

Lewis Beals (1779–1829) carried on an active cabinetmaking business in St. Albans, Vermont, from 1800 until his death. Although his shop inventory indicates a substantial business, with hundreds of tools and various unfinished pieces, only a single signed example is presently known. This is a massive late Federal mahogany sideboard inscribed in pencil

This sidbord Made at St. Albans in the Stait of Vermont/By/Lewis Beals
Ref.: Robinson; *Antiques,* October 1970.

BEAR, JOHN

A Chippendale walnut chest of drawers bears the red chalk signature

Johan Bear
for John Bear (working c. 1786–1803), a Mennonite from Earl Township, Lancaster County, Pennsylvania, where he was first listed as a joiner in 1786. He left the county in 1803. Ref.: *Antiques,* May 1984.

Detail of pencil signature, "J. Beale," appearing on a drawer bottom in the Federal secretary desk by Joseph Beale. Courtesy, Bernard and S. Dean Levy, Inc., New York.

BEARY, CHRISTIAN

The Chester County, Pennsylvania, craftsman Christian Beary is known for a Chippendale cherry slant-front desk that is stamped in several places

C. BEARY

Beary worked in Coventry Township from 1797, when he was listed as a joiner on the tax rolls, until his death in 1833. His inventory included cabinet wood and numerous tools. Ref.: Schiffer.

BECK, D.

The underseat of a sack-back armchair attributed to Massachusetts is stamped

D. BECK

which may be the name of an as yet undocumented chairmaker. Ref.: Santore II.

BEDELL, J. W.

A rare set of matching bamboo-turned rod-back Windsor side chairs, each of which

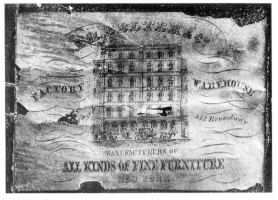

Detail of the label of John Henry Belter illustrating his factory and warehouse. This label was used during the period 1854–1861. Courtesy, Museum of the City of New York.

is impressed beneath the seat

J.W. BEDELL

was sold at a Skinner's auction, January 2, 1987. They are thought to be the work of a presently unknown New England chairmaker.

BEDORTHA, CALVIN

At Historic Deerfield there is a bow-back Windsor side chair bearing the label of Calvin Bedortha of West Springfield, Massachusetts. Bedortha stated in an 1800 advertisement that he had ". . . commenced the chair-making business in West Springfield. . . ." He appears to have carried on until at

A pair of bamboo-turned rod-back Windsor side chairs stamped beneath the seats with the mark of the New England turner J. W. Bedell. Courtesy, Skinner, Inc., Bolton, Mass.

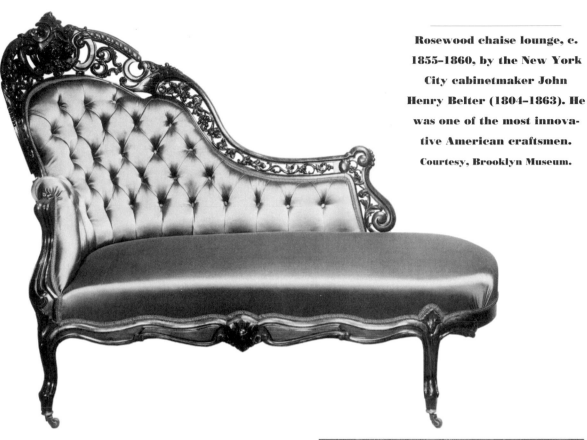

Rosewood chaise lounge, c. 1855–1860, by the New York City cabinetmaker John Henry Belter (1804–1863). He was one of the most innovative American craftsmen. Courtesy, Brooklyn Museum.

least 1815. Ref.: *Springfield Furniture, 1700–1850* (Springfield, Mass.: Connecticut Valley Historical Museum, 1990).

BELDEN, GEORGE

A Chippendale cherry secretary in a private collection is inscribed within the top drawer

GEORGE BELDEN/HARTFORD/
May 6, 1791

George Belden (1770–1838) worked in Windsor, outside of Hartford, Connecticut, c. 1790–1810. Ref.: *Connecticut Furniture, Seventeenth and Eighteenth Centuries* (Hartford: Wadsworth Atheneum, 1967).

BELT, BENJAMIN MIDDLETOWN

See James Robinson.

BELTER, JOHN HENRY

One of the most important nineteenth-century American cabinetmakers (known for developing laminated, carved Rococo Revival furniture), John Henry Belter (1804–1863) was born in Germany and first appeared in New York City in 1844, when he was operating a cabinet shop at 40½ Chatham Square. Within a few years he had moved to Broadway, where he had both shop and showroom for his Rococo Revival furniture until the factory was reestablished on a grand scale at Third Avenue and Seventy-sixth Street.

Despite the general belief that identifiable Belter furniture is rare, a surprising variety of marks is known. The first of these date to the period 1853–1856, when the business was located at 547 Broadway. A rosewood center table at the Newark Museum bears a partial label reading,

**CABINET MANUFACTURER/
547 BROADWAY/ NEW YORK**

From 1856 until 1861 the showrooms were at 552 Broadway and the workshop (after 1854) was at Third Avenue and Seventy-sixth Street. Although there is a rosewood center table that is signed simply

Impressed mark of John Henry Belter on a c. 1856–1863 rosewood bedstead. This stamp, reading J. H. BELTER/ PATENT/AUGUST 19, 1856/N.Y., reflects Belter's patent on construction of a two-piece bedstead. Private collection.

J.H. Belter/552/Broadway
pieces more often bear a paper label engraved with a representation of Belter's showrooms and the wording

**J.H. BELTER & Co./FACTORY/3rd Avenue
76th St./WAREHOUSE/552 Broadway/
MANUFACTURERS OF/ALL KINDS OF
FINE FURNITURE/ NEW YORK**

It was during this, the high period of his career, that Belter also patented two designs for serpentine bedsteads. Beds made under the first, four-piece construction patent are impressed

**J. H. BELTER/ PATENT/
AUGUST 15, 1856/ N.Y.**

while ones conforming to Belter's two-piece

Patent model made by John Henry Belter to accompany his application for an 1858 patent for the laminating process used in constructing his furniture. Courtesy, the Smithsonian Institution.

Detail of stenciled mark of Bembe & Kimbel

on the oak armchair, c. 1850–1870.

Private collection.

construction patent are stamped

J.H. BELTER/PATENT/
AUGUST 19, 1856/N.Y.

There is also yet another patent from this period, for a bureau, this impressed simply

J.H. BELTER/PATENT/NEW YORK

Following Belter's death in 1863, several brothers-in-law continued the business, and the rare inscription

J.H. Belter & Co.

may date from this period. However, in 1865 the new proprietors changed the firm name to Springmeyer Brothers (see their entry) and the stenciled logo to

SPRINGMEYER BRO'S/ J.H. BELTER &
CO./722 BROADWAY,/ NEW YORK

It didn't help. The firm went into bankruptcy

Carved and turned oak armchair bearing

the stenciled mark of Bembe & Kimbel, a

firm of New York City cabinetmakers active

c. 1850–1870. This chair was made in 1857

for the U. S. House of Representatives and

used there until 1859. Courtesy, the Henry

Ford Museum, Dearborn, Mich.

in 1867. Refs.: Bjerkoe; Schwartz, Stanek, and True; *Antiques,* September 1948, May 1981.

BEMAN, REUBEN, JR.

A Chippendale cherry chest on chest at Winterthur bears the chalk inscription

Reuben Beman Junr.

and is the work of Reuben Beman, Jr., a relative of the well-known Windsor chair maker Ebenezer Tracy (see his entry). Beman (b. 1742) is first listed as a cabinetmaker in Kent, Connecticut, in 1785. The date 1801, which also appears on the piece, may indicate when it was made. Refs.: Bjerkoe; Downs.

BEMBE & KIMBEL

The firm of A. Bembe and A. Kimbel, active c. 1850–1870, made massive Victorian furniture, some of which, in the

Renaissance Revival style, was stenciled

**BEMBE & KIMBEL/
928/BROADWAY/NEW YORK**

Among their products were a suite of carved and turned chairs made in 1857 for use in the U.S. House of Representatives. Not found suitable by the House membership, these chairs were auctioned in 1859. Among the buyers was the photographer Mathew Brady, who later photographed President Lincoln in one of them. Ref.: Bishop.

BENDER, LEWIS

A Philadelphia sack-back armchair, c. 1780–1800, bears the impressed mark

L. BENDER

for the Windsor chair maker Lewis Bender, who is listed as working in Philadelphia in 1794. Ref.: Santore II.

BENJAMIN, A.

A c. 1790–1800 Hepplewhite worktable in mahogany and satinwood with silk bag at the Henry Ford Museum has the name

A. Benjamin

written in chalk. The piece is thought to be of Massachusetts origin, but nothing is known of Benjamin. He (or she) may well be a former owner.

BENNET, J.

The inscription

J. BENNET, PORT BYRON

beneath the seat of a midnineteenth-century rocking chair may be that of either the maker or an owner.

BENNETT, COTTON

Cotton Bennett (1786–1859), originally from New Market, New Hampshire, was in Salem, Massachusetts, by 1808. In 1817 he bought land for a shop on Cabot Street in nearby Beverly. He is thought to have worked there for the remainder of his productive life. Presently, the only piece from his hand that can be identified is a Federal mahogany and satinwood secretary or desk and bookcase, which is inscribed three times in ink

Cotton Bennett

and dated 1809. It is at the Essex Institute in

New England Hepplewhite mahogany and satinwood worktable, c. 1790–1800, with the chalk signature of A. Benjamin, who could have been either the maker or an owner. Courtesy, the Henry Ford Museum, Dearborn, Mich.

Salem. Ref.: *Essex Institute Historical Collections,* July 1964.

BENT, S., & BROS.

According to the brand beneath its chair seats,

S. BENT & BROS., INC. 1867,
GARDNER, MASS.

this was a firm of some antiquity. However, its products seem to have consisted of c. 1880–1910 mass-produced Colonial Revival–style Windsor chairs. Some of these also bear a paper label reading,

PROGRESSIVE CHAIRMAKERS/
S. BENT & BROTHERS, INC./
GARDNER, MASS

Refs.: Fairbanks and Bates; Kane.

BERKEY & GAY

One of the major producers of "Grand Rapids" furniture, Berkey & Gay grew out of a cabinet shop established by Julius Berkey in the 1860s. The firm became Berkey & Matter in 1862 and by the 1870s commanded a wide business as Berkey & Gay. Numerous marked examples are known, including a line of Colonial Revival furnishings appropriately labeled

Patent Antique/BERKEY & GAY/
Grand Rapids, Michigan/U.S.A.

BERNARDA, VALENTI

See Paul Cermenati.

BERRY, JAMES A.

A cherry wardrobe bearing in the top drawer the pencil inscription

Detail of the impressed mark
J. BERTINE/N.YORK, beneath the seat of
the braced bow-back Windsor side chair.
Private collection.

James A. Berry Maker this 26 day of/
August 1842

was produced by cabinetmaker James Berry (working c. 1840–1850) of Robertson County, Tennessee. Ref.: Williams and Harsh.

BERRY, W. J.

A set of six painted step-down arrow-back Windsor side chairs are marked beneath the seat

W.J. Berry Fayette Corner, Maine

This may be either the maker's or an owner's mark. Ref.: *MAD,* December 1977.

BERTINE, JAMES

Of Huguenot ancestry, the Manhattan chairmaker James Bertine came from a New Rochelle, New York, family. He is listed in New York City directories as working at Pearl and Queen streets from 1790 through 1797. Among the Windsor chairs marked by him are continuous-arm chairs and braced bow-back side chairs. All are impressed beneath the seat

J.BERTINE/N.YORK

Ref.: Bjerkoe; *Antiques,* May 1981.

BEST, ALBERT, & CO.

A privately owned walnut marble-top center table in the Victorian Renaissance Revival style is stenciled

MANUFACTURED BY/Albert Best & Company/BUFFALO, NEW YORK

The table appears to date c. 1870–1900. Nothing is known of the maker.

Victorian Renaissance Revival walnut marble-top center table bearing the stenciled mark of Albert Best & Company, Buffalo, New York, c. 1870–1900. Private collection.

BIGELOW, JABEZ

An early-nineteenth-century grain-painted blanket chest over drawer in a private collection is inscribed beneath the lid

Jabez Bigelow/South Groton

which may be the name of the maker, the decorator, or an owner. The chest is of New England form and may be from Connecticut or Massachusetts. Both states have communities named Groton. Ref.: *Antiques,* June 1957.

Braced bow-back Windsor side chair bearing the impressed mark of James Bertine, a New York City Windsor chair maker, active at Pearl and Queen streets, c. 1790–1797. Private collection.

BILLINGS, P. P.

A late Federal paint-decorated "fancy" rocker formerly in the Lipman collection is stenciled

P.P. BILLINGS, N.Y.

for either the maker or the decorator.

BIRD, JONATHAN

A Federal inlaid cherry wood tilt-top table impressed

J. BIRD

and with the incised date "1792" is attributed to the cabinetmaker Jonathan Bird of Charleston,

Detail of impressed mark J. BIRD of Jonathan Bird. Courtesy, George Michael, Merrimack, N.H.

South Carolina. Bird, a native of Yorkshire, England, was active in Charleston, c. 1777–1807. A few other similarly marked pieces are known. Ref.: Bjerkoe.

BIRDSEY, JOSEPH, JR.

A fan-back Windsor side chair in a private collection bears the partial label of Joseph Birdsey, Jr., a craftsman who worked in Ridgefield or Huntington, Connecticut, c. 1790–1805. The oval label reads,

Federal inlaid cherry wood tilt-top table dated 1792 and branded by Jonathan Bird, a cabinetmaker active in Charleston, South Carolina, c. 1777–1807. Courtesy, George Michael, Merrimack, N.H.

Joseph Birdsey, Jur./ Cabinet Maker/ with at least one further line obscured. No complete label is known. Ref.: Santore II.

BISHOP, AMOS

A pine chest of drawers illustrated in *Antiques,* January 1933, was inscribed

Lucy Bishop's Case. Made by A.B.
April 3, 1817

It is attributed to the Shaker carpenter Amos Bishop (1780–1857) of Mount Lebanon, New York. Ref.: Rieman and Burks.

BISHOP, LEMUEL

A Federal inlaid mahogany lampstand bearing the oval label

Made By/Lemuel Bishop/Charlotte/1815

is by the Charlotte, North Carolina, cabinetmaker Lemuel Bishop, active c. 1810–1820. Refs.: Bjerkoe; *Antiques,* May 1951.

BISPHAM, J. M.

The impressed mark

J.M. BISPHAM

appears on a bamboo-turned bow-back Windsor child's side chair illustrated in *Antiques* for August 1980. Both maker and origin remain uncertain. Ref.: Santore II.

BLACK, ROBERT

The Tennessee cabinetmaker Robert Black is known only for a Sheraton cherry chest of drawers inscribed in red joiner's pencil

Robert Black/Dixon's Springs/
21st April, 1819/for Manson Young

Black was active in the town of Carthage, Smith County, Tennessee, from 1806 until his death in 1820. Refs.: Coleman and Harsh; *Antiques,* September 1991.

BLAKE, JAMES G.

A late Federal mahogany dressing mirror (c. 1810–1840) bears the stenciled inscription

FROM/JAMES G. BLAKE/
UPHOLSTERY/AND FURNITURE/
12 to 20 Cornhill/BOSTON

Blake may have been a furniture maker, but it is more likely that he was simply a merchant. Ref.: *Antiques,* February 1976.

BLAKE, JUDSON

A late Federal carved mahogany pedestal-base flip-top card table bears the possibly unique printed paper label

JUDSON BLAKE,/ CABINET MANU-
FACTORY/PRESIDENT.STREET/
Providence, (R.I.)

Although the piece would date c. 1810–1840, nothing is presently known of the maker. Ref.: *Antiques,* January 1975.

BLAKELY, ERASTUS

The Shaftsbury, Vermont, turner Erastus Blakely (1785–1831) is credited with a child's fancy chair, now at the Bennington Museum, that is inscribed with his initials

E B

Ref.: Robinson.

BLANCHARD, EPHRAIM

The New Hampshire cabinetmaker Ephraim Blanchard (1778–1841) ran a shop in Amherst, c. 1800–1830. His printed paper label,

ALL KINDS OF/CABINET FURNI-
TURE,/MADE AND SOLD BY/EPHRAIM
BLANCHARD,/AMHERST, N.H.

has been found on Pembroke and dressing
tables, a Federal desk and bookcase, and two
Empire chests of drawers. Refs.: Currier;
Antiques, May 1979, July 1986.

BLANCHARD, SETH

A walnut, birch, and pine counter with
drawers is inscribed in pencil

Seth Blanchard Born/October 21-1784/
Erected this case April 21-1853/
Aged 68 years 6 Months

Blanchard (1784–1868), a Shaker resident at
the Harvard, Massachusetts, community, is
known only for this signed piece. In the 1850
census he was described as a "carpenter." Ref.:
Rieman and Burks.

BLANCHARD & CO.

Edwin C. Blanchard, the principal in
Blanchard & Co., took over the business
upon the death of his father in 1859, operating
it until he sold out in 1878 to J. M. Jones. His
walnut furniture in late Federal and Empire
modes is stenciled

From/BLANCHARD & CO./
Manufacturers/& Dealers In/FURNITURE./
Planing.Matching./&/UNDERTAKING/
GRANVILLE, O.

Ref.: *Made in Ohio.*

BLATT, BENJAMIN

A paint-decorated step-back cupboard at
the Landis Valley Museum is inscribed

Benj. Blatt 1841

The piece has a Berks County, Pennsylvania, history, but no cabinetmaker by this name is presently recorded. Ref.: *Antiques,* September 1986.

BLAUCH, CHRISTIAN C.

Among the cabinetmakers working in
the Soap Hollow area of Johnstown,
Pennsylvania, was Christian C. Blauch (active
c. 1845–1860), a maker of brightly painted,
stencil-decorated furniture. He is remembered
for a six-board chest with plain bracket feet (at
the Henry Ford Museum) and a late Sheraton-
type chest of drawers, both stenciled

MANUFACTURED BY CHRISTIAN
BLAUCH

as well as another chest, which is stenciled
across the front,

ET 1852 and MF.BY.CCB

Refs.: Fales, *American Painted Furniture; Antique
Review,* November 1993; *Antiques,* May 1983.

BLINN, HENRY C.

An elder in the Canterbury, New Hampshire, community, Henry C. Blinn
(1824–1905) was an accomplished cabinetmaker to whom several pieces are attributed.
However, his name appears only on a mixed-
woods sewing desk inscribed

These two Sewing desks were/made from
Mother Hannah's Butternut/trees, grown
South of Ministries Shop. Were cared for
by her when saplings./Made by
Elder Henry C. Blinn.

Ref.: Rieman and Burks.

BLISS, LUTHER

A cherry desk and bookcase or secretary in a private collection is inscribed **William Lloyd/Luther Bliss/1804** Bliss was apparently a sometime apprentice to the well-known Springfield, Massachusetts, cabinetmaker William Lloyd (see his entry). Bliss later became a tanner. Ref.: *Springfield Furniture, 1700–1850* (Springfield, Mass.: Connecticut Valley Historical Museum, 1990).

BLISS, PELATIAH

The craftsman Pelatiah Bliss worked in Springfield, Massachusetts, c. 1800–1815. In an advertisement placed in the *Hampshire Federalist* for February 15, 1810, he notified the public that ". . . he still carries on the cabinet-making business at his old stand one fourth mile north of Bridge lane. . . ." Known examples from his hand include a Chippendale chest of drawers and both card tables and chests of drawers in the Federal manner. All bear an oval printed label reading,

PELATIAH BLISS/A few rods north of L.& F. Stebbins Store,/Springfield, Ms./CARRIES ON THE/Cabinet Business,/IN ITS VARIOUS BRANCHES

Refs.: Bjerkoe; *Springfield Furniture, 1700–1850* (Springfield, Mass.: Connecticut Valley Historical Museum, 1990); *Antiques, September 1930.*

BLISS, RALPH AND LEWIS

The firm of Ralph and Lewis Bliss (distant cousins) made massive late Federal and Empire furniture in Springfield, Massachusetts, from 1828 until 1832. A sofa bearing their label is at the Wadsworth Atheneum in Hartford, Connecticut. Ref.: *Springfield Furniture, 1700–1850* (Springfield, Mass.: Connecticut Valley Historical Museum, 1990).

BLISS & HORSWILL

The Boston craftsmen Thomas Bliss and John W. Horswill were partners in the cabinetmaking business in Charlestown, Massachusetts, from December 1797 until June 1798. A single labeled piece, an upholstered Federal easy chair, survives to mark this association. Its label reads,

Bliff & Horfwill,/CABINET AND CHAIR MAKERS/FROM BOSTON,/Have taken a stand in Charleftown oppo-/site Mr. Oliver Hall's Store, where they/will carry on the aforfaid busineff, in its various/forms. They make Mahogany and Cherry/ furnishings of all kinds, such as Fancy Chairs,/. . . . .

Ref.: *The Decorative Arts of New Hampshire, 1725–1825* (Manchester: Currier Gallery of Art, 1964).

BLOOM, J.

The Windsor chair maker John Bloom is listed from 1790 until 1840 in census records for the community of Bloom's Corners near Milford, Orange County, New York. He is known for a bow-back Windsor side chair at the New York State Museum, which is impressed beneath the seat

J.BLOOM

Ref.: Scherer.

BLOOM, MATHIAS

The little-known Manhattan Windsor chair maker Mathias Bloom (active 1787–1793)

is remembered for a pair of braced bow-back Windsor side chairs stamped beneath the seat

M.BLOOM/NEW YORK

Refs.: *Antiques,* May 1981; *MAD,* January 1976.

BLYTHE, THOMAS

Little is known of the cabinetmaker Thomas Blythe, who arrived in South Carolina around 1733 and died in Charleston in 1762. A mahogany chest on chest from his hand is said to have been signed

Blythe

Ref.: Bjerkoe.

BOARDMAN, L.

A Federal mahogany bowfront chest of drawers, c. 1790–1800, with birch banding is chalk-signed under the top

L. Boardman

The piece is attributed to Portsmouth, New Hampshire, but it is not known if Boardman was an owner or the maker. Ref.: *Bee,* July 29, 1994.

BOARDMAN, SAMUEL

A Massachusetts Federal mahogany corner washstand, c. 1790–1810, offered at a Weschler's sale January 15, 1994, bore a label inscribed

Saml. Boardman

It is not known if this is a maker's or an owner's name.

BOND, FRANCIS L.

The Tarboro, North Carolina, cabinetmaker Francis L. Bond (1820–1890), active in the 1830s and 1840s, left behind several identifiable pieces in the late Federal style, including a secretary bookcase branded

F.L.BOND/MAKER/TARBORO

and a bureau with looking glass, which is inscribed on a drawer back

F.L. Bond Maker NC 1839

Ref.: Bivins.

BOND, LEWIS

Lewis Bond (1770–1858), father of Francis (see previous entry), is known for a Federal inlaid desk made while he was working at Greenville, North Carolina. A paper label attached to this piece is inscribed

**Lewis Bonds Cabinet/Furniture,
Greenville,/July the 26th 1815**

Bond later moved his business to Tarboro, North Carolina. Ref.: Bivins.

BOOTH, J.

A late Federal sofa (c. 1815–1835), in mahogany with heavily carved feet, bears the signature

J. Booth, Hartford

This could be the name of either a cabinetmaker or an owner. Ref.: *Bee,* January 20, 1994.

BOSTON FURNITURE COMPANY

The Boston Furniture Company of Boston, Massachusetts, produced various examples of Victorian "patent" furnishings during the 1860–1880 period. Its folding walnut armchairs with tapestry upholstery were labeled

**Boston Furniture Co./
Patented Nov. 19, 1867, Aug. 6, 1868**

Later examples with labels including an 1879

Detail of stenciled label of Michael Bouvier. His shop was at 91 South Second Street from 1823 until 1861. Courtesy, Donald L. Fennimore.

patent date also are known. Refs.: Fairbanks and Bates; *MAD,* April 1990.

BOUVIER, MICHAEL

Though a wealthy and important Philadelphian and a leading cabinetmaker of his day, Michael Bouvier (1792–1874) is known for only a single piece of marked furniture, a c. 1823–1840 early Empire maple and mahogany card table stenciled

M. BOUVIER,/Keeps constantly on hand,/CABINET WARE,/Mahogany, hair

---

Victorian Renaissance Revival walnut upholstered folding armchair bearing the label of the Boston Furniture Company, Boston, Massachusetts, active c. 1860–1880. This label has an 1868 patent date. Other examples dated 1867, 1869, and 1879 are known. Private collection.

seatings &c./At No. 91 So: 2d St./PHILADA Bouvier was born and trained in France. In Philadelphia, he established himself in 1819 at Fifth and Walnut streets. In 1823 he moved to 91 South Second Street, where his shop remained until the business was dissolved around 1861. Refs.: *Antiques,* February 1962, April 1973.

BOWEN, JAMES

The New Jersey cabinetmaker James Bowen arrived in Cumberland County around 1780 and appears to have spent most of his working life there. Nevertheless, his only known piece is a Chippendale walnut wardrobe over chest of drawers bearing the branded signature **James Bowen**

Ref.: *Early Furniture Made in New Jersey, 1690–1870* (Newark: Newark Museum Association, 1958).

BOWEN, NATHAN

Nathan Bowen (1752–1837) of Marblehead, Massachusetts, had a long and productive career, leaving behind several identifiable pieces. These include a Chippendale mahogany block-front chest on chest at the Detroit Institute of Arts, which is inscribed

N B 1774

a Chippendale mahogany reverse-serpentine slant-front desk with the inked signature

Nath Bowen/19th Sept 1780

offered at Christie's in October 1985, and a Federal mahogany and bird's-eye maple chest of drawers inscribed

Bowen

Refs.: Bjerkoe; *Antiques,* August 1974.

BOWEN, WILLIAM

The Philadelphia chairmaker William Bowen had a shop at 83 North Front Street, c. 1786–1810. His impressed mark

W. BOWEN

appears on bow-back Windsor side chairs. Bowen appears to have also worked in Cumberland County, New Jersey, after 1810. Refs.: Santore II; *Early Furniture Made in New Jersey, 1690–1870* (Newark: Newark Museum Association, 1958).

BOWEN & HAYES

A c. 1785–1805 low-back Windsor knuckle-arm settee that sold at auction in the fall of 1994 was branded beneath the seat

BOWEN & HAYES

Empire mahogany and maple card table, c. 1823–1840, bearing the stenciled label of Michael Bouvier (1792–1874), active in Philadelphia, c. 1819–1861. Courtesy, Donald L. Fennimore.

This previously unlisted mark may be that of the Philadelphia turner William Bowen (active c. 1786–1810) and an unknown partner. Ref.: *MAD,* December 1994.

BOWEN & MARTIN

The Marblehead, Massachusetts, joiners Nathan Bowen (1752–1837, see his entry) and Ebenezer Martin, Sr. (c. 1735–1800, see his entry), were associated at various times in their careers. The one piece they are known to have collaborated on is a Chippendale mahogany oxbow-base chest on chest at the Museum of Fine Arts, Boston. It is inscribed

E.M. 1780/ Feb. 26 1780/ Martin/Que est Fecit hic/E.M./Nath Bowen/Fecit Invt.

Ref.: Randall.

BOWLES, W.

A small c. 1780–1800 Hepplewhite mahogany desk and bookcase or secretary in a private collection is branded
W.BOWLES
The piece is attributed to Massachusetts, but it is not known if the mark is that of an owner or the maker.

BOYD, HENRY

The African-American cabinetmaker Henry Boyd (1802–1886), born into slavery in Kentucky, purchased his own freedom and came to Cincinnati, Ohio, where by 1836 he had established a successful bed-making shop at the corner of Broadway and Eighth streets and had developed several innovations in furniture construction. A substantial number of his walnut and cherry bedsteads branded
H.BOYD, CINI OHIO
survive. Boyd remained active until 1862. Ref.: *Made in Ohio.*

BOYER

A c. 1850–1870 bootjack-back painted side chair inscribed in paint beneath the seat
B/Roann, Ind.
has been attributed to a craftsman named

Boyer who worked in Roann, Wabash County, Indiana.

BRADLEY, AMOS

A Hepplewhite mahogany and cherry chest of drawers with French feet advertised in *Antiques* for May 1958 is inscribed
Easthaven, Connecticut/October 23, 1801/ Amos Bradley made this
East Haven is now part of greater New Haven. Nothing further is known of this Connecticut cabinetmaker.

Hepplewhite mahogany desk and bookcase or secretary, c. 1780–1800, attributed to Massachusetts and branded W.BOWLES. It is not known if Bowles was an owner or the maker. Courtesy, Israel Sack, Inc., New York.

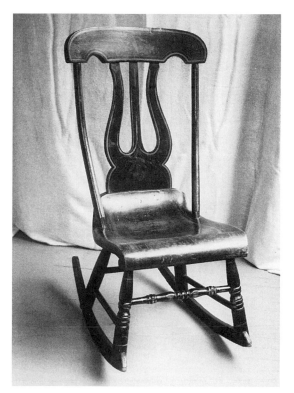

Bootjack-back painted side chair, c. 1850–1870, initialed "B" for Boyer, a Roann, Wabash County, Indiana, chairmaker. Private collection.

BRADLEY, HARRISON, & SON

Harrison Bradley advertised himself as a chairmaker in Alexandria, Virginia, newspapers as early as 1835. Around 1840 he took a son into the business. A c. 1840–1850 Classical mahogany pier table at the Smithsonian Institution bears a label reading,

H. BRADLEY & SON'S,/CABINET, CHAIR AND SOFA/ MANUFACTORY,/CORNER OF KING AND PATRICK

STREETS/Alexandria, D.C./H.B. & SON have constantly on hand, and offer to the Pub-/lic on the lowest terms, an excellent assortment of Cabinet Ware, So-/fas, and Chairs of every variety, which for dur-/ability and finish, can-/not be surpassed. Ref.: Fitzgerald.

BRAUWERS, JOSEPH

One of the lesser-known émigré cabinetmakers is Joseph Brauwers of Manhattan, whose label reading,

JOSEPH BRAUWERS,/No. 163 William-Street, New-York,/(EBENIST, FROM PARIS)/CABINET-MAKER,/With the Richest Ornaments just im-/ported from France.

Detail of mark, B/Roann/Ind., applied in paint to underside of seat of bootjack-back side chair. The "B" is thought to stand for Boyer. Private collection.

has been found on two Classical card tables (one at Winterthur) as well as on an unusual Classical mahogany cellarette offered at Christie's, January 22, 1994. Joseph Brauwers does not appear in early Manhattan directories, but in 1814 a John Brauwer is listed at 163 William Street. Because early directory compilers tended to simplify and alter names to suit themselves, it is likely that this is the cabinetmaker. Refs.: Fairbanks and Bates; Montgomery.

BRECK, J.

A birdcage rod-back Windsor chair bearing under the seat the signature
J. Breck
is in a private collection. The mark may be that of the maker or an owner. Ref.: *MAD,* September 1978.

BREWSTER, G.

A Chippendale mahogany side chair with Gothic latticework back owned by the

Detail of label of Harrison Bradley & Son on the Classical mahogany pier table.
Courtesy, Richard H. Howland, Washington, D.C.

Society for the Preservation of New England Antiquities is inscribed at the base of the splat
G.Brewster/Portsmouth N.H. 1832
Because the mark is very late for the chair, it is likely to be that of an owner. Ref.: *Antiques,* May 1978.

BRIGGS, CORNELIUS

A late Federal mahogany veneer card table with double-lyre pedestal, under the top of which is written in pencil
. . . 1825/C.Briggs 578 Washington Street
is attributed to Cornelius Briggs, a Boston cab-

Classical mahogany pier table, c. 1840–1850, bearing the paper label of Harrison Bradley & Son. Bradley was working as a cabinetmaker in Alexandria, Virginia, as early as 1835. His son entered the business around 1840. Courtesy, Richard H. Howland, Washington, D.C.

inetmaker living at 2 Temple Place in 1817. The piece was offered at Christie's, October 13, 1984. A Federal-Sheraton mahogany sewing or worktable branded

C.BRIGGS

is thought to be by the same maker. Refs.: Bjerkoe; *Antiques,* April 1986.

BRIGGS, ELIPHALET

Eliphalet Briggs (1788–1853), a member of an extended family of cabinetmakers, opened a shop on Washington Street in Keene, New Hampshire, in 1810. Active until at least 1849, he was involved in several partnerships and various building projects but is primarily known now for a Federal mahogany and cherry bowfront chest of drawers, which bears the pencil inscription

Eliphalet Briggs jr,/Keene January 19th 1810,/Made this . . . $19 Doll

Detail of the label on a Classical mahogany cellarette of the New York City cabinetmaker Joseph Brauwers. He worked on William Street in Manhattan, probably c. 1810–1820. Courtesy, Ginsburg & Levy, New York.

It was sold at Sotheby's dispersal of the Little collection, January 29, 1994. A Federal mahogany and rosewood card table inscribed beneath the top

E. Briggs

is also attributed to him. Refs.: Hewitt, Kane, and Ward; *Antiques,* May 1979.

BRIGGS, LYMAN

A son of the New Hampshire cabinetmaker Eliphalet Briggs (see previous entry), Lyman Briggs (b. 1803) moved to Montpelier, Vermont, where he carried on the family trade from 1825 until at least 1850, in partnership during 1826–1829 with his brother Joseph G. Briggs. A washstand in a private collection is labeled

Cabinet Furniture made in the most Fashionable and Durable manner, and sold Wholesale and Retail by, Lyman Briggs, Montpelier, Vt./All orders duly acknowledged and promptly attended to.

Ref.: Robinson.

BRIGHAM, EZEKIEL, JR.

The cabinetmaker Ezekiel Brigham, Jr. (1789–1848), of Grafton, Massachusetts, made a Hepplewhite mahogany slant-front desk with French feet now in the collection of Old Sturbridge Village. It bears a paper label with Brigham's name and the date "February 1816." Refs.: Comstock, *American Furniture; Antiques,* May 1993.

BRIGHT, GEORGE

Known to his contemporaries as "the neatest workman in town," George Bright (1726–1805) had a shop on Fish Street in

Boston, where he produced a variety of fine furniture, including an extraordinary bombé desk and bookcase or secretary inscribed in chalk

Ge . . . Bright

It is now at the Museum of Fine Arts, Boston. Bright also made a group of leather-upholstered bergère-form armchairs, c. 1797, for the Massachusetts State House in Boston. He was active c. 1750–1800. Refs.: Bjerkoe; Montgomery; Randall.

BRIGHT, I.

An eighteenth-century Queen Anne maple side chair with seat and back upholstered in leather bears on the back splat the brand

I B

which may be the mark of John Bright, Sr. (1681–1786), one of a prolific family of Boston chair- and cabinetmakers. Ref.: Bernard and S. Dean Levy, Catalog 4 (New York: By-Art Publishing Company, 1984).

BRIGHT, JOHN AND WILLIAM

A Chippendale mahogany sofa advertised in *Antiques* for November 1965 is signed on the crest rail

J. & W. Bright

for John and William Bright, Boston cabinetmakers and sons of George Bright (see his

---

Leather-upholstered Federal bergère armchair, c. 1797, made by the Boston craftsman George Bright (1726–1805). This is one of a group made for the Massachusetts State House. Courtesy, the Henry Ford Museum, Dearborn, Mich.

entry). They are listed in the 1797 Boston directory as working at 44 Marlborough Street. Ref.: Bjerkoe.

BROCAS, JOHN

A japanned high chest of drawers or highboy in a private collection is inscribed

Brocas

on a drawer interior. This is the signature of either John Brocas, Sr. (working 1701–1740), or John Brocas, Jr. (working 1728–1751). Both were Boston cabinetmakers with a shop on Union Street. Refs.: Bjerkoe; *Antiques,* May 1979, January 1984.

127 FULTON ST. COR. SANDS BROOKLYN, N.Y.

Lithograph of the cabinet warehouse of the cabinetmaker Thomas Brooks (1811–1887), on Fulton Street, Brooklyn, New York, c. 1856–1876. Courtesy, *The Magazine Antiques.*

BROOK

A c. 1790–1810 fan-back Windsor chair branded

BROOK

on the underside of the seat was advertised in *MAD* for July 1979. The mark may be that of the maker or an owner.

BROOKS, F.

A painted half-spindle variation of the rod-back Windsor side chair now at Old Sturbridge Village is marked

F.Brooks, Warranted

The chair would date c. 1830–1850, and the mark is probably that of a Connecticut manufacturer. A set of four similarly marked thumbback side chairs was sold at a 1994 auction. Ref.: Kenney.

BROOKS, JONATHAN

T o Jonathan Brooks (1745–1808), a New London, Connecticut, cabinetmaker, is attributed a cherry bonnet-top high chest of drawers or highboy inscribed in red ink

1769/Made by John Brooks

which was sold at Sotheby's November 27–30, 1979. Brooks had a long career, advertising in New London newspapers several times between 1768 and 1801. Refs.: Bjerkoe; *New London County Furniture, 1640–1840* (New London, Conn.: Lyman Allyn Museum, 1974).

BROOKS, THOMAS

S ome of the most spectacular Victorian Renaissance Revival furniture was produced by Thomas Brooks (1811–1887), who was in business by 1841 and established at Nos. 127 to 129 Fulton Street in Brooklyn, New

York, by 1856. His label on a bedstead reads **FROM/T. BROOKS/cabinet/x/ UPHOLSTERY/WAREHOUSE/127 Fulton St. cor Sands St./Brooklyn, N.Y.** At some point the firm name became Thomas Brooks & Co., with Brooks remaining controlling partner until he retired in 1876. Among the pieces bearing his stenciled mark **Thomas Brooks & Co./ 127 Fulton Street/Brooklyn, N.Y.** are a set of chairs at the Brooklyn Museum, a bookcase presented to the singer Jenny Lind, marble-top washstands, étagères, and a lady's writing desk. Refs.: Bjerkoe; Fitzgerald.

Stenciled mark of the Brooklyn cabinetmaker Thomas Brooks on the Renaissance Revival bedstead.
Courtesy, Neal Auction Company.

BROOKS BROS.

Edward and William Brooks established their cabinetmaking partnership in 1878 at 123 Mill Street in Rochester, New York, where they remained until 1884, when they took new quarters on West Street, continuing there into the 1890s.

Specializing in Victorian Eastlake chamber or bedroom furniture, they marked their wares with a printed paper label reading, **FROM/BROOKS BROS.,/ MANUFACTURERS OF/FURNITURE/ 123 Mill Street., ROCHESTER, N.Y.** Ref.: Scherer.

Walnut Victorian Renaissance Revival bedstead, c. 1860–1870 bearing the stenciled mark of Thomas Brooks (1811–1887), active on Fulton Street in Brooklyn, New York, c. 1841–1876.
Courtesy, Neal Auction Company.

BROWER, JOHN L.

A pair of late Federal carved saber-leg side chairs offered at Christie's, June 4, 1988, are inscribed on the front rails

J.L.(?) Brower Maker 181 Chambers St. New York

The maker's initials are hard to read, but it is likely that they are those of John L. Brower, listed in New York City directories as maintaining a "Cabinet-Warehouse," c. 1810–1830.

BROWN, CHESTER

A Federal cherry reverse-serpentine chest of drawers offered at auction in March 1994 by Swinebord-Denton, of Lexington, Kentucky, bears the signature

Chester Brown

This may be the mark of either an owner or the maker.

BROWN, DAVID

A Chippendale shell-carved mahogany slant-top desk bears the penciled inscription **Manufactured by David Brown for his brother-in-law Enoch Greenleaf, 1782**
The maker was the brother of Samuel Brown (1720–1798), a Newburyport, Massachusetts, cabinetmaker. Ref.: Bernard and S. Dean Levy, Catalog 5 (New York: Cosmos Communications, 1986).

BROWN, G.

The Sterling, Massachusetts, chairmaker G. Brown is known for a decorated flat-top Windsor side chair as well as a set of four "rabbit ear" Windsors advertised in *MAD* for September 1978. All are branded

G. BROWN/WARRANTED

and date c. 1820–1840. Ref.: Fales, *American Painted Furniture*.

BROWN, ISRAEL

Israel Brown (1800–1860) of Montgomery, Ohio, was a prominent local politician who also made furniture, leaving behind an Empire cherry chest of drawers signed

ISRAEL BROWN

Ref.: Hageman I.

Chippendale mahogany slant-top desk with shell-carved interior, with the pencil signature "Manufactured by David Brown for his brother-in-law Enoch Greenleaf, 1782." Brown was a Newburyport, Massachusetts, cabinetmaker. Courtesy of Bernard and S. Dean Levy, Inc., New York.

BROWN, LEMUEL P.

A privately owned late Sheraton chest of drawers bears the printed label of the cabinetmaker Samuel S. Noyes (see his entry) of East Sudbury, Massachusetts, which has written across it in ink

**January 14, 1825/Warted
{Warranted}/Made by Leml. P. Brown,
Jourman**

indicating that Brown, an employee of the Noyes firm, produced it. No other pieces by Brown are known. Ref.: *Antiques,* June 1966.

BROWN, ROBERT T. S.

A Federal two-drawer stand, c. 1800–1820, advertised in *MAD* for September 1978, is inscribed on the top drawer bottom

Robt. T.S. Brown

No cabinetmaker of this name is known, and it is probably an owner's mark.

BROWN, T.

A stencil-decorated Salem rocker, c. 1810–1830, is impressed twice on the underside of the seat

T. BROWN

Stylistically, the piece would relate to Connecticut, and the stamp is more likely that of the maker than that of an owner.

BROWN, WILLIAM

A Sheraton cherry bowfront chest of drawers in a private collection is inscribed in ink on the bottom of the top drawer

**Wm Brown/Cabinet/Maker
May 15th 1815/Joel & Purity**

Probably made for a wedding couple, this piece could be attributed to one of three cabinetmakers named William Brown, one from Boston, a second from Baltimore, and a third from New London, Connecticut. Ref.: *Antiques,* July 1972.

BRUMLEY, JOSEPH

Joseph Brumley, then of Mount Holly, New Jersey, made a tall case clock case for the clockmaker William Hudson, inscribing it

J. Brumley, 1785

Brumley later worked in Trenton, New Jersey (c. 1798), and by 1800 he was in Washington, D.C. Ref.: *Antiques,* August 1984.

BRUNER & MOORE

The brothers Henry and Peter Bruner, cabinetmakers from Prussia, formed with a man named Moore the firm Bruner & Moore, which was located from 1853 until 1876 at 75–77 King Street in Manhattan. Several pieces of Renaissance Revival walnut furniture from this period bear the stencil

**BRUNER & MOORE/
FURNITURE/WAREHOUSE/
75 & 77 KING ST./NEW YORK.**

In 1876 the shop and factory was moved to 41 West Fourteenth Street, where it remained until 1891, when the business was sold to one George C. Flint (see his entry). Refs.: Comstock, *American Furniture; Antiques,* May 1974, May 1975.

BRUNNER, WILLIAM

A decorated poplar blanket chest in the Chippendale manner, now part of the Abby Aldrich Rockefeller Folk Art Collection, is inscribed in red pencil

Wm. Brunner

It is thought to date c. 1820–1835 and to have been made by William Brunner, a Wythe County, Virginia, craftsman. Ref.: *Antiques,* March 1974.

BUCKTROUT, BENJAMIN

lthough he is known for only a single piece of furniture, Benjamin Bucktrout (working 1766–1779, d. 1813) of Williamsburg, Virginia, is one of our most published cabinetmakers. His spectacular Masonic master's armchair now at Colonial Williamsburg has been photographed numerous times. This massive chair, which incorporates in its design various bits of Masonic regalia, is stamped

BENIMAN/BUCKTROUT
and dates c. 1767–1770. Refs.: Bjerkoe; Cooper; Fairbanks and Bates; Fitzgerald; *Antiques,* August 1978, June 1984, October 1989.

BUDD, JOHN

lthough the cabinetmaker John Budd of Manhattan was in business as early as 1817 and was still listed in the city directory in 1840, I know of only two labeled pieces by him: a mahogany card table with rope-twist legs and an unusual two-drawer writing table. Both are late Federal, dating c. 1820–1830. Budd's labels read,

JOHN BUDD/CABINET MAKER,/
NO. 118 FULTON-STREET,/
BETWEEN WILLIAM AND NASSAU
STREETS,/NEW-YORK,/Has constantly
for sale a general assortment of Cabinet
Ware,/on the most reasonable
terms./Orders from southern ports
immediately attended to, and/all furniture
warranted. May, 1817.

Refs.: Bjerkoe; *Antiques,* February 1961, April 1976.

BULLOCK, EZEKIAL

he Carlisle, Pennsylvania, chairmaker Ezekial Bullock took over his father's shop in 1819, continuing the business until around 1845. He advertised ". . . fancy and Grecian chairs together with settees and sociables. . . ." One of the former, a country Empire painted and gilded chair at the Cumberland County Historical Society, is stamped on the underseat

E. BULLOCK
Ref.: *Antiques,* September 1979.

BUNNELL, H. C.

pair of child-size plank armchairs in the so-called Adirondack style offered for sale in the May 1994 issue of *MAD* were marked

MFD. H. C. BUNNELL,
Westport, N.Y./Pat. July 16, 1905,
Improved July 6, 1922
Bunnell, of Westport, a small community on Lake Champlain, was one of many producing these popular and inexpensive camp chairs.

BURBANK

wo late-eighteenth-century Chippendale mahogany slant-front desks, Boston-Salem area in design, have been found to bear the inscribed signature

Burbank
The existence of two such pieces raises the distinct possibility that this is the mark of an as yet unknown Massachusetts cabinetmaker. Ref.: *Antiques,* April 1968.

BURCHALL & WICKERSHAM

For a firm that was in business only from 1822 (when they advertised ". . . a general assortment of Fancy, Rushbottom and Windsor chairs . . .") until 1824, the chairmakers Burchall and Wickersham of West Chester, Pennsylvania, have left behind a surprising number of examples bearing the label

BURCHALL & WICKERSHAM/FANCY AND WINDSOR/CHAIR-MAKERS/Next door to P & S Kendall's Store/ WEST CHESTER, PA

These chairs include arrow-back Windsors, painted rod-backs, and bamboo-turned "fancy chairs." Ref.: Schiffer.

BURCHSTED, J.

A carved Chippendale mahogany tilt-top tea table, c. 1770–1780, offered at Sotheby's, April 29–May 1, 1981, is stamped

J. BURCHSTED

The piece is attributed to Massachusetts in style, but it is not known if the mark is that of a cabinetmaker.

BURDEN, JOSEPH

A variety of marked Windsors are known from the Philadelphia chairmaker Joseph Burden (1793–1839). These include rod-back side chairs and settees, medallion-back side chairs, and birdcage armchairs. Two brands exist:

J. BURDEN

and

J.BURDEN/PHILADA

Burden had a shop with various partners on South Third Street in Philadelphia, c. 1796–1816. Refs.: Santore II; *Antiques,* May 1991.

BURLING, SAMUEL AND WILLIAM S.

The Manhattan cabinetmakers Samuel and William Burling are known for a Federal mahogany chest of drawers with

Chippendale cherry block-front slant-front desk signed and dated 1769 by the Colchester, Connecticut, cabinetmaker Benjamin Burnham (c. 1737–1773).

Courtesy, *Index of American Design,* Metropolitan Museum of Art.

French feet, which is labeled

Samuel & Wm. S. Burling,/CABINET-MAKERS,/No. 25, BEEKMAN-STREET,/NEW-YORK.

Manhattan directories reveal that the Burlings worked at 25 Beekman Street during the period 1805–1808. Ref.: *Antiques,* May 1973.

BURLING, THOMAS

Thomas Burling (working 1769–1797) was one of New York City's most important eighteenth-century cabinetmakers, working for, among others, President George Washington and producing a formidable array of labeled furniture, including secretaries, sideboards, chairs, commodes, and kneehole and slant-front desks. Nearly all of these, in the Chippendale and early Federal manner, bear an elaborately engraved label illustrated with tables, a desk, and a chest of drawers and reading,

THO.s BURLING/Cabinet & Chairmaker/No. 36 Beekman Street/ New York

However, there are at least two pieces—a mahogany Queen Anne tilt-top tea table and a Chippendale slant-front desk—that have a different and almost certainly older label. It is circular and reads,

Made and fold by/ THOMAS BURLING,/ in Chappel Street,/NEW.YORK

Because Burling's advertisement of February 17, 1772, in the *New York Gazette* states that he is a chairmaker in Beekman Street ". . . commonly called Chapel Street . . . ," it seems clear that this rare label marks the period in the early 1770s when street names were in flux. By 1793 the city directory lists Burling's address at Beekman Street. Refs.: Bjerkoe; Joseph Downs and Ruth Ralston, *New York State Furniture*

(New York: Metropolitan Museum of Art, 1934); *Antiques,* January 1978.

BURNELL, NATHAN

Nathan Burnell (1790–1866), a Massachusetts cabinetmaker who worked in Swanton and Milton, Vermont, produced rather sophisticated Federal furniture resembling in style that made in the Portsmouth, New Hampshire, area. A mahogany and maple drop-panel chest of drawers is inscribed

N. Burnell/Swanton/May 13th 181 . . .

Because another signed Burnell piece—"made by N. Burnell 1847" (at the Vermont Historical Society)—is known, it would appear he had a rather long career. Refs.: *MAD,* October 1993; Robinson.

BURNHAM, BENJAMIN

A Chippendale cherry block-front slant-front desk at the Metropolitan Museum of Art bears the ink inscription

This desk was maid in the/year of 1769 by Benjn Burnam/that sarvfed his time in Felledlfay.

Although there have been several candidates for the honor of producing this fine desk, it is today generally agreed that the most likely is Benjamin Burnham (c. 1737–1773) of Colchester, Connecticut. It should be noted that there is also a Queen Anne walnut flat-top high chest of drawers or highboy that is inscribed in chalk

Benjamin/Burnham

but authorities do not consider this the work of the same cabinetmaker. Refs.: Fitzgerald; Heckscher; *Antiques,* July 1959.

BURNS & TRAINQUE

A Victorian Elizabethan Revival side chair in a private collection bears the partial label of this Manhattan firm, reading,

. . . ./BURNS &
TRAINQUE/CABINETMAKERS &
UPHOLSTERERS,/435 Broadway/
New York

The chair dates to the 1850–1860 period, and the firm is listed at 435 Broadway in the 1850–1851 Manhattan directory. A Peter Trainque continued to be listed in the city throughout the 1850s.

BURPEE, EPHRAIM

A thumb-back Windsor side chair, c. 1830–1850, bears the extremely rare label (illustrated in *MAD,* October 1993) of the hitherto unknown Vermont Windsor maker Ephraim Burpee. The oval label reads,

WINDSOR CHAIRS, MADE &

SOLD/BY/EPHRAIM BURPEE,/
Weathersfield Vermont.

However, the word *Springfield* has been inked over "Weathersfield," indicating that Burpee had moved some five miles southwest to the larger community. Ref.: Robinson.

BURROUGHS, CALEB

A Classical mahogany sideboard with carved hairy paw feet and spiral columns, which was illustrated in *MAD* for January 1995, was signed

Caleb C. Burroughs/January 24, 1820
Burroughs (1799–1885) was a New Jersey cabinetmaker, active in the community of Madison, Morris County. He is also known for a signed Federal mahogany slant-top desk with inlay in bird's-eye maple. Ref.: Walter H. Van Hoesen, *Crafts and Craftsmen of New Jersey* (Rutherford, N.J.: Fairleigh Dickinson University Press, 1973).

BUSH

A c. 1830–1850 Pennsylvania-type painted settee with a view of the Susquehanna River, which was illustrated in *Antiques* for May 1986, is signed

Bush/Harrisburg
This could be the name of either the maker or the decorator.

Chippendale mahogany bombé slant-front desk, c. 1760–1770, bearing the branded mark G.CADE, believed to be that of an unknown Boston, Massachusetts, cabinetmaker. Courtesy, Israel Sack, Inc., New York.

BUTH

A c. 1820–1840 carved Empire pedestal-foot drop-leaf table in the New York manner is reported to be stamped twice

BUTH

The mark is probably that of an owner. Ref.: *Antiques,* June 1939.

BUTLER & GILL

The partnership of the Lincoln County, Tennessee, cabinetmakers William C. Butler and Sam Gill (c. 1835–1850) is memorialized in an Empire cherry Jackson press signed

William C.B his hand and Sam Gill

Ref.: Williams and Harsh.

C

CADE, G.

A Chippendale mahogany bombé slant-front desk, c. 1760–1770, branded

G.CADE

is attributed to an unknown Boston, Massachusetts, cabinetmaker.

CAFFREY, J. P., & CO.

The firm of J. P. Caffrey & Co. consisted of at least three Caffreys: J.P., whose full name is unknown, and Charles P. and William A. During the 1840s and '50s this Waterville, Maine, shop turned out inexpensive painted pine and poplar tables and stands stenciled

J.P.CAFFREY/& CO./
Cabinet Makers/Waterville, Me.

Ref.: *MAD,* November 1978.

CAIN, T.

The brand

T.CAIN

appears on the underside of the seat of a c. 1810–1820 New England rod-back side chair. Although the mark appears to be that of an unknown maker, he has not yet been identified. Ref.: Santore II.

CALDWELL, JOHN

A late-eighteenth-century New York–style continuous-arm Windsor chair is impressed beneath the seat

J-CALDWELL

and is attributed to the Manhattan chairmaker John Caldwell, active in the 1790s. Ref.: Santore II.

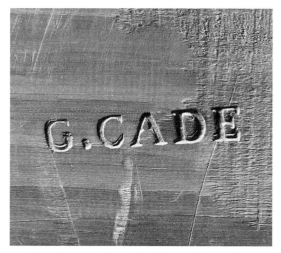

Detail of the brand of G. Cade on the Chippendale mahogany bombé slant-top desk. Courtesy, Israel Sack, Inc., New York.

CALVER, JAMES VALENTINE, JR.

James Valentine Calver, Jr. (1839—?), was a member of the Shaker community at New Lebanon, new York, until he withdrew from the order in 1871. A privately owned ocher-stained pine washstand inscribed in pencil under drawer

Made by/James V. Calver/April 1862

is attributed to him. It was made less than a year after he transferred from gardening to the community joiners' shop. Refs.: Rieman and Burks; Sprigg.

CALWELL, ————

See Alanson Winston.

CAMERON, CHARLES P.

A Federal cherry and mahogany chest of drawers with French feet, which was advertised in *Antiques* for July 1978, is inscribed

Charles P. Cameron, Sheperdstown
July 27, 1808

It is possibly by a West Virginia cabinetmaker

CAMP, WILLIAM

William Camp, an important Baltimore maker of Federal furniture, was active on Water Street in that city from 1802 until 1823. His attractively engraved label or trade card is illustrated with representations of high-style chairs, tables, and sideboards and reads,

William Camp,/Cabinet Maker and
Upholsterer,/at No. 25,/Water Street/
BALTIMORE/Orders/for the West Indies

or/any part of/the/Continent/neatly executed &/attended to with/Punctuality
Refs.: Bjerkoe; *Antiques,* February 1977.

CAMPBELL, JAMES

The Spring Lane, Boston, cabinetmaker James Campbell (d. 1809) was in partnership with one Moses Ward in Boston in 1791. Campbell is credited with an upholstered wing chair inscribed on the frame

J. Campbell

Ref.: Bjerkoe.

CANE, M.

A c. 1800–1820 Windsor stool with an oval top and bamboo turned legs that was offered at a Christie's auction, October 18, 1986, was branded

M. CANE

on the underside of the top. It is not known if this is the mark of a maker or an owner.

CARDWELL, JOHN

The Vermont cabinetmaker John Cardwell (Cardwill) is known for a tall chest of drawers at the Shelburne Museum, inscribed

Made in the year 1800, By John Cardwill
For Mr. Willis Griswold of Middletown
Sp Vermont

Cardwell's name appears in the 1810 Federal census for Middletown, Vermont. Ref.: Robinson.

CARLILE, JOHN

The Providence, Rhode Island, cabinetmaker John Carlile (1727–1796) had six sons, two of which at least joined him in the business. Most active was John Carlile, Jr. (see next entry). Although their father died before 1800, it appears that the sons continued to use well into the nineteenth century a label reading,

MADE AND SOLD, BY/JOHN CARLILE & SONS./ALL Kinds of CABINET WORK done, in/ the beft Manner, and at the fhorteft/Notice, at their Shop, juft Southward of the/Market in PROVI-DENCE, State of Rhode-/Ifland, &c.

Several Federal mahogany shield-back side chairs bearing this label are known. Refs.: Cooper; *Antiques,* June 1980, May 1982.

CARLILE, JOHN, JR.

John Carlile, Jr. (1762–1832), took over the Providence cabinet shop at his father's death in 1796 (see previous entry) and within the year moved it from the old stand on Main Street near the public market to a new building at 357 Benefit Street. Here he remained until his death. Only a single piece, a Chippendale mahogany slant-front desk signed

Providence August 6th 1785/John Carlile junr. of/said town/joyner.

can be assigned with certainty to him, but he is thought to have made many of the pieces of Federal furniture bearing the John Carlile & Sons label. Refs.: Bjerkoe; *Antiques,* May 1982.

Chippendale mahogany high chest of drawers or highboy, c. 1760–1770, signed twice in chalk by the New York City cabinetmaker Robert Carter (working c. 1760–1785). Courtesy, Bernard and S. Dean Levy, Inc., New York.

CARTER, MINOT

The New Ipswich, New Hampshire, turner Minot Carter (1812–1873) was related by marriage to Josiah P. Wilder (see his entry), who owned a chair factory in that town and appears to have made chairs there "on shares." A group of six painted thumb-back Windsor side chairs at Winterthur as well as another group of four sold at Bourne's auction gallery, May 17, 1983, bear Carter's label:

WARRANTED CHAIRS/MADE BY/MINOT CARTER./WILDER'S CHAIR

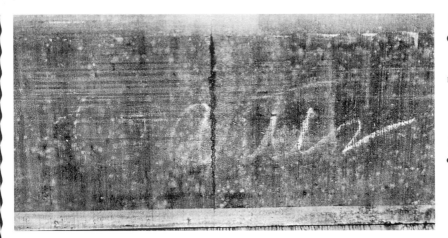

Chalk signature, "R. Carter," on a drawer of the Chippendale mahogany high chest of drawers made by Robert Carter. The piece is signed a second time on the backboards. Courtesy, Bernard and S. Dean Levy, Inc., New York.

FACTORY/NEW-IPSWICH, N.H.

Carter is believed to have been active c. 1826–1841. Ref.: Santore II.

CARTER, ROBERT

The New York City cabinetmaker Robert Carter (working c. 1760–1785), at one point a partner of Thomas Burling (see his entry), was the maker of a Chippendale mahogany high chest of drawers or highboy (c. 1760–1770) upon which his name,

R. Carter

is signed twice in chalk. Carter carried the banner of the Manhattan guild of cabinetmakers in the parade celebrating the ratification of the Constitution in 1788. Refs.: Fairbanks and Bates; *Antiques,* April 1980.

CARTER, SAMUEL

Two Classical worktables with carved legs bear the stenciled mark

Sam'l Carter/Cabinet Maker/
51 Beekman Street/New York

Carter was active in Manhattan, c. 1827–1834. One of his tables is in the Lincoln Sitting Room at the White House. Ref.: *Antiques,* December 1974.

CARTER & YOUNG

A c. 1800–1820 Federal bowfront chest of drawers in cherry and curly maple, which was advertised in *Antiques* for December 1966, is branded

J. Carter & M. Young, Belcher

There is a Belchertown in western Massachusetts, and it is possible that Carter and Young were cabinetmakers in that area.

Stenciled mark of Samuel Carter on a drawer of the Classical worktable. This table is in the Lincoln Sitting Room at the White House. Courtesy, White House Collection.

CARTERET, DANIEL

The Windsor chair maker Daniel Carteret, active c. 1793–1820, stamped his work, including settees,

D. CARTERET

Carteret is known to have worked on Shippen and South Front streets in Philadelphia. Ref.: Santore II.

CARWITHEN, WILLIAM

A c. 1732–1740 walnut Queen Anne slant-front desk at MESDA is stamped four times

W/CARWITHEN

for William Carwithen (1704–1770), a cabinetmaker active in Charleston, South Carolina, as early as 1729. Ref.: *Antiques*, May 1994.

CARY & MARCH

The firm of Cary & March, once located in Fryeburg, Maine, has left behind a c. 1820–1830 grain-painted country Empire chest of drawers in birch, which bears the following label:

Cabinet Furniture Shop,/CARY & MARCH,/Having taken a shop at Fryeburg corner, respectfully/inform their friends and the public that they carry on the/Cabinet Furniture Business/in all its various branches and hope by paying the strict-/est attention to their business and using their best en-/deavours to satisfy their customers, they shall merit and/receive a share of public patronage./Old FURNITURE REPAIRED at the/shortest notice./Fryeberg, November 12, 1823.

Ref.: *Antiques*, October 1970.

CASE, A. G.

A remarkable set of twelve matching bow-back Windsor armchairs, some of which are branded beneath the seats

A.G. CASE

which were advertised in *Antiques* for October 1969, are attributed to the Norwich, Connecticut, turner A. G. Case (1769–1828), active from around 1790 until his death. Ref.: Santore II.

Classical mahogany two-drawer worktable with carved legs, bearing the stenciled mark of Samuel Carter, a New York City cabinetmaker, active at 51 Beekman Street c. 1827–1834. Courtesy, White House Collection.

CASSELL, JAMES

In a private collection there is a late Federal mahogany sofa with heavily carved feet, which is inscribed in pencil

Cass(ell)/Furniture/
743 Boylston/Boston/Mass.

It is attributed to the cabinetmaker James Cassell, who was listed in the Boston city directory from 1816 until 1823. Ref.: *Antiques,* May 1991.

CATE, H.

A Windsor child's sack-back armchair illustrated in Ormsbee, *The Windsor Chair,* is twice branded beneath the seat

H. CATE

The piece is attributed to Boston or Rhode Island, c. 1770–1780, but nothing is known of the maker. Refs.: Santore II; Thomas H. Ormsbee, *The Windsor Chair* (New York: Deerfield Books, 1962).

CATES, J. W.

A nineteenth-century side chair in a private collection is stenciled

J.W. CATES/Boston

Nothing further is known of its origin.

CAWLEY, J. C.

A mahogany sewing box inlaid in ivory and ebony now in the collection of the New Jersey State Museum is inscribed

Made by/J.C. Cawley Swedsbrow/
gloster County N.J./August 10th 1858

CERMENATI, BARNARD

The much-traveled picture frame and mirror manufacturer Barnard Cermenati was in Newburyport, Massachusetts, c. 1807–1809, during which time he labeled his products as follows:

LOOKING GLASSES/BARNARD CERMENATI,/Carver, Gilder, Picture-Frame and Looking-Glass Manufacturer/ No. 10, State-Street, Newburyport/Keeps constantly for sale, at the most reduced prices/A COMPLETE ASSORTMENT OF/LOOKING-GLASSES, Picture Glasses, Prints, Spy-Glasses,/Thermometers, Glazier's Diamonds of the first quality-drawing Paper, Paints, Pencils, &c&c./Ladies Dressing Glasses of all

Grain-painted country Empire birch chest of drawers, c. 1820–1830, bearing the label of Cary & March, cabinetmakers of Fryeburg, Maine. Courtesy, Bernard and S. Dean Levy, Inc., New York.

Detail of label of Paul Cermenati and Company on the c. 1805 Federal looking glass. The firm made picture frames as well as mirrors. Courtesy, Bernard and S. Dean Levy, Inc., New York.

sizes—Looking Glass Plates/of all sizes to fit old frames. WINDOW GLASS of all sizes./With all kinds of FRAMES in his line./Ladies Needle Work handsomely framed in the most/modern style, and the shortest notice, at as cheap a rate as can be done in BOSTON/Old FRAMES new gilded./Ladies and Gentlemen will gratify Mr. C. by calling and/examining the above articles whether they purchase or not.

By December 1809 Cermenati was in Salem, Massachusetts, and by 1812 in Portsmouth, New Hampshire. In 1813 he entered a partnership in Boston. Refs.: Helen Comstock, *The Looking Glass in America, 1700–1825* (New York: Viking Press, 1964); *Antiques,* May 1968.

CERMENATI, PAUL

The picture frame and looking glass maker Paul Cermenati was in partnership with Valenti Bernarda on Boston's North Row from 1803 until 1806. A Federal looking glass from this shop is labeled

V.Bernarda & Cermenati,/CARVERS & GILDERS,/No.10, NORTH-ROW, BOSTON:/ALL kinds of LOOKING-GLASS and PICTURE-FRAMES, neatly made and Gilt,/a large affortment of LOOKING-GLAESSS [*sic*]/of all fizes, on the moft Reafonable terms. En-/ameling on glafs, executed in the beft manner./LIKEWISE, a variety of TELESCOPES, and/THERMOMETERS of all forts./THERMOMETERS REPAIRED.

In 1806 Paul Cermenati entered a new partner-

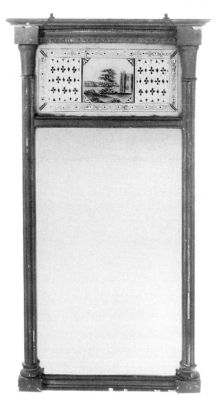

Federal looking glass, pine with traces of gilding and eglomise panel, by Paul Cermenati and G. Monfrino, 2 State Street, Boston, Massachusetts, c. 1806. Private collection.

ship at No. 2 State Street, Boston, with G. Monfrino. An engraved oval label on a gilded frame memorializes this venture:

Ladies needlework fram'd and Glaz'd in the neatest manner/Cermenati & Monfrino/CARVERS, GILDERS, PICTURE FRAME and/Looking Glafs Manufacturers/No. 2 STATE STREET/South Side of the old State House/BOSTON/Where they keep constantly for sale a large and/elegent afsortment of looking glafses, Prints/ from the best Masters in Europe/Also Telescopes, Barometers and Thermometers/made and Repaired in the/best manner./Old Looking Glafs new silvered.

These ventures and at least one other, remembered for several Sheraton mirrors labeled indistinctly P. CERMENATI & CO./ 64 or 65 Cornhill, Boston, apparently did not pan out, because by 1807 Cermenati was in Salem, Massachusetts, in partnership (only until 1808) with another Bernarda, John, and producing looking glasses labeled

CERMENATI & BERNARDA/Carvers, Gilders, Picture Frame and Looking Glass/ MANUFACTURERS—ESSEX STREET, SALEM,/Keep constantly for sale, at the most reduced prices, a/complete assortment of Looking Glasses . . . PICTURE GLASSES . . . PRINTS . . . PENCILS &c.&c.—with all kinds of/FRAMES in their line. ALSO/Ladies Needle Work handsomely framed in the most/modern style, and at the shortest notice.
OLD FRAMES, new gilded.

Another version of this label exists, which reads, Cermenati & Bernarda,/Gilders and Looking-Glass Manufacturers,/ opposite Albert Gray's Hat-Store, Essex Street,/Salem—/Where they keep constantly for sale, at the most reduced prices a complete assortment of/Looking Glasses—Pictures—Night or Day

Engraved label of Paul Cermenati and G. Monfrino on the c. 1806 Federal looking glass. Other products of the firm are also illustrated. Private collection.

Gilded Federal looking glass with eglomise panel by Paul Cermenati and Company, Boston, Massachusetts, c. 1805. Cermenati worked at various addresses and in several Boston partnerships. Courtesy, Bernard and S. Dean Levy, Inc., New York.

Telescopes—Thermometers—/Paint Boxes, Drawing Paper, Pencils, Etc.Etc.Etc./Looking Glass and Picture Frames made in the/best manner./Ladies' Needle Work handsomely framed and/glazied in the most modern style and at the shortest notice.

It should be noted that a great deal of uncertainty still remains regarding the various Bernarda, Cermenati, and Monfrino partnerships, as to dates, names of partners, and relationship to the several extant labels. Refs.: *Antiques,* March 1926, May 1981, May 1982.

CERMENATI & BERNARDA

See Paul Cermenati.

CERMENATI & MONFRINO

See Paul Cermenati.

CHADWICK, S.

A Hepplewhite demilune dressing table illustrated in the program for the 1973 New York City Winter Antiques Show is inscribed

S.Chadwick Portland, Maine

It is likely that this is an owner's rather than the maker's name.

CHALFANT, JAMES

An Empire mahogany veneer chest of drawers and a similar mirrored bureau, both in private collections, are stenciled

FROM/JAMES CHALFANT/
Cabinet Maker,/Unionville, Pa.

Chalfant (b. 1799) worked as a cabinetmaker in Unionville, East Marlboro Township, Pennsylvania, from 1829 until 1857. In 1838 he advertised that he made ". . . Sideboards, Sofas, Secretaries, Bureaus, Side and Centre Tables, Ladies' dressing Tables &c. . . ." Ref.: Schiffer.

CHALK, JULE

A pair of painted maple vase-back side chairs at the Henry Ford Museum are stamped on the underside of the seats

JULE CHALK

They are attributed to an Ohio chairmaker of that name thought to have been active c. 1850–1870. Ref.: Bishop.

CHAMBERLAIN, C. D.

An Empire two-drawer worktable of cherry and flame birch with square or so-called New York legs is inscribed

Stamping or branding hammer used by Jule Chalk. Courtesy, the Henry Ford Museum, Dearborn, Mich.

C.D. Chamberlain/Maker/ March the 20th 1843/ Burlington, Vt. Chamberlain is thought to have worked in Burlington, c. 1840–1850. Ref.: *MAD*, October 1993.

CHAMPLIN, H. P.

Santore lists the impressed stamp

H.P. CHAMPLIN

as a mark found on Windsors, possibly of Rhode Island origin, c. 1780–1800. Ref.: Santore II.

CHANDLER, THOMAS

A Federal tapered-leg sideboard in mahogany and white pine, which is privately

Painted maple vase-back side chair, c. 1850–1870, with the impressed mark of the Ohio chairmaker Jule Chalk. Courtesy, the Henry Ford Museum, Dearborn, Mich.

owned, bears the inscription

**Made by Thomas Chandler/York/
July 25. 1810.**

Chandler worked in York, Maine, but his sophisticated design indicates Massachusetts or New Hampshire training. Ref.: *Antiques,* May 1992.

CHAPIN, AMZI

Amzi Chapin (1768–1835), a younger brother of the well-known Connecticut cabinetmaker Aaron Chapin, is known for a single marked piece, a Federal mahogany demilune card table, c. 1790–1800, at Old Deerfield. It is stamped

AMZI/CHAPIN

Ref.: Fales, *Historic Deerfield.*

CHAPIN, ELIPHALET

Though one of Connecticut's better-known cabinetmakers, Eliphalet Chapin (1741–1807) of East Windsor does not appear to have signed his work. A Federal bureau desk is inscribed

**THIS DESK was made By Elapot [sic]
Chapin/IN THE YEAR OF OUR LORD
1802/ IN THE STATE OF CONNETICUT
[sic],/FOR PONTIUS WINSLOWE**

but since Eliphalet knew how to spell his own name, this is almost certainly the hand of an owner. Refs.: Bjerkoe; *Antiques,* April 1939, February 1941.

CHAPIN, SILAS

Silas Chapin, distant cousin of Aaron Chapin, was born in Gilsum, New Hampshire, in 1793. He migrated to Big Flats, Tioga County, New York, where he died in 1828. His only identified work is a late Sheraton drop-leaf table, which is labeled

**. . . . . . . .MANUFACTURES/MADE
AND SOLD/BY/SILAS CHAPIN,/BIG
FLATS/TIOGA COUNTY/ NEW YORK**

Refs.: Bjerkoe; *Antiques,* June 1930.

CHAPMAN, JOHN

A rod-back Windsor armchair now at Independence National Historical Park bears beneath the seat the brand

I. CHAPIN

for John Chapin, who worked in Philadelphia on Eighth and Cherry streets, c. 1793–1808. Ref.: Santore II.

CHAPPEL, WILLIAM

A tall case clock in the collection of the Connecticut Historical Society in Hartford is labeled

**WILLIAM CHAPPEL,/CABINET &
CHAIR MAKER,/DANBURY,/Makes all
kinds of CABINET WORK,/and CHAIRS,
warranted, of the neat-/eft and moft
approved fafhions.**

The label appears to be dated 1796 in ink, which would seem appropriate to the early Federal piece. Nothing else is presently known of this Danbury, Connecticut, craftsman.

CHASE, CHARLES

The best-known Nantucket, Massachusetts, Windsor chair maker was Charles Chase (1731–1815). Chase, who seems to have specialized in fan-back Windsor side and armchairs (including brace-backs), branded his work

C. CHASE

Marked examples are at Winterthur and

Colonial Williamsburg. Refs.: Charles H. and Mary Grace Carpenter, *The Decorative Arts of Nantucket* (New York: Dodd, Mead, 1987); *Antiques,* May 1988.

CHENEY

A Queen Anne cherry and maple side chair, c. 1740–1760, at Winterthur is signed in chalk on the slip seat

CHENEY

It is not known if this is the maker's or an owner's mark. The piece is much too early to be the work of the Litchfield, Connecticut, craftsman Silas E. Cheney (1776–1821).

CHESNUT, JARED

A prolific maker of bamboo-turned rodback Windsor side and armchairs (some with medallion backs), Jared Chesnut went into business first in Christina, Delaware, around 1800, but by 1804 he had a shop on Hemphill's Wharf in Wilmington. By 1814 he was at 20 Market Street, and he continued to make chairs there until at least 1832. His impressed mark is

J.CHESNUT/WILMINGTON/DEL.
Refs.: *Plain and Ornamental;* Santore II.

CHIPMAN, JOHN

The Salem, Massachusetts, cabinetmaker John Chipman (1746–1819) is credited with three signed pieces of Chippendale mahogany furniture. These include a fine c. 1770–1790 block-front desk and bookcase or secretary inscribed

Made by John Chipman/Salem
an oxbow-front four-drawer bureau or chest of

Chippendale mahogany block-front desk and bookcase or secretary, c. 1770–1790, signed by the Salem, Massachusetts, cabinetmaker John Chipman (1746–1819). Chipman had shops on Liberty Street and at the Salem Turnpike entrance.
Courtesy, Israel Sack, Inc., New York.

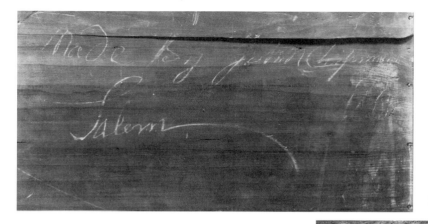

drawers signed

Made by/John Chipman/Salem 1794

and a slant-front desk with straight bracket feet, which is signed twice

Made by/John Chipman/Cabinet m. Salem Newengland

and

Made by/John Chipman/Salem/ Augt 179——/Price 30 ——llars

Chipman, who had a shop first on Liberty Street in Salem and later at the Salem Turnpike entrance, was part of the group of Salem cabinetmakers shipping goods overseas as venture trade. The desk described here was found in Durban, South Africa. Refs.: Bjerkoe; *Antiques,* December 1987, November 1988.

CHISHOLM, ARCHIBALD

See Shaw & Chisholm.

CHOATE, D. C.

A c. 1780–1800 New England Chippendale mahogany chest of drawers with ball-and-claw feet and unusual line inlay is stamped numerous times

D.C. CHOATE

No cabinetmaker of this name is presently known, and the mark may be that of an owner.

CHOATE & MARTIN

The cabinetmakers Robert Choate (1770–?) and George Whitfield Martin (1771–1810) were in partnership in Concord, New Hampshire, ". . . opposite Mr. Harris's store . . ." from 1794 until 1796. The known fruit

of this union is a Federal mahogany card table bearing a paper label reading,

MADE/By/Choate & Martin/
Concord, New Hampshire

Ref.: Hewitt, Kane, and Ward.

CHRISTIAN, CHARLES

The cabinetmaker Charles Christian was active at 90 Fulton Street in Manhattan, c. 1810–1815. He is known for two pieces: a Federal mahogany reeded-leg Pembroke table in a private collection and an Egyptian-style desk made for the mayor's office at New York's City Hall. Both bear the following printed label:

CHARLES CHRISTIAN'S/SOUTHERN AND WEST INDIA/Cabinet Furniture/ Warehouse,/NO.90 Fulton STREET,/ NEAR PEARL-STREET,/NEW-YORK/ HE/SOLICITS THE PATRONAGE OF THE MERCHANTS.

Refs.: Tracy; Christie's catalog, sale of January 22, 1994.

CHURCHILL, F. A.

A c. 1820–1830 mahogany portable medicine chest in a private collection bears the following printed paper label:

New England Chippendale inlaid mahogany ball-and-claw-foot chest of drawers, c. 1780–1800, with the impressed mark of D.C. Choate. He may be either the maker or an owner of the piece. Private collection.

Portable Desks, Medicine/Chests Instrument Cases,/Work and Dressing Boxes,/made and sold by/ F.A. CHURCHILL,/Cincinnati.

Nothing further is known of this Cincinnati, Ohio, craftsman. Ref.: Letter, Kenneth Wilson to Katherine Hagler, November 10, 1975.

CHURCHILL, LEMUEL

Two c. 1805–1815 Federal upholstered mahogany lolling chairs (one of which is

Detail of the interior of the mahogany medicine chest labeled F.A. Churchill. The blown-glass bottles are original. Private collection.

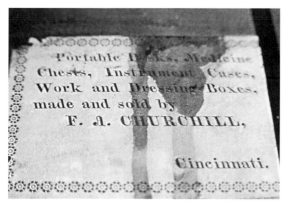

Label of the Cincinnati, Ohio, craftsman F. A. Churchill found on a c. 1820–1830 mahogany portable medicine chest. Churchill was a cabinetmaker, though clearly a highly specialized one. Private collection.

Label of Lemuel Churchill on the Federal lolling chair. Only two labeled pieces of Churchill's furniture are known. Courtesy, Leigh Keno, New York.

at Winterthur) bear the damaged partial label **LEMUEL CHURCHILL,/MAKES AND SELLS/Cabinet-Furniture and Chairs,/OF THE NEWEST FASHIONS AND BEST OF WORK,/ AT HIS/SHOP IN NEWBURY STREET** Churchill (working c. 1805–1828) was located on Orange, High, and Washington streets in Boston as well as at the Newbury Street address. Refs.: Montgomery; Analysis report, Leigh Keno, January 1994.

Federal upholstered mahogany lolling chair, c. 1805–1815, with the label of the Newbury Street, Boston, chair- and cabinetmaker Lemuel Churchill. Courtesy, Leigh Keno, New York, Richard P. Goodbody, Inc.

CINCINNATI STEAM BUREAU MANUFACTURING CO.

A c. 1850–1860 Empire mahogany veneer chest of drawers or bureau in a private collection is stenciled

Cincinnati Steam Bureau Manufacturing CO./Successors to Walter and Meader/ Front and South Sts./Warranted Good.

Nothing further is known of this mid-nineteenth-century Ohio concern. Ref.: Coleman and Harsh.

CLARK, E. M.

A n attractive c. 1790–1810 Portsmouth, New Hampshire, Federal mahogany secretary or desk and bookcase sold at Skinner's, February 6, 1994, is branded

E.M. CLARK

Research indicates that Enoch M. Clark (1764–1815) was a deacon and a teacher but probably not a cabinetmaker. Ref.: *MAD,* April 1994.

CLARK, JAMES

A Windsor chair at Old Sturbridge Village that is branded

I. CLARK

is attributed to the turner James Clark (1782–1858), who worked in New Braintree before 1822 and thereafter in West Brookfield, Massachusetts. Ref.: *Antiques,* May 1993.

CLARK, ROBERT

T he Newburyport, Massachusetts, cabinet-maker Robert Clark (or Clarke) is known for a late Sheraton mahogany lady's desk, c. 1820–1830, which is labeled indistinctly

. . . . AND . . . /FURNITURE,/OF ALL KINDS,/MADE AND SOLD BY/ROBERT CLARK,/AT HIS CABINET

Sheraton mahogany lolling chair, c. 1800–1815, with the signature "R. Clarke" of Robert Clark (1775–1846), a cabinetmaker who worked on Middle Street in Newburyport, Massachusetts, c. 1800–1820. Courtesy, Bernard and S. Dean Levy, Inc., New York.

Detail of the signature
**W. Clark/Cabinetmaker/Providence,
R.I./1828, as inscribed on the lady's desk by
William Clark. Courtesy, Israel Sack, Inc.,
New York.**

FURNITURE STORE/MIDDLE-STREET NEWBURYPORT.

There is also a Sheraton mahogany Martha Washington lolling chair, which is signed in chalk

R. Clarke

and attributed to the same craftsman. Robert Clark (1775–1846) advertised for an apprentice in 1817, at which time his shop was at the Middle Street address. Refs.: Bjerkoe; *Antiques,* January 1972, August 1978.

**Sheraton inlaid mahogany and cherry
lady's desk, with the inscribed signature of
William Clark, a Providence, Rhode Island,
cabinetmaker, and the date 1828. Courtesy,
Israel Sack, Inc., New York.**

CLARK, WILLIAM

A very fine Sheraton inlaid mahogany and cherry lady's desk with swelled reeded legs is inscribed on a drawer

W.Clark/Cabinetmaker/
Providence, R.I./1828

William Clark, who is listed as a cabinetmaker in the 1828 Providence directory, may not have been long in business.

CLARKE, JONAS

A primitive Windsor-type armchair advertised in the *Bee* for August 13, 1976, is said to bear an old paper label reading,

Jonas Clarke—Worster, Mass. 1776
Nothing is known of Clarke. If a chairmaker, he was a poor one.

CLAY, DANIEL

The cabinetmaker Daniel Clay (1770– after 1831) was active in Greenfield, Massachusetts, from 1794 until 1829, turning out a variety of labeled furnishings, including card tables, clock cases, Pembroke tables, secretaries, and chests of drawers. Most were of cherry, often stained to resemble mahogany. His earliest identifying mark is the signature

Daniel Clay/Greenfield

on a Chippendale cherry card table. At a later date he employed two printed paper labels. The first simply read,

MADE BY/DANIEL CLAY/
Greenfield, Maffachufetts

This appears on a Sheraton bowfront chest and a c. 1800–1810 Pembroke table. More common is Clay's elaborate (for the area) 1794 label:

CABINET WORK,/DANIEL CLAY,/AT
HIS SHOP IN GREEN-/FIELD,/MAKES
all kinds of/Cabinet and Shop Join-/ery
Work, and conftantly/ keeps an affortment
on hand/which he will fell on
reafonable/terms, for Cafh, all kinds of
Country Produce & Lumber,/or approved
Credit.Every/favour will be duly acknowl-/
edged, by their humble fer-/vant,/
DANIEL CLAY./November 4, 1794

Refs.: Fitzgerald; *Antiques,* April 1934, June 1966, December 1992.

CLEMENT, SAMUEL

A dated 1726 William and Mary high chest of drawers or highboy in red gum, ash, and elm now at Winterthur is inscribed on the backboards

This was made in ye year 1726/ By
me Samuel Clement of flushing/Junc ye

and attributed to Samuel Clement of Flushing,

William and Mary red gum, ash, and elm high chest of drawers or highboy signed and dated 1726 by the joiner Samuel Clement (working c. 1715–1726) of Flushing, Queens County, New York. Courtesy, Bernard and S. Dean Levy, Inc., New York.

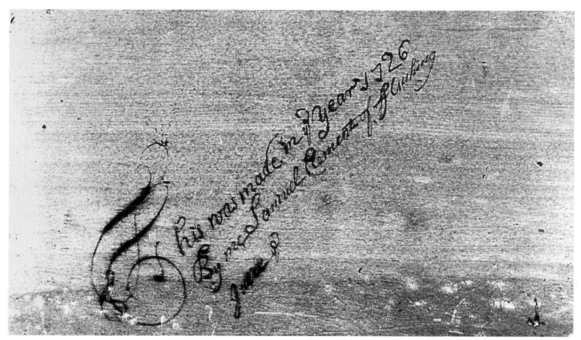

Detail of inscribed signature of Samuel Clement on the backboards of the William and Mary high chest of drawers or highboy. Courtesy, Bernard and S. Dean Levy, Inc., New York.

Queens County, New York (working c. 1715–1726). The "ye" may actually be an 8. Refs.: Fairbanks and Bates; *Antiques,* December 1988.

CLEMENTS, JOHN

A cherry Hepplewhite slant-front desk advertised in *Antiques,* May 1994, was signed on the lid

Liberty John Clements 1816

The piece is believed to have originated in Kentucky, but no cabinetmaker by this name is presently known.

CLEVELAND, JEREMIAH C.

Jeremiah C. Cleveland (1794–1836) appears to have been an apprentice to Aaron Chapin and his son, Laertes, at their shop in Hartford, Connecticut, c. 1808–1818. During this period he made an upholstered Sheraton easy chair, which is inscribed on the crest rail back

Aaron Chapin & Son/
Jeremiah B. Cleveland

In 1819 Cleveland settled in Batavia, Ohio. Although he is said to have continued his career, no marked pieces are known.

CLIFTON, HENRY

The Philadelphia cabinetmaker Henry Clifton (d. 1771) was a partner of the well-known James Gillingham (see his entry), c. 1761–1768. Thereafter until his death he was located on Arch Street in the city. He is remembered for a dressing table at Williamsburg, which is signed

Henry Clifton/1753

Refs.: Bjerkoe; Hornor; *MAD,* August 1993.

CLODFELTER, JESSE

The cabinetmaker Jesse Clodfelter was born in Friedberg, North Carolina, in 1804. He worked near Wachovia until 1848, when he left for Indiana. Two signed Clodfelter pieces are known: a walnut chest of drawers in the Federal style but signed

February 11, 1842/February 15, 1842/
Jesse Clodfelter

and a corner cupboard in the same wood with Chippendale details, which is inscribed

Jesse Clodfelter/July 31, 1844

Ref.: *The Swisegood School of Cabinetmakers* (Winston-Salem, N.C.: Museum of Early Southern Decorative Arts, 1973).

CLOSTERMAN, H.

A c. 1878–1885 walnut Victorian Renaissance Revival writing desk, sold at auction in Flomaton, Alabama, June 17–18, 1994, is stenciled within a drawer

H. CLOSTERMAN/Manufacturer
OF/CHAIRS/PARLOR
FURNITURE/TABLES/HATRACKS,
LOUNGES &/CINCINNATTI, O./PAT'D
FEB'Y 12th. 1878

Closterman was active in Cincinnati during the 1870s and '80s. Ref.: *MAD,* September 1994.

CLOWES, GEORGE H.

See George W. Gates.

COCHOIS, J. B.

A c. 1810–1820 Classical mahogany bed in the "French Style" is stamped in eight places

C.H. LANNUIER/J.B. COCHOIS

Cochois was a cabinetmaker employed in New York City by the furniture manufacturer Charles-Honoré Lannuier (see his entry). Ref.: Fitzgerald.

CODMAN, I.

A Chippendale mahogany oxbow-front chest of drawers with ball-and-claw feet, advertised in *Antiques* for August 1974, is inscribed on the back

I. Codman

The piece dates c. 1765–1775, but no cabinetmaker by this name is presently known.

CODMAN, WILLIAM C.

A lady's writing table, chair, and desk designed by William Codman (1839–1912) and produced by the Gorham silver company won a grand prize at the St. Louis World's Fair of 1903. The pieces were inscribed

W.C. Codman 1903

Refs.: Bishop; Monkhouse and Michie.

COE, ADAM S.

The Newport cabinetmaker Adam S. Coe (1782–1862) is known for a single marked piece, a Chippendale mahogany sofa at Winterthur, which is inscribed in red chalk

Made by Adam S. Coe April 1812 for
Edw W. Lawton/Newport

Coe was described as a cabinetmaker in Newport, Rhode Island, as early as 1810. He sold his shop on Long Wharf in 1847. Refs.: Bjerkoe; Downs.

COFFIN, JOB B.

A c. 1810–1825 Classical saber-leg footstool in curly maple offered at Christie's, March 10, 1978, is branded

JOB B. COFFIN

It is possible that the maker was the turner Job B. Coffin of Fishkill, New York. A chair by Coffin is at the Art Institute of Chicago. Ref.: *Antiques,* May 1981.

COGSWELL, JOHN

Although his career in Boston extended at least from 1769 until 1789, the cabinetmaker John Cogswell is known for only a single marked piece, a magnificent Chippendale mahogany bombé chest on chest inscribed

**Made by John/Cogswell in
midle Street/Boston 1782**

However, a Chippendale easy chair sold at auction in 1994 is said to have borne the chalk inscription ". . . Cogswell, Boston." A man of means and holder of various public offices, Cogswell lived and worked on Middle Street in Boston's North End. Refs.: Bjerkoe; Fairbanks and Bates; *Antiques,* September 1981, May 1989; *MAD,* January 1995.

COGSWELL, T.

Chippendale tiger maple serpentine-front secretary or desk and bookcase inscribed

T (?) Cogswell/1799/Gilmanton

is one of three similar pieces having a Gilmanton, New Hampshire, history. There is, however, no evidence that this Cogswell was a cabinetmaker. Ref.: Heckscher.

COIT, JOB

The Boston cabinetmaker Job Coit (1692–1742) was the maker of the earliest known dated piece of American block-front furniture, a Chippendale walnut desk and bookcase at Winterthur, which is inscribed twice

Job Coit Jr./1738

and

J. Coit 1738

Coit was working at his craft in Boston as early as 1725. His home, and presumably his shop, was on Ann Street. Ref.: *Antiques,* June 1971.

COLE, JACOB

The Baltimore, Maryland, turner Jacob Cole branded his bamboo-turned rod-back Windsor chairs

J. COLE

Known examples include a side chair at the Baltimore Museum of Art and a bench or settee offered at auction in Maine, May 12, 1979. The latter was branded

J. COLE/WARRANTED

Cole's shop was on Front Street in Baltimore's Old Town section, where he first advertised in 1794. He died in 1801. Refs.: Elder and Stokes; *MAD,* May 1979.

COLES, WILLIAM

The New York City turner William Coles (1803–1862) arrived in Springfield, Ohio, in 1832, establishing a chairmaking shop on East Main Street, which was continued by his sons after Coles's retirement in 1856. William Coles produced three chair types: half-spindles, cane-seated Hitchcocks, and a modified klismos. All were decorated with stenciling and freehand painting and stenciled beneath the seat

MADE.BY: W.-COLES.
SPRINGFIELD, OHIO.

or

W.COLES. CHAIRMAKER/
SPRINGFIELD. O.

Refs.: Hageman, I, II; *Made in Ohio.*

COLES, W. AND G.

A paint-decorated chair offered at a New Hampshire auction on August 8, 1977, was described as being marked

W. & G. COLES SPRINGFIELD, OHIO

Assuming this is a correct transcription of the mark, it may represent a partnership, c. 1852–1856, between William Coles of Springfield, Ohio (see previous entry), and one of his sons. However, no son with the initial *G* is known. Possibly, it was a *J* for son J. W. Coles. Ref.: Hageman I.

COLLADAY, W.

A Chippendale mahogany tray-top tea table with ball-and-claw feet illustrated in *Antiques* for August 1963 is branded

W. COLLADAY

The table is Philadelphia in style, but the mark is probably that of an owner rather than a manufacturer. However, the existence of four c. 1750 Queen Anne side chairs, which were illustrated in *Antiques* in January 1995 and which bore the same mark, raises the possibility that Colladay was a cabinetmaker.

COLLIER, ALFRED

Alfred Collier (1823–1884), a Shaker brother and a member of the Harvard, Massachusetts, community, is credited with a green-painted high or clerk's desk signed in chalk under the lid

Alfred Collier

Painted and decorated Hitchcock-type fancy chair, c. 1840–1855, with the stenciled mark "MADE. BY: W.-COLES.SPRINGFIELD. OHIO." William Coles (1803–1862) made chairs in Springfield from 1832 until 1856. Courtesy, the Henry Ford Museum, Dearborn, Mich.

Collier's cabinetmaking activities are referred to in several Shaker journals. Ref.: Rieman and Burks.

COLLIER, GEORGE

A Massachusetts Federal card table in mahogany and dating c. 1805–1815 is signed in pencil

Geo. Collier

This is believed to be an owner's signature.

COLLIGNON CHAIR COMPANY

The Collignon Chair Company was located in Closter, New Jersey. During the last quarter of the nineteenth century, it produced a variety of Victorian chairs, many of which were marked

Collignon Patent

Ref.: *Spinning Wheel,* February 1976.

COLTON, B.

B. Colton (probably a relative of the Hartford, Connecticut, cabinetmaker Aaron Colton) was an apprentice or journeyman employee of the Hartford firm of Aaron and Laertes Chapin when he inscribed a Sheraton sideboard

Made by B. Colton for A.Chapin & Son, Sept. 1801

New England braced bow-back Windsor side chair, c. 1790–1810, of mixed woods, branded R. COLTON beneath the seat. Colton is thought to have been an as yet unidentified turner. Private collection.

This inscription would indicate that the formal association between Aaron Chapin and his son, Laertes, began several years before the date given in Bjerkoe.

COLTON, R.

A braced bow-back Windsor side chair, c. 1790–1810, of mixed woods with bamboo turnings, is branded on the underside of the seat

R. COLTON

which is thought to be the name of a heretofore unidentified New England chair turner.

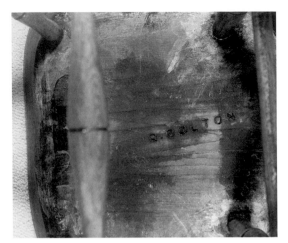

Brand of R. COLTON on the underside of the seat bottom of the braced bow-back Windsor side chair. Private collection.

CONKLIN, HENRY

A nineteenth-century mahogany desk and bookcase or secretary sold at auction in June 1994 is said to have borne the label of Henry Conklin. Nothing further has been learned of this cabinetmaker. Ref.: *Bee,* June 3, 1994.

CONNELL, WILLIAM

A Chippendale walnut tall case clock at Winterthur is labeled by the little-known Philadelphia cabinetmaker William Connell:
MADE and SOLD, by/WILLIAM CON-NELL,/CABINET-MAKER,/In Third-Street, the Corner of Spruce-/Street, PHILADELPHIA; where may be/had, all Sorts of Cabinet and Chair/Work, on the fhorteft Notice.
Connell, who is believed to have made this clock case c. 1760–1775, signed the receipt book of his fellow Philadelphia joiner Benjamin Randolph (see his entry) in 1769 and was listed as a joiner on the 1774 tax list. Nothing more is known of him. Refs.: Downs; Hummel.

CONNELLY, HENRY

One of Philadelphia's most influential cabinetmakers, Henry Connelly (1770–1826) is known for a variety of late Federal and Empire furniture, including chairs, sofas, sideboards, card and dining tables, and even a music stand. Throughout his career he used the same label, an engraving illustrated with a Federal bowfront chest of drawers, knife box, and card table, below which in an oval first appeared
H. Connelly/CABINET & CHAIRMAKER/ No. l6/Chesnut: Street/PHILADa.
This label was used at Connelly's first shop, 16 Chestnut Street, where he worked from 1800 through 1802. When in 1803 he moved to 44 Spruce Street, the label was changed in only one particular, by substituting "No. 44/Spruce Street" for "No. 16/Chesnut: Street." In 1808 Connelly moved again, to 72 South Fourth Street, where he remained until retiring in 1824. Again, the same label was used, with "No.72/South.Fourth.Street" replacing the Spruce Street address. Refs.: Bishop; Bjerkoe; Montgomery; *Antiques,* May 1991.

CONSTANTINE, THOMAS, & Co.

The firm of Thomas Constantine and Company (working 1815–1839) produced late Federal and Empire furniture in Manhattan. A Federal mahogany two-part dining table and an Empire pier table in mahogany and marble bear the printed paper label
T.CONSTANTINE & Co./(Cabinet Makers)/ 157/FULTON; Late PARTITION St./

Opposite St.Paul's Church Yard/
NEW YORK

Constantine was at this address from 1817 to
1824. In 1825 the company was at 538 Green-
wich Street, and from 1826 to 1839 he operated a mahogany yard at 503 Pearl Street.
Refs.: *Antiques,* May 1979, June 1987.

COOK & PARKIN

A highly ornate Empire mahogany sideboard at the Baltimore Museum of Art
bears the rare label of this Philadelphia firm:

**COOK & PARKIN/Cabinet and Chair
Makers/NO.58/Walnut Street/Between
Park & Third Streets/South Side/Philada.**

Cook and Parkin were in business together
c. 1820–1825. Although little is known of
Cook, the other partner is probably Richard
Parkin, whose label appears on a pair of Phila-
delphia Empire footstools of the same period.
Refs.: Bjerkoe; *Antiques,* May 1993.

COOKE, JAMES H.

James H. Cooke, who was working in Litchfield, Connecticut, in 1822, was in Manhattan
by 1825, being listed as a cabinetmaker at 38
Beekman Street. By 1832 he had a store on
Broadway, which he maintained at various
addresses until 1864. An Empire mahogany
one-drawer stand at the New York State Museum is stenciled

**FROM/JAMES H. COOKE/
92/BROADWAY/NEW-YORK**

This was Cooke's location from 1845 until
1850. Ref.: Scherer.

COOPER, THOMAS

An inlaid mahogany Queen Anne slant-top
desk sold at Christie's on October 18,
1986, bore a piece of paper mounted under
glass on the prospect door which read

Thomas Cooper August ye 1770

**Mahogany Federal sofa, c. 1795–1810, bearing the engraved label of Henry Connelly
(1770–1826), a cabinetmaker who worked at various addresses in Philadelphia,
c. 1795–1825. Private collection.**

Cooper was a cabinetmaker who worked in Southampton, Long Island, New York, in the 1770s.

COOPER, WILLIAM

A small table owned by the Society for the Preservation of Long Island Antiquities is marked

Wm. COOPER/SAG-HARBOR

for the Long Island, New York, cabinetmaker William Cooper, active c. 1797–1830. Ref.: *Antiques,* May 1981.

COREY, WALTER

One of the largest chair factories in Maine was run c. 1836–1866 by Walter Corey (1809–1889) of Portland. Corey, who also produced a variety of cabinet furniture, operated at several addresses in Portland and employed various marks. Chairs were often simply stenciled

W.COREY.PORTLAND,ME.

or

W. Corey-Portland.

From 1836 to 1841, when Corey's shop was at 19 Exchange Street, both furniture (usually in a heavy Empire mode) and chairs might be stenciled

WALTER COREY/19 EXCHANGE STREET/PORTLAND ME./WARRANTED

or (in an oval)

WALTER COREY/FURNITURE WARE-HOUSE/Feather Store/& Chair Factory/ 19 Exchange Street/PORTLAND.

From 1842 until 1866, when the entire complex was destroyed by fire, Corey's factory was at 52–54 Exchange Street, and the stencil read,

WALTER COREY./52 & 54/ EXCHANGE ST./PORTLAND. ME.

or

WALTER COREY/Manufacturer/52 & 54/ EXCHANGE ST./PORTLAND. ME.

Chippendale mahogany sofa, c. 1757–1760, labeled by the cabinetmaker Joseph Cox, active at various addresses in New York City, c. 1756–1775.
Courtesy, *Index of American Design*, Metropolitan Museum of Art.

Refs.: Fales, *American Painted Furniture; Antiques,* May 1982.

COSGRAY, JAMES

A painted Victorian side chair in a private collection is marked

James Cosgray/Waynesburg, Pa.

Nothing is known of the originator of this mark.

COTTON, L.

A Federal mahogany inlaid card table, c. 1790–1810, offered at Christie's, January 18, 1992, is branded

L. COTTON

It is not known if this is the mark of the maker or an owner.

COUCH, ALBERT G.

The Massachusetts cabinetmaker Albert G. Couch (1819–1903) established a furniture shop in Wellington, Lorain County, Ohio, in 1843. His son, George, entered the business around 1875 and became owner upon Albert's retirement in 1883. Albert Couch's painted Victorian cottage furniture is often marked in paint

A.G. COUCH/MAKER/WELLINGTON, O.

A washstand may be seen at the Ohio Historical Society, Columbus. Refs.: *Made in Ohio; Antiques,* February 1984.

COURTRIGHT, CHARLES

The obscure New York City cabinetmaker Charles Courtright is represented by a c. 1790–1810 Hepplewhite mahogany card table at Gracie Mansion in Manhattan, which is labeled in an oval

MADE AND SOLD BY/CHARLES

COURTRIGHT/At The Sign of the Four Stars/in Pine St./NEW YORK

No information about Courtright has been found, and some have questioned the age of the label. Ref.: Hewitt, Kane, and Ward.

COUTANT, DAVID

The turner David Coutant (name spelled variously Coutont, Coutong), who worked in New York City and New Rochelle, New York, c. 1780–1800, made a variety of chairs, including banister-back armchairs, vase-splat "Yorker" side chairs, and bow-back and continuous-arm Windsors. All were stamped

D. COUTONG

David Coutant worked at his father's chair factory in New Rochelle until 1786, when he moved to Manhattan, where he was active on Broad Street and Broadway until 1794, when, upon the death of his father, he returned to New Rochelle, continuing the factory into the early 1800s. Refs.: Santore II; Scherer; *Antiques,* May 1981.

COX, JOSEPH

Although he described himself as an "upholsterer" and is known for only a single piece—a Chippendale mahogany sofa, c. 1757–1760, at the Metropolitan Museum of Art that once bore his label—Joseph Cox is regarded as one of earliest known Manhattan furniture makers. His engraved label,

Jofeph Cox, Upholfterer,/From LONDON,/ At the Sign of/The Royal-Bed,/In Dock-Street, near Countjies's-Market, New-York;/MAKES all Sorts of Beds, both for Sea and Land;/likewife, Window Curtains, Mattreffes, Eafy/Chairs, Sophies, French Chairs, and Chairs of all Sorts,/in the neweft Fafhion.

specifically mentions that he makes "Sophies" as well as other seating furniture. After living on Hanover Square in 1756, Cox was at the Dock Street address from 1757 to 1760, and the sofa is assumed to date from that period. He moved to Wall Street in 1760. He was last mentioned in 1775. Refs.: Bjerkoe; Heckscher.

COX, WILLIAM

The turner William Cox (d. 1811) worked in Newcastle, Delaware, and from 1767 until around 1804 on Second Street in Philadelphia. Several Windsor forms, including bamboo-turned bow-back side chairs (some upholstered) and armchairs, bear his brand:

W. COX

Examples are at Independence National Historical Park, Philadelphia. Cox also made rush-bottom chairs. Ref.: Santore II.

CRANDALL, THOMAS

The cabinetmaker Thomas Crandall had a shop at the corner of Second Street and Fourth Alley in Lynchburg, Virginia, during the years 1813–1817. Before and after that time he was in business in Richmond. Associated with Crandall's stay in Lynchburg are two pieces, a Sheraton mahogany sideboard inscribed

Thomas Crandall/Maker of this work/Lynchburg, Virginia/1813

and a mahogany sideboard blending Gothic and Sheraton characteristics. This is inscribed in a like manner:

I Thomas (Cran)dall/maker of this work/Lynchburg 1813

Refs.: Piorkowski; *Antiques,* November 1982.

CRIPPS, WILLIAM McLEAN

A mahogany and mahogany veneer toilet table at the Smithsonian Institution and a chest of drawers in the same materials in a private collection both bear the stenciled mark

Wm.McL.CRIPPS/ Cabinet & Sofa/Manufacturer,/ 11th St. bet E St. & Pa. Ave.

Both these Empire pieces were produced by Cripps, who was located at this address or on Pennsylvania Avenue in Washington, D.C., from 1827 until the late 1840s. Ref.: *Antiques,* May 1975.

Renaissance Revival burl walnut marble-top chest of drawers, c. 1865–1870, bearing the label of the furniture manufacturers George Croome & Co., working in Boston, c. 1861–1874. Courtesy, E. J. Canton.

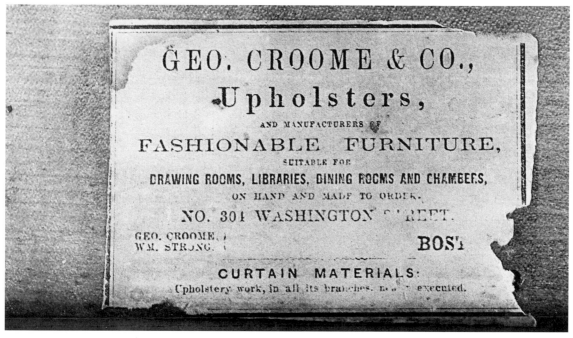

GEO. CROOME & CO.,

Upholsters,

AND MANUFACTURERS OF

FASHIONABLE FURNITURE,

SUITABLE FOR

DRAWING ROOMS, LIBRARIES, DINING ROOMS AND CHAMBERS,

ON HAND AND MADE TO ORDER.

NO. 304 WASHINGTON STREET.

GEO. CROOME,
WM. STRONG.

BOS'

CURTAIN MATERIALS:

Upholstery work, in all its branches, neatly executed.

Detail of the label of George Croome & Co., as it appears on the Renaissance Revival chest of drawers. The firm, on Washington Street, also did upholstery work. Courtesy, E. J. Canton.

CROOME, GEORGE, & CO.

The furniture manufacturer and upholsterer George Croome was active in Boston at 304 Washington Street from 1861 to 1874. Three pieces, Victorian with French influence, bear his label. These are a carved mahogany candle stand offered at Sotheby's, January 28–31, 1981, a Rococo Revival mahogany, rosewood étagère, and a Renaissance Revival chest of drawers. All are labeled

GEO.CROOME & CO.,/Upholsters,/AND MANUFACTURERS OF/FASHIONABLE FURNITURE,/SUITABLE FOR/DRAWING ROOMS, LIBRARIES, DINING ROOMS AND CHAMBERS,/ON HAND AND MADE TO ORDER./NO.304 WASHINGTON STREET./GEO. CROOME,/WM. STRONG,/BOSTON/

CURTAIN MATERIALS:/Upholstery work, in all its branches, neatly executed. Refs.: Fairbanks and Bates; *Antiques,* September 1981.

CROSBY, NATHAN

A Chippendale cherry serpentine-front desk and bookcase, c. 1760–1780, offered at Skinner's, February 6, 1994, is inscribed

Nathan Crosby Lowell Mass

a mark thought to be that of an owner rather than a manufacturer.

CROSMAN, ROBERT

Robert Crosman (1707–1799), a carpenter and drum maker of Taunton, Massachusetts, is considered to be the maker of a miniature William and Mary paint-decorated pine chest of drawers, which is marked in paint

TaunTon,/R.C./1729

as well as other full-size chests bearing similar decoration. Ref.: Bjerkoe; Fales, *American Painted Furniture; Antiques,* April 1933.

CULBERTSON, JOSEPH

A Federal curly maple bowfront chest of drawers with French feet from the Valley of Virginia, c. 1800–1820, signed

Joseph Culbertson

and illustrated in *Antiques* in October 1969, is so similar in design to another cherry serpentine-front chest of drawers of the same period illustrated in *Antiques* for January 1967 and bearing the same signature that one may suspect they are the work of the same unidentified Virginia cabinetmaker.

CUMMINGS, WILLIAM

A labeled Vermont curly maple desk sold at auction in 1993 was attributed to William Cummings of East Dorset. Ref.: *Bee,* November 19, 1993.

CURTIS, JOEL

A late Sheraton mahogany tripod-base writing table in the manner of Duncan Phyfe

bears the label of Joel Curtis, who was working at 153 Chambers Street in Manhattan, c. 1821–1823. The label, engraved with what appear to be Masonic symbols, is unique:

J.CURTIS,/CABINET MAKER/
153/Chambers Street,/NEW YORK.

Ref.: Tracy.

Massachusetts Federal mahogany desk and bookcase or secretary, c. 1800–1820, inscribed "J. Davenport, Gloucester." It is not known if this is the name of the maker or an owner. Courtesy, Frank and Barbara Pollack.

CUSTER, JESSE

The turner Jesse Custer was working in Vincent Township, Chester County, Pennsylvania, as early as 1796. He appeared in nearby Coventry Township tax records two years later. His Windsor chairs, which include sack-back and comb-back armchairs, are branded beneath the seat

J. CUSTER

Ref.: Schiffer.

❧D❧

DALEY, JOHN L.

A New England Sheraton cherry and maple short sideboard in a private collection is inscribed

John L. Daley/March 6. 1820/What is left is left done/Left Case/Rutland Vermont/Back

It is thought to be the work of Rutland, Vermont, cabinetmaker John Daley, active c. 1815–1825.

DANE, S.

A matching pair of c. 1790–1810 Sheraton mahogany games tables with shaped tops and reeded legs offered at auction in October 1994 was inscribed

S. Dane

They have been attributed to the cabinetmaker Samuel Dane of Beverly, Massachusetts. However, Dane died in 1777, well before the date of these chairs. Refs.: Bjerkoe; *Bee*, October 28, 1994.

DANFORTH, D.

A New England fan-back Windsor side chair illustrated in *Antiques* for June 1960 is impressed beneath the seat

D.DANFORTH

No chairmaker by this name is known. However, several Danforths worked as cabinetmakers in the Manchester, Massachusetts, area.

DANFORTH, WILLIAM

A country Chippendale maple slant-front desk in a private collection is inscribed within the case

Wm.Patten, His Desk, Made by Wm.Danforth/in the Year 1760

Danforth, born in Billerica, Massachusetts, in 1737, appears to have spent his life as a farmer rather than a cabinetmaker. Ref.: *Antiques,* May 1924.

DANIEL, URSUAL

A Chippendale mahogany block-front desk at the Museum of Fine Arts in Richmond, Virginia, is said to have the label of Ursual Daniel, a Halifax, North Carolina, cabinetmaker, active c. 1780–1800. The label, pasted within a hidden drawer, is inscribed

Ursual M. Daniel/Halifax, N.C.

Ref.: Bjerkoe.

DAVENPORT, A. H., & CO.

Albert H. Davenport (1845–1906) bought his employer's Boston business in 1880, converting it into a "Mammoth Furniture Establishment" at 96–98 Washington Avenue, which furnished portions of the White House and the Iolani Palace in Honolulu. The furniture, in various eclectic styles and a variety of woods, was sometimes impressed

H.A. DAVENPORT—BOSTON— NEW YORK

The New York address reflects the existence there of a warehouse. Refs.: *Antiques,* May 1976, November 1984.

DAVENPORT, J.

A Massachusetts Federal mahogany desk and bookcase or secretary with writing slide, c. 1800–1820, is inscribed upon the slide

J. Davenport, Gloucester

It is likely that this is an owner's mark, although there is a possible connection to John Davenport (1791–1842), a Newburyport cabinetmaker. Ref.: Bjerkoe.

DAVEY, JOHN

Although he is listed in the Philadelphia directories throughout the period 1797–1822 (primarily at 12 Christian Street), the cabinetmaker John Davey is known for only a single piece, a remarkable c. 1805–1810 Federal secretary-bookcase in mahogany, inlaid in satinwood and with oval mirrors. It has several penciled inscriptions:

John Davey

three times,

John Davey, Philadelphia

three times,

John Davey, Maker

and

John Davey, Jr.

and

John Davey, Jr. Philadelphia

Refs.: Fairbanks and Bates; *Antiques,* April 1964.

DAVEY, JOHN, JR.

As noted under the previous entry for his father, the signature of John Davey, Jr., appears twice on a Philadelphia secretary-bookcase. Because the piece has been dated to a period when Davey Jr. was just finishing his apprenticeship in the cabinetmaking trade, it is likely that he served as assistant to his father on the project. Ref.: Fairbanks and Bates.

DAVIDSON, JAMES

A Chippendale mahogany side chair with Gothic back and Marlborough legs, part of a 1947 exhibition of Baltimore furniture, is stamped on the back seat rail

I D

thought to be the mark of James Davidson, a cabinetmaker active in Baltimore, c. 1785–1806. Ref.: William Voss Elder III, *Maryland Queen Anne and Chippendale Furniture of the Eighteenth Century* (Baltimore: Baltimore Museum of Art, 1968).

DAVIES, S.

A Hepplewhite mahogany card table, c. 1790–1800, is inscribed beneath the top

S. Davies

and is credited to Samuel Davies, a Boston cabinetmaker known to have been working at No. 57 Newbury Street, c. 1792. Refs.: Bjerkoe; *Antiques,* August 1974.

DAVIS, ABNER

A Sheraton mahogany bowfront chest of drawers offered at Christie's on January 21, 1984, is signed in chalk on the underside of the top

Abner Davis

and is attributed to a Pennsylvania cabinet-maker of that name active c. 1790–1810.

DAVIS, ABRAHAM

A c. 1740–1760 Queen Anne curly maple flat-top high chest of drawers or highboy offered in *Antiques* for May 1973 is inscribed

Abraham Davis/Boston

It is not known if this is the signature of the maker or an owner.

DAVIS, C. E. R.

A paint-decorated plank-seat fancy chair in the collection of the Cumberland County Historical Society, Carlisle, Pennsylvania, is stamped beneath the seat

C.E.R. DAVIS

Davis was a Carlisle turner active c. 1831–1842. Ref.: *New York–Pennsylvania Collector,* December 1984.

DAVIS, H.

T wo c. 1800–1820 bamboo-turned bird-cage Windsor side chairs illustrated in *Antiques* for April 1986 are branded

H. DAVIS

This may be the name of an unknown turner.

DAVIS, JOSEPH

J oseph Davis (working c. 1726–1751) was an apprentice to the Boston cabinetmaker Job Coit (1692–1741, see his entry) and later worked both in Boston and in Portsmouth, New Hampshire. A Queen Anne walnut dressing table (c. 1740–1760) inscribed in chalk

Joseph Davis

is thought to be his work, as is an unusual c. 1730–1760 Queen Anne mahogany block-front cupboard on chest signed

Davis

and a c. 1730–1750 Queen Anne walnut veneer high chest of drawers, which bears the chalk signature

J. Davis

Refs.: Fairbanks and Bates; *Old Time New England Furniture* (Boston: Society for the Preservation of New England Antiquities, 1987); *Antiques,* December 1987; Christie's, sale of January 18, 1992.

DAVIS, MOSES

A pine blanket chest in old paint is inscribed in chalk on the bottom

Made March 28th/1820/by Moses Davis

Davis was born December 8, 1800, in Milford, Massachusetts, and married November 27, 1818, in Pelham, Massachusetts, where he carried on his craft.

DAVIS, WILLIAM

A Federal mahogany and white pine five-leg card table, c. 1795–1810, inscribed in chalk beneath the top

W. Davis

is attributed to William Davis, a cabinetmaker who may have worked in Annapolis and Baltimore and who was advertising his shop in Raleigh, North Carolina, in 1812. He died the following year. Davis was from Rhode Island, and he may be the William Davis described as a "joyner" in a Newport account book of 1772. Refs.: Bivins; Bjerkoe.

**Empire mahogany looking glass,
c. 1830–1839, bearing the label of the
mirror and frame maker Charles Del
Vecchio, active in New York City,
c. 1813–1844. Courtesy, Bernard and
S. Dean Levy, Inc., New York.**

DAYTON, BREWSTER

The Stratford, Connecticut, cabinetmaker Brewster Dayton is known for two nearly identical Queen Anne high chests of drawers or highboys in cherry and poplar. One, at Winterthur, is inscribed in chalk

**August 1784 Brewster Dayton made these
draws/in Stratford**

The other, in a private collection, has several chalk inscriptions:

Jan thee 24, 1784/Brewster Dayton
made draws/B. Dayton/1784
Right Hand draw/B. Dayton/1784

and

BD 1784

Dayton, who was born on Long Island, was working in Stratford as early as 1762. He died there in 1796. Refs.: *Antique Monthly,* June 1973; *Antiques,* January 1984.

DECKMAN, GEORGE

George Deckman (1833–1901) of Philadelphia came to Ohio in 1858 and established a furniture manufactory in Minerva, which he removed to Malverne, Carroll County, in 1862. At his death control passed to a son, Stephen George Deckman, who maintained the business into the 1920s. George Deckman's products, including paint-decorated balloon-back chairs, were stenciled

From/Geo. Deckman/
Manufacturer/Bedsteads, Bureaus/
Tables & c./Malverne, O.

Ref.: *Made in Ohio.*

DeFOREST, JACOB

A c. 1850–1870 grain-painted pine "cottage"-type chest of drawers illustrated in *MAD* for February 1975 is signed in pencil

Jacob DeForest, Schenectady, N.Y.

It is likely that this is the name of an owner.

DeFOREST & GARVIN

A Victorian Renaissance Revival walnut bureau with marble top at the New York State Museum is inscribed in crayon and paint

DeForest & Garvin, Fort Edward, N.Y.

Label on the Empire mahogany looking glass. It is in Spanish, reflecting Del Vecchio's extensive South American trade. He was at 44 Chatham Street, the address listed, from 1830 through 1839. Courtesy, Bernard and S. Dean Levy, Inc., New York.

Garvin is thought to have been a c. 1873–1879 partner of Edgar and Alfred E. DeForest, who described themselves in 1879 as "Manufacturers and Dealers in Parlor, Library, Hall, Kitchen and Chamber furniture . . ." at 139 Broadway in Fort Edward. The firm was continued until 1929. Ref.: Scherer.

DEL VECCHIO, CHARLES

An Empire mahogany dressing glass bears the most common label of Charles Del Vecchio (d. c. 1847), a looking glass and picture frame manufacturer active in New York City from at least 1813 to 1844. This label has the 44 Chatham Street address, Del Vecchio's location from 1830 until 1839:

CHARLES DEL VECCHIO'S/Looking Glass/AND PICTURE FRAME/ MANUFACTORY,/NO. 44 CHATHAM-STREET,/New-York,/Where he has constantly on hand, a general assortment of/PIER, CHIMNEY, & DRESSING GLASSES,/Framed in the neatest and most fashionable Patterns./Portrait Frames of all descriptions made to order./Old Looking Glasses . . . . and Frames Re-gilt./OLD PAINTINGS CLEANED AND REPAIRED.

Reflecting an extensive South American trade, Del Vecchio also used a similar label printed in Spanish. There is also what appears to be an ear-

**Maple ladder-back side chair, impressed
CAD on the front posts, for Charles A.
Demarest, a turner who worked in
Bergen County, New Jersey, c. 1800–1825.
Private collection.**

lier Del Vecchio label, this one simply reading
**From/DEL VECCHIO/Looking Glass &
Picture/Frame Manufacturer**
The bottom line is illegible. Ref.: Montgomery.

**Sweet gum and poplar kas or wardrobe
bearing the signature of the
Schraalenburgh, New Jersey, joiner and
carpenter Roelof D. Demarest. Courtesy,
Bernard and S. Dean Levy, Inc., New York.**

DEMAREST, CHARLES A.

A pair of turned maple slat-back, rush-seat side chairs offered at Sotheby's, January 23–25, 1992, are stamped on the top of the front legs

C A D

the cipher of Charles A. Demarest, a Bergen County, New Jersey, turner, active c. 1800–1825.

DEMAREST, ROELOF D.

A large c. 1795–1805 sweet gum and poplar kas or wardrobe in a private collection is signed in chalk
Made by Roelof Demarest/March 17.
The piece is generally attributed to Roelof D. Demarest (1769–1845), a carpenter from Schraalenburgh, Bergen County, New Jersey, who also worked in New York City, c. 1797–

Signature of the cabinetmaker Roelof D. Demarest as it appears on the inside of the top of the kas. Courtesy, Bernard and S. Dean Levy, Inc., New York.

1815. Refs.: Cooper; Peter M. Kenny, Frances G. Safford, and Gilbert T. Vincent, *American Kasten: The Dutch-Style Cupboards of New York and New Jersey, 1650–1800* (New York: Metropolitan Museum of Art, 1991); *Antiques,* July 1986.

DEMING, OLIVER

Two Connecticut cherry reverse-serpentine chests of drawers are signed by Oliver Deming (1774–1825), a cabinetmaker who worked in Wethersfield, Connecticut, before moving to New Haven around 1800. One is signed twice

    Oliver Deming Feby 17th 1796

while the other is simply inscribed

    Oliver Deming

Ref.: *MAD,* March 1993.

DEMING, SIMEON

An outstanding pair of Hepplewhite ma-hogany and gilt mirrors, c. 1790–1800,

A pair of c. 1790–1800 Hepplewhite gilded mahogany mirrors, each of which is signed on the back "S. Deming," for Simeon Deming (1769–1855), a cabinetmaker active in New York City from 1793 until 1798. Courtesy, Israel Sack, Inc., New York.

Victorian Eastlake oak marble-top shaving stand, c. 1870–1880, bearing the label of Derleth Brothers, furniture makers in Manhattan, c. 1865–1880.

Private collection.

from the Israel Sack Collection are signed in ink on the backs

S. Deming

for Simeon Deming (1769–1855), a Wethersfield, Connecticut, cabinetmaker who moved to New York City in 1793, remaining there in partnership with William Mills until 1798 (see Mills & Deming). Ref.: Bjerkoe.

DENMARK, N. S.

An unusual grained and stenciled rod-back Windsor side chair in a private collection bears a paper label reading,

N.S. Denmark, Canton, Pa.

The Pennsylvania chair would date c. 1840–1860, but we do not know if Denmark was a cabinetmaker or an owner.

DENWIDDIE, H.

A pair of grained and stenciled plank-seat fancy chairs in the collection of the Hershey Museum of American Life, Hershey, Pennsylvania, are impressed

H. Denwiddie

Denwiddie was a turner active in Gettysburg, Pennsylvania, c. 1835–1855. Ref.: *New York–Pennsylvania Collector,* December 1984.

DERBY, DEXTER

An Empire bureau in mahogany and maple at the Sheldon Museum is signed twice

Dexter Derby/1836

Derby (1805–1875), a Bridport, Addison County, Vermont, cabinetmaker born in Orford, New Hampshire, was active c. 1835–1850. Ref.: *Old Time New England Furniture* (Boston: Society for the Preservation of New England Antiquities, 1987).

DERLETH BROTHERS

An oak marble-top shaving stand, c. 1870–1880, in the Victorian Eastlake manner, which is in a private collection, bears the printed label of Derleth Brothers, active in Manhattan, c. 1865–1880:

**FROM/DERLETH BROS./
MANUFACTURERS OF/Furniture &
Upholstery,/WAREROOMS:/821 to 829
Sixth Avenue,/Cor. 47th Street,
NEW YORK./FACTORY,
176 ELIZABETH STREET**

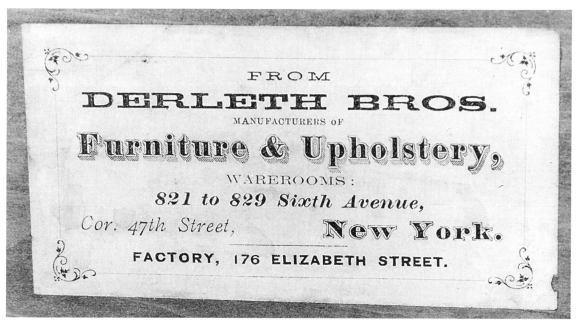

Label of Derleth Brothers, on the Eastlake oak shaving stand. Note that their showrooms were in the fashionable uptown area, while the factory was in the immigrant-filled Lower East Side. Private collection.

DESSOIR, JULIUS S.

A rosewood étagère at the Metropolitan Museum of Art and a walnut and mahogany hall chair in the New York State Museum both are stenciled in an oval

JULIUS S. DESSOIR/
Manufacturer/543/Broadway/
New York

Dessoir worked at several addresses in Manhattan from 1842 until 1865. He was at 543 Broadway between 1851 and 1864, when these pieces were made. Ref.: Scherer.

DETROIT CHAIR FACTORY

A walnut rocking chair in the Elizabethan Revival mode is impressed beneath the seat

DETROIT CHAIR FACTORY

This factory in Detroit, Michigan, was in business c. 1865–1878. Ref.: *Antiques,* March 1965.

DEWEY, GEORGE

The Connecticut craftsman George Dewey was in business in Litchfield as early as 1830, continuing until around 1850. Among his labeled works are an Empire carved mahogany and mahogany veneer bureau at the Stowe-Day Foundation and two Empire cherry one-drawer stands. His label features a gambrel-roof warehouse and three pieces of Empire furniture: a sideboard and two saber-leg chairs. It reads,

GEORGE DEWEY/LITCHFIELD/AT HIS
WARE ROOMS, TWO DOORS WEST OF
THE COUNTY HOUSE,/KEEPS ON

HAND,/CABINET FURNITURE,/Made of good materials, and in a fashionable style, which he/is offering on as good terms as can be purchased at/any other Establishment./CHAIRS, manufactured and sold at the same place.

Ref.: *Litchfield County Furniture, 1730–1850* (Litchfield, Conn.: Litchfield County Historical Society, 1969).

DEWEY, HENRY F.

Henry Freeman Dewey (1800–1882) from Windham, Connecticut, was advertising in Bennington, Vermont, in the 1820s. He appears to have remained active there for nearly two decades, as a maple rocking chair at the Bennington Museum is inscribed in pencil

H.F. Dewey/Chairmaker/East Bennington/Sept. 15, 1838/1838/$ 4.50

Another in the same collection is simply stamped

H. DEWEY.

Ref.: *Antiques,* August 1993; Robinson.

DEWEY & OLMSTEAD

The partnership of Dewey and Olmstead in Springfield, Massachusetts, is remembered for a pair of c. 1850–1870 Victorian Rococo Revival walnut side chairs inscribed on their frames

Dewey and Olmstead/Springfield

Nothing more seems to be known of the firm. Ref.: *Springfield Furniture, 1700–1850* (Springfield, Mass.: Connecticut Valley Historical Museum, 1990).

DE WITT, JOHN

Although he was in business in Manhattan for only a few years (1794–1799), the Windsor chair maker John De Witt left behind several identifiable examples of his work. Most, including bow-back side chairs and continuous-arm chairs (including brace-backs), bear De Witt's printed paper label of 1796–1797, which, appropriately enough, illustrates a continuous-arm chair with the wording

JOHN DE WITT/Windfor Chair Maker,/
No. 47, Water-Street, near/
Coenties Slip, NEW YORK

However, the Sotheby's sale of February 1–4, 1978, offered a very similar continuous-arm

Walnut center table with spiral-turned legs with inscription attributed to the Hartford, Connecticut, joiner Nicholas Disbrowe (1612–1683). Private collection.

chair, which was branded beneath the seat

I. DE WITT

and very likely reflects other periods in De Witt's career, when he worked on Whitehall, William, and Pearl streets. Refs.: Santore I, II; *Antiques,* July 1952.

DIAMOND, THOMAS L.

A rare Massachusetts Chippendale mahogany bombé tea caddy illustrated in *Antiques* for May 1953 is inscribed

**Thomas L. Diamond made
in the year 1765**

Nothing is known of Thomas Diamond.

DIKEMAN, JOHN

Two labeled pieces of furniture by the Manhattan cabinetmaker John Dikeman are known. These are a Chippendale mahogany chest of drawers and a Hepplewhite Pembroke table of mahogany banded in rosewood and boxwood inlaid. Though stylistically different, both pieces are labeled

**JOHN DIKEMAN/Cabinet & Chair
Maker,/No. 167, William-Street,/
NEW-YORK.**

Dikeman is listed at this address in the 1795 New York City directory. The prior year, 1794, he had advertised ". . . a handsome assortment of fashionable furniture. . ." from 48 Beekman Street. From 1796 to 1806 he was listed as a grocer. Refs.: *Antiques,* April 1974, May 1981.

DILWORTH, THOMAS

A privately owned Hepplewhite fall-front bureau desk in mahogany inlaid with maple is signed

made by Thomas Dilworth 1801

and is attributed to the Pennsylvania cabinetmaker Thomas Dilworth, who was working in Chester County, c. 1801–1805. Refs.: Schiffer; *Antiques,* October 1965.

DINSMORE & BATCHELDER

A fine Federal boxwood-inlaid mahogany secretary-desk at Winterthur, dating c. 1800–1820, bears the printed paper label

**MAHOGANY/AND BIRCH
FURNITURE,/OF ALL KINDS, AND
OF THE LATEST/FASHIONS,
MANUFACTURED/DINSMORE &
BATCHELDER,/Brunswick, (Maine.)**

No other pieces from this firm have been identified.

DINWOODEY, H.

A Boston-type rocker in the collection of Pioneer Trail State Park, Salt Lake City, Utah, is stenciled beneath the seat

**H.DINWOODEY/Furniture and Bedding,
Wallpaper, Carpets, etc./
Salt Lake City, Utah.**

The piece dates c. 1875–1900, and it is likely that the name is that of a wholesaler rather than a manufacturer.

DISBROWE, NICHOLAS

A curious walnut center table with spiral-turned legs and shaped-cross stretcher in a private collection is inscribed

**CUTTE & JOYNED BY
NICH DISBROWE—X— HIS MARK for
DEPUTY GOV. WILLIAM BRADFORD**

The letter *X* in chalk also appears in various places on the piece. Nicholas Disbrowe (1612–

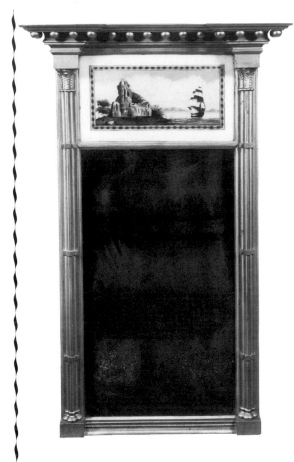

Gilded Federal mirror with reverse-painted panel, c. 1805–1815, labeled by John Doggett (1780–1857), a cabinetmaker active on Market Street in Roxbury, Massachusetts, c. 1802–1835. Courtesy, Israel Sack, Inc., New York.

1683), an early Connecticut joiner, worked in Hartford from the 1630s until his death. He has been associated with a carved oak chest inscribed
Mary Allyns Chistt Cutte and/ joyned by Nich: Disbrowe

This inscription has been proven not authentic, and it is highly doubtful that the inscription on the table is any more valid. Refs.: Bjerkoe; *Antiques,* May 1933, December 1966.

DIXON, F.

A country Chippendale maple high chest of drawers, c. 1790–1820, illustrated in *MAD* for December 1977, is signed on the backboard
F. Dixon Taunton, Mass.
This is probably an owner's name.

DODGE, THOMAS

Thomas Dodge was a member of the Dodge furniture-making family in Manchester, Massachusetts. Their business was established in 1841 and continued into the twentieth century. Marked examples include late Empire furnishings as well as Colonial Revival pieces in the Queen Anne, Chippendale, and Federal styles. The usual mark is
T. DODGE
impressed, although the signature
Thomas Dodge
is also known. Refs.: *Antiques & Arts Weekly,* July 16, 1993; *MAD,* January 1994.

DOGGETT, JOHN

John Doggett (1780–1857) of Roxbury, Massachusetts, is thought of primarily as a gilder and maker of picture frames and mirrors. However, he was a remarkably versatile craftsman, whose elaborate label, set in a foliate circle surmounted by an eagle and reading
JOHN DOGGETT/Gilder,/Looking Glafs & Picture Frame/Manufacturer/Roxbury/ Constantly for sale/a large afsortment of/Looking Glafses

Label of John Doggett, on the back panel of the Federal mirror. Unlike most looking glass manufacturers, Doggett made a wide variety of furniture.

Courtesy, Israel Sack, Inc., New York.

may be found also on dressing tables, fire screens, dressing glasses, clock cases, and bed cornices, some of which he made, others he gilded. Doggett was active on Market Street in Roxbury at various addresses from 1802 until at least 1835. Refs.: Fales, *American Painted Furniture;* Montgomery; *Antiques,* May 1992.

DOLAN, JOHN T.

The cabinetmaker John T. Dolan is listed in the Manhattan directories for the period 1805–1810, first at 65 Beekman Street, the location found on his label, which appears on a Sheraton mahogany Pembroke table sold at Weschler's in Washington, D.C., in January 1994:

JOHN T. DOLAN'S/CABINET & CHAIR/Warehouse,/NO. 65, BEEKMAN-STREET,/NEW-YORK.

and in 1810 at 30 Beekman Street, which may be only a change in municipal street numbering. In any case, Dolan simply changed the number on his old label. Among the very few known labeled Dolan examples are a Hepplewhite chest of drawers, two card tables (one at the Museum of the City of New York), an unusual lift-top single-drawer writing table, and the above-mentioned Pembroke table. Refs.: Comstock, *American Furniture; Antiques,* October 1961, June 1966; *MAD,* March 1993, March 1994.

DOMINY, FELIX

Felix Dominy (1800–1868) continued the family clock and cabinetmaking business on Main Street in East Hampton, Long Island, New York. He is known for four clocks, marked respectively

F D/ 1818/ Augst 4
Felix Dominy/ 1824
DOMINY

and

F. Dominy, 1827

Ref.: Hummel.

DOMINY, NATHANIEL, IV

Nathaniel Dominy IV (1737–1812), the most active clockmaker among the Dominy clan of East Hampton, New York, produced a variety of signed examples. Among the existent marks are

N.DOMINY, 1790, E. HAMPTON
N. DOMINY, E. HAMPTON, 1804
also the same mark with 1807 and 1809 dates
N. DOMINY
Nath Dominy. E. Hampton/1780
Made by Nath Dominy/E. Hampton
Long Island 1787
N.D. 1789
Made by Nathaniel Dominy/of
East Hampton Long Island
N. Dominie fecit 1791 Nov./
for John Lyon Gardiner $ 70
N. Dominy 17 E. Hampton 95
N. Dominy/1795
N. Dominy, 1798
DOMINY/1803
Ref.: Hummel.

DOMINY, NATHANIEL, V

Nathaniel Dominy V (1770–1852) inherited his father's business on Main Street in East Hampton, New York. He is known for an unusual mahogany low-back Windsor chair, which is marked beneath the seat
NAT DOMINY/MAKg 10/
Nov 11, 1794/WR
and a Chippendale mahogany desk bearing the penciled inscription
Nathaniel Dominie, Junr. fecit Jan 4-

Victorian Renaissance Revival walnut bureau with marble fittings and mirror, c. 1860–1880, which bears the partial mark of James Donohoe, a cabinetmaker working at the time on Cherry Street in Philadelphia. Private collection.

1802—/For John Lyn Gardiner, Esqr.—
Price $ 27
Ref.: Hummel.

DONN, GEORGE W., & COMPANY

The Washington, D.C., cabinetmaker George W. Donn was in business on Pennsylvania Avenue near the White House as early as 1836. Although it is not known who the "& Co." consisted of, the firm remained in business at various Washington addresses until

after 1860. Their heavy walnut and mahogany furniture, late Sheraton and Empire in style, was stenciled

DONN & CO./SOFA/&/CABINET
MANUFACTURERS/PA AVE/
Near the Capitol,/Washington City
Ref.: *Antiques,* May 1975.

DONNELL, GEORGE O.

The Shaker chairmaker George O. Donnell (b. 1823) was a member of the Mount Lebanon, New York, community. He is known for a patent model of a miniature ladder-back chair fitted with brass tilters in brass sleeves. It was submitted to the U.S. Patent Office in 1852 and is stenciled on the lower slat

GEORGE, O DONNELL

Donnell later left the Shaker order, and there is no evidence that chairs of this sort were ever produced. Refs.: Rieman and Burks; Sprigg.

DONOHOE, JAMES

A Victorian Renaissance Revival walnut bureau with marble fittings and mirror, dating c. 1860–1880, bears the indistinct mark

Select Council/Philadelphia 1868/
James Donohoe/. . . . Cabinet Ware
Manufacturer/304 Cherry—
Philadelphia, Pen.

Nothing more is presently known of this manufacturer.

DOW, I.

A Rhode Island bow-back Windsor side chair, c. 1800–1820, is branded twice

I. DOW

It is not known if this is an owner's or the maker's mark. Ref.: Santore II.

Gilded Chippendale mahogany mirror, c. 1770–1790, with the label of Hosea Dugliss, a looking glass manufacturer working at 11 Chatham Row in Manhattan. Courtesy, the Henry Ford Museum, Dearborn, Mich.

DOWDNEY, NATHANIEL

A tall case clock by William Huston of Philadelphia (working 1754–1771) bears within its case the handwritten label

Nathaniel Dowdney No. 24

Dowdney (c. 1736–1793) was a "joyner" from Hopewell Township, Cumberland County, New Jersey, who worked on Third Street in Philadelphia from 1764 until 1770. Refs.: Bjerkoe; *Antiques,* March 1955.

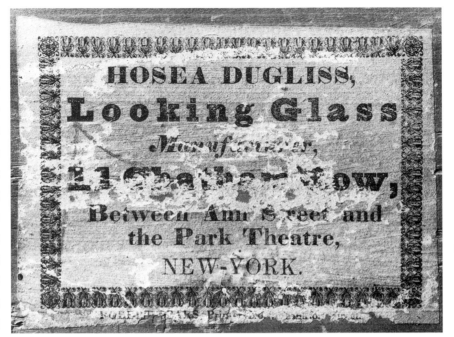

DOWNS, D.

An unusual c. 1800–1810 Federal cherry bookcase over bowfront case of drawers in a private collection is signed in chalk

D. Downs

believed to be the name of a cabinetmaker working in eastern Kentucky during the early nineteenth century. Ref.: *Antiques,* November 1947.

DRAKE, T.

A well-made c. 1790–1800 brace-back continuous-arm Windsor chair with New York characteristics, which was part of the Garvan Collection sold at Parke Bernet, October 31, 1970, is branded

T.DRAKE.N.Y.

It is likely that this is the mark of a hitherto unknown Manhattan turner. Ref.: *Antiques,* June 1936.

DRUM, PHILLIP

A vase-splat plank-bottom chair in a private collection is inscribed beneath the seat

MADE BY PHILLIP DRUM/BETHEL/OHIO/1847/FOR SAMUEL SIMPSON

Drum apprenticed to the turner Robert McGinnis and worked in Bethel, Clermont County, Ohio, c. 1845–1850. Ref.: Hageman I.

DUGLISS, HOSEA

An ornate gilded Chippendale mahogany mirror with applied eagle and foliate inlay in the collection of the Henry Ford Museum bears a label reading

HOSEA DUGLISS/Looking Glass/ Manufacturer,/11 Chatham Row,/ Between Ann Street and/the Park Theatre,/ NEW-YORK.

The mirror dates c. 1770–1790, but nothing further is known of the manufacturer.

DULIN, WILLIAM H.

William H. Dulin apprenticed to the cabinetmaker David H. Stayton in Camden, Delaware, in 1841, remaining with him until at least 1850. Dulin thereafter worked on his own as cabinetmaker and undertaker until 1874. He is known for a Victorian walnut "cottage" bureau inscribed

Wm. H. Dulin/Camden/made this bureau
and
William H. Dulin 1869/Made this Buruo
Ref.: *Plain and Ornamental.*

DUNBAR, SAMUEL

country Federal maple chest of drawers advertised in *Antiques* for July 1975 bears the signature

Samuel Dunbar
Nothing is presently known of this individual.

DUNCAN, I.

A c. 1770–1790 Chippendale mahogany Marlborough-leg side chair with pierced Gothic splat illustrated in Hornor is inscribed
I. Duncan
It is likely that this is an owner's mark. Ref.: Hornor.

DUNHAM, WATSON

c. 1830–1840 carved Classical three-drawer marble-top mahogany stand in a private collection is branded
WATSON DUNHAM MAKER
The piece is attributed to the Albany, New

York, area, but nothing is known of the maker.

DUNLAP, DAN

Dan Dunlap (1792–1866), cousin of the well-known New Hampshire cabinetmaker John Dunlap II (see his entry), was born in Bedford, New Hampshire, but moved to Antrim in 1812. We do not know how long he made furniture there, and only a single piece from his hand, an ordinary c. 1830–1850 pine and maple drop-leaf table signed in pencil

Dan Dunlap/Antrim/N.H.
is known. Ref.: *Antiques,* July 1964.

DUNLAP, JOHN

Major John Dunlap (1746–1792), born in Chester, New Hampshire, moved to Goffstown in 1769 and established his cabinetmaking shop at Bedford near Manchester in 1777. He is known for a Queen Anne maple chest on chest mounted on bandy legs and with characteristic Dunlap carving. Incised on the back is

John Dunlap/1784
Ref.: *The Dunlaps and Their Furniture* (Manchester, N.H.: Currier Gallery of Art, 1970).

DUNLAP, JOHN, II

The New Hampshire cabinetmaker John Dunlap, Jr. (1784–1869), was in business in Antrim in 1805. Before moving to Zanesville, Ohio, in 1844 he produced a substantial quantity of marked furniture, ranging from ordinary rod-back side chairs and rockers stamped
JOHN/DUNLAP/1830
to sophisticated Hepplewhite cherry card tables inlaid in birch and grain-painted tall

clock cases. These were typically marked with a paper label signed in brown ink

John Dunlap, 1807/Cabinet and Chairmaker/Antrim

A single card table labeled simply

John Dunlap

is also known, but because part of the paper has been torn off, it is possible that it was originally identical to the above. Refs.: *The Dunlaps and Their Furniture; Antiques,* August 1979, May 1982.

DUNLAP, ROBERT E.

Robert E. Dunlap (1779–1865), son of Maj. John Dunlap (see his entry), worked at the family shop in Bedford, New Hampshire. His only known signed piece is a typical Dunlap Queen Anne maple chest on chest on frame, which is initialed on the bottom

R.E.D.

Ref.: *The Dunlaps and Their Furniture.*

DUNLAP, SAMUEL

Lieutenant Samuel Dunlap (1752–1830), brother of John Dunlap, Sr. (see his entry), worked in Goffstown, Henniker, and Salisbury, New Hampshire. His initials,

S.D.

appear twice in paint on the back of a Queen Anne maple high chest of drawers or highboy

---

Hepplewhite inlaid cherry high chest of drawers, signed and dated under the top, "George Dyer 1808." Dyer was a cabinet-maker working in Manheim, Pennsylvania, during the early nineteenth century.

Courtesy, Israel Sack, Inc., New York.

in a private collection. Ref.: *The Dunlaps and Their Furniture.*

DURANT, THOMAS

The cabinetmaker and chairmaker Thomas Durant is known only for a Federal walnut and yellow pine chest of drawers signed in ink

. . . . . . **Durant**

which is at Travelers' Rest Historic House in Nashville, Tennessee. Durant had a shop in Carthage, Smith County, Tennessee, c. 1819–1823. Ref.: Williams and Harsh.

DYER, GEORGE

The early-nineteenth-century Manheim, Pennsylvania, cabinetmaker George Dyer signed a Hepplewhite cherry high chest of drawers with double eagle inlay

William and Mary maple Spanish-foot, cane-back armchair, c. 1700–1720, marked EE for Edmund Edes, who was working in Boston from 1709. Private collection.

George Dyer 1808

Although little is known of its maker, the piece indicates a high level of skill.

EACHUS, VIRGIL

The cabinetmaker Virgil Eachus (d. 1839) worked in Thornbury, Middletown, and Haverford townships, Chester County, Pennsylvania, c. 1785–1839. A Chippendale walnut tall chest of drawers on frame in a private collection signed

Virgil Eachus 1785

is attributed to him. Ref.: Schiffer.

EARLE, JAMES S.

James S. Earle, active at 212 Chestnut Street, Philadelphia, c. 1820–1840, is credited with a gilded Empire overmantel mirror offered at Christie's, January 22, 1985. It bears a printed paper label reading

JAMES S. EARLE'S/Gallery of Paintings,/LOOKING GLASS WORKS/AND/Picture Frame Manufactory/212/Chestnut Street, opposite Girard House/PHILADELPHIA

EASTWOOD, MOSES

A pine bookcase on desk or plantation desk offered in *Antiques* for September 1979 is signed

M.E./1852

and attributed to Moses Eastwood, a Shaker joiner thought to have been associated with an Ohio or a Kentucky community

EATON, W. P.

The stenciled name

W.P. Eaton

is occasionally found on painted and stenciled New England chairs and rockers. However, Eaton (1819–1904) was a decorator, not a turner. He worked in Boston and near South Weare, New Hampshire. Refs.: *Antiques*, August 1949, June 1975.

EDES, EDMUND

Edmund Edes, who was working in Boston as early as 1709, left a William and Mary

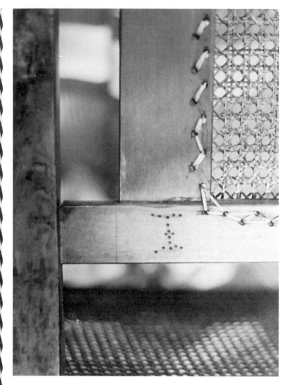 

LEFT: Unusual punchwork mark of Edmund Edes on the lower back rail of the William and Mary armchair. Private collection. RIGHT: Punchwork mark on a William and Mary maple cane-back side chair attributed to the Boston turner Edmund Edes. This has been described as either a capital *I* with cross-serif or two *E*'s placed back-to-back. Courtesy, Bernard and S. Dean Levy, Inc., New York.

maple Spanish-foot cane-back armchair and a similar side chair. Both are c. 1700–1720 and are marked with a punchwork design resembling two *E*'s placed back-to-back. Refs.: Bjerkoe; *Antiques,* September 1984.

EDGE, WALTER

The Gilmanton, New Hampshire, cabinet-maker Walter Edge is represented in the collection of the Currier Gallery of Art, Manchester, by a Chippendale oxbow-front desk and bookcase or secretary in curly maple, which is inscribed in chalk

Walter Edge, Gilmanton, N.H. dated June 5, 1799

Ref.: Currier.

EDSON, SIMEON WILLARD

The turner Simeon Willard Edson worked in Peth, Orange County, Vermont, from 1834 until he moved to Wisconsin in 1850. His label "S.W. EDSON/PETH" appears on a

Octagonal label of the cabinetmaker Matthew Egerton on the Federal tall clock case. Courtesy, C. L. Prickett, Yardley, Pa.

maple and tiger maple one-drawer stand. Ref.: *MAD,* October 1993.

EGERTON, MATTHEW

Matthew Egerton, Sr. (1739–1802), of New Brunswick, New Jersey, is regarded as one of the Garden State's finest craftsmen. His well-known oval printed label:

MATTHEW EGERTON,/CABINET MAKER,/IN BURNET STREET./ NEW BRUNSWICK, (N.J.)

has been found on a variety of Sheraton and Hepplewhite inlaid mahogany furniture, including sideboards, clock cases, end and Pembroke tables, slant-front desks, linen presses, and even a barometer. Refs.: Bjerkoe; *Antiques,* September 1928.

Federal mahogany inlaid tall clock case, c. 1790–1800, labeled by the cabinetmaker Matthew Egerton (1739–1802), who worked on Burnet Street in New Brunswick, New Jersey. Courtesy, C. L. Prickett, Yardley, Pa.

EGERTON, MATTHEW, JR.

Matthew Egerton, Jr., followed in his father's (see his entry) footsteps at the old shop on Burnet Street in New Brunswick, where he worked until his death in 1837. Active as early as 1785, Matthew Jr. had pur-

chased a lot adjoining his father's shop in 1793. His usual printed label:

MADE AND SOLD BY/MATTHEW EGERTON, Junior,/JOINER and CABINETMAKER,/New-Brunswick,/ NEW-JERSEY/—No.—

may be found on a variety of Federal furnishings similar in style to those made by his father. These include sideboards and buffets, console and card tables, and, of course, clock cases, such as the one at the Newark Museum. However, he also made and marked large archaic kas or clothespresses in a style more suitable to the early eighteenth century. There is also a single clock case bearing an ink-inscribed paper label reading,

Made and Sold by/Matthew Egerton, Jr./ In New Brunswick

This may date to the earliest period of Matthew Jr.'s career. Refs.: Bjerkoe; *Antiques,* November 1928.

EHLE, GEORGE M.

A c. 1840–1860 grain-painted pine six-board chest at the New York State Museum in Albany is inscribed

George M. Ehle Maker/Freys Bush

Ehle (1826–1883) is described as a "carpenter" in the 1850 and 1855 census reports. He lived in Freys Bush, Montgomery County, New York. Ref.: Mary Antoine de Julio, *German*

Federal inlaid mahogany Pembroke table, c. 1795–1805, bearing the label of Matthew Egerton, Jr. (d. 1837), working in New Brunswick, New Jersey, c. 1785–1837. Courtesy, Bernard and S. Dean Levy, Inc., New York.

Folk Art of New York State (Albany: Albany Institute of History and Art, 1985).

EISENBRAG, JOHN

A Federal mahogany slant-front desk with French feet advertised in *Antiques* December 1969 is signed

John Eisenbrag, 1794, Maker

A similar unsigned desk is at Winterthur. Nothing further is known of the maker.

ELIAERS, AUGUSTUS

S everal Victorian Renaissance Revival–style leather-upholstered oak or mahogany library chairs (one at the Chicago Historical Society), which convert to stepladders, are stamped

A. ELIAERS/PATENT

Augustus Eliaers, a native of France, worked in

Boston from 1849 until 1860, designing unusual seating, including invalid chairs and railway benches. In 1858 he was described in *Ballou's Pictorial Magazine* as ". . . not merely a cabinetmaker, in the usual sense of the word; he is an artist, a designer, and inventor. . . ." Refs.: Bishop; *Antiques,* September 1981.

ELLIOTT, J.

Although there is apparently no firm evidence that the well-known Philadelphia looking glass sellers John Elliott (1713–1791) and John Elliott, Jr. (1739–1810), made the mirrors they so frequently labeled (despite the fact that the father, at least, was a cabinetmaker), there is another Philadelphia Elliott who did claim to manufacture mirrors. A c. 1810–1830 Federal mahogany dressing glass illustrated in *Antiques* for October 1967 is labeled

J. ELLIOTT,/Comb and Looking Glass/MANUFACTURRER,/No.1, NORTH THIRD STREET,/PHILADELPHIA/ RESPECTFULLY informs his friends, and

the public/in general,/that he has constantly for sale, a large assort-/ment of COMBS AND LOOKING GLASSES, finish-/ed in the best manner, which he will sell at reduced prices.

A variant of this label appears on the reverse, making it perhaps the only known double-sided American manufacturer's label. This J. Elliott is probably the John Elliott who was listed as having a shop on Market Street from 1808 until 1839, long after both John Elliott and John Elliott, Jr., were dead. He may also be the maker of a Chippendale mahogany mirror branded

ELIOT

illustrated in *Antiques* for April 4, 1966. Refs.: Montgomery; *Antiques,* October 1967.

ELLIS, JOHN A.

A Sheraton mahogany two-drawer sewing table with cookie corners illustrated in *Antiques* for April 1968 bears the printed paper label

JOHN A. ELLIS,/Manufactures all types

of/FIRST CLASS/FURNITURE/GORE STREET/. . . . ./EAST CAMBRIDGE. The piece would appear to date c. 1800–1820, but little is known of the East Cambridge, Massachusetts, maker.

ELY, JOHN W. M.

A late Federal walnut desk and bookcase or secretary inlaid in maple and cherry is signed in pencil

January the 20th 1836/John W.M. Ely and is attributed to the cabinetmaker John Ely of Greene County, Tennessee, who was active as early as 1830. Ref.: Williams and Harsh.

ELY, SMITH

A turner who later became a very successful merchant, Smith Ely (1800–1884) produced a variety of Empire cane-seated chairs at his shops on Broad and New streets in Manhattan, c. 1823–1837. They are impressed upon the rear seat rail

S. ELY

or

S. ELY.N.Y.

Among Ely's customers was the Portland, Maine, chair manufacturer Walter Corey (see his entry), whose shop bought and decorated unfinished Ely chairs. Refs.: Monkhouse and Michie; *Antiques,* June 1982.

EMERY, D.

A pair of bamboo-turned bow-back Windsor side chairs offered at Skinner's, March 30, 1984, are branded beneath the seats

D. EMERY

This is possibly the mark of an unknown New England turner. Members of the Emery family were engaged in cabinetmaking in the Newbury/ Newburyport area of Massachusetts.

Classical mahogany veneer sideboard, c. 1818–1825, labeled by Thomas Emmons and George Archibald, cabinetmakers who worked at 39 Orange Street in Boston from 1813 through 1825. Courtesy, Skinner, Inc., Bolton, Mass.

Stenciled mark of Emmons & Archibald on the Classical mahogany veneer sideboard.

Courtesy, Skinner, Inc., Bolton, Mass.

EMMONS & ARCHIBALD

The partnership of Thomas Emmons (d. 1825) and George Archibald was active from 1813 to 1825 at 39 Orange Street in Boston, Massachusetts. They produced a substantial number of late Classical or Empire furnishings, including card and pier tables and sideboards, many of which were in mahogany or rosewood with ormolu mounts and ebonized areas. Their stenciled mark

EMMONS & ARCHIBALD/No.39
Orange Street/(BOSTON)/Cabinet,
Chair & Upholstery/Manufactory

is found on five pieces in the collection of the Museum of Fine Arts, Boston. Refs.: Cooper; Fairbanks and Bates; *Antiques,* September 1981, May 1992.

ENGLISH, WILLIAM

A c. 1790–1810 Hepplewhite mahogany, rosewood, and birch tambour secretary illustrated in *Antiques* for February 1962 is signed in chalk

William English

and attributed to William English, a cabinet-maker documented as working in Boston in 1809. Ref.: Bjerkoe.

ENOS, THOMAS THOMPSON

Apprenticed in 1831 to the Smyrna cabinetmaker Alexander Faries, Thomas Thompson Enos (1817–1889) established his own shop in Odessa, Delaware, in 1840, continuing until at least 1874. He is known for a pine pie safe with punchwork-decorated panels, including his mark

Thomas T. Enos/June 30th/1845

and painted poplar half-spindle side chairs inscribed in pencil beneath the seats

T.T. ENOS/Odessa/Del 2

Ref.: *Plain and Ornamental.*

EPRIGHT, R.

An eighteenth-century New England fan-back Windsor side chair, illustrated in *Antiques* for May 1966, is stamped five times beneath the seat

R.EPRIGHT

This may be the mark of an owner or of the maker.

ERMENTROUT, E.

A six-foot-long paint-decorated Pennsylvania settee, c. 1830–1850, which was sold at Parke Bernet November 12–13, 1971, is branded several times beneath the seat

E. ERMENTROUT

Nothing is known of this maker or owner.

ESTEY MANUFACTURING COMPANY

A late-nineteenth-century golden oak commode with mirror in the collection of the Henry Ford Museum is labeled

FROM/ESTEY MANUFACTURING CO./MANUFACTURERS OF THE/STANDARD LINE OF FURNITURE/. . . . NO . . . . . OWOSSO, MICHIGAN

EUSTIS, EBENEZER

A fine Federal mahogany secretary-bookcase with satinwood inlay illustrated in the Bernard and S. Dean Levy catalog V of 1986 is inscribed

Victorian Eastlake oak chest of drawers or bureau, c. 1870–1900, with the label of the Estey Manufacturing Company, Owosso, Michigan. A typical example of "Grand Rapids"–type furniture. Private collection.

EUSTIS 1808

and attributed to the cabinetmaker Ebenezer Eustis of Salem, Massachusetts, who had a shop on North Street in 1824. He was on Essex Street a year later and was still working there in 1837. Ref.: Bjerkoe.

Federal inlaid mahogany secretary-bookcase inscribed EUSTIS 1808 and ascribed to the Salem, Massachusetts, cabinetmaker Ebenezer Eustis. Courtesy, Bernard and S. Dean Levy, Inc., New York.

Brand of Edward Evans on a drawer in the William and Mary secretary-desk or writing cabinet. Courtesy, Colonial Williamsburg.

EVANS, DAVID

The Philadelphia cabinetmaker David Evans made a variety of Chippendale and Federal furniture at the shop on Arch Street that he occupied c. 1774–1814. His account books covering most of this period are now at the Historical Society of Pennsylvania. A Chippendale mahogany dining table illustrated in *Antiques* for October 1972 bears his impressed mark

D.EVANS

It is also possible that the impression

D.E.

on a Chippendale mahogany Marlborough-leg side chair in a private collection reflects his manufacture. Ref.: Bjerkoe.

William and Mary walnut fall-front secretary-desk or writing cabinet bearing the mark of Edward Evans and the date, 1707. The joiner Edward Evans worked in Philadelphia, c. 1701–1715. Courtesy, Colonial Williamsburg.

EVANS, EDWARD

A William and Mary walnut fall-front secretary-desk or writing cabinet at Colonial Williamsburg, which is stamped within a drawer

EDWARD EVANS 1707

is the earliest signed and dated piece of Pennsylvania furniture known. Evans (d. 1754), described as a "joiner" in contemporary records, was working in Philadelphia c. 1701–1715. Among his patrons was the family of William Penn. Refs.: Fairbanks and Bates; *Antiques*, January 1960.

Sack-back Windsor armchair, c. 1786–1800, of mixed woods, marked and labeled by Ephraim Evans of Alexandria, Virginia. Evans, who had worked in Philadelphia, was in Alexandria by 1786. Courtesy, Bernard and S. Dean Levy, Inc., New York.

EVANS, EPHRAIM

The Windsor chair maker Ephraim Evans was working on Front Street in Philadelphia in 1785 but by the next year had moved to Alexandria, Virginia. His rare impressed mark is

E. EVANS

Ref.: Santore II.

EVANS, ISAAC

The Kentucky cabinetmaker Isaac Evans was born in what is now West Virginia in 1771 and came to Maysville, Kentucky, in 1796. He later owned land in Bath and Rowan counties. His only known work is a Federal cherry desk and bookcase or secretary at the Museum of Early Southern Decorative Arts, which is inscribed within the case

Made by my hans/Isaac Evans, Maysville, K

Refs.: *Antiques,* April 1974; *Antiques Journal,* February 1994.

EVANS, JOHN

A c. 1800–1810 Chippendale cherry slant-front desk in a private collection is signed in ink within a document box

John Evans

Evans lived in the area of Delaware known as White Clay Creek Hundred and is described in an 1806 deed as a "cabinetmaker." Nothing further is known of his career. Refs.: *Plain and Ornamental; Antiques,* May 1985.

EVANS, W.

A c. 1740–1760 Queen Anne cherry drop-leaf dining table in a private collection is branded

W.EVANS

It is not known if the mark is that of the maker or an owner.

EVENTON, MARDUN VAGHN

All that remains from the rather lengthy career of the Virginia cabinetmaker

Mardun Vaghn Eventon is a Chippendale walnut and yellow pine desk and bookcase or secretary inscribed in chalk

made by Mardun V. Eventon

Eventon was located as early as 1762 in Dumfries, Prince William County, and was advertising as late as 1777 from Chesterfield County. Refs.: Bjerkoe; Gusler.

F

FAIRBANKS, JONATHAN, JR.

The cabinetmaker Jonathan Fairbanks, Jr. (1788–1881), was working in Harvard, Massachusetts, by 1816 and still active in 1832, when he was in partnership with Sylvester Priest. Three marked pieces of Fairbanks's furniture are known, including a Sheraton mahogany card table at Old Sturbridge Village, which is inscribed

J. Fairbanks/Harvard

Another, similar card table offered at a New Hampshire auction house sale of August 1979 bears the chalk signature

Fairbanks Harvard

Refs.: *Antiques,* May 1980, May 1993.

FAIRCHILD, ANSON T.

A c. 1790–1810 Sheraton mahogany and satinwood sideboard in a private collection is signed in pencil

**Anson T. Fairchild, Northampton, 1815/—
made for Ames Clark**

Fairchild, a Northampton, Massachusetts, cabinetmaker, is listed in the 1790 census for that community. Ref.: *Antiques,* May 1959.

FELDMAN'S

A set of Empire-style mahogany vase-back saber-leg side chairs dating to the early twentieth century, which were sold at the New Orleans Auction Galleries in 1993, are stamped

**Feldman's Handmade/Furniture/
New Orleans**

This was evidently a company producing good-quality reproductions.

Impressed mark, E. EVANS, and barely distinguishable paper label of Ephraim Evans. Courtesy, Bernard and S. Dean Levy, Inc., New York.

FENN, WILLIAM W.

A simple country Sheraton pine stand in a private collection is inscribed in paint beneath the seat

This Stand was made/By Wm. W. Fenn Son of/H.C. Fenn of the Firm of/Brewster & Fenn on the 3 of/April 1850 and presented By/Him to Mrs. Colsen his worthy/Grandmother/Rochester,/N.Y.

From the appearance of the piece, its maker was not particularly skilled.

FERRIS, JOHN, III

Son and grandson of cabinetmakers, John Ferris III (1801–1882) ran a successful "cabinet warehouse" on Shipley Street in Wilmington, Delaware, from the early 1820s until he retired in 1853. An Empire pillar-and-scroll mahogany veneer and tulipwood desk and bookcase or secretary in a private collection is inscribed

Made by/John Ferris/. . . . 1841

Ref.: *Plain and Ornamental.*

FETTER, JACOB

Windsor chairs bearing beneath the seats the impression

I.FETTER

are attributed by Santore to the turner Jacob Fetter (1756–1833), who worked in Lancaster, Pennsylvania. Ref.: Santore II.

Country Sheraton pine stand with the inscribed name of the maker, William W. Fenn, and date April 3, 1850, on the underside of the top. Private collection.

FIES, PETER

An unusual Pennsylvania walnut spice or seed chest advertised in *Antiques & Arts Weekly* for September 2, 1994, is signed within each drawer

Peter Fies, 1837

It is not known if Fies was owner or maker of this piece.

FISHER, GEORGE

The Woodstock, Vermont, cabinetmaker George Fisher (1820–1896) is known for an Empire mahogany veneer card table, dating c. 1840–1850, now at the Dana House in Woodstock. The piece bears a label reading,

GEORGE FISHER,/MANUFACTURER OF AND DEALER IN,/Sofas, Mahogany Chairs and Tables/AND EVERY VARIETY OF/HOUSEHOLD FURNITURE,/Pleasant Street/ WOODSTOCK, VT.

Ref.: *Antiques,* December 1980.

FISHER, THOMAS

A small dressing box or shaving mirror illustrated in *Antiques and Art Weekly* for May 13, 1994, is signed

T. Fisher 1887

It is the only presently known marked work of the Shaker brother and cabinetmaker Thomas Fisher (1823–1902) of Enfield, Connecticut. Ref.: Rieman and Burks.

FISHER & McLOUGHLIN

The cabinetmakers Jacob Fisher and Thomas McLoughlin were active in Woodstock, Vermont, from 1823 until at least 1833 selling sofas, beds, bureaus, and chairs. One source (*The History of Woodstock, Vermont,* 1899) describes the firm as doing ". . . more business than all other cabinet-shops round put together." Their mark

Fisher & McLoughlin/Woodstock/
Oct. 28, 1829

appears on a mahogany sewing table or work-table at the Woodstock Historical Society. Jacob Fisher may have been the father of George Fisher (see his entry) who worked in Woodstock at a later date. Ref.: Robinson.

FISKE, SAMUEL

Samuel Fiske (1769–1797), a cabinetmaker born in Waltham, Massachusetts, worked in Dorchester with Stephen Badlam (see his

Chalk signature of Samuel Fiske on the underside of the inlaid mahogany Hepplewhite card table. Courtesy, Israel Sack, Inc., New York.

entry) and had a shop in Salem, probably from the 1780s. By the 1790s he was in Boston on Washington Street. He is known for several marked pieces, including a Hepplewhite mahogany card table signed in chalk

S. Fisk/Cabinate Maker/Bofton

and a pair of c. 1790–1795 Hepplewhite mahogany shield back side chairs stamped

S.F.

Ref.: Montgomery.

Pair of Hepplewhite mahogany shield-back side chairs, c. 1790–1795, each of which is branded "S.F." for Samuel Fiske. Courtesy, Israel Sack, Inc., New York.

Pair of c. 1820–1840 Classical mahogany breakfast tables, each of which bears the stenciled mark of the Boston cabinetmaker William Fiske (1770–1844), who worked at the family shop on Washington Street, c. 1798–1844. Courtesy, Skinner, Inc., Bolton, Mass.

FISKE, WILLIAM

Brother of Samuel Fiske (see previous entry) and a notable cabinetmaker in his own right, William Fiske (1770–1844) worked in his brother's Boston shop from around 1793 until the former's death in 1797. He appears to

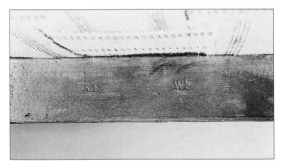

Impressed brands SF and WF for Samuel and William Fiske as they appear on the rail of the Hepplewhite shield-back side chair. Courtesy, Israel Sack, Inc., New York.

have continued the Washington Street business until well after 1830. His later work, such as a Classical mahogany drop-leaf table (c. 1820–1830) with rope-turned legs, was stenciled within an oval

**Wm FISK./Cabinet Maker/
Washington St. ./BOSTON**

A pair of Classical mahogany dressing tables inscribed in chalk

Fisk

are also thought to be from this period. Some earlier examples, such as a Hepplewhite mahogany shield-back side chair at the Museum of Fine Arts, Boston, are simply stamped

WF

These may have been made c. 1788–1793, when Fiske was working in Salem, Massachusetts, probably with members of the Sanderson family of cabinetmakers. Refs.: Hewitt, Kane, and Ward; Montgomery; *Antiques,* April 1948, March 1981.

FISKE & BADLAM

At some point in his career (probably the early 1780s) Samuel Fiske worked in Dorchester, Massachusetts, with another cabinetmaker, Stephen Badlam (see his entry). This relationship is memorialized in two Federal chairs impressed

S. Badlam/S.F.

Ref.: Montgomery.

FISKE & FISKE

During the period c. 1793–1797, the cabinetmakers Samuel and William Fiske were in partnership in Boston, Massachusetts, producing among other pieces a Hepplewhite mahogany card table and a Hepplewhite shield-back side chair in the same material, both of which are stamped

SF WF

Ref.: Hewitt, Kane, and Ward.

Brand WF for William Fiske (1770–1844) on a Hepplewhite mahogany shield-back side chair generally believed to have been made by Fiske while working in Salem, Massachusetts, c. 1788–1793. However, the piece may also have been produced in his Boston Neck shop after 1793. Courtesy, Israel Sack, Inc., New York.

FITTS, GEORGE

See Spooner & Fitts.

FITZGERALD, R.

Several in a set of ten c. 1790–1800 matching bow-back Windsor side chairs with a Notoway County, Virginia, provenance are branded

R. FITZGERALD

The chairs were sold at auction in Virginia in April 1994. It is not known if Fitzgerald was the maker or an owner. Ref.: *MAD,* April 1994.

Hepplewhite mahogany shield-back side chair marked with the initials of Samuel and William Fiske, working together in Salem, Massachusetts, c. 1780–1790, and Boston, c. 1793–1797. Courtesy, Israel Sack, Inc., New York.

FLAGG, WILLIAM

The cabinetmaker William Flagg (1773–1859) advertised the opening of his shop in Hartford, Connecticut, ". . . two doors North of Mr. Elisha Babcock's Printing Office, . . ." in July 1796. He worked in Hartford and East Hartford for some years, leaving a Chippendale-Federal transitional desk and bookcase or secretary signed

William Flagg

as well as two other similar pieces, a chest and a chest on chest, all of which are incised with the maker's initials:

W.F.

Refs.: Bjerkoe; *MAD,* March 1993.

FLEETWOOD, DAVID

A late Federal mahogany marble-top dressing bureau, illustrated in *Antiques* for September 1987, bears the label of David Fleetwood, a Philadelphia cabinetmaker working c. 1830–1840.

FLINT, ARCHELAUS

The obscure Charlestown, Massachusetts, cabinetmaker Archelaus Flint (working c. 1803–1814) left three pieces of Hepplewhite satinwood-inlaid mahogany furniture: a bow-front chest of drawers, a card table, and a corner washstand. All bear a printed paper label reading,

HOUSE FURNITURE,/Of the most approved fafhions and beft kind,/MADE, SOLD AND EXCHANGED/BY/ ARCHELAUS FLINT,/CABINET MAKER,/At his shop in Basin Street, near the Square/Charlestown.

Refs.: Bjerkoe; *Antiques,* April 1962.

FLINT, GEORGE C., & CO.

An unusual mahogany curio cabinet in the Art Nouveau manner (rare in American furniture), which is part of the collection of the Metropolitan Museum of Art, bears a pressed-metal label reading,

TRADE/FFF MARK/GEO C. FLINT CO./ WEST 23RD. ST. N.Y.

The Flint firm was established in Manhattan in 1868 but did not move to Twenty-third Street until 1894. This address covers 1909–1913; the cabinet may be presumed to date from then.

FLINT & HORNER

A carved mahogany partner's desk in the late-Victorian manner, which was sold at auction in 1994, was marked

FLINT & HORNER

This rare mark reflects a partnership between the Manhattan furniture makers George C. Flint and R. J. Horner, both of whom were listed after 1894 as having establishments on West 23d Street. Another known mark is

FOUNDED 1840/FLINT & HORNER CO. FURNITURE, DECORATIONS & RUGS/NEW YORK

and a variation is

FOUNDED 1840/FLINT'S FINE FURNI- TURE/FLINT & HORNER CO., INC. NEW YORK

It seems likely that Horner eventually took over the Flint business, which had been established in 1868. Ref.: *Bee,* November 16, 1994.

FLOPFER, C. F., & CO.

A c. 1830–1850 Empire walnut and poplar worktable with square "New York" legs

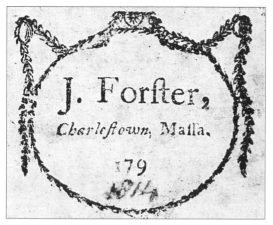

Printed paper label of Jacob Forster as it appears on a Sheraton mahogany sewing table. Courtesy, Bernard and S. Dean Levy, Inc., New York.

is stenciled within a drawer

Manufactured by/C.F. Flopfer & Co.,/Cor.
of Penn. & Wayne St.,/Pittsburg, PA.

Nothing further is known of the manufacturer.

FOLGER, G.

A small footstool with heavy turned Sheraton legs is stamped

G. FOLGER

No cabinetmaker of this name is currently known, and the mark is probably that of an owner. The piece is attributed to Nantucket, Massachusetts.

FOLSOM, G. P.

A pair of midnineteeenth-century thumb-back Windsor side chairs, advertised in *Antiques & Arts Weekly* for August 7, 1981, are signed

G.P. FOLSOM

and are credited to Dover, New Hampshire. This turner may be related to the Josiah Folsom

of Portsmouth, New Hampshire, mentioned by Santore. Ref.: Santore II.

FONDEY, JOHN, JR.

A c. 1790–1800 mahogany knife box illustrated in *Antiques* for March 1962 is branded on the base

I. FONDEY JUNr

for John Fondey, Jr., an Albany, New York, resident and owner of the box.

FORD, WILLIAM

A circa 1750–1760 maple Queen Anne high chest of drawers or highboy, illustrated in *Antiques and Arts* weekly for September 2, 1994, and attributed to Connecticut, is signed on the backboards

Wm. Ford

This could be the name of either the maker or an owner.

FORRESTER, RALPH E.

A late Sheraton or Classical mahogany worktable in the collection of the Baltimore Museum of Art is signed

R.E. Forrester, No. 61 St. Patrick's/Row, Baltimore

Forrester was in Baltimore, on Water Street, in 1814, and he worked at the St. Patrick's Row address from 1816 to 1821. The piece may be dated to that period. He remained in Baltimore until at least 1829. Ref.: Elder and Stokes.

FORSTER, JACOB

The cabinetmaker Jacob Forster (1764–1838) was in Charlestown, Massachusetts, by 1781 and bought land for his shop at the corner of Main and Union streets in 1793. His earlier and rather rare label dating to this period reads,

J. Forfter,/Charleftown, Maffa./179
This label appears to have been used over a long period of time, for it is found not only on a Chippendale mahogany serpentine-front chest of drawers but also with addition of the inked-in date 1814 on both a Sheraton mahogany sewing table and a Sheraton two-drawer stand in the same material as well as a Hepplewhite shield-back side chair. Most of his Federal pieces, including inlaid mahogany card tables (one at Winterthur, another at Yale), portable desks, and an unusual basin stand, are, however, labeled

JACOB FORSTER,/Cabinet
Maker,/CHARLESTOWN,
Maffachufetts,/Where are Made,/Tables of
All Kinds,/In the neweft and beft
mode,/Defks, Book Cafes, Mahogany
Chairs, Sofas,/Lolling & Eafy Chairs,
Clock Cafes, &c.
Refs.: Fairbanks and Bates; Hewitt, Kane, and Ward; Montgomery.

FOSTER, J. W.

A Sheraton mahogany library table, c. 1790–1810, illustrated in *Antiques* for July 1964, is signed beneath the top

J.W. Foster/Portsmouth/NH
Although several Fosters worked as cabinetmakers in Massachusetts, it is not known if this is the name of a craftsman rather than an owner.

FOSTER, JESSE

A matched set of six nine-spindle bow-back Windsor side chairs, illustrated in *Antiques* for September 1985, are branded

J. FOSTER
for the Boston, Massachusetts, turner and cabinetmaker Jesse Foster, active c. 1795–1800. Ref.: Bjerkoe.

FOSTER, JOHN W.

The Pennsylvania cabinetmaker John W. Foster had a shop in Londongrove Township, Chester County, ". . . one mile and a half west of Londongrove Meeting House . . ." from 1820 until at least 1824. By 1827 he was in West Chester Township, where he made an Empire mahogany veneer chest of drawers inscribed

John Foster/W.Chester/April 10, 1827
In 1832 he moved again, to Marshallton, West Bradford Township. Ref.: Schiffer.

FOSTER, THOMAS

The little-known Boston cabinetmaker Thomas Foster is associated with a single

Chippendale mahogany reverse-serpentine-front chest of drawers, c. 1790–1795, bearing the label of the cabinetmaker Jacob Forster (1764–1838), working in Charlestown, Massachusetts, c. 1793–1820. Courtesy, Israel Sack, Inc., New York.

marked piece, a Federal mahogany and satinwood inlaid card table, c. 1790–1800, which bears a paper label reading,

Thomas Fofter,/Cabinet-Maker,/
BSOTON [*sic*]

Ref.: *Antiques,* July 1972.

FOSTER, W. H.

The Gorham, Maine, cabinetmaker W. H. Foster produced a c. 1805–1815 Sheraton mahogany and bird's-eye maple card table offered at Sotheby's, January 23–25, 1992. It is inscribed in pencil

Made W.H. Foster, Gorham

This may be the same piece advertised in *Antiques* for May 1988 and described as being signed

W.H. Foster Maker Gorham

FRANCIS, J.B., & Co.

John B. Francis (1813–c. 1893) learned the cabinetmaking trade in Hartford, Connecticut. By 1837 he was in Waterloo, Seneca County, New York, and in 1842 he established a furniture shop in Canandaigua, New York, which he ran for many years. A late Sheraton cherry and maple two-drawer stand at the New York State Museum is labeled

J.B. FRANCIS & CO.,/Manufacturers of all kinds of/CABINET FURNITURE,/such as/SOFAS, CENTRE TABLES, WARDROBES, BUREAUS, LOCKERS,/TABLES AND STANDS,/of every size and pattern usually found in such an establishment./Also all kinds of/Chairs always on hand and furnished to order and/warranted./Also, READY-MADE COFFINS of every size and quality./Canandaigua Oct. 1851
J.B. FRANCIS/ORRIN HART.

Francis's partner was his father-in-law, Orrin Hart (b. 1789), a Bristol, Connecticut, cabinetmaker. Ref.: Scherer.

FRANCIS, JOSEPH

Joseph Francis was listed in 1789 as a cabinetmaker on Water Street in Boston, Massachusetts. He is said to have been the maker of a marked lolling chair in a private collection. Refs.: Bjerkoe; *Boston Block Front Furniture* (Boston, 1974, Vol. 48, Publications of the Colonial Society of Massachusetts).

FRANCIS, SIMON

An unusual Federal transitional mahogany bowfront chest of drawers with ball-and-claw feet, illustrated in *Antiques* for January 1975, is signed

Simon Francis/BOSTON

and is attributed to the Simon Francis who was listed in 1800 as a cabinetmaker at 40 Middle Street. Ref.: Bjerkoe.

FRENCH, ALBERT

A Pennsylvania paneled and painted pine blanket chest on frame with Sheraton legs has incised on an inset cherry name block

ALBERT.FRENCH/JANUARY.1854

This may be the name of either an owner or the maker. Ref.: *Antiques,* April 1974.

FREY, JACOB

The cabinetmaker Jacob Frey is thought to have worked in the vicinity of Milton, Pennsylvania, c. 1790–1810. Two pieces are attributed to him, a Chippendale walnut high chest on frame inscribed on a drawer

Jacob Frey 1795

and inlaid on the front

1795 J.F.

and a Chippendale bracket-foot slant-front desk, which bears the inlaid mark

Jacob Frey 1800

Refs.: *Antiques,* March 1933, September 1963.

FROST, PETERSON & CO.

A Victorian Gothic Revival walnut rocker with perforated plywood back at the Harris County (Texas) Heritage Society in Houston has punched into it the mark

FROST, PETERSON & CO./N.Y./FROST MANU'S PATENT/Dec.20, 1865/NOV. 18, 1868.

The firm of Frost, Peterson & Co. was in business in Manhattan, c. 1868–1880.

FROTHINGHAM, BENJAMIN

Major Benjamin Frothingham (1734–1809), son of the cabinetmaker Benjamin Frothingham, Sr. (1708–1765), was trained at his father's shop on Milk Street in Boston. By 1754 he was independently established in Charlestown, where he maintained a shop intermittently until his death. Despite long periods of military service and the burning of his Charlestown shop by the British in 1775, Frothingham produced a large number of pieces in Queen Anne, Chippendale, and Federal styles. The great majority of these are labeled

Benjn. Frothingham/Cabinet Maker/ IN/CHARLES-TOWN. N E.

There are, however, a few inscribed pieces, including a c. 1790–1795 Federal mahogany side chair signed in ink

Mr.Benja n Frothingham/Charlestown

a Chippendale mahogany block-front slant-front desk inscribed

Benj/Frothingham/1781

a mirror back signed

Made by/Benj. Frothingham/ Charlestown N.E./1773

a maple high chest of drawers incised

B.F. Boston 1778

and a Queen Anne mahogany high chest of

Chippendale mahogany bombé desk and bookcase or secretary bearing the pencil signatures of the Boston cabinetmaker Benjamin Frothingham (1708–1765) and one Sprage, who may have been an apprentice or journeyman, as well as the date 1753. Courtesy, Israel Sack, Inc., New York.

Label of the Philadelphia turner George Fry, who made Windsor and fancy chairs on North Front Street, c. 1800–1820.

Courtesy, the Newark Museum.

drawers or highboy signed in chalk

Benjamin Frothingham

Refs.: Bjerkoe; Fairbanks and Bates; Fitzgerald; Montgomery.

FROTHINGHAM, WALTER

A c. 1770–1780 Chippendale mahogany block-front chest of drawers in a private collection bears the signature

Walter/Frothingham/Charlestown

No member of the cabinetmaking Frothingham family is known to have had this name, but the piece is, in construction and style, similar to the work of Benjamin Frothingham (see previous entry). Ref.: *Antiques,* June 1953.

FROTHINGHAM & SPRAGE

What is thought by some to be the earliest dated piece of American bombé furniture, a Chippendale mahogany desk and bookcase or secretary, is inscribed in pencil at several points

Do DS /Benj. Frothingham/Benj.

Frothingham/Do Sprage/1753

The piece is generally ascribed to Maj. Benjamin Frothingham (see his entry), although it is early enough to have been done by his father, Benjamin Sr. Indeed, because Benjamin Jr. was only nineteen at the time, it seems more likely to be the father's work. Sprage has been variously described as an apprentice or an owner. Refs.: Lovell; *Antiques,* May 1989.

FRY, GEORGE

The North Front Street, Philadelphia, Pennsylvania, turner George Fry, active c. 1800–1820, is known for bamboo-turned rod-back birdcage Windsor side chairs, which are labeled

GEORGE FRY,/WINDSOR & FANCY CHAIR-MAKER,/No.88, NORTH FRONT STREET,/Between Arch and Race, West side,/PHILADELPHIA,/Continues the said business in all its various branches./ CABINET WARE,/ MAY BE HAD AT THE SAME PLACE,/ Orders punctually attended to.

Examples of Fry's work are in the collection of the Newark Museum. Ref.: Fales, *American Painted Furniture.*

FURBER, THOMAS GERRISH

A dated 1834 dwarf tall case clock sold at Sotheby's, January 29, 1994, is inscribed in pencil on an interior panel

Madd & Warranted by T.G. Furber, Newington, N.H. clocks

Thomas Gerrish Furber was born in 1811 in Newington, where he spent over fifty years working as a cabinetmaker. Clock cases were one of his specialties. Ref.: *Antiques,* March 1968.

G

GAGE, AUSTIN E.

Though listed as a "house carpenter" in the 1877 Pittsfield, Massachusetts, directory, Austin E. Gage was also a cabinetmaker who produced some thirty cupboards and cases of drawers for use in the Shaker community at Hancock, Massachusetts. Not himself a Shaker, Gage made furniture for the growing settlement. One of the cupboards, now part of the Mount Lebanon Shaker Collection, is signed in pencil

A.E. Gage, 1877

Ref.: Rieman and Burks.

GALBRAITH, WILLIAM

The cabinetmaker William Galbraith was active in Knoxville, Knox County, Tennessee, when he made a Hepplewhite

cherry slant-front desk incised

Knoxville/January 12th 1815/
William Galbraith 1815

and in another place

1814/William Galbraith January 9th

By 1820 he was working in Roane County, Tennessee. Nothing further is known of his career. Ref.: Williams and Harsh.

GALE, HUBBARD C.

A Hepplewhite mahogany bowfront chest of drawers with French feet in a private collection is labeled within a drawer

HUBBARD C. GALE,/ CABINET AND
CHAIR-MAKER,/CONCORD, N.H./
Price 20$ 1804

Hubbard C. Gale (1780–1805) had a brief career in Concord, New Hampshire. Already ill in 1804, he advertised that one Levi Bartlett (see his entry) would run the business ". . . in his absence. . . ." Refs.: *The Decorative Arts of New Hampshire, 1725–1825* (Manchester: Currier Gallery of Art, 1964); *Antiques,* July 1968.

GANSEVOORT, PETER

A set of Chippendale mahogany side chairs at Cherry Hill in Albany, New York, are said to bear the impressed name of the turner Peter Gansevoort of Albany. Ref.: *Antiques,* July 1951.

Victorian Eastlake mahogany and cast-iron patent adjustable reading table or work-table, c. 1880–1885, bearing the label of Clowes & Gates Manufacturing Company, Waterbury, Connecticut (Philadelphia after 1880). Private collection.

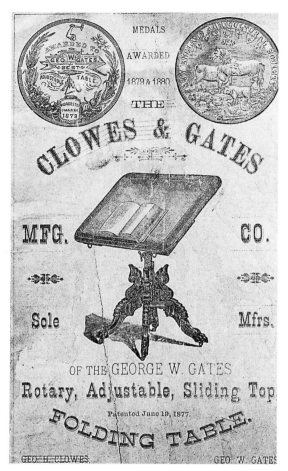

Label of Clowes & Gates on the Eastlake patent reading table or worktable. Ink changes indicate that Clowes left the firm and Gates moved the business to Philadelphia after 1880. Private collection.

GARDINER, SAMUEL

The cabinetmaker Samuel Gardiner had a shop in Geneseo, Livingston County, New York, c.1830–1850. Several pieces, including an Empire dining table, a footstool, and a two-drawer sewing table, bear his label:

CABINET FURNITURE/IN ALL ITS VARIETY/Made and Sold by/ SAMUEL GARDINER/Geneseo, N.Y./ (two doors south of E. Hill's drug store).
Also, a well-carved c. 1830–1840 Empire mahogany sofa at the New York State Museum is signed on the frame
Samuel Gardiner
Refs.: Scherer; *Antiques,* October 1923.

GARDNER, CALEB

A walnut and maple upholstered easy chair at the Metropolitan Museum of Art is signed on the crest rail
Gardner Junr/Newport May/1758
possibly the signature of Caleb Gardner, working as an upholsterer in Providence, Rhode Island, in the late eighteenth century. Refs.: Cooper; Fitzgerald; Jobe and Kaye.

GARNSEY, ISAAC

A Chippendale mahogany slant-front desk in a private collection has a brass keyhole cover engraved
Made/By/Isaac Garnsey/Febr. 12th/1790
Nothing further is known of Garnsey. Ref.: *Antiques,* September 1971.

GARRETT, BENJAMIN

A c. 1795–1805 Chippendale mahogany clock case housing a tall case clock is signed
Benj. Garrett Goshen
Benjamin Garrett (1771–1856) was the son of joiner Joseph Garrett and was himself referred to in Goshen Township, Chester County, Pennsylvania, records as a "joiner" and as having a "join shop." Ref.: Schiffer.

GATES, GEORGE W.

An unusual piece of patent furniture, a Victorian Eastlake mahogany and cast-iron adjustable reading table or worktable, bears a large engraved label including an illustration of the table and both sides of a medal awarded the design in 1879 by the New England Agricultural Society. The label reads, **MEDALS/AWARDED/1879 &1880/THE CLOWES & GATES/MFG. CO./Sole Mfrs./OF THE GEORGE W. GATES/Rotary, Adjustable, Sliding Top,/Patented June 19, 1877./FOLDING TABLE./GEO. H.CLOWES GEO. W. GATES/Waterbury, Conn./AGENTS WANTED EVERYWHERE.** Clowes's name has been scratched out wherever it appears and a new address, "Washington Ave and 17th St. Philada/Penna," substituted, indicating that Gates renounced his partnership and moved from Waterbury to Philadelphia sometime after 1880.

GATES, M. L.

A c. 1850–1870 decorated fiddle-back side chair is inscribed in paint on the lower splat **MADE/BY/M.L.GATES/BOSTON** while a similarly decorated spindle-back side chair is stenciled **FROM M.L. GATES BOSTON** It is possible that Gates was a decorator rather than a turner. Ref.: Zilla Rider Lea, *The Ornamented Chair: Its Development in America* (Rutland, Vt.: Charles E. Tuttle, 1960).

GAVET, JONATHAN

A pair of Hepplewhite inlaid mahogany card tables, illustrated in *Antiques* for May 1987, are inscribed in chalk beneath their tops **J G** for Jonathan Gavet (1761–1806), a cabinetmaker who worked in Salem, Massachusetts, c. 1784–1806. Ref.: Mabel Swan, *Samuel McIntire, Carver, and the Sandersons, Early Salem Cabinetmakers* (Salem, Mass.: Essex Institute, 1934).

GAW, GILBERT

The Philadelphia turner Gilbert Gaw (working c. 1795–1834) had a shop on Front Street from 1800 until 1815. He made a variety of bamboo-turned Windsor chairs, including bow-back side and armchairs. These were usually branded beneath the seat **G. GAW** However, at least one chair bears a partial printed label reading, **Windsor Chairs/Made and Sold/By/ GILBERT GAW/No. 90 N. Front Street/ twelve doors above Mulberry Street/ PHILADELPHIA** Refs.: Santore II; *Antiques,* May 1991.

GAW, ROBERT

Brother to the turner Gilbert Gaw (see previous entry), Robert Gaw was active on Front and Second streets in Philadelphia as a chairmaker from around 1796 until 1833, when he moved to Havana, Cuba. His mark, **R. GAW** appears on bamboo-turned bow-back Windsor side chairs, a child's birdcage side chair with medallion, and an unusual birdcage medallion settee. Far rarer is his engraved paper label, an example of which is on a chair at Mount Vernon. It reads, **ALL KINDS OF/WINDSOR CHAIRS,/MADE AND SOLD/BY**

ROBERT GAW,/No. 280, South Second,
and No. 88,/ North Front-ftreets,
PHILADELPHIA.

Refs.: *Annual Report,* 1971, Mount Vernon
Ladies' Association of the Union, Mount
Vernon, Va.; *Antiques,* May 1991.

GAW, GILBERT AND ROBERT

Although they later ran separate shops, the
brothers Gilbert and Robert Gaw (see
previous entries) of Philadelphia were working
together in May 1796, when they billed
President George Washington $44 for two
dozen "ovel Back Chairs" (bow-back Windsors)
for the East Portico at Mount Vernon. Their
products, rarely found today, include a bow-
back high chair and a settee, both bamboo-
turned and branded

G & R GAW

Santore also mentions "remnants" of a Gilbert
and Robert Gaw label, but I know of no complete example. Refs: Kane; Santore II.

GAYLORD, WELLS M.

Wells M. Gaylord had a looking glass manufactory on Genesee Street in Utica,
New York, from at least 1826 until 1845. His
earliest label, dated April 1826, reads,

Looking-Glass Factory & Store,/W.M.GAY-
LORD,/No. 55, Genesee St., two doors
above Wm.Clarkes Lottery Office/and
nearly opposite the Ontario Branch
Bank./Has for sale at reduced prices, a
very elegant and complete assortment
of/Gilt and Mahogany Framed/Looking-
Glasses/Also—Bed and Window Cornices
made to order. Pictures, Framed
and/Glazed with neatness and dispatch.

And every description of Ornamental
Gild-/ing, common in his line of business,
executed with taste.

There is also a later, simplified version of this
label, giving Gaylord's address as 56 rather
than 55 Genesee Street. Also, in 1839 Edwin
Gaylord, presumably a son, entered the business. A partial label on a late Federal mirror
from that period reads,

W.M. & E. GAYLORD/LOOKING GLASS
FACTORY/No. 55 Franklin Square,
Utica,/NEXT DOOR BELOW THE BANK
OF CENTRAL N.YORK,/and directly
opposite the Franklin House./The
Subscribers have on hand the most com-
plete/assortment of fashionable styles
of/LOOKING GLASSES/with which the
market has ever been supplied./They
invite their friends and the public in gen-
eral/Merchants in . . . . . . Northern,
New/York, would do well to supply themselves from this establish-/ment./JOB
WORK/Such as Bed and Window
Cornices, Portrait, and/Picture Framing,
New Plates set in Old Frames, Regilding,
Burnishing and Repair generally of Old
Work, done on/short notice and at
Reasonable Prices./Looking Glass plates by
the box or single. Gold/beat by the pack or
book./N.B. The Subscribers have on hand
a good supply of French plates,/which they
will frame to order as cheap as they can be
had in New York./Utica May 1st, 1841

W.M. & E. GAYLORD

Edwin Gaylord took over the business in 1845, continuing to 1849. Refs.: Scherer; *Antiques,* May 1981.

GEER, JOHN WHEELER

The Connecticut cabinetmaker and turner
John Wheeler Geer (1753–1828) worked

in Preston and Griswold after completing his apprenticeship around 1774. He was still active in 1816. Among his marked pieces are several country Chippendale maple bracket-foot blanket chests signed in paint

J.W.G.

He is also known from his account book, now at the Connecticut Historical Society, to have made chairs, bedsteads, candle stands, and knife boxes. Ref.: *New London County Furniture, 1640–1840* (New London, Conn.: Lyman Allyn Museum, 1974).

GEFFROY, NICHOLAS

Although he was listed as a joiner in Newport, Rhode Island, around 1800, Nicholas Geffroy's label, found on a Chippendale scroll-crested mahogany example, indicates that he focused more on mirrors:

LOOKING-GLASS MANUFACTORY,/Looking-Glasses, of the newest fashions, in/gilt and mahogany frames, pillar and plain; mahogany do./Old Glasses new framed and new silvered; gilt/Frames for paintings, needle-work and profiles, of/all sizes, made at short notice, by/NICHOLAS GIFFROY,/No. 127 Thames-Street, Newport,R.I./I further give notice that I have invented a/Composition which will prevent Glass from being/damaged, even against the water, as the Composi-/tion lies back of the quicksilver. Two thirds of/the Glasses are generally spoilt in this climate by/the dampness of the air which produces/that effect. Confident of the efficy of my Com-/position I shall Warrant my Looking-Glasses to the purchaser for the space of ten years; if damaged in that time, to be new silvered gratis. I also/shall warrant the gilding to be genuine gold leaf free from tarnish. The additional charge for the/guarantee will not exceed 75 cents for the largest size, and so down to 25, warranted and signed.

Geffroy (1761–1839) is also thought to have been a silversmith. Ref.: *Antiques,* September 1948.

GERRISH

Windsor chairs bearing beneath the seat the stamped impression

GERRISH

are reported. It is not known if this is the name of a maker or an owner. Ref.: *Antiques,* April 1945.

GETTYS, LEANDER

Leander Gettys (1832–left, 1865) was a Shaker cabinetmaker living at Pleasant Hill, Kentucky. He is known for two signed pieces: a cherry worktable inscribed in red paint beneath the top

L. Gettys, Oct. 4, 1860

and a one-drawer stand in the same material identified in black paint as by

L. Gettys, Jan. 1861

Ref.: Rieman and Burks.

GIBBS, J. N.

A set of four matching c. 1790–1810 bamboo-turned birdcage Windsor side chairs, illustrated in *Antique Collecting* for April 1979, are branded beneath the seats

J.N.GIBBS

This may be the mark of either a manufacturer or an owner.

GIBBS, JOHN

A Queen Anne mahogany corner or round-about chair in a private collection is branded

GIBBS

and is attributed to the craftsman John Gibbs, who was working as a joiner in Newport, Rhode Island, c. 1742–1750. Ref.: Bjerkoe.

GIEBNER, S.

An unusual decorated arrow-back writing-arm Windsor rocker in a private collection is impressed twice beneath the seat

S. GIEBNER

The piece dates c. 1840–1870, and it is thought that Giebner was an Indiana craftsman.

GILLERD, JAMES

An Empire mahogany and mahogany veneer card table with heavily carved pedestal-and-paw feet is attributed in part (the base may be later) to the Manhattan cabinet-maker James Gillerd, whose label is affixed to the top:

JAMES GILLERD,/CABINET & CHAIR-MAKER,/No. 74 CHATHAM-STREET,/ NEW-YORK.

Gillerd's shop was at 74 Chatham Street from 1803 to 1807. Previously, 1801–1802, he was located on Beekman Street, and by 1808 he was a coach maker at the Chatham Street address. His final entry is as a cabinetmaker in 1810 on William Street. Ref.: Scherer.

GILLETT, BENJAMIN CATLIN

Only a single piece, a Federal inlaid mahogany five-leg card table, at the Wadsworth Atheneum, can be traced to the Hartford, Connecticut, cabinetmaker Benjamin Catlin Gillett (working c. 1802–1812). The table is inscribed within an inlaid oval

B. C. Gillett

and is also dated under the top in pencil

Hartford 1802

Refs.: Hewitt, Kane, and Ward; *Antiques,* April 1969.

Carved Chippendale mahogany side chair by James Gillingham (1736–1781), who was active in Philadelphia from 1761 until 1773. The attached label lists Gillingham at a Second Street address, where he worked from 1768 until 1773. Courtesy, White House Collection.

Low-back Windsor chair of mixed woods impressed beneath the seat with the mark T.GILPIN for Thomas Gilpin (1700–1766), a West Chester County and Philadelphia, Pennsylvania, turner active c. 1721–1756. Courtesy, Bernard and S. Dean Levy, Inc., New York.

GILLINGHAM, JAMES

The famed Philadelphia cabinetmaker James Gillingham is known for his Chippendale mahogany side and arm chairs, one of which is in the White House collection. Gillingham (1736–1781) was working as a cabinetmaker in Philadelphia by 1761. In 1768 he took a cabinet shop on Second Street, where he remained until 1773. His uncommon engraved label, so far found only on chairs, reads,

James Gillingham/Cabinet and Chair-

Maker/In Second Street/Between/Walnut & Chesnut Streets/PHILADELPHIA. Refs.: Bjerkoe; *Antiques,* June 1946, November 1959.

GILLINGHAM, WILLIAM

William Gillingham (1783–1850), a turner from Morrisville, Pennsylvania, is credited with Windsor chairs stamped beneath the seat

W. GILLINGHAM

Ref.: Santore II.

GILPIN, THOMAS

The Windsor chair maker Thomas Gilpin (1700–1766) worked in Birmingham Township, West Chester County, Pennsylvania, from 1721 until 1726, thereafter in Thornbury Township, and finally in Philadelphia, where he remained active until 1756. His brand,

T.GILPIN

is thought to be one of the earliest Windsor marks. Refs.: Santore II; Schiffer.

GLADDING, JONATHAN

A set of matching braced bow-back Windsor armchairs, illustrated in *Antiques* for February 1987, contains an example stamped beneath the seat

J. GLADDING

the mark of Jonathan Gladding, a Newport, Rhode Island, turner active c. 1770–1780. Ref.: Santore II.

GLAEVER, HENRYK

A pair of seventeenth-century turned banister-back side chairs at the New

Jersey State Museum in Trenton are marked

H G

on the rear legs and attributed to Henryk Glaever, a turner working in the Crosswicks Creek area of New Jersey, c. 1690–1710. Ref.: *Furniture and Furnishings from the Collection of the New Jersey State Museum* (Trenton: New Jersey State Museum, 1970).

GLAPION

On the bottom of a large walnut and cypress armoire in a private Louisiana collection is the chalk signature

Glapion

This may refer to Celestin Glapion, a free African American who was listed in the 1838 New Orleans directory as a carpenter at 179 St. Ann Street. Ref.: *Early Furniture of Louisiana: 1750–1830* (New Orleans: Louisiana State Museum, 1972).

GLASS, PETER

Peter Glass (1824–1901) worked in Leonminster, Massachusetts; New York City; and for many years in Scott, Sheboygan County, Wisconsin. He was one of the foremost makers of American marquetry furnishings, producing tables, stands, and workboxes, and winning numerous American and European prizes for his work. Among extant examples are a center table at the Smithsonian Institution inlaid

Peter/Glass/Maker/Town/Scott/
Wisconsin/U.S./of/America

another in a private collection inlaid

Peter Glass/Barton/Wisconsin/
U.S. of America

several marquetry work stands inlaid

Peter Glass/Beechwood/Wisconsin/
U.S.O./America/1895

and a group of four work stands inlaid either

In Memory of/
Peter/Glass/Beechwood/Wisconsin/1897

or

1898

Refs.: *Antiques,* December 1973, September 1974.

GLENDENING, ADAM

A Chippendale walnut raised-panel high chest of drawers, illustrated in *MAD* for June 1993, is signed on the bottom drawer

Adam Glendening

Glendening worked in West Fallowfield Township, Chester County, Pennsylvania, c. 1780–1800. Ref.: Schiffer.

Chippendale mahogany shell-carved block-front kneehole chest, c. 1755–1764, inscribed in chalk "Daniel Goddard—His Draugh," for the Newport, Rhode Island, joiner Daniel Goddard (d. 1764). Courtesy, Israel Sack, Inc., New York.

GLOVER, ICHABOD

A Chippendale mahogany porringer-top tip table, illustrated in *Antiques* for January 1980, is branded

I. GLOVER

probably for Ichabod Glover (c. 1747–1801), a Salem, Massachusetts, chair- and cabinetmaker. His advertisement of June 19, 1798, in the *Salem Gazette* stated that ". . . he makes chairs and other furniture on reasonable terms. . . ." He appears also to have been a ship's carpenter. Ref.: Bjerkoe.

GODDARD, DANIEL

One of the first-generation Goddard family cabinetmakers, the Newport, Rhode Island, craftsman Daniel Goddard died in a

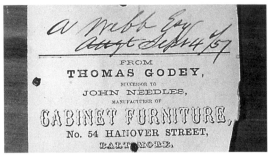

Label of Thomas Godey, as it appears on the marble-top Rococo Revival bureau. Godey's shop on Hanover Street was formerly occupied by the cabinetmaker John Needles. Courtesy, E. J. Canton.

building accident in South Kingston, Rhode Island, in 1764. A mahogany shell-carved block-front kneehole chest or "bureau table" on loan to the Philadelphia Museum of Art is inscribed in chalk

Daniel Goddard—His Draugh

and attributed by some to Daniel, although others feel it was made by John Goddard I (see his entry). The piece is thought to date c. 1755–1764. Refs.: Bjerkoe; *Antiques,* May 1984.

GODDARD, JAMES

James Goddard, Jr. (1727–?), a second-generation Newport, Rhode Island, cabinetmaker, is sometimes credited with a c.

Rococo Revival rosewood veneer marble-top bureau, c. 1857–1860, bearing the label of Thomas Godey, a cabinetmaker who worked in Baltimore, Maryland, from 1850 until well into the 1870s. Courtesy, E. J. Canton.

1765–1785 Chippendale mahogany block-front chest of drawers inscribed

James Goddard, Jr.

The name

John

also appearing on this piece could be that of his brother, John Goddard I (1723–1785, see next entry). Refs.: Bjerkoe; *Antiques,* October 1986.

GODDARD, JOHN, I

Best known of the Goddard family of cabinetmakers in Rhode Island, John Goddard I (1723–1785), son of Daniel (see his entry), had his own shop by 1748. It was located at what was later 72 Washington Street in Newport. He is credited with several marked pieces. Among these are two plain Chippendale mahogany slant-front desks inscribed respectively

Made by/John Goddard/
in Newport Rhode Isle

and

John Goddard 1754

and in ink on a paper label on a Queen Anne mahogany desk

Made by John Goddard of/
Newport on Rhoadisland in Newengland/
in the year of our Lord 1745

There is also a Chippendale mahogany desk and bookcase or secretary inscribed

Made by John Goddard 1761

and a block-front shell-carved chest of drawers

Chippendale mahogany slant-front desk, inscribed "John Goddard 1754." The cabinetmaker, John Goddard I (1723–1785), was active in Newport, Rhode Island, c. 1745–1765. Courtesy, Israel Sack, Inc., New York.

at the Metropolitan Museum of Art labeled within a drawer

Made by John Goddard Rhode Island 1765

Refs.: Bjerkoe; *Antiques,* September 1968, February 1973.

GODDARD, STEPHEN AND THOMAS

Stephen (1764–1804) and Thomas (1765–1858) Goddard, sons of John Goddard I (see previous entry), were working together as cabinetmakers in Newport, Rhode Island, as early as 1787. However, only a single labeled piece by them, a Hepplewhite inlaid mahogany card table at the Metropolitan Museum of Art, is known. The damaged label on this piece reads in part,

. . . ./Stephen & Thos
Goddard/Cabinetmakers/Carries on faid
busineff/. . . . . .in NEWPORT

Refs.: Bjerkoe; Hewitt, Kane, and Ward.

GODEY, THOMAS H.

The cabinetmaker Thomas Godey (working c. 1850–1875) took over John Needles's

old shop (see his entry) on Hanover Street in Baltimore before 1857, continuing into the 1870s. The firm was still active as Godey & Sons in 1892. Godey's furniture, primarily in the Renaissance Revival mode, was marked in several ways. Early pieces bore a plain printed label:

FROM/THOMAS GODEY,/SUCCESSOR TO/JOHN NEEDLES,/MANUFACTURER OF/CABINET FURNITURE,/No. 54 HANOVER STREET,/BALTIMORE.

By the 1860s an elaborate engraved label featuring a view of the manufactory was being employed. It read,

THOMAS GODEY/MANUFACTURER OF/CABINET FURNITURE/No. 41 Hanover St./BALTIMORE.

There is also a Renaissance Revival walnut armchair, which is stamped on the seat rail

T.& H. GODEY, BALTIMORE, MD.

reflecting the c. 1875 entrance into partnership of one of Godey's sons. Refs.: Fitzgerald; *Antiques,* May 1975, May 1976, October 1983.

GOOD

A Chippendale cherry tall chest of drawers illustrated in *Antiques* for January 1972 is signed

Good 1795

No cabinetmaker of that name is presently known.

GOODELL, DAVID

Although little is known of his life, the Pomfret, Connecticut, cabinetmaker David Goodell attached his label to two c. 1790–1800 Chippendale-Federal transitional cherry tall case clocks. Engraved with illustrations of a high chest of drawers, a desk and bookcase, a Pembroke table, and a ladder-back chair at the corners, it reads,

David Goodell/CABINET/and/ CHAIR-MAKER,/Pomfret

There is also a Chippendale cherry tripod stand with a center medallion inscribed

G

which is attributed through Goodell family history to David. Ref.: *Antiques,* July 1936.

GOODELL, J. W.

A nineteenth-century grain-painted pine wall cupboard, illustrated in the *Bee* for May 21, 1993, is signed on the back

J.W. Goodell, Honeyoye, Ontario Co., NY

Sheraton wing chair, c. 1805–1815, in mahogany, poplar, and pine, signed twice on the frame by the New York City cabinetmaker Isaac Goold. Courtesy, Bernard and S. Dean Levy, Inc., New York.

The penciled inscription Isaac Goold/Cabinet Maker as it appears on the Sheraton wing chair. Courtesy, Bernard and S. Dean Levy, Inc., New York.

This may be the name of either the maker or an owner.

GOODMAN, JOHN

Unlike most pianomakers, John Goodman, whose mark,

John Goodman/Frankfort/Ky./1801

is found on an early-nineteenth-century pianoforte, appears to have been a cabinetmaker who produced his own piano cases. He advertised his cabinetwork in Lexington, Kentucky, in 1799 and was established in Frankfort soon after 1800. Ref.: *Antiques,* April 1974.

GOODRICH, ANSEL

The Massachusetts turner Ansel Goodrich (c. 1773–1803) had a shop on King Street in Northampton from 1795 until his death. He employed up to five men and turned out a variety of fan-back and bow-back Windsors, many of which bore his primary label:

Anfel Goodrich,/HAS on hand and keeps/constantly for sale, a quan-/tity of warranted Chairs,/a few rods North of the/Court-Houfe Northamp-/ton.

However, a few examples will be found with a later, much less common label:

Ansel Goodrich,/HAS ON HAND, AND KEEPS CON-/STANTLY/FOR SALE/ A QUANTITY OF WARRANTED/CHAIRS./A few rods north of the Court House/NORTHAMPTON.

Three labeled Windsors by Goodrich are at Historic Deerfield. Refs.: *Antiques,* July 1930, May 1980.

GOOLD, ISAAC

A c. 1805–1815 Sheraton wing chair of mahogany, poplar, and pine is signed twice on the frame

Isaac Goold/Cabinet Maker

for the New York City craftsman of that name who was active in Manhattan during the first quarter of the nineteenth century. Goold's work is uncommon.

GOSTELOWE, JONATHAN

Although he was well known and highly respected for his skills, few marked examples from the hand of the Philadelphia cabinetmaker Jonathan Gostelowe (1745–1795) are known. Among these are a Chippendale walnut serpentine-front chest of drawers and a ribbonback side chair, both labeled

Jonathan Goftelowe,/CABINET AND CHAIR-MAKER/At his fhop in CHURCH ALLEY, about midway between/Second and Third-streets, .../BEGS leave to inform his former Cuftomers and the/Public in general, That he hath again resumed his/occupation at the above mentioned place. A renewal of their/favors will

be thankfully received, and his beft endeavors/fhall be ufed to give fatifaction to thofe who pleafe to employ/him.

Gostelowe was at the Church Alley address from 1783 until 1789 (he had been on Front Street before joining the Continental Army in 1776) and then worked at 66 Market Street until his retirement in 1793. Refs.: Bjerkoe; Montgomery.

GOULD, DAVID W.

A Chippendale mahogany chest of drawers, c. 1770–1780, illustrated in *Antiques* for October 1965, is signed

David W. Gould, Cohoes, N.Y.

The signature style is much later than the piece, and it is likely that of an owner.

GOULD, JOHN, JR.

A Sheraton cherry and mahogany chest of drawers in a private collection is labeled

JOHN GOULD, JR./CABINET

MAKER,/Near the Meetinghouse, in New/Ipswich, manufactures in the/Newest Stile, all kinds of/ CHERRY & MAHOGANY/FURNITURE/ Cash or Furniture given for/ Cherry Boards and Planks.

John Gould, Jr. (1793–1840), was active for several decades in New Ipswich, New Hampshire. The brand

J.G.h

on a Hepplewhite mahogany sideboard has also been attributed to him. Refs.: *The Decorative Arts of New Hampshire, 1725–1825* (Manchester: Currier Gallery of Art, 1964); *Antiques,* July 1968.

GOULD, N.

A rather crude comb-back Windsor armchair offered at Sotheby's, November 16–18, 1972, is stamped beneath the seat

N. GOULD

This could be one or the other of the Salem, Massachusetts, joiners named Nathaniel Gould listed in Bjerkoe. Ref.: Bjerkoe.

GOULD, ROYAL.

A Federal card table at the Art Institute of Chicago is signed

Royal H. Gould/Chester

Chippendale mahogany serpentine-front chest of drawers, c. 1783–1789, which has the rare label of Jonathan Gostelowe (1745–1795), a Philadelphia cabinetmaker who worked in the city c. 1773–1793. Courtesy, Bernard and S. Dean Levy, Inc., New York.

Rod-back birdcage Windsor side chair of mixed woods marked by Samuel Gragg, a Boston chairmaker, c. 1800–1806. Chairs like this were Gragg's usual product before he developed experimental bentwood examples. Courtesy, Gary Davenport.

and is attributed to a Vermont craftsman active c. 1820–1830 in Rutland and Burlington. Ref.: Robinson.

GOULD & CO.

A Victorian étagère or whatnot stand dating c. 1862–1865 at the Ebenezer Maxwell Mansion in Philadelphia is labeled

From/Gould & Co.,/Union/Furniture
Depot,/N.E. cor. Market and Ninth Sts.,
Philadelphia.

Because this firm advertised whatnots in the *Philadelphia Inquirer* in 1863, it is possible that they made only this item. Ref.: *Antiques,* December 1981.

GRAGG, SAMUEL.

Samuel Gragg, one of the most innovative of American turners, began his career in Boston around 1800. At this point he was a maker of Windsor chairs, a rare example of which, an ordinary bamboo-turned birdcage side chair branded

S. GRAGG/BOSTON

is in a private collection. From 1806 to 1807 he was in partnership with his future brother-in-law William Hutchins, presumably making similar seating furniture. However, in 1808 Gragg received a patent for an "elastic" or bentwood chair, a design far in advance of later efforts by Belter and Thonet. From 1809 until 1830, while located at various shop sites in Boston—Common Street, Tremont Street, and finally Market Street—Gragg produced a substantial number of bentwood side and armchairs as well as a few rare settees. Most were branded

S. GRAGG/BOSTON

or, more often,

S. GRAGG/BOSTON/PATENT

**Branded mark of Samuel Gragg on the rod-back, birdcage Windsor side chair.
Courtesy, Gary Davenport.**

These marks may be found on two chair types: one with curving saber legs, the other with turned cylindrical legs. Both are painted in the manner of contemporary fancy chairs. Refs.: Fales, *American Painted Furniture;* Kane; Montgomery; *Antiques,* January 1983.

GRAND RAPIDS CHAIR COMPANY

The Grand Rapids Chair Company, operating in Grand Rapids, Michigan, at the end of the nineteenth century, was one of many similar firms mass-producing household furniture of oak or other native woods. Its Victorian chairs and dining and parlor sets are stenciled in an oval

GRAND RAPIDS CHAIR CO./WAR-RANTED/GRAND RAPIDS, MICH.

GRANT, ERASTUS

The prolific Massachusetts cabinetmaker Erastus Grant (1774–1865) spent his life in Westfield in the Connecticut Valley, where he turned out furnishings in the Chippendale, Federal, and Empire styles. Most of these, like the c. 1795–1815 Hepplewhite mahogany chest of drawers at Historic Deerfield, are labeled

CABINET FURNITURE,/OF ALL KINDS/MADE AND SOLD BY/ ERASTUS GRANT/WESTFIELD, MASS.

There are also signed pieces. A Chippendale cherry serpentine-front chest of drawers is signed in three places

E Grant/Oct 11 1799

and

Grant/Novr 2, 1799

also

E. Grant Cabinet Maker

and a Federal mahogany bowfront chest of drawers is signed

E. Grant/Jan. 16, 1804 Westfield

There is in addition an Empire sideboard in mahogany, which is inscribed on a drawer bottom

E Grant Westfield 15 Nov. 1833

Refs.: *Antiques,* October 1979, December 1992; *New York–Pennsylvania Collector,* June 1987.

Branded mark of the Grand Rapids Chair Company on the c. 1870–1890 maple side chair. Private collection.

Maple slat-back side chair with caned seat, c. 1870–1890, bearing on the underside the brand of the Grand Rapids (Michigan) Chair Company. Private collection.

GRANT, T.

A Hepplewhite maple and maple veneer chest of drawers, c. 1800–1810, offered at Christie's, January 21, 1984, is signed beneath the top in red chalk

T. Grant

The piece is attributed to Pennsylvania, but it is not known if Grant was a cabinetmaker.

GRATIGNY, L. B.

A c. 1840–1870 urn-back country side chair at the Henry Ford Museum is stenciled beneath the seat

L.B. GRATIGNY./BEALSVILLE O.

Beallsville is a small community in southeastern Ohio, near the West Virginia line. Nothing further is known of the manufacturer.

The brand of B. Green on the underside of the Windsor braced continuous-arm chair.

Courtesy, the Henry Ford Museum, Dearborn, Mich.

GRAY, I.

A Windsor bow-back side chair with cross-stretcher branded

I. GRAY

is attributed to an unknown Boston, Massachusetts, turner. Ref.: Santore II.

GRAY, RICHARDSON

The obscure New Jersey cabinetmaker Richardson Gray is known for a late-

---

Windsor braced continuous-arm chair, c. 1790–1810, branded B. GREEN, a mark attributed to a South Windham, Connecticut, turner. Courtesy, Bernard and S. Dean Levy, Inc., New York.

eighteenth-century Chippendale cherry chest on chest offered in *Antiques* for June 1978. It is labeled twice

MADE & SOLD/BY/
RICHARDSON GRAY,/Cabinetmaker,/
Elizabeth.Town, New Jerfey

GREEN

An elaborate c. 1760–1790 Boston Chippendale mahogany bombé chest of drawers in the Dietrich Fine Arts Collection, Philadelphia, is inscribed in chalk within the case

Green

It is likely that this is the name of an owner. Ref.: Cooper.

GREEN, B.

Several Windsors, including bow- and fan-back side chairs and a braced continuous-arm chair, are impressed beneath the seat

B. GREEN

which Santore attributes to a B. Green of South Windham, Connecticut, an apprentice of Amos D. Allen (see his entry), working c. 1810–1820. The chairs, however, look earlier than the dates given. There is also the problem of a Chippendale cherry chest of drawers dating c. 1780–1790, which was illustrated in *Antiques* for July 1968. It too bears the stamp "B. GREEN." Was Green a cabinetmaker as well as turner? Refs.: Santore II; *MAD,* March 1994.

GREEN, J. D.

A country Federal decorated tall clock case owned by the Henry Ford Museum is signed

J.D. Green/1832

Though possibly a maker's name, this is more likely the mark of a decorator. Ref.: Fales, *American Painted Furniture.*

GREEN, T.

A Sheraton mahogany with birch and mahogany veneer card table, c. 1805–1815, is branded

T. GREEN

The style of the piece indicates a rural Massachusetts or New Hampshire origin, but we do not know if Green was the maker or an owner.

GREENOUGH, JOHN

A group of six rod-back Windsor side chairs offered for auction in Massachusetts in

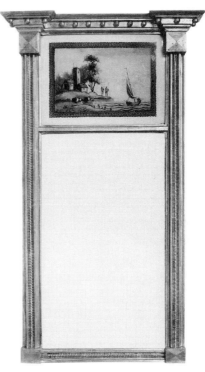

Gilded Sheraton pine mirror with reverse-painted panel bearing the label of Peter Grinnell & Son of Providence, Rhode Island. Grinnell (d. 1836) was active on Main Street in Providence, c. 1800–1825. Courtesy, Bernard and S. Dean Levy, Inc., New York.

September 1994 was labeled by the turner, John Greenough, of Portsmouth, New Hampshire. Ref.: *MAD,* September 1994.

GREGORY, PETER M.

A late Sheraton mahogany two-drawer work-table with rope-twist legs, c. 1810–1820, is inscribed in pencil

Made by Peter M. Gregory/New York late from Cork/D.P. I. Elliott

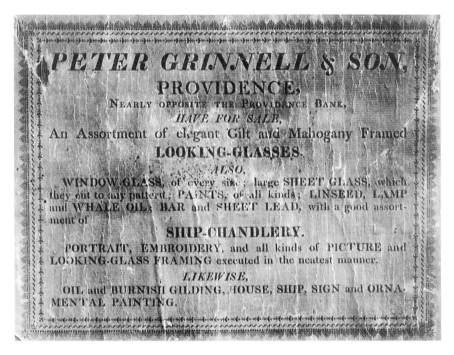

Label of Peter Grinnell & Son, on the Sheraton mirror. The Grinnells appear to have originally made their own mirrors, later selling the products of others. Courtesy, Bernard and S. Dean Levy, Inc., New York.

One might surmise that this was an early piece by an immigrant cabinetmaker. However, nothing more is known of his work. Ref.: *Antiques,* October 1970.

GRINNELL, PETER, & SON

Several well-made early Federal mirrors (c. 1790–1800) are labeled
LOOKING-GLASS & PICTURE-FRAME/MANUFACTORY,/PROVIDENCE,/Looking-Glasses in Gilt and Mahogany Frames, of/the newest fashions, constantly on hand, at wholesale/and retail; Gilt Frames and Glasses for all kinds of Needle Work, Portraits and Pictures; Looking-Glass/Plates, Window-Glass of every size, Linseed, Lamp and Whale Oil, with a large assortment of Paints,/ Ship-Chandelry and Hard Ware./ PETER GRINNELL & SON,/Main-Street, nearly opposite the Providence Bank.

Although this would indicate that Peter Grinnell (d. 1836) and his son, William T., were makers of looking glasses, it should be noted that another label of theirs, found on late Federal and Empire mirrors, offers looking glasses for sale but makes no mention of their manufacture. Perhaps the Grinnells, who were in business on South Main Street in Providence by 1823, found it more profitable to wholesale

Stenciled mark of W. H. Grove on the base of the walnut sewing or spool cabinet. Private collection.

than to manufacture. Refs.: Helen Comstock, *The Looking Glass in America, 1700–1825* (New York: Viking Press, 1964); *Antiques,* March 1978.

GROVE, W. H.

A Victorian walnut sewing or spool cabinet (c. 1872–1880) in a private collection is stenciled

**Patented May 2nd 1872/W.H.GROVE
113 Nth 4th St./PHILADA**

Although Grove may have been a manufacturer, it is also possible that he assigned his patent rights to a furniture company.

GRUBBS, LEROY MADISON

A c. 1850–1860 poplar pie or food safe with tin panels punch-decorated with eagles and Masonic symbols also bears the punched-in name

L.M. Grubbs

Leroy Madison Grubbs (1825–1867) was a Marshall County, Tennessee, cabinetmaker and house carpenter. Refs.: Coleman and Harsh; Williams.

Victorian walnut sewing or spool cabinet, c. 1872–1880, with stenciled mark of patentee, W. H. Grove of Philadelphia. Private collection.

GRUEZ, JOHN

The French cabinetmaker John Gruez was employed in Manhattan as shop foreman to the well-known cabinetmaker Charles-Honoré Lannuier (see his entry). Upon Lannuier's death in October 1819, Gruez took over the firm. His only known marked piece is a Classical mahogany extension dining table, which bears Lannuier's label altered in ink to list Gruez as "Successor." Apparently trading on his master's name was not enough. After several moves to other Manhattan addresses, Gruez disappeared from the New York directories in 1827. Ref.: Bjerkoe.

GUILD, ABNER

A Sheraton mahogany serving table, illustrated in *Antiques* for February 1966, is inscribed

A.G. Decr. 12, 1818, 17 Broad St.

and is attributed to Abner Guild, a cabinetmaker working in Boston, c. 1800–1820. He was also active in Dedham, Massachusetts. Ref.: Bjerkoe.

GUILD, C.

A c. 1780–1800 sack-back Windsor armchair in a private collection is branded beneath the seat

C.GUILD

**Federal mahogany tall case clock,
c. 1790–1800, with the partial label of the
New York City cabinetmaker James Hallett.
Courtesy, Bernard and S. Dean Levy, Inc.,
New York.**

The chair appears to be from the Boston area with a Roxbury history and may be by a heretofore unknown turner.

H

HAGEN, ERNEST F.

The cabinetmaker Ernest F. Hagen bridged the gap between early-nineteenth-century furniture making and the mass production of the late 1800s. Apprenticed in Manhattan in 1844, he was still making and selling furniture, much of it reproductions of Classical pieces, in the 1890s. His printed labels:

**ERNEST F. HAGEN, FURNITURE &
UPHOLSTERY,/213 East 26th Street,/
Near Third Avenue/NEW YORK**

or at a later date

**FROM/ERNEST F. HAGEN/Furniture &
Antiques/213 E. 26th St./NEW YORK**

can be found on chairs, tables, and sideboards otherwise almost indistinguishable from period examples. Refs.: *Antiques,* December 1943, December 1945; *MAD,* November 1988.

HAGGET, AMOS

The Charlestown, Massachusetts, turner Amos Hagget produced a variety of Windsor chairs, c. 1800–1815, including continuous-arm chairs and birdcage side chairs. These were branded

A: HAGGET

or

A: HAGGET/CHARLESTOWN

Refs.: Santore II; *Antiques,* February 1982; *MAD,* May 1977.

HAHN, A.

Santore records the incised mark
A.HAHN
appearing beneath the seat of a c. 1760–1780

fan-back side chair attributed to Philadelphia or Bucks County, Pennsylvania. This seems most likely to be an owner's name. Ref.: Santore II.

HAINES, ADAM

The Philadelphia cabinetmaker Adam Haines (1768–after 1820) had a shop on North Third Street near Vine from 1793 until he moved to Market Street in 1797 and in 1803 to Berks County. His North Third Street label found on a pair of mahogany armchairs in the French style owned by the Society for the Preservation of New England Antiquities reads,

**ALL KINDS OF/CABINET AND CHAIR-
WORK/DONE BY/ADAM HAINES,/
NO.135, NORTH THIRD-STREET/
PHILADELPHIA.**

Haines also branded some of his products. An elaborate Chippendale mahogany breakfast table at Winterthur is impressed

A.HAINS/PHILa fecit

Refs.: Bjerkoe; Cooper; Downs.

HAINES, EPHRAIM

Though famous as the maker of a set of ebony wood parlor furniture for Stephen Girard, the Philadelphia cabinetmaker Ephraim Haines (1775–1837) seems to have only a single marked piece attributed to him, a heavy Classical mahogany chest of drawers, c. 1815–1825, signed

E. Haines

which was illustrated in *Antiques* for August 1982. Ref.: Bishop.

Detail of James Hallett's engraved label as it appears on the Federal tall case clock.

Courtesy, Bernard and S. Dean Levy, Inc., New York.

HAINES, JEREMIAH

A Chippendale mahogany chest of drawers, c. 1770–1790, which was illustrated in *Antiques* for January 1956, is inscribed on the bottom

Made and Sold by Jeremiah Haines
Nothing is known of the maker.

HALE, ASA

A Federal sideboard in a private collection which is branded
ASA HALE
is attributed either to Asa Hale (1759–1843), who was in Rutland, Vermont, by 1772, or his son Asa Hale, Jr. (1794–1885), who worked in the same community until at least 1835. Ref.: Robinson.

HALE, KILBURN & CO.

The Philadelphia firm of Hale, Kilburn & Co. was in business at least from the 1870s until around 1910. In 1874 they patented an unusual walnut and walnut burl folding bed in the Victorian Renaissance Revival style. This piece was labeled
Champion Folding Bedstead/Hale, Kilburn & Co./40–50 N. 6th St. Phila. Pa.
The Brooklyn Museum owns a set of carved Colonial Revival side chairs by the same firm, which date c. 1910. Ref.: Bishop.

HALL, E.

A three-part Chippendale mahogany banquet table, c. 1775–1785, which was illustrated in *Antiques* for November 1987, is branded
E. HALL
It is not known if this is the mark of the maker or an owner. However, two Edward Halls worked as cabinetmakers: one in Boston, c. 1796, the other in Baltimore, c. 1804. Ref.: Bjerkoe.

HALLETT, JAMES

A Federal mahogany tall case clock, c. 1790–1800, bears an engraved label reading,

Pencil signature of Supply Ham and date 1812 on the Federal mahogany drop-front secretary. Courtesy, Israel Sack, Inc., New York.

JAMES HALLETT,/Cabinett & Chair Maker
No. 9, Beekman's Street, New-York/
N.B. Joinery . . . . ./of all kinds for sale.
Hallett is probably the son of the eighteenth-century Manhattan wheelwright of the same name. Ref.: Rita S. Gottesman, *The Arts and Crafts in New York, 1726–1776* (New York: J. J. Little & Ives, 1938).

HALLIBURTON, A.

A Salem, Massachusetts, Sheraton mahogany and satinwood card table, c. 1790–1800, illustrated in *Antiques* for February 1949, is branded upon the frame

A. HALLIBURTON

This is thought to be an owner's mark.

Federal mahogany drop-front secretary-desk signed in pencil by Supply Ham, a cabinet-maker who worked in Portsmouth, New Hampshire, in the early nineteenth century. The piece is dated 1812. Courtesy, Israel Sack, Inc., New York.

HAM, SUPPLY

A Federal mahogany drop-front secretary-desk, illustrated in *Antiques* for December 1967, is signed in pencil

Supply Ham/1812

as well as being branded in several places

S.HAM.

It is the work of Supply Ham, a Portsmouth, New Hampshire, cabinet- and clockmaker.

HAMMOND, THOMAS, JR.

A tripod-base cherry and poplar c. 1825–1835 candle stand is inscribed in pencil
Made by Thomas Hammond—Annie W. 1883
Thomas Hammond, Jr. (1791–1880), was one of the leading cabinetmakers in the Shaker community at Harvard, Massachusetts. He had, however, been dead for three years in 1883; and the inscription is not from his hand but rather is that of Annie Walker, the last eldress at Harvard. Ref.: Rieman and Burks.

HAMTON, ABRAHAM

See Always & Hamton.

HANCOCK, WILLIAM

William Hancock (b. 1794), active in Boston c. 1819–1849, was a well-known upholsterer who also sold furniture and, some argue, may have made or at least designed it. An unusual form of Empire mahogany sofa with drawers in the arms is signed in a drawer
William Hancock
More often seen on upholstered Empire sofas and arm and side chairs is Hancock's paper label reading,
WILLIAM HANCOCK,/Upholsterer,/39 & 41 MARKET STREET,/BOSTON.

Stencil-decorated ladder-back side chair bearing the stenciled mark of William D. Hann, a New Jersey turner, active in Flemington, c. 1880–1895.

Courtesy, the Newark Museum.

Hancock was at this address from 1825 until 1829. He had started out on Orange Street in 1819, continuing there until 1825. He remained on Market Street until moving to Cornhill around 1836. Although he continued to be listed in Boston directories until 1849, little is known of Hancock after the dissolution of the partnership of Hancock, Holden & Adams (see next entry) in 1837. Refs.: *Antiques,* May 1976, May 1991.

HANCOCK, HOLDEN & ADAMS

During the period 1836–1837, the Boston cabinetmaker and upholsterer William

Stenciled mark of William D. Hann on the ladder-back side chair.

Courtesy, the Newark Museum.

Hancock was in partnership with two men named Holden and Adams. An Empire sofa and a footstool in private collections bear the firm's elaborate label featuring a Grecian or "fainting" couch and the legend

FURNITURE/AND/UPHOLSTERY WAREHOUSE./HANCOCK, HOLDEN & ADAMS,/UPHOLSTERERS,/No. 37 CORNHILL . . . late of Market Street,/BOSTON,/Have on hand, and are constantly manufacturing, every article in the/CABINET AND CHAIR LINE./Orders gratefully received and faithfully executed./Upholstery Goods/of all kinds, and the business as usual attended to in all its branches./FEATHERS of every description./BEDS, MATTRESSES, etc.

Ref.: *Antiques,* May 1976.

HANN, WILLIAM D.

A pair of stencil-decorated ladder-back side chairs in the collection of the Newark Museum bear the stenciled mark

WM. D. HANN/CHAIR MAKER/ FLEMINGTON, N.J.

William D. Hann was a turner, active in Flemington, c. 1880–1895.

HARBISON, W. P.

A c. 1820–1840 decorated rocking chair with scroll seat in a private collection is stenciled beneath the seat

W.P. HARBISON/WILMINGTON

This may be the William Harbison listed by Santore as working c. 1814 at 46 King Street in Wilmington. Refs.: Santore II; *Plain and Ornamental.*

HARDY, P. J.

An upholstered Victorian Renaissance Revival walnut reclining chair fitted with an iron and wood writing arm is stamped twice

Pat. Dec. 11 60, P. J. Hardy

Although Hardy patented this c. 1860 chair, it may have been manufactured by others. Ref.: *Bee,* August 5, 1994.

HARRELL, T.

A braced bow-back Windsor side chair, c. 1790–1800, illustrated in *MAD* for March 1975, is impressed beneath the seat

T. HARRELL

It is not known if this was the maker or an owner.

HARRIS, JOHN

The Newburyport, Massachusetts, joiner John Harris (active 1750–1775) is known for two pieces: a Queen Anne mahogany spinet, which bears the inlaid mark

John Harris Boston New England fecit.

and which may be dated to 1769 from an article about it published September, 18, 1769, in the *Boston Gazette and Country Journal,* and a

Chippendale mahogany camel-back sofa offered at Sotheby's, January 30–31, 1986, which bears the chalk inscription

John Harris

Refs.: Bjerkoe; *Antiques,* November 1952.

HARRIS, WILLIAM, JR.

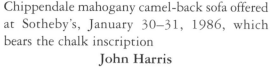

Several braced bow-back Windsor side chairs are labeled

CHAIRS/MADE and SOLD by/ WILLIAM HARRIS, jun./In New London

William Harris, Jr., advertised himself as a Windsor chair maker in the *New London Gazette* for November 14, 1788, and the chairs date 1785–1795. Refs.: Bjerkoe; Santore II.

HART, ORRIN

See J. B. Francis & Co.

HART, R.

The name R. Hart is associated with over a dozen marked pieces of Chippendale mahogany furniture, all dating c. 1760–1780. Most are branded

R. HART

although a wing chair is signed in white paint

R. Hart

These pieces have generally been attributed to

Pair of c. 1785–1795 braced bow-back Windsor side chairs in mixed woods, each labeled by William Harris, Jr., of New London, Connecticut.

Courtesy, C. L. Prickett, Yardley, Pa.

**Detail of paper label of William Harris, Jr.,
of Portsmouth, New Hampshire on the
bottom of a braced bow-back Windsor side
chair. Courtesy, C. L. Prickett, Yardley, Pa.**

an unknown cabinetmaker from the Newburyport, Massachusetts–Portsmouth, New Hampshire, area. However, an alternative theory is that the mark is that of an owner, the wealthy merchant Richard Hart of Portsmouth. Refs.: Bjerkoe; *Antiques,* May 1978; *MAD,* July 1994.

HART, ROBERT, & CO.

Asmall Victorian walnut one-drawer stand with splash back and Elizabethan turn-

**Chippendale mahogany side chair,
c. 1760–1780, marked by and attributed to
a cabinetmaker or owner named R. Hart
from the Portsmouth, New Hampshire, area.
Courtesy, Israel Sack, Inc., New York.**

ings, illustrated in *MAD* for April 1994, bears the following label:

FROM/ROBERT HART & CO./Manufacturers and Wholesale Dealers in all Kinds of/CABINET WARE & CHAIRS/MANUFACTORY, CORNER OF TENTH & SCHOOL STREETS/BUFFALO

The table would appear to date c. 1870–1900, but so far nothing has been learned of its Buffalo, New York, manufacturer.

HART, WARE & CO.

One of the most important makers of painted Victorian "cottage" furniture was

Stenciled mark, R. HART, on the frame of the Chippendale side chair.

Courtesy, Israel Sack, Inc., New York.

Hart, Ware & Co. of Chestnut Street, Philadelphia. The trend-setting (for the day) *Godey's Lady's Book* cited them in 1852 for a ". . . most splendid display, . . ." and a year later they exhibited at New York's Crystal Palace. Nevertheless the firm vanished from Philadelphia directories in 1854, having apparently moved to Baltimore, Maryland, where they used the label

HART, WARE & CO./MANUFAC-TURERS/OF/Cottage Furniture/ No. 10/ Nth Charles St/BALTIMORE, MD.

It is not known how long the firm was active in Baltimore. Refs.: Comstock, *American Furniture;* Fales, *American Painted Furniture; Antiques,* October 1979.

HARTING, RICHARD

AChippendale mahogany chest on chest with Boston characteristics, which was illustrated in *Antiques* for July 1969, is inscribed

---

Signature R. Hart in white paint on the frame of a c. 1780–1790 Chippendale mahogany wing chair. This name is believed to be connected to the branded mark R. HART. Courtesy, Israel Sack, Inc., New York.

May 6th Day 1767 Richard Harting

There is no record of a cabinetmaker by this name, and it is likely that the inscription is that of an owner.

HARTSHERN, EBENEZER

An important Queen Anne high chest of drawers or highboy in walnut veneer at the Museum of Fine Arts, Boston, is signed

E. Hartshern/1739

The maker was Ebenezer Hartshern (1689–1781), who was working as a "joyner" in Charlestown, Massachusetts, as early as 1729, continuing until 1742, when he moved briefly to Brattle Street, Boston, and then, in 1746, to Concord, Massachusetts, where he spent the remainder of his life. Refs.: Fairbanks and Bates; *Antiques,* January 1965.

HARTWICK, C. J.

An unusual c. 1850–1880 side chair with open yoke back and turned legs, illustrated in *Antiques* for June 1937, is stamped beneath the seat

C.J. HARTWICK

This could be the mark of either the maker or an owner.

HARVEY, D.

A c. 1810–1830 paint-decorated Windsor cradle found in the Passumsic, Vermont, area is branded

D. HARVEY/PASSUMSIC

for Darvins Harvey (b. 1801), active in Barnet, Vermont, until 1832. Ref.: Robinson.

HARVEY, GEORGE

An Empire mahogany tall case clock in the collection of the New York State Museum bears the following label:

CABINET MAKER/
AND/UNDERTAKER/
GEORGE HARVEY,/BURLINGHAM
(3 MILES NORTH OF BLOOMING-/
BURGH) SULLIVAN COUNTY, N.Y./
Orders for Mahogany Coffins, and Cabinet
Furniture,/executed on the shortest
notice—An extensive/assortment of Fash-
ionable/Furniture & Looking Glasses,/will
be kept constantly on hand for sale./
March 23, 1824

George Harvey (working c. 1820–1830) made coffins as well as furniture, not unusual at a time when there was often more demand for the former than for the latter. Ref.: Scherer.

HASBROUCK, J. M.

A c. 1780–1810 Windsor continuous-arm chair at the Art Institute of Chicago is stamped beneath the seat

J.M. HASBROUCK/
KINGSTON/NEW YORK

It is not known if this is the maker's or an owner's mark.

HASKELL, NATHAN

See Newburyport Chair Factory.

HASKELL, WILLIAM

The Salem, Massachusetts, cabinetmaker William Haskell (1791–1860) is known for an unusual pair of c. 1815–1820 Sheraton mahogany side tables with marble tops. A printed label reads,

MADE AND WARRANTED BY,/
WILLIAM HASKELL/SALEM, Mass.

Haskell was working on Essex Street in Salem, c. 1817–1859. Refs.: Bjerkoe; Montgomery.

HASKELL & SONS

A c. 1820–1840 decorated backless Windsor bench with bamboo turnings in a private collection is marked

HASKELL & SONS

Although this seems likely to be a maker's mark, no further information has been obtained.

HASKINS, ORREN

The Shaker cabinetmaker Orren Haskins (1815–1892), of the New Lebanon, New York, community, defied Shaker conventions by producing a number of marked pieces. These include a pine cupboard and case of drawers inscribed

March 27, 1833 Made by Orren H.

a pine lap desk signed in pencil

O.H. June 6, 1834

and another marked

Febuary 6, 1837 O.H.

a cupboard signed

January 6, 1837 O.H.

a workbench with drawers inscribed

O H February 1853

a work stand signed

Cornelia French/May 17, 1874 O.H.

and a set of six drawers added to a worktable and inscribed

**O.N.H., June 11, 1881,
Mount/Lebanon/Columbia Co., N.Y.**

Refs.: Rieman and Burks; Sprigg.

HATCH, J. K.

A Hitchcock-type decorated half-spindle plank-bottom side chair, probably from Connecticut, c. 1840–1870, bears the printed paper label

J.K. Hatch/Warranted

Another similar chair bears the same mark but in the form of a brand. Nothing is presently known of the maker. It should also be noted that one source gives the initials as "J.B." rather than "J.K." Ref.: Zilla Rider Lea, *The Ornamented Chair: Its Development in America* (Rutland, Vt.: Charles E. Tuttle, 1960).

HAUSCHILD

A patented Victorian Eastlake walnut daybed in the form of a Grecian or "fainting" sofa in a private collection bears an oval embossed brass tag reading,

**HAUSCHILD'S/
IMPROVED PATENT/BED LOUNGE/
PAT'D JAN.2, 1877/CHICAGO, ILL.**

The bed was purchased c. 1890, indicating the firm was still in business then. Nothing further is known of the manufacturer.

Victorian Eastlake upholstered bed-lounge or daybed bearing an embossed brass tag with the name of the manufacturer, Hauschild, of Chicago, Illinois. The bed dates c. 1877–1890. Private collection.

HAWKINS, WILLIAM

The cabinetmaker William Hawkins (1807–1839) was active in Cincinnati, Ohio, from 1829 until 1838, when he sold his shop on Fourth Street to the firm of Jones & Rammelsberg. A spectacular Empire desk and bookcase or secretary in crotch-maple veneer, now at the Cincinnati Art Museum, bears his stenciled label:

Wm HAWKINS/Manufacturer/of the most Fashionable/Cabinet Furniture/ on Fourth St./Between Main & Sycamore/ CINCINNATI,O.

A brand superimposed upon this label reads,

WM. HAWKINS, MAKER/ CINCINATTI, OHIO

Refs.: *Made in Ohio; Antiques,* July 1969.

HAY, EDMUND AND WILLIAM

The brothers and Boston cabinetmakers Edmund and William Hay are known for a Federal inlaid mahogany demilune card table signed

Messr. Hay James St.

It is not known when they were working on James Street, but Edmund was listed as a cabinetmaker on Congress Street in 1807. The table would date c. 1790–1810. Ref.: Bjerkoe.

HAYWARD, THOMAS COTTON

The Charlestown, Massachusetts, turner Thomas Cotton Hayward (working c. 1790–1820) placed his brand,

T. C. HAYWARD

beneath the seats of a wide variety of Windsor chairs, including continuous-arm chairs, bow-

Low-back Windsor writing-arm chair, branded under the seat T. C. HAYWARD for Thomas Cotton Hayward, a turner working c. 1790–1820 in Charlestown, Massachusetts. Courtesy, the Henry Ford Museum, Dearborn, Mich.

back side chairs, and a low-back, writing-arm chair. He may also have produced fancy chairs, as his advertisement in the *New England Palladium* for July 11, 1817, illustrates one of these. No marked examples are known. Refs.: Bishop; Bjerkoe; *Antiques,* June 1924.

HAZARD, SIMEON

The Newport, Rhode Island, cabinetmaker Simeon Hazard (1817–1855) was in business at No. 1 Church Street before 1847, when he took over Adam S. Coe's old shop (see his entry) at 23 Church Street, continuing at that site until his death in 1855. His brothers, James L. and George A. Hazard, continued the business into the 1880s. An ornate c. 1835–1845 Empire mahogany sewing or workbox by Hazard is labeled

FURNITURE/and/Upholstery Warehouse/SIMEON HAZARD/ UPHOLSTERER/No.1 CHURCH STREET/NEWPORT, R.I./Has on hand and is constantly manufacturing every article in the/Cabinet and Chair line./ Upholstery Goods/of all kinds, and the business as usual attended to in all its branches/Orders thankfully received and faithfully executed.

Refs.: Monkhouse and Michie; *Antiques,* July 1980.

HAZZEN, MOSES

The little-known Weare, New Hampshire, turner and cabinetmaker Moses Hazzen labeled a c. 1790–1820 birch tall clock case

MADE/BY/MOSES HAZZEN,/Joiner & Cabinet Maker,/Weare New Hampfhire

He is also credited with a pair of birdcage Windsor side chairs illustrated in *MAD* for August 1978, which are stamped

M.H.

HEINY, CHRISTIAN

The Windsor chair maker Christian Heiny had a shop at 496 North Second Street in Philadelphia in 1791. It is not known how long he remained in the city. Among his products are bow-back side chairs branded

C. HEINY

Ref.: Santore II.

HELMSKY, JOHN & SON

A privately owned c. 1875–1885 cherry side chair in the Victorian Aesthetic or Anglo-Japanese style is labeled

From/JOHN HELMSKY & SON/ NEW YORK

Nothing is known of the firm, which may have been maker or seller. Ref.: Fairbanks and Bates.

HEMPSTEAD, JOSHUA

A pine, oak, and ash six-board chest owned by the Antiquarian and Landmarks Society of Connecticut bears the initials

I H

believed to be those of Joshua Hempstead (1678–1758), who was working in New London, Connecticut, c. 1710–1735. Ref.: *New London County Furniture, 1640–1840* (New London, Conn.: Lyman Allyn Museum, 1974).

HENKELS, GEORGE J.

George J. Henkels (1819–1883), one of the more important cabinetmakers of the Victorian era, worked in Philadelphia c. 1843–1877, making furniture (some of laminated wood) in the Rococo and Renaissance Revival modes. Henkels employed several marks. A c. 1845–1855 child's Elizabethan-style walnut side chair has a fragmentary printed paper reading simply,

GEORGE J. HENKELS

while a stamped-metal label on a walnut drop-front desk in the French manner proclaims

GEORGE J. HENKELS/CABINET MAKER/211 Sth 12th St. PHILA.

This was Henkels's address from 1874 through 1877. Also, a set of Rococo Revival parlor furniture is signed in paint

G.J. Henkels Philadelphia/
809–811 Chestnut Street

Henkels was at this address on Chestnut Street from 1862 until 1867. He also occupied other space on Chestnut as well as a shop on Walnut Street. Most recently discovered, and illustrated in the May 1994 *Antiques,* is the signature

G.J. Henkels

on a c. 1860–1865 carved fall-front secretary.

Henkels's most unusual label is in the form of a notarized affidavit attached to a bizarre-looking bonnet-top washstand made from portions of an ancient maple tree that stood in Independence Square. This reads,

I CERTIFY/That this piece of furniture is made from the wood of a/Maple Tree that grew in Independence Square and was cut down/to make room for improvements in September 1875. By counting the/yearly circles of growth it proved to be/OVER TWO HUNDRED YEARS OLD./It was thus over One Hundred Years Old at the time of the Declarat-/ion of Independence./The tree was very much decayed, as the wood shows; By cutt-/ing the best part into veneers it was suitable for Furniture, and is/Susceptible of a fine finish./ GEO. J. HENKELS/ CABINET MAKER/ 211 S. Twelfth Street, Philadelphia.

Refs.: *Antiques,* May 1976, August 1976; *New York–Pennsylvania Collector,* December 1979.

HENNE, H.

An Empire wardrobe in a private collection is stamped twice

H. HENNE

and dated in pencil 1826. The piece is attributed to Wayne County, Ohio, but it is not known if Henne was the maker or an owner. Ref.: Hageman II.

HENNINGER, CONRAD

A ladder-back armchair, with stretchers and stiles turned in part in egg form, is signed
Conrad Henninger/Lebanon 1887
The piece is thought to have been made in Lebanon, Ohio, probably by an amateur rather than a professional turner.

HENSHAW, GEORGE, SONS

The English furniture maker George Henshaw arrived in New Orleans in 1844 and by 1847 had established a factory in Cincinnati, where he worked until his death in 1881. The firm was taken over by his sons, who continued the business using a brass plate on certain pieces of their furniture that read,
E.J. Smiths Elastic Settee/Pat Mar. 80, Feb. 82, by G. Henshaw Sons Cincinnati, O.
Ref.: *Collectors News,* March 1978.

HENZEY, JOSEPH

Joseph Henzey (1743–1796), a Philadelphia chairmaker, had shops on South Eighth Street and Almond Street during the period 1770–1795. At some point he was in partnership with Joseph Burden (see his entry). His products, including bow-back Windsor side and armchairs, fan-back side chairs, and comb-back high chairs and armchairs were usually branded

I. HENZEY

including a child's bow-back side chair stamped

I. HENZEY, I.S.I. 1787

However, a rare bow-back side chair, illustrated in *MAD* for August 1979, is impressed beneath the seat

I. HENZEY/CITY & COUNTY OF PHi.

Henzey had a son of the same name, who made and decorated Windsor chairs c. 1802–1806, but none of the marked chairs is attributed to him. Refs.: Bjerkoe; Hornor; Santore II.

HERENDON, A. S., & Co.

A Victorian Eastlake parlor table in walnut with a marble top bears a printed paper label reading,

A.S. Herendon & Co./ MANUFACTUR-ERS AND DEALERS IN/Furniture, Mirrors—Mattresses and . . . . . ./ 114 Bank Street CLEVELAND.

The Herendon firm was in business in Cleveland from at least 1871 until 1885, always at a Bank Street address. Ref.: *Made in Ohio.*

HERRCK, S. N.

A Windsor sack-back armchair, c. 1780–1800, offered at Sotheby's, January 28–31, 1981, is stamped beneath the seat

S.N. HERRCK

a mark Santore attributes to a turner from the Albany, New York, area. Ref.: Santore II.

HERTER, GUSTAVE

A c. 1860 Victorian library table in rosewood and bird's-eye maple, which was offered at auction in New Orleans in the summer of 1994, is inscribed

Gustave Herter, New York

The German-born cabinetmaker Gustave (Gustav) Herter (b. 1830) opened a shop in New York City in 1851, working alone until 1864, when he was joined by his brother, Christian. The firm then became Herter Brothers (see following entry). Gustave's individual mark is quite rare. Ref.: *MAD,* September 1994.

Fan-back Windsor child's high chair in mixed woods, branded I. HENZEY for Joseph Henzey (1743–1796), a chair turner working in Philadelphia, c. 1770–1795. Courtesy, Bernard and S. Dean Levy, Inc., New York.

HERTER BROTHERS

A mong the most influential decorators and furniture designers of the late nineteenth century, Gustave and Christian Herter decorated the homes of the wealthy, including New York's Vanderbilt Mansion and Jay Gould's Lyndhurst at Tarrytown, New York. Their business was established in 1851 by Gustave (b. 1830, see previous entry), joined in 1864 by Christian (1840–1883), who assumed sole control in 1870, running the firm until his retirement in 1880. Herter furniture ranged over a variety of Victorian styles, favoring the Aesthetic or Anglo-Japanese and the Eastlake while featuring complex marquetry, inlaid tile, gilding, and ebonization. These spectacular pieces were modestly stamped

HERTER BRO'S

Refs.: Fairbanks and Bates; *Antiques,* May 1979, October 1983; *MAD,* November 1994.

HERTS BROTHERS

Long active in New York City (1872–1937), the firm of Herts Brothers produced high-quality furniture primarily in the Aesthetic movement manner. Cabinets, cupboards, and tables featured inlays in metals and semiprecious stones against a background of rosewood, mahogany, or walnut. The firm's identifying brand was

HERTS BROTHERS/
BROADWAY & 20 St N.Y.

Victorian Anglo-Japanese desk and bookcase or secretary, c. 1870–1880, in ebonized hardwood with porcelain plaque and bearing the mark HERTER BRO'S of Gustave and Christian Herter, a cabinetmaking firm active in New York City, c. 1851–1880. Courtesy, Dubrow Collection.

HESS, GEORGE

One of numerous skilled cabinetmakers active in New York City after the Civil War, George Hess (working c. 1864–1882) is known for a Victorian Eastlake marquetry-decorated walnut worktable, which is impressed within the writing drawer

GEO. HESS/PAT.FEB.8.76

Ref.: *Antiques,* May 1983.

Federal mahogany mirror with reverse-painted panel having the stenciled mark of T.Hillier, who made looking glasses on Ninth Street in Pittsburgh, c. 1800–1820.

Private collection.

HEYWOOD BROTHERS & CO.

Active in Gardner, Massachusetts, c. 1826–1897, Heywood Brothers & Co. produced a variety of household furniture, often combining oak with caned seats and backs and patented iron features. One such piece, a rocker in a private collection, bears two stamped brass medallions reading,

HEYWOOD BROS. & CO.
GARDNER MASS./PAT JAN. 7, 1873

The firm also had a Chicago factory, established in 1884, and a set of late-nineteenth-century pressed-back oak side chairs is labeled

No . . . . ./HEYWOOD BROS. &
Company/CHICAGO, ILL. U.S.A.

In 1897 Heywood Brothers was merged with the Wakefield Rattan Company and the Heywood & Morrill Rattan Company. Refs.: *A Completed Century, 1826–1926* (Boston: Heywood-Wakefield Company, 1926); *Antiques,* March 1981.

HIBBS, ADIN G.

Adin G. Hibbs established a chair manufactory in Columbus, Franklin County, Ohio, in 1833, describing himself in the *Columbus Daily Advertiser* as a maker of ". . . Windsor and Fancy chairs of every description. . . ." An example of his work, a painted arrow-back Windsor side chair, is branded

A.G. HIBBS

Hibbs continued to make chairs at least until 1837, later becoming wealthy as a mill owner. Ref.: Hageman I.

HICKS

A c. 1790–1810 Federal mahogany fall-front butler's desk in a private southern collection is branded

HICKS

It is likely that this is an owner's name, although Bjerkoe does mention the cabinetmaking firm of Hicks & Law, active in Baltimore, Maryland, c. 1796. Refs.: Bjerkoe; *Antiques,* January 1936.

HICKS, PAUL A.

A country cherry two-drawer stand, c. 1840–1870, in a private Ohio collection is signed within a drawer

Paul A. Hicks, Centerburg, Knox County

It is not known if this is a maker's signature. Ref.: Hageman II.

HILL, BILLIOUS

A rare Chippendale cherry bonnet-top desk and bookcase or secretary offered at Christie's, June 17, 1992, is signed on the upper case

BILLIOUS HILL

Billious Hill was a craftsman working in Woodbury, Connecticut, c. 1765–1778. He is described as a cabinetmaker in local account books.

HILL, I.

A Massachusetts Queen Anne walnut center table, dating c. 1720–1740, with marble top is stamped

I HILL

The piece is in the Winterthur collection. No cabinetmaker with this name is presently recorded, although Downs thought that the piece might be associated with a John Hill of Boston. Ref.: Downs.

HILLHOUSE

An early-nineteenth-century card table in a private Ohio collection is inscribed on the bottom

Hillhouse

The piece has a Chillicothe, Ross County, Ohio, history, but it is not known if the name is that

Stenciled mark of the looking glass and frame manufacturer T.Hillier on the back panel of the Federal mirror.

Private collection.

of the maker rather than an owner. Ref.: Hageman I.

HILLHOUSE, T.

A Federal mahogany Pembroke table, c. 1790–1800, which was illustrated in *Antiques* for October 1954 and April 1963, bears beneath the top the painted inscription

T.Hillhouse No.5 Lodge Street, Albany

There is presently no evidence that Hillhouse was a cabinetmaker.

HILLIER, T.

A c. 1800–1820 Federal mahogany mirror with reverse glass painting bears the stenciled mark of its maker:

**T.HILLIER/No.7 NINTH STREET/
Looking Glass & Picture Frame/
MANUFACTURER/PITTSBURGH**

Stencil-decorated cane-bottom fancy chair bearing the mark of Lambert Hitchcock (1795–1852), a chair manufacturer in Hitchcocksville (Riverton), Connecticut, c. 1818–1829. Courtesy, the Hitchcock Chair Company, Riverton, Conn.

Hillier appears to be one of the earliest Pittsburgh, Pennsylvania, mirror makers.

HILLS, M.

An Empire column-front mahogany chest of drawers, c. 1830–1850, sold at auction in New Hampshire in July 1994, is said to have borne the label of the furniture maker M. Hills. Nothing further is presently known. Ref.: *Bee,* July 29, 1994.

HITCHCOCK, LAMBERT

Arguably the best-known American chairmaker, Lambert Hitchcock (1795–1852) established a turning shop in 1818 at a spot on the Farmington River that by 1821 bore his name, Hitchcocksville. His factory, built in 1825, turned out large numbers of Sheraton-type fancy chairs, stencil decorated and grain painted, with rush, cane, or plank seats, as well as rockers and settees. These were stenciled

L. HITCHCOCK.HITCHCOCKS-VILLE, CONN.WARRANTED

Forced into bankruptcy in 1829, Hitchcock reorganized and by 1832 had taken his brother-in-law, Arba Alford (1807–1881), into partnership (see next entry). In 1843 Hitchcock withdrew from this firm (which had been incorporated in 1841) and opened another fac-

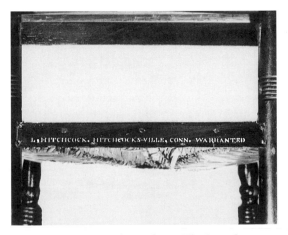

Stenciled mark of Lambert Hitchcock on a painted and stencil-decorated rush-bottom fancy chair, c. 1818–1829. Courtesy, the Henry Ford Museum, Dearborn, Mich.

Engraving, 1836, of Hitchcocksville (Riverton), Connecticut, site of Lambert Hitchcock's chair factory. Courtesy, the Hitchcock Chair Company, Riverton, Conn.

tory in Unionville, Connecticut, which he operated sporadically until his death. There is no evidence that Unionville products (which included case furniture as well as chairs) were ever marked. Refs.: Kenney; Montgomery; *The Connecticut Antiquarian,* July 1966.

HITCHCOCK, ALFORD & Co.

ambert Hitchcock (1795–1852, see previous entry), who had established the chair factory at Hitchcocksville, Connecticut (now Riverton), in 1818, took his brother-in-law, Arba Alford (1807–1881), into the business sometime between 1829 and 1832. Chairs made by this firm were stenciled

HITCHCOCK.ALFORD & CO.HITCH-COCKS-VILLE.CONN./WARRANTED

or less commonly

HITCHCOCK & ALFORD.HITCHCOCK-VILLE.CONN./WARRANTED

Hitchcock withdrew from the business in 1843, and it was continued under their own names until 1864 by Arba and Alfred Alford. Refs.: Kenney; Montgomery; *The Connecticut Antiquarian,* July 1966.

HOBBS, T.

A set of five c. 1790–1810 bamboo-turned bow-back Windsor side chairs, illustrated in *MAD,* November 1975, are impressed beneath the seats

T. HOBBS

This is thought to be the mark of a previously unrecognized maker.

HOBSON, JOHN

An unusual country Chippendale walnut chest with slanting lift top, an interior with drawers, and bracket feet and thought to date c. 1760–1780 is inscribed

Made by John Hobson

The piece is attributed to North Carolina, but nothing is known of the manufacturer. Ref.: Paul Burroughs, *Southern Antiques* (New York: Bonanza Books, 1981).

HODGES, T. N., & CO.

Thomas Nelson Hodges (1818–1865) arrived in Hitchcocksville (Riverton), Connecticut, around 1842. A year later he purchased a local stone cutter's shop, which he may have converted to a chair factory. His rare signed pieces, including Boston-type rockers, date c. 1845–1850 and are stenciled

T.N. HODGES & Co.
HITCHCOCKVILLE.CT.

Ref.: Kenney.

Painted and stencil-decorated rod-back Windsor side chair bearing the stenciled mark of Lambert Hitchcock (1795–1852) and Arba Alford (1807–1881), in business together as chair manufacturers at Hitchcocksville (Riverton), Connecticut, c. 1829–1848. Courtesy, the Hitchcock Chair Company, Riverton, Conn.

HOLDEN, JOSHUA

The chairmaker and ornamental painter Joshua Holden is credited with several c. 1815–1830 Federal-Empire transitional side chairs marked

J. HOLDEN

Holden had a shop on Washington and Orange streets in Boston, c. 1810–1835. More problematical are a set of eight Classical painted side chairs offered at Sotheby's, January 30–February 2, 1980, which were branded simply

HOLDEN'S

Sotheby's attributed these to Asa Holden, a Manhattan chairmaker, but it seems more

Pair of painted and decorated Classical klismos-form side chairs stenciled HOLDEN'S and attributed to the chairmaker Joshua Holden, who worked in Boston, c. 1810–1835. Courtesy, Israel Sack, Inc., New York.

likely that they too were made, probably c. 1810–1820, by Joshua Holden. Refs.: Kenney; Scherer.

HOLLBROOK

A c. 1820–1840 rod-back Windsor armchair with crest illustrated in the *Bee* for August 26, 1994, was signed beneath the seat

Hollbrook

This is probably the name of an owner.

HOLLISTER, HENRY

Henry Hollister (1838–1919), a member of the Mount Lebanon, New York, Shaker community, is known for a butternut and pine case of drawers, which is inscribed in pencil

No.6/Henry Hollister/January 61/Tis only he that has no/credit to loose that

can/afford to work in this style Ref.: Rieman and Burks.

HOLMES, A.

A paint-decorated and stenciled arrow-back Windsor rocker with comb is stenciled

A. HOLMES

and attributed to a North Jay, Maine, chairmaker of that name, working c. 1830–1850.

HOLMES, GEORGE W.

George W. Holmes was a cabinetmaker living in Sturbridge, Massachusetts, c. 1825–1840. Only a single piece from his hand has been identified, a Sheraton cherry bowfront chest of drawers signed

George W. Holmes

Refs.: *Antiques,* October 1979, May 1993.

Detail of Joshua Holden's mark as it appears on the pair of Classical side chairs.

Courtesy, Israel Sack, Inc., New York.

HOLMES & HAINES

Edward Holmes (working in Manhattan at 48 Broad Street since 1821) and Simeon Haines (working at 20 Beaver Street) went into partnership in 1825, remaining together at various addresses until 1830. An Empire mahogany two-drawer stand at the New York State Museum bears their printed paper label: **HOLMES & HAINES/Cabinet Makers/Nos. 48 Broad & 20 Beaver St./NEW YORK** They were at this number only from 1825 until 1827. A much more spectacular piece, an Empire mahogany veneer dressing bureau with carved animal feet, has a partial label reading, **H & H/ No. 154** This, too, is thought to be a Holmes & Haines label, dating perhaps to the 1828–1829 period, when the firm was at 151 Broadway. Refs.: Fales, *American Painted Furniture;* Scherer.

Unusual paint-decorated and stenciled arrow-back Windsor rocker with comb, stenciled A. HOLMES for a North Jay, Maine, chairmaker of that name, active c. 1830–1850. Private collection.

HOLMES & ROBERTS

Rufus Holmes, a farmer, and the chair-maker Samuel Roberts ran a chair factory in Robertsville, Colebrook Township, Connecticut, not far from Hitchcockville, from 1835 until 1839, when they sold out to Lam-

bert Hitchcock (see his entry). Their painted fancy chairs, similar to Hitchcock's work, were stenciled

**HOLMES & ROBERTS.
COLEBROOK.CONN./
WARRANTED**

Refs.: Kenney; *Antiques,* September 1925.

HOLSTEIN & HAMMER

A Victorian walnut mirrored bureau in the Renaissance Revival style is labeled

**HOLSTEIN & HAMMER
CINCINNATI, O.**

The piece, in a private collection, dates c. 1860–1880, but nothing is known of the manufacturer.

HOLT, T. K.

A c. 1830–1850 pine red-painted schoolmaster's desk with slant top and unusual pullout writing slide below two drawers is stamped

T. K. HOLT

It is not known if Holt was the maker or an owner. Ref.: *Antiques,* October 1953.

HOMER, ANDREW

A Chippendale-style mahogany Pembroke table of uncertain age at the Henry Ford Museum is labeled

ANDREW HOMER/Court-Street

and has been attributed to a supposed Boston cabinetmaker on the basis of an accompanying bill of sale. But an article in *MAD* for February 1985 argues persuasively that Homer was a dry goods merchant rather than a furniture maker, and that the label and bill of sale were designed to induce collectors to buy a much later piece of furniture in the belief that it had been made by an eighteenth-century cabinetmaker. This, however, doesn't resolve the matter of a second piece, a Chippendale mahogany slant-front desk, c. 1770, sold at Sotheby's, June 26, 1986. This example is signed on a lid support

View of the home in North Jay, Maine, of A. Holmes. Private collection.

Unusual porcelain plaque used by the firm of R. J. Horner & Company to mark their products. Private collection.

Andrew Homer

Could the piece have been owned by Homer the dry goods merchant, or is there more to the story of "Andrew Homer, cabinetmaker"? Ref.: *MAD,* February 1985.

HOPKINS, GERRARD

The cabinetmaker Gerrard Hopkins was trained in Philadelphia and had a shop on Gay Street in Baltimore by 1767. He remained there until his death in 1796. Although many of his products have been identified through bills and family records, his only known labeled piece is a late-eighteenth-century Chippendale high chest of drawers at the Baltimore Museum of Arts. The faded label reads in part,

GERRARD HOPKINS/Cabinet and Chair-maker/At the sign of the Tea-Table and Chair in Gay St./BALTIMORE

Ebonized wood desk in the Aesthetic Movement manner with ormolu attachments. Made and marked by R. J. Horner & Company, New York City, c. 1890–1900. Private collection.

TOWN,/MAKES and Sells . . . .
Refs.: Bjerkoe; *Antiques,* September 1934.

HORNER, R. J., & Co.

The firm of R. J. Horner & Company, active in Manhattan during the late-nineteenth and early-twentieth centuries, made a variety of furniture, particularly in the style of the Aesthetic Movement. Their products were usually identified by an unusual porcelain plaque reading,

FROM/R.J.HORNER & CO.,/FURNITURE MAKERS,/61, 63 & 65 West 23rd St., N.Y. which was nailed to the pieces. However, a paper label reading,

From/R. J. Horner & Co./
Furniture Makers/and importers/
61, 63 & 65 West 23rd St. New York City

Detail of the Classical ormolu mounts on the Aesthetic Movement desk by R. J. Horner & Company. Private collection.

appears on a mahogany center table sold at auction in 1994. Ref.: *MAD,* June 1994.

HORTON, SAMUEL H.

Little is known of the Boston turner Samuel H. Horton other than that he was listed as a chairmaker on Boston Neck in 1807. A c. 1800–1820 birdcage Windsor side chair formerly in the author's collection bore his brand:

S.H. HORTON

beneath the seat. Ref.: Bjerkoe.

HORTON, W. H.

A set of three bow-back Windsor side chairs, offered at a Richard A. Bourne auction on November 30, 1974, are stamped beneath the seats

W.H. HORTON

They date c. 1790–1810 and are the work of the Boston turner and cabinetmaker W. H. Horton.

HOUSTON, WILLIAM

A maple high chest of drawers or highboy made in the shop of Maj. John Dunlap (see his entry) at Bedford, New Hampshire, c. 1780–1790, is signed in chalk

Willm Houston

and attributed to William Houston, who was apprenticed to Dunlap in 1775. He later worked for John Dunlap II. Ref.: *Antiques,* June 1970.

HOW, BATES

Little is known of the career of Bates How, a Connecticut cabinetmaker born in

Canaan, 1776, and the maker of a Chippendale cherry serpentine-front chest of drawers inscribed in pencil on the back

This Buro was Made/in the year of our Lord/1795/By Bates How

It is thought that How worked in Kent, Connecticut, and that the chest, now at the Yale University Art Gallery, was made there. Ref.: *Litchfield County Furniture, 1730–1850* (Litchfield, Conn.: Litchfield County Historical Society, 1969).

HOWARD, DANIEL

An Empire mahogany and birch chest of drawers at the Maine State Museum is marked by Daniel Howard, who had a furniture shop in Belfast, Maine, c. 1845.

HOWARD, WILLIAM

A set of three matching arrow-back Windsor side chairs in a private collection is branded on the underside of the seat

Wm. HOWARD/S. EVERETT, VT.

Howard is believed to have been a mid-nineteenth-century Vermont chair turner.

HOWE, ARA

The Vermont cabinetmaker Ara Howe (1797–1863) was active in Brookfield from 1841 until 1850 when he moved to Northfield, where the business was continued

Arrow-back Windsor side chair, c. 1830–1850, branded by William Howard, a turner working in South Everett, Vermont. Private collection.

by his sons Amos E. and Lyman until after 1863. Ara Howe is known for several marked pieces, all bearing his printed label

MANUFACTURED BY/ARA/HOWE,/ BROOKFIELD, VT./Warranted.

A pair of labeled fancy chairs are at the Shelburne Museum. Refs.: Robinson; *MAD,* October 1993.

HOWE, JOHN

A Queen Anne–Chippendale transitional walnut side chair with pierced back splat and trifid feet, illustrated in *Antiques* for April 1974, is inscribed

Oct. 8, 1761/John Howe married Susannah Greeves and made this wedding chair

Nothing is known of this cabinetmaker. The chair is thought to be from Boston.

HOWE FOLDING FURNITURE COMPANY

A c. 1900 folding hardwood table bears a partial paper label reading,

HOWE FOLDING FURNITURE Co./
. . . . **New York, New York**

Utility tables of this sort were widely made at the turn of the century. Nothing further is known of this manufacturer.

HOWLAND, S. R.

A c. 1835–1845 Empire mahogany secretary or desk and bookcase illustrated in *MAD* for October 1994 was signed

S.R. Howland/Venice Centre New York

It is not known if Howland was the maker or an owner of the piece.

HOXIE

S antore reports a c. 1790 Rhode Island–type brace-back Windsor armchair, which is branded

HOXIE

Nothing is known of the maker. Ref.: Santore II.

HOYT, BERNARD

B ernard Hoyt (1792–1876), a Danville, Vermont, turner, active c. 1834–1860, is known for chairs, including rockers, branded

B. HOYT

Ref.: Robinson.

HOYT, N.

A Federal inlaid mahogany serpentine-front card table, c. 1790–1800, illustrated in *Antiques* for September 1953, is signed

N. Hoyt

It is not known if this is the maker's or an owner's mark.

HUBBARD, J. C.

T he Boston chairmaker J. C. Hubbard was in business c. 1828–1884, producing a wide variety, from rod-back side chairs through "firehouse Windsor" armchairs to long rod-back meetinghouse benches. His not uncommon products are branded

J.C. HUBBARD

A slightly different mark,

J.C. HUBBARD/BOSTON

appears on a rod-back armchair said to have been made in 1884 for Capt. Charles W. Fisher of Nantucket. Refs.: Charles H. and Mary Grace Carpenter, *The Decorative Arts of Nantucket* (New York: Dodd, Mead, 1987); *Antiques,* October 1979; *MAD,* December 1974.

HUBBARD & WHITE

A set of twelve pine rod-back side chairs offered at auction February 10, 1994, in Watertown, Massachusetts, are branded beneath the seats

Made by/HUBBARD & WHITE

This apparently reflects a c. 1820–1830 partnership between one William White and the Boston chairmaker J. C. Hubbard (see previous entry). Refs.: Santore II; *Antiques & Arts Weekly,* February 4, 1994.

HUDSON & BROOKS

A painted and decorated arrow-back Windsor rocking chair with comb and mahogany arms, illustrated in *Antiques & Arts Weekly* for August 26, 1983, bears beneath the seat a paper label reading,

HUDSON & BROOKS/PORTLAND

The chair, from Portland, Maine, dates c. 1815–1823. Brooks may be F. Brooks, maker of a painted fancy chair now at Old Sturbridge Village.

HUEY, JAMES

James Huey (b. 1805) worked as a chairmaker in Zanesville, Ohio, from 1828 until at least 1851. He had a substantial shop, employing twenty men at the time of the 1850 census. His stenciled mark:

J.HUEY/ZANESVILLE

appears on the bottom of an elaborately decorated arrow-back Windsor settee. Refs.: Hageman I; *Antiques,* February 1984.

Federal inlaid mahogany card table, c. 1790–1800, marked W. HUNT. It is not known if Hunt was a cabinetmaker or an owner of the piece. Courtesy, Estate Antiques, Charleston, S.C.

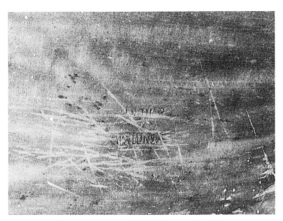

Branded mark W. HUNT on the Federal mahogany card table. Courtesy, Estate Antiques, Charleston, S.C.

HUEY, JOHN

Possibly the father of James Huey (see previous entry), John Huey was a Washington County, Pennsylvania, cabinetmaker, active c. 1793–1808. He is known for a Federal inlaid walnut slant-front desk, which is inscribed within a drawer

James Boyer his Desk/made June 1808 By me J. Huey/Washington County & State of/Pennsylvania DESK for Mr. James Boyer
John Huey is also probably the maker of a similar Federal desk owned by the Historical Society of Western Pennsylvania. This one is signed

J. Hughey, Washington County/1808
Refs.: *Made in Ohio; Antiques,* August 1972, May 1983.

HUGHES, J. E.

A c. 1820–1840 country Chippendale walnut wardrobe at the New York State Museum bears on its back a paper label inscribed in ink

J.E. Hughes/Black River, N.Y.
Scherer suggests that the maker might be cabinetmaker John E. Hughes of Little Falls, New York. Ref.: Scherer.

HUMESTON, JAY

The Windsor chair maker Jay Humeston or Humiston is known for a bow-back Windsor side chair branded beneath the seat
J. HUMESTON/HALIFAX/WARRANTED
Humeston worked in Charleston, South Carolina, in 1798 and again in 1802 and in Savannah, Georgia, in 1800. By 1804 he appears to have moved to Halifax, Nova Scotia. Refs.: Santore II; *Antiques,* January 1967.

HUMPHREVILLE, ALEXANDER D.

The cabinetmaker Alexander D. Humphreville (1836–1923) spent his career working in Mt. Pleasant, Jefferson County, Ohio. Among the pieces from his shop is a walnut two-drawer stand in a vernacular rendering of the Victorian Louis XVI style. It is labeled
From/A.D.Humphreville,/
CABINET MAKER/and Undertaker/
Mt. Pleasant, Ohio
Ref.: *Made in Ohio.*

HUNT, JOSEPH RUGGLES

The Windsor chair manufacturer Joseph Ruggles Hunt (1781–1871) worked in Eaton (now Madison), New Hampshire, c. 1811–1860. His chairs are stamped beneath the seat

J.R.HUNT/MAKER.
Ref.: Santore II.

HUNT, TIMOTHY, & CO.

This firm consisted of the brothers Timothy (d. 1874) and Simon H. Hunt. Timothy Hunt was working as a cabinetmaker in Boston as early as 1819, retiring in 1836. Simon too appeared in Boston in 1819 and was still running a "furniture ware house" in 1841. During the period 1819–1827, they worked together as Timothy Hunt & Co. at various addresses, including 85 Newbury Street, the location given on their stenciled mark:

T.HUNT & CO./Cabinet & Chair/Manufacturers/No. 85 Newbury St./BOSTON

They produced heavily carved late Classical or Empire furniture, generally of mahogany. Labeled desks and bookcases, card tables, and chests of drawers are known. Refs.: *Antiques*, May 1976, May 1992.

HUNT, W.

A Federal inlaid mahogany card table, c. 1790–1800, in a private collection is stamped twice

W. HUNT

It is not known if this is the maker or an owner. Bjerkoe lists a New York City cabinetmaker Ward Hunt in 1774. Ref.: Bjerkoe.

HUNZINGER, GEORGE

The German-born and -trained cabinet- and chairmaker George Hunzinger settled in Brooklyn, New York, in the 1850s, opening his own shop there in 1866. In 1870 he moved the business to Manhattan, where he remained active at various addresses until his death in 1899. His sons continued the business into the 1920s. Although Hunzinger obtained twenty patents in the furniture field and produced an array of highly eclectic pieces, blending Victorian Eastlake and Renaissance Revival styles with machinelike elements, he is known primarily for two chair design patents. The first of these was for a reclining or folding armchair, and such chairs are branded

HUNZINGER/N.Y./PATENTED/1866

or

Upholstered walnut folding chair with the impressed mark of George Hunzinger, a maker of unusual chairs who worked in New York City from 1870 to 1899. Many of Hunzinger's products bear 1866 or 1869 patent dates, obtained while he was located in Brooklyn, 1866–1870. Courtesy, E. J. Canton.

HUNZINGER/New York/Pat. Feb.6/1866
Even more common are chairs with a patented diagonal brace connecting the front feet to the upper back. These are stamped
HUNZINGER/N.Y./PAT
MARCH 30/1869
or
G. HUNZINGER, N.Y. Patented
30 March 1869
or
GEO. HUNZINGER, patented
Mar. 30, 1869

Chippendale mahogany serpentine-front bonnet-top desk and bookcase or secretary, attributed to Salem, Massachusetts, c. 1770–1780. It is inscribed John Hurd/George Hurd. If the Hurds were cabinetmakers, they have not yet been identified. Courtesy, Israel Sack, Inc., New York.

Refs.: Scherer; *Art and Antiques,* January–February 1980.

A Chippendale mahogany serpentine-front bonnet-top desk and bookcase or secretary is incised

John Hurd/George Hurd
The piece is attributed to Salem, Massachusetts, c. 1770–1780. It is not known if these are the names of owners or the makers.

HUSE, E.

A Chippendale mahogany serpentine-front bureau or chest of drawers, c. 1770–1780, is branded

E. HUSE
It is not known if Huse was a cabinetmaker. A John Huse, cabinetmaker (1783–1827), lived in Newburyport, Massachusetts. Ref.: Bjerkoe.

HUTCHINGS, E. W.

The Manhattan cabinetmaker E. W. Hutchings (b. 1810) specialized in ornate Victorian Rococo Revival furnishings. Among the pieces bearing his stenciled mark:

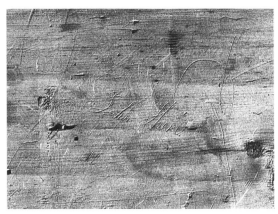

Incised signatures of John and George Hurd on top of the desk portion of the Chippendale mahogany desk and bookcase. Courtesy, Israel Sack, Inc., New York.

FROM/E.W.HUTCHINGS/CABINET-WARE ROOMS/475 BROADWAY, N.Y. are a marble-top sideboard, a rosewood server, and a rosewood lady's desk. The last is at the Munson-Williams-Proctor Institute in Utica, New York. Hutchings, who was born around 1810, was in business in Manhattan for some fifty years. He was at 475 Broadway from 1845 until 1869. His son continued the business until 1892. Refs.: *Antiques,* October 1970, May 1972.

Chippendale mahogany serpentine-front bureau or chest of drawers, c. 1770–1780. It is branded E. HUSE, which may be a maker's or an owner's name. Cabinetmakers named Huse were active in Newburyport, Massachusetts. Courtesy, Israel Sack, Inc., New York.

HUTCHINS, ZADOCK, JR.

During his brief career in Pomfret, Connecticut, the turner Zadock Hutchins, Jr. (1793–1830), produced a few rod-back Windsor side chairs and Salem rockers branded

Z. HUCHENS

One marked chair is at Winterthur. Refs.: Santore II; *Antiques,* January 1983.

I

IDEN, HENRY

The Manhattan cabinetmaker Henry Iden is known for two marked Victorian Rococo Revival étagères. One is inscribed

H. IDEN/NEW YORK

while a nearly identical example is stenciled

**IDEN/CABINET MANUFACTURING/
194 & 196 HESTER ST., NEW YORK**

Iden worked in New York City at various addresses from 1850 until 1866. He was at the Hester Street address from 1854 on. Ref.: *Antiques,* May 1984.

Victorian Rococo Revival rosewood lady's desk, c. 1850–1860, bearing the stenciled mark of the maker, E. W. Hutchings (b. 1810). Hutchings had a shop on Broadway in New York City from 1845 until 1869. Courtesy, Munson-Williams-Proctor Institute, Utica, New York.

ILSLEY, G. L.

The turner G. L. Ilsley is known for medallion-back birdcage Windsor side chairs with the unusual oval brand

G.L.ISLEY/EXETER, N.H.

Brand E. HUSE on the Chippendale mahogany bureau or chest of drawers. Courtesy, Israel Sack, Inc., New York.

He worked in Exeter, New Hampshire, c. 1800–1820. Ref.: Santore II.

INGALS, SILAS

A rod-back fancy side chair with curved seat similar to that found on Boston rockers is stamped beneath the seat

S.I.

for Silas Ingals (1786–1854), who worked in Danville, Caledonia County, Vermont, c. 1815–1850. Refs.: *Old Time New England Furniture* (Boston: Society for the Preservation of New England Antiquities, 1987); Robinson.

INGRAHAM, JOHN S.

A c. 1750–1760 Queen Anne mahogany block-front desk at the Museum of Fine Arts, Boston, and a table at Historic Deerfield, both branded

J.S. INGRAHAM

are attributed to John S. Ingraham of Boston and New Haven, Connecticut, who may have been associated with the Coit family of cabinetmakers. Ref.: Lovell.

❧J❧

JACKSON, C.

A Sheraton cherry chest of drawers or bureau in a private collection is signed beneath the top

 Made/December/the 23rd/1824/C.Jackson

Jackson worked in the Pleasant View area of Cheatham County, Tennessee. Ref.: *Antiques,* October 1971.

JACKSON, FRANCIS

An arrow-back Windsor armchair, c. 1820–1840, owned by the State Museum of Pennsylvania and pictured in the *New York–Pennsylvania Collector* for December 1984, bears a label reading,

Francis Jackson's Chair Manufactory, Easton, Pennsylvania

Nothing further is known of Jackson's shop.

JACOBS, E. H., MFG. CO.

An unusual folding triangular chair with high slotted back bears a paper label depicting people using the chair in various locales and reading,

The/WIGWAM/CHAIR/Country/Sea Shore/Veranda PATENTED/E.H.JACOBS MFG. CO.,/Danielson, Conn.

Another example of Victorian patent furniture, it dates c. 1880–1910. Nothing is known of the manufacturer.

JACQUES, S.

A Windsor bow-back armchair offered at Sotheby's, February 2, 1985, is described as being branded beneath the seat

S.JACQUES

It is possible that this is a misreading of "R.Jacques," for the Windsor manufacturer Richard Jacques listed by Santore as working in New Brunswick, New Jersey, c. 1775. It could also be another member of the same family. Ref.: Santore II.

JAHN, JOHANN MICHAEL

The Pomeranian cabinetmaker Johann Michael Jahn migrated to the United

Walnut tripod-base pedestal table or stand, c. 1850–1855, marked JJ and attributed to Johann Michael Jahn of New Braunfels, Texas. Jahn worked there from 1846 until after 1880. Private collection.

a Chippendale clock case at the Philadelphia Museum of Art, both of which are labeled **Made and Sold by/EDWARD JAMES/Cabinet and Chair Maker in/Swanson street near Swedes Church/Philadelphia** James was first listed as a joiner in the Southwark area of Philadelphia in 1760, and he was still working there, on Queen Street, in 1796. Refs.: Bjerkoe; *Antiques,* February 1931; *International Studio,* February 1929.

JAMES, FISHER

One of a pair of matching c. 1780–1800 Hepplewhite mahogany worktables is inscribed

Fisher James Paternal Elder, Elder Family This appears to refer to an owner.

States in 1844, setting up shop in New Braunfels, Texas, in 1846 and continuing to work into the 1880s. A walnut tripod-base pedestal table or stand exhibited at the San Antonio Museum in 1973 and initialed in ink

JJ

is attributed to him. It is dated c. 1850–1855. A similarly marked rocking chair is known, as well as various unsigned pieces. Ref.: *Antiques,* May 1974.

JAMES, EDWARD

The Philadelphia cabinetmaker Edward James (d. 1798) is known for a Chippendale walnut birdcage tripod-base tea table and

Detail of the underside of the walnut pedestal table by Johann Michael Jahn, showing partial view of the maker's initials, JJ. Private collection.

Upholstered Victorian Renaissance Revival rosewood armchair, c. 1860–1870, by John Jelliff & Company, Newark, New Jersey. Courtesy, the Newark Museum.

JANVIER, JOHN

The well-known Delaware cabinetmaker John Janvier (1749–1801) left a substantial number of marked pieces. Janvier, son and father of cabinetmakers, was established at Elkton, Cecil County, Maryland, by 1770. His only printed label is from this period and appears to be an advertisement used as a label:

ADVERTISEMENT/JOHN JANVIER/CABINET AND CHAIR-MAKER/FROM PHILADELPHIA,/Takes this method to inform the Public that he

carries on/the Joiner's bufineff, in all its various branches, at the head/of Elk in Cecil county, MARYLAND, in the shop which/Caleb Ricketts formerly occupied, where he makes and fells all forts/of Joiner's work, in the neateft and beft manner, and neweft fafhions;/such as desks of various forts, chefts of drawers; card, dining, cham-/ber, Pembroke and tea tables &c.; parlour, eafy, and elbow chairs, &c./clock-cafes, couches, bed-fteads, and many other pieces of furniture/too tedious to mention: all of which he will engage to be equal in neat-/nefs and ftrength to Philadelphia work; he therefore hopes, that he/will meet with fuitable encouragement in his bufinefs, as he intends to/make it his study to give the greatest fatisfaction that lays in his/power to all thofe who will pleafe to favor him with their cuftom./He likewife intends to keep a general affortment of fcrews, fprigs, nails,/locks, hings &c. fuch as are necefary in the Joiner's trade, and which/he intends to fell as low as poffible, for cafh only.

Apparently Janvier did not meet with "fuitable encouragement," for by 1777 he was at Cantwell's Bridge (now Odessa), New Castle County, Delaware, where he worked until his death. A Chippendale walnut tall clock case made here bears the handwritten label

Cabinet work & Chairs/Of the Newest Fashion/Made in the Best manner,/By the Subscriber at Cantwell's Bridge/ May 29th 1795 John Janvier

There is also a c. 1800 Chippendale mahogany chest of drawers signed in chalk

John Janvier at Cantwell's Bridge
Ref.: *Antiques,* April 1981, May 1983.

JANVIER, JOHN, JR.

After his father's death (see previous entry), John Janvier, Jr. (1777–1850), took over the family shop at Cantwell's Bridge in Delaware's New Castle County. He had been working alone as a cabinetmaker from at least 1794 and had, among others, made furniture for the Philadelphia craftsman Daniel Trotter. Although he was active until his death, only two pieces of furniture bear his mark. One is a Chippendale mahogany desk and bookcase or secretary inscribed in ink

Made by John Janvier/Appoquinimink—
Delaware/November 1805/
For F.D. Janvier—Princeton

the other, a late Sheraton mahogany sideboard,

which is signed

Made by John Janvier at Cantwell's Bridge
New Castle County/Delaware 1812

Refs.: *Plain and Ornamental; Antiques,* January 1942.

JANVIER, PEREGRINE

Yet another son of John Janvier, Sr. (see his entry), Peregrine Janvier (1781–1863 or '65) was trained at the family shop in Cantwell's Bridge (Odessa), Delaware. The only marked piece from his hand is a Chippendale-Hepplewhite transitional mahogany bowfront chest of drawers, which is inscribed in ink

Made by Peregrine Janvier at
Appoquinimink—July 1804

The piece is also stamped

P.I.

and bears a scratched-in notation

Made August 1804/By Peregrine
Janvier/Appoquinimink/for/
Mr. David Wilson.

The discrepancy in dates probably reflects the time it took to make the piece. Ref.: *Plain and Ornamental.*

JELLIFF, JOHN

John Jelliff (1813–1893), New Jersey's best-known nineteenth-century cabinetmaker, was in partnership with Thomas L. Vantilburg

Carved Victorian Rococo Revival rosewood desk, dated 1855 and inscribed with the name and location of John Jelliff, a Newark, New Jersey, cabinetmaker working c. 1836–1860.
Courtesy, the Newark Museum.

from 1836 until 1843 and then established his own shop at 301–303 Broad Street in Newark. A Victorian Rococo Revival mahogany lady's writing desk with étagère at the Newark Museum is inscribed

1855 J. Jelliff Co./Sep 29 301 or 303 Broad St/R.W. W.G.W. Newark N.J.

and

John Jelliff & Co.

More frequently encountered on Jelliff's Victorian furnishings is the simple brand

J.J. Co.

The "Co." was Henry H. Miller, who took over the firm after Jelliff's retirement in 1860, running it under his former employer's name until 1890. Ref.: *Antiques,* May 1986.

JENKINS, ANTHONY HEARN

Anthony Hearn Jenkins (1814–1884), eldest son of the Baltimore craftsman Michael Jenkins (see his entry), took over the shop on Light Street in Baltimore following his father's death in 1832, running it alone until 1837, when he took his brother, Henry (see Jenkins & Jenkins), into partnership. The firm was dissolved in 1857. A mahogany pedestal-base card table in the collection of the Baltimore Museum of Art is incised on the skirt and till respectively

AHJ

and

A.H.JENKINS

There is also a chair at the Maryland Historical Society that is stenciled

A.H. JENKINS/Cabinet Maker/ No.18 Light St.,/Balto.

Ref.: Elder and Stokes.

JENKINS, HENRY W., & SONS

The Jenkins family firm in Baltimore, Maryland, was operated into the twentieth century by Henry Worthington Jenkins and his sons. Although they ceased to make furniture after 1904, the associated undertaking establishment continued until it was sold out of the family in 1958. During the 1880s the business was expanded to include office furnishings. Oak and walnut rotary armchairs from this period were often marked in a circle

HENRY W. JENKINS & SONS/Cabinet Makers &/ Interior Decorators/Establish'd A.D.1793/310 N. Charles St. Balto, Md.

A much earlier piece, a c. 1860–1870 Victorian Rococo Revival mahogany desk with fold-out writing surface, bears the rare chalk signature

Jenkins

Ref.: *Antiques,* May 1986.

JENKINS, MICHAEL

Michael Jenkins (1778–1832), patriarch of Baltimore's Jenkins cabinetmaking family, was active in the city as early as 1799, founding a business that was to continue in the family until 1904. However, although he is listed in Baltimore directories until 1820, only a single marked piece from his shop has been identified. This is a Federal mahogany fall-front desk inscribed

Baltimore June 18 6 Was Made at Mr./Michial Jenkins Shop No.18 Light Street/Baltimore

The date is probably June 18, 1806. Ref.: *Antiques,* May 1986.

JENKINS & JENKINS

Anthony Hearn Jenkins (1814–1884, see his entry) and his brother, Henry Worthington Jenkins, were in business together at the family shop on Light Street in Baltimore from 1837 until 1857. Among the many pieces of massive Empire furniture they produced is a mahogany writing table and bookcase, illustrated in the *Bee* for November 12, 1993, which is inscribed

H. & A. Jenkins

Ref.: Elder and Stokes.

JEWETT, AMOS

Amos Jewett (1753–1834), a Shaker brother of the Mount Lebanon, New York, community, is credited with a simple poplar tall clock case in a private collection, which has written on the wooden dial

1809 Amos Jewett/Lebanon No.

Jewett's name also appears on several other clock dials. It is thought that he was a clock-maker who also made his own cases. Ref.: Rieman and Burks.

JOHN, DAVID OR DANIEL

A c. 1720–1725 William and Mary walnut and poplar desk and bookcase or secretary, which is inscribed in chalk

D John 6/20

is attributed to either David or Daniel John, sons of the Philadelphia joiner Philip John. Ref.: *Antiques,* July 1976.

JOHN, G.

A Chippendale walnut slant-front desk, c. 1760–1780, offered at Parke Bernet

Galleries, January 30–February 1, 1975, is stamped twice

G. JOHN

It is attributed to a cabinetmaker or owner from Chester County, Pennsylvania.

JOHN, ROBERT

A Chippendale walnut slant-front desk owned by the Chester County Historical Society is inscribed beneath the base

Made by Robert John 1797

Son of the joiner Reuben John, Robert is listed as a cabinetmaker in Uwchlan Township, Chester County, Pennsylvania, tax records for the period 1796–1799. Ref.: Schiffer.

JOHN, SQUIRE JAMES

One of Cincinnati's largest nineteenth-century furniture factories (employing fifty people in 1850) was owned by Squire James John, who came to the city in 1829 and opened his own shop, on Third Street, in 1844, remaining active until his death in 1859. John's Victorian furnishings, which included a popular patent extension table, were stenciled

S.J. JOHN/Fashionable/Cabinet,/Chair & Sofa/WARE ROOMS/3rd ST bet/Main & Sycamore/CINCINNATI, O.

A marked desk and bookcase or secretary is at the Western Reserve Historical Society in Cleveland. Ref.: *Made in Ohio.*

JOHNSON, C. JOSEPH

The Shaker craftsman C. Joseph Johnson (1781–1852) was a member of the Enfield, New Hampshire, community. He is known for a two-drawer birch table signed in pencil

C.J.Johnson/March 23, 1850

Ref.: Rieman and Burks.

JOHNSON, CHESTER

An unusual Sheraton painted and decorated settee, which converts to a bed, was patented in 1827 by Chester Johnson of Albany, New York. Examples of this piece are at the New York State Museum and the Munson-Williams-Proctor Institute in Utica, New York. Both are signed within the decoration

C. Johnson's/ Patent

Chester Johnson appears in the Albany directories for the years 1820–1827. Refs.: Fales, *American Painted Furniture;* Scherer.

JOHNSON, EDMUND

The prolific Massachusetts cabinetmaker Edmund Johnson (d. 1811) was active on River Street in Salem, c. 1793–1811, producing a variety of Federal furniture identified in several ways. A c. 1790–1795 inlaid mahogany card table is pencil-signed

Edmund Johnson

and a pair of rare mahogany knife boxes are inscribed

E. Johnson 1795

while a Heppelwhite mahogany tambour-front desk is branded

E. JOHNSON

However, the majority of Johnson's identifiable work bears a printed paper label reading,

ALL KINDS OF/CABINET FURNITURE/MADE & WARRANTED/By EDMUND JOHNSON,/Federal-Street, SALEM

Refs.: Bjerkoe; Montgomery.

JOHNSON, FORD, & CO.

A Victorian patent child's carriage, convertible to a sled, is stenciled

Ford Johnson & Co./Manufacturers/ Johnson City, Ind./Patent Oct/17 '76

The carriage dates c. 1875–1900, but nothing is known of the manufacturer. Ref.: *Antiques,* April 1936.

JOHNSON, GEORGE T.

The Virginia Windsor chair maker George T. Johnson (b. 1796) worked at various locations in Lynchburg, c. 1819–1850. His wares were labeled

Windsor Chairs,/Cribs, Cradles and Settees/MADE AND WARRANTED

Pair of Federal mahogany knife boxes bearing the signature of the Salem, Massachusetts, cabinetmaker Edmund Johnson (d. 1811) and the date 1795. Courtesy, Diplomatic Reception Rooms, U.S. State Department.

BY/GEORGE T. JOHNSON/Main Street, 4 Doors above the Market House/ LYNCHBURG, VA.

Ref.: Piorkowski.

JOHNSON, JAMES

A bow-back Windsor side chair in a private collection is stamped

J. JOHNSON

for the Wilmington, Delaware, turner and cabinetmaker James Johnson, active c. 1805–1813. Ref.: *Antiques,* April 1981.

JOHNSON, SAMUEL W.

A cherry sugar chest on frame containing a drawer in a private collection is signed twice on a drawer back

Samuel W. Johnson

for Samuel W. Johnson, a cabinetmaker who was in Giles County, Tennessee, before 1840 and worked in Lawrence County, c. 1841–1860. Ref.: Williams and Harsh.

JOHNSTON, F. T.

A miniature Empire mahogany marble-top side or serving table at the Henry Ford Museum is inscribed in ink on the back

Made and Presented by/F.T. JOHN-STON/Cabinet Maker/No.343 South Fort Below Almond/March 29th, 1834

Neither the identity of this craftsman nor his location is presently known.

JONES, G. D.

An Empire mahogany cradle with sleigh bed characteristics, illustrated in *Antiques* for September 1990, is labeled

G.D. Jones No.62 S 4th St. Phila.

The piece would date c. 1820–1840, but nothing is known of the manufacturer.

JONES, HORACE

A Federal gilt looking glass offered at Christie's, January 21–22, 1994, bears the label of Horace Jones, who worked in Troy, New York, from 1820 until his death in 1828:

LOOKING/GLASSES./HORACE JONES,/Manufacturer of Gilt & Ma-/hogany LOOKING GLASSES;/Framer of Prints, Paint-/ings & Embroidery. Old/frames repaired—Look-/ing Glass plates silvered. Country Merchants & oth-/ers supplied with Looking/Glasses as cheap as can be/purchased in the U. States,/of the same quality, whole-/sale and retail at his China,/Glass, Earthen-ware and LOOKING GLASS STORE,/River-Street TROY.

The text is set within an engraving of a looking glass identical to the one on to which the label was glued!

JONES, JOSEPH

The turner Joseph Jones (d. 1868) ran a chairmaking shop in West Chester, Pennsylvania, from 1817. He produced a wide variety of Windsor, fancy, and rush-bottom chairs as well as settees and advertised regularly. He gave up the chair shop in 1846 to concentrate on an iron business he had previously developed. Chairs bearing Jones's label:

JOSEPH JONES,/FANCY & WINDSOR/CHAIR-MAKER,/Nearly opposite the Academy,/WEST-CHESTER

are relatively common. Ref.: Schiffer.

JONES, MAHLON

An Empire walnut and walnut veneer desk and bookcase or secretary inscribed

Made by Mahlon Jones/In the year of our lord 1849/february 23rd and the 56th year of the makers age, in the Burough of Oxford, North Carolina

is the only known marked piece by Mahlon Jones, a Baltimore-trained craftsman who worked in North Carolina, c. 1825–1850. He was in Oxford, Granville County, in 1849. Ref.: Bivins.

JONES, THOMAS

A rare Chippendale walnut desk and bookcase or secretary, illustrated in *Antiques* for May 1987, is signed

Thomas Jones

Jones was an English cabinetmaker who came to Philadelphia in 1773 to work for the well-known craftsman Jonathan Gostelowe (see his entry). The piece would date c. 1773–1780.

JONES, WILLIAM

The cabinetmaker William Jones was trained in Perquimans County, North Carolina, and appears to have worked there as well as in Virginia. He is known for a Classical mahogany drop-leaf dining table signed in chalk

W Jones/1801

A Federal walnut corner cupboard signed in block letters

W. JONES

is also attributed to him. Ref.: Bivins.

JUDKINS & SENTER

To the well-known Portsmouth, New Hampshire, cabinetmaking firm of Judkins & Senter is attributed a Sheraton mahogany sideboard inscribed in pencil

Made & . . . . /January 22/1815/
by J. & Senter

The partners worked together, c. 1808–1826, producing a substantial quantity of high-style furniture. This sideboard is at Strawbery Banke, Portsmouth. Ref.: *Antiques,* May 1979.

KARPEN, S., & BROS.

The Chicago firm of S. Karpen & Bros. active during the early twentieth century, produced a variety of furnishings, from Arts and Crafts pieces resembling those made by the Stickleys (see Gustav Stickley) to overstuffed sofas and chairs in a vaguely French manner. These bear stamped metal tags reading

Karpen/Guaranteed Upholstered
Furniture/Chicago

Ref.: *Antiques & Arts Weekly,* February 11, 1994.

KEELER & CO.

A set of c. 1870–1880 walnut Victorian Eastlake bedroom furniture offered for sale in December 1994 was marked

Keeler & Co./Boston, MA

This is probably the name of a furniture dealership rather than a manufacturer.

KELLER, FERDINAND

The German-born cabinetmaker Ferdinand Keller established a firm in Philadelphia that from 1882 until 1970 produced and sold reproductions of classical furniture styles, both American and European. Over the years the shop was at various locations in the city. A Chippendale mahogany side chair in a private collection is labeled

FERDINAND KELLER/ANTIQUE
FURNITURE,/Silver, China and Delft/
216-218-220 S. 9th St./Philadelphia, Pa.

Keller was at this address from 1885 until 1910.

KEMPEN, A.

The Austin, Texas, cabinetmaker A. Kempen (c. 1870–1890) produced high-quality Victorian furniture in a generally Rococo Revival mode, though with the addition of Renaissance and Gothic Revival elements. A mahogany lady's desk is labeled

A.KEMPEN/CABINETMAKER/PICTURE
Frames/MOULDINGS/WIRE CORD/
Tassels and Nails/kept always on
hand/FRAMES/and WINDOW
CORNICES,/made to order on
short/notice/ALSO THE HANGING
OF/Window Shades and Cur-/tains, repairing and var-/nishing of Furniture,/Musical/instruments, etc./FURNITURE/made
to order/CONGRESS AVENUE/next to
Berryman's Store, opposite Bengener's
tin shop./AUSTIN, TEXAS.

Ref.: *MAD,* May 1976.

KENDRICK, HASTINGS

The Shaftsbury and Bennington, Vermont, cabinetmaker Hastings Kendrick (working c. 1824–1831) is known for a Classical mahogany sideboard, which is inscribed in pencil within a drawer

Shaftsbury/Oct. 7, 1825 AD H.K.

Kendrick was in Shaftsbury only until 1829, when he moved to Bennington. He left his shop there in 1831. Refs.: Robinson; *Antiques,* August 1993.

KENNEDY & REDDIN

The New York City firm of Kennedy and Reddin, active on Maiden Lane in Manhattan, c. 1820–1830, is known for a labeled Classical mahogany dressing glass. We have

not been able to obtain the wording of this label.

KENT, EBENEZER

A Chippendale mahogany serpentine-front chest of drawers, offered at Sotheby's January 31–February 3, 1979, is inscribed on the backboard

Kent

It is attributed to Ebenezer Kent, a cabinetmaker active in Charlestown, Massachusetts, c. 1775. Ref.: Bjerkoe.

KERWOOD, WILLIAM

Two pieces from the hand of the Trenton, New Jersey, cabinetmaker William Kerwood (b. 1779) are known. One is a Sheraton mahogany drop-leaf table, the other an upholstered mahogany wing chair with reeded Chippendale legs. Both are labeled

WILLIAM KERWOOD./CABINET & CHAIR-MAKER,/Nearly Opposite the Government House, Trenton,/executes in the neatest manner, on reasonable terms,/all orders in the line of his BUSINESS, and constantly/keeps on hand for sale,/A VARIETY OF CABINETWARE,/Such as, Desks, BUREAUS, Tables, Clock-/Cases, &c.&c./N.B. Sophas, Easy Chairs, Venitian Blinds, &c./made in the newest style and shortest notice.

Upholstered Chippendale mahogany wing chair, c. 1800–1810, bearing the label of William Kerwood (b. 1779), a cabinetmaker active in Trenton, New Jersey, c. 1803–1825. Courtesy, C. L. Prickett, Yardley, Pa.

Printed paper label of William Kerwood on the Chippendale wing chair. Courtesy, C. L. Prickett, Yardley, Pa.

Kerwood, who served his apprenticeship in Philadelphia, was established in Trenton, New Jersey, by 1803, remaining in business there for several decades. Refs.: Bjerkoe; *Antiques,* August 1932.

KIBLING, GEORGE O.

A group of three painted and stencil-decorated fancy side chairs with cane seats, which were offered at Sotheby's January 28–31, 1981, are stenciled on the front rail

GEO. W. KIBLING

Kibling had a chairmaking shop in Ashburnham, Massachusetts, c. 1820–1830.

KIDD, THOMAS

A Queen Anne oval-top tavern table, illustrated in *Antiques* for January 1957, is inscribed

Manufactured by Thos. Kidd/Queen St. Exeter 1743

Nothing further is known of this Exeter, New Hampshire, craftsman.

KIDDER, ELI

The Shaker brother and cabinetmaker Eli Kidder (1783–1867) spent his life as a member of the Canterbury, New Hampshire, community. He is known for two signed mixed-woods sewing stands. The first, at the Philadelphia Museum of Art, is inscribed in ink

Made by Br. Eli Kidder at 77 years for Almira Hill at 40 yrs. January 1861 Chh Canterbury N.H./U.S.A.

The second, in the collection of the Shaker Museum, Old Chatham, New York, is signed

Work Stand Made by Bro. Eli Kidder aged 77 years/Jan. 1861/Moved into by MEH Jan 18, 1861

Ref.: Rieman and Burks.

KIDDER & CARTER

Several c. 1810–1825 Sheraton gilded looking glasses with reverse-painted panels bear the label of John Kidder (1753–1835) and Joseph Carter, who became Kidder's partner

The brand of the turner Stephen Kilburn (1787–1867) beneath the rod-back Windsor side chair. Private collection.

around 1811. Their label reads,

KIDDER & CARTER/MANUFACTURE AND SELL LOOKING-GLASSES & TIN-FOIL,/Wholesale and Retail, at their Store,/MAIN STREET,/CHARLESTOWN, (Mass.)/ALSO—Old Looking-Glasses New Silvered./Embroidery and Pictures Framed. Nothing more is presently known of this firm. Refs.: Comstock, *The Looking Glass in America; Antiques,* November 1983.

KILBURN, STEPHEN

The turner Stephen Kilburn (1787–1867) was born in Massachusetts, lived in New York State, and settled in the village of New London, Huron County, Ohio, in 1840. His shop, operated by the proprietor and various family members, remained active until around 1870. Kilburn must have had a substantial business, because rod-back Windsor and painted fancy chairs branded

S. KILBURN

have been found from Ohio to New England. The author discovered one in a secondhand shop in Byram, Connecticut. Ref.: Hageman II.

KIMBALL, JEREMIAH

A Federal card table in mahogany and mahogany veneer described in the *Bee* for January 3, 1995, is said to have been inscribed

Rod-back Windsor side chair, c. 1840–1870, branded on the underside of the seat S. KILBURN for Stephen Kilburn, who made chairs in New London, Ohio. Private collection.

Ebonized hardwood
tête-à-tête with inlay
and gilding, labeled by
the New York City
cabinetmaking firm of
Anthony Kimbel and
Joseph Cabus, working
together c. 1865–1882.
Courtesy, Cooper Union.

by the early-nineteenth-century cabinetmaker Jeremiah Kimball of Ipswich, Massachusetts, working c. 1790. Ref.: Bjerkoe.

KIMBALL, JOHN

A Chippendale maple slant-front desk at the New Hampshire Historical Society in Concord bears on its back the large painted inscription

February/23. 1762/John Kimball

It is the work of the cabinetmaker John Kimball (1739–1817), made in Derryfield (now Manchester), New Hampshire, before he moved to Concord in 1764. Once owned by the Revolutionary War hero Gen. John Stark, the desk is believed to be the oldest existing piece of documented New Hampshire furniture. Ref.: *Antiques*, May 1979.

KIMBALL, JOSEPH

Chippendale maple slant-front desk, illustrated in *MAD* for June 1975, is signed on the back in chalk

Joseph Kimball

It is thought to be by the cabinetmaker Joseph Kimball, who was working in Canterbury, New Hampshire, around 1812. Ref.: Bjerkoe.

KIMBALL & SARGENT

A late Sheraton mahogany and mahogany veneer washstand at the Essex Institute bears the following label:

Kimball & Sargent,/CABINET MAKERS,/ESSEX STREET . . . OPPOSITE UNION STREET,/SALEM/Cabinetwork of all kinds made at short/notice, and the work Warranted.

The partnership of Abraham Kimball and Winthrop Sargent was in business on Essex Street in Salem, Massachusetts, by 1821. They moved to Holyoke Place in 1831 and went out of business in 1842. Refs.: Bjerkoe; Fales, *Essex County Furniture*.

KIMBEL, ANTHONY, & SONS

Following dissolution of his partnership with Joseph Cabus (see next entry), the

Manhattan cabinetmaker Anthony Kimbel went into business with his sons. The firm (active 1882–1941) produced a variety of late Victorian furniture, primarily in the Aesthetic and Gothic modes. A cherry étagère at the Metropolitan Museum of Art is labeled

A. Kimbel & Sons/Cabinet Makers and Decorators/New York

Ref.: *Antiques,* May 1992.

KIMBEL & CABUS

The Manhattan firm of Anthony Kimbel and Joseph Cabus (working together, c. 1865–1882) produced a substantial quantity of Victorian furniture during the second half of the nineteenth century. Best known for their "Modern Gothic" style, they also produced furnishings in the Eastlake, Renaissance Revival, and Aesthetic modes. An ebonized cherry library table in the collection of the Hudson River Museum, Yonkers, New York, bears a partial Kimbel & Cabus label. A larger label, featuring an elaborate Gothic sideboard, reads,

KIMBEL & CABUS,/7 & 9/East 20th St./ New York/Cabinet Manufacturers and Decorators.

Ref.: Bishop.

KING, D.

A sack-back writing-arm Windsor chair, illustrated in *Antiques* for January 1967, is inscribed

D. King/Richmond, Va.

No turner of this name is recorded, and it is thought that the name is that of an owner.

KING, E.

A Queen Anne burl walnut veneer high chest of drawers or highboy, sold at Sotheby's May 1975, is signed within a drawer

E. King/1736

The piece is thought to be from Boston or Salem, Massachusetts, but it is not known if the name is that of the maker or an owner.

KING, EDWIN

A Queen Anne mahogany and cherry high chest of drawers or highboy sold at auction in Sandwich, Massachusetts, November 27, 1993, bears the signature

Edwin King

said to have been an eighteenth-century cabinetmaker in New Bedford, Massachusetts. Ref.: *Antiques & Arts Weekly,* January 7, 1994.

KING, WILLIAM

The Salem, Massachusetts, cabinetmaker William King (b. 1754) is known for a fine Chippendale mahogany serpentine-front chest of drawers, c. 1775–1785, which is labeled simply

Made and Sold by/W. KING/Salem

and a mahogany tripod-base, tilt-top candle stand of the same period branded

W. KING

which was sold at Sotheby's, November18–20, 1976. Though a fine craftsman, King was not much of a homebody, deserting his Salem family on a regular basis. He was last heard of in Hanover, New Hampshire, in 1806. Refs.: Bjerkoe; *Antiques,* September 1927.

KINGMAN & MURPHY

A Victorian Renaissance Revival marble center table with Sienna marble top at the Newark Museum is labeled

KINGMAN & MURPHY/Cabinet Furniture/Warerooms, 93 Bleecker St/One Block West of Broadway/NEW YORK

while a set of six apparently late-eighteenth-century Federal mahogany side chairs offered at Sotheby's, June 30–July 1, 1983, are labeled

**KINGMAN & MURPHY/
MANUFACTURERS/OF CABINET
FURNITURE/Warerooms,
93 Bleecker Street, NEW YORK.**

Because the firm of Sumner Kingman and H. G. Murphy was at 93 Bleecker Street, Manhattan, only from 1868 until 1872, it would appear that the chairs either are reproductions or were being sold as used furniture. Ref.: *Antiques,* May 1983.

KINGSBURY, EBENEZER

A Federal tall case clock in a private collection is reported to bear the handwritten label of the cabinetmaker Ebenezer Kingsbury (married 1797) of Shrewsbury and Spencer, Massachusetts. Kingsbury was still active in the latter town around 1810. Ref.: *Antiques,* May 1993.

KINNAMAN & MEAD

The firm of Alexander Kinnaman and States Mead had a furniture shop in New York City, c. 1813–1830. A Classical mahogany secretary-bookcase offered at Sotheby's, January 27–30, 1982, bears a partial label indicating that they were at No. 94 Broad Street, Manhattan, and that they

. . . had on hand a complete assortment of elegent and highly finished furniture.

KINNIE, JAMES C.

A Federal inlaid mahogany dressing glass offered at Christie's, March 10, 1978, bears the rare label

James C. Kinnie/JOINER AND CABINET-MAKER/MONTICELLO,/NEW YORK

Kinnie worked in the Sullivan County town of Monticello, c. 1800–1815.

KINSELA, THOMAS

A New York State banister-back side chair in a private collection is stamped

T/KINSELA

on each front post. A Thomas Kinsela of Schenectady, listed in the 1810 and 1820 federal censuses, is thought to have been either the maker or an owner. Ref.: *Antiques,* May 1981.

KIPP, GEORGE W., & CO.

A c. 1880–1890 pine and maple worktable with heavily turned legs, now owned by the Sleepy Hollow Restorations, is marked under the top

G. W. Kipp and Co. Sing Sing

It was made by the firm of George and Arthur Kipp, listed as furniture manufacturers at the corner of Spring and St. Paul's streets in Ossining, New York, during the 1880s. They may be sons of the Henry Kipp who worked in Manhattan, c. 1820–1840. Ref.: *A Celebration of Westchester* (Scarsdale, N.Y.: New York Historical Society, 1981).

KIPP, HENRY, & SON.

An Empire mahogany desk and bookcase or secretary, c. 1820–1840, in a private collection bears the stenciled mark of the Manhattan concern Henry Kipp & Son.

HENRY KIPP & SON,/Cabinet, Mahogany,/Chair and Sofa/WARE-HOUSE/No.7 Chatham Square,/Corner of East Broadway,/NEW-YORK

It is possible that Kipp was a dealer in furniture rather than a cabinetmaker.

KIRKPATRICK, SHEPLEY HOLMES

Shepley Holmes Kirkpatrick (1816–after 1870) was a carpenter and furniture maker in Pike Township, Knox County, Ohio. He is known for a spectacular tiger maple bed with carved eagle headboard that is inscribed in red crayon

Made by Shepley Holmes Kirkpatrick Dec 22 AD 1841/Knox Co Pike TP/Ohio
Ref.: *Made in Ohio.*

KITCHELL, ISAAC

A braced bow-back Windsor side chair in the collection of the Newark Museum is branded beneath the seat

Ic KITCHEL

and was made by the turner Isaac Kitchell, active in New York City, c. 1789–1812. A marked comb-back Windsor armchair by the same maker was illustrated in *Antiques* for May 1981. Ref.: Santore II.

KNAGY, JACOB

The Amish cabinetmaker Jacob Knagy (1796–1883) was born and spent his working life on a farm in Somerset County, Pennsylvania. A substantial number of painted, stencil-decorated chests and chests of drawers bearing his mark remain. These include an 1851 blanket chest and an 1882 chest of drawers, both with the stenciled initials

J. K.

Ref.: *Antique Review,* April 1991.

KNAPP, JOHN

An elaborately inlaid mahogany Pembroke table, c. 1790–1800, illustrated in *An-*

Carved Classical card table with brass attachments, c. 1820–1840, with stenciled mark of Henry Kipp & Son of Chatham Square, New York City. Courtesy, Post Road Antiques, Larchmont, N.Y.

Stenciled mark of Henry Kipp & Son on the Classical card table. Courtesy, Post Road Antiques, Larchmont, N.Y.

articles of houfehold/Furniture, viz—/ SWELL'D front and plain Defks, with or without/Book-cafes, Swell'd and plain Bureaus, Clock-/Cafes, Cafes of Drawers, Merchant's writing Defks,/Dining Tables, Tea, Card, Pembroke and Tray/ditto, Tea and Dining Trays, Ladies wafh Stands,/Fire Screens, Parlour Chairs, Chamber ditto, Sofas,/Eafy Chairs, Elbow ditto, and Chairs of various o-/ther kinds; High poft, Camp and common Bedfteads,/Light Stands, Back-Gammon Boxes, Ches and Crib-/bage Boards, Looking-Glafs Frames, plain or gilt;/Alfo Furniture of various other kinds made of Cher-/ry-Tree or Mehogahy; on rea-fonable terms; at his/Shop, a few yards north of the Bridge./Hartford: August 14, 1786. Ref.: *Connecticut Historical Society Bulletin,* April 1955.

KNEELAND & ADAMS

tiques for September 1968, is signed

John Knapp

within a drawer. It is not known if this is the maker's or an owner's mark.

KNEELAND, SAMUEL

The cabinetmaker Samuel Kneeland (1755–1828) worked in Hartford, Connecticut, from 1786 until sometime after 1795. By 1798 he was occupying a shop in nearby Farmington. He died in Genesee, New York. Although labeled furniture from Kneeland's partnership with Lemuel Adams (1792–1795) is relatively plentiful, I know of only a single piece, a mahogany punch bowl case at the Connecticut Historical Society, bearing his earlier label:

SAMUEL KNEELAND,/Cabinet-Maker,/Makes and Fells the following

The well-known Hartford, Connecticut, cabinetmakers Samuel Kneeland (see previous entry) and Lemuel Adams were in partnership from 1792 until 1795, using a distinctive engraved label featuring a desk and bookcase, mirror, side table, and tall case clock and reading,

KNEELAND & ADAMS,/Cabinet and Chair-Makers, Hartford,/Have constantly on hand, MAHOGANY FURNITURE, of the firft quality;/beft warranted CLOCKS and TIME-PIECES, elegant LOOKING-GLASSES of/their own manufacturing; CABINET WORK of every kind may be had on very/fhort notice, warranted equal to any made in America.

Among the many pieces bearing the partners' labels are Chippendale and Federal tall case clocks, chests of drawers, chairs, and looking glasses. Refs.: Bjerkoe; Downs; Montgomery.

KNEMMULE, WILLIAM

See George Ackerman.

KNOWLES, SIMON

A pair of braced fan-back Windsor side chairs, c. 1790–1810, illustrated in *Antiques* for March 1957, are signed

Simon Knowles

It is not known if this is the name of the maker or an owner.

KNOWLTON, CALEB

The cabinetmaker Caleb Knowlton (d. 1860) worked in Manchester, Essex

County, Massachusetts, from sometime before 1808 until 1814, when he moved to Brandon, Vermont, where he remained active until the 1840s. A Federal mahogany gentleman's secretary at the Essex Institute is inscribed on a shelf

Made in Manchester 1808
by Caleb Knowl

Refs.: Fales, *Essex County Furniture; Antiques,* August 1965.

KNOWLTON, EBENEZER

The Boston cabinetmaker Ebenezer Knowlton (1769–1810) established a shop on Ann Street in 1796. After several moves he settled on Fish Street, where he remained until his death. The only known marked example of his work is a Sheraton mahogany tambour-front desk and bookcase or secretary, which is labeled

EBENEZER KNOWLTON/Makes and has for sale at his shop in Fore-Street/ at the head of Moore's Wood-Wharf/ BOSTON/Cabinet Furniture and Chairs of all kinds./On reasonable Terms for Cash.

Ref.: Bjerkoe.

KOERBEL, R.

A c. 1880–1910 pine food or pie safe with wire screen panels, exhibited at the San Antonio Museum in 1973, is signed on a back panel in blue carpenter's chalk

R. Koerbel/Lacoste

Pine food or pie safe with wire screen panels, c. 1880–1910, with the blue chalk signature of R. Koerbel of La Coste, Texas. It is likely that Koerbel was the maker of this piece. Private collection.

Comb-back Windsor armchair of mixed woods branded LAMBERT beneath the seat. The turner John Lambert (d. 1793) was active in Philadelphia, c. 1786–1793. Courtesy, Bernard and S. Dean Levy, Inc., New York.

La Coste, Texas, is a small community established in 1881. Nothing is known of R. Koerbel.

KRAUSE, LOUIS

A late Victorian walnut desk and bookcase with fall-front writing surface and in a style combining elements of several period modes is labeled

Louis Krause/S.W. Corner 5th and Green/Philadelphia

Nothing more is known of Krause.

L

LAIDEN, JOSEPH

A Classical-style mahogany, basswood, and white pine fall-front desk is inscribed **June 13 Joseph Laiden 472 Washington . . . Boston 1826** The European-trained cabinetmaker Joseph Laiden is listed in the 1830 Boston directory as having a workshop at 472 Washington Street.

LAM, E. K.

A c. 1830–1850 Empire chest of drawers with mahogany veneer sold at auction in September 1994 was signed

E.K. Lam

It is not known if this is the name of owner or maker. Ref.: *MAD*, September 1994.

LAMBERT, JOHN

The Philadelphia turner John Lambert (d. 1793) is listed in local records as working c. 1786–1793. He is known for Windsor bow-back side chairs and comb-back armchairs branded

LAMBERT

His chairs have unusual bamboo-turned stretchers. Refs.: Santore II; *MAD*, December 1988.

LAMMERT, MARTIN

A heavily carved Renaissance Revival rosewood bedstead and a marble-top chest of drawers, offered by the New Orleans Auction Galleries in 1993, are stenciled

FROM/MARTIN LAMMERT/

MANUFACTURER/WHOLESALE/& RETAIL/DEALER IN/FURNITURE/4112/ . . . . ./ST.LOUIS, Mo.

Lammert is believed to have been active in St. Louis, Missouri, c. 1855–1875. Ref.: *MAD,* October 1993.

LAMSON, B.

A Hepplewhite inlaid mahogany bowfront chest of drawers with French feet, c. 1790–1810, illustrated in *Antiques* for September 1980, is stamped

B. LAMSON

possibly for Benjamin Lamson, a cabinetmaker listed in the Boston directory for 1830. Ref.: Bjerkoe.

LANE, JOSHUA

A c. 1770–1780 Chippendale maple chest on chest sold at Sotheby's, January 27–28, 1983, is signed in red paint on a backboard

Made by Lane . . . .

It is attributed to the New Hampshire cabinetmaker Joshua Lane, who worked in Poplin and Fremont in the 1770s.

LANE, SAMUEL

The joiner Samuel Lane (1698–1776) of Hampton, New Hampshire, is thought to be the maker of a painted pine chest over drawer signed in red paint

Sam Lane/1719

Refs.: Fales, *American Painted Furniture; Antiques,* April 1930.

LANE & CROOME

The partnership of W. J. Lane and George Croome operated on Washington Street in Boston, Massachusetts, from 1835 until 1842. They are known for a set of six Empire mahogany side chairs, all of which are stenciled within the back rail

LANE & CROOME

Ref.: Edwin C. Skinner, letter of February 21, 1994.

Carved Classical mahogany bedstead, c. 1810–1819, with the impressed mark of Charles-Honoré Lannuier (1779–1819), a well-known New York City cabinetmaker, working 1804–1819. Private collection.

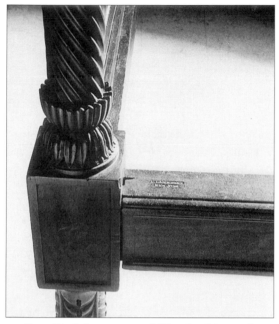

Detail of the stamp of Charles-Honoré Lannuier on the Classical mahogany bedstead. Private collection.

LANGDON, J.

A Queen Anne walnut side chair with upholstered seat, c. 1750–1770, at Old Sturbridge Village, is branded

J. LANGDON

thought to be the name of a Portsmouth, New Hampshire, turner. Ref.: Ralph and Terry Kovel, *American Country Furniture, 1780–1875* (New York: Crown, 1965).

Carved and gilded Classical mahogany sofa table, c. 1805–1815, labeled by Charles-Honoré Lannuier, working at 60 Broad Street, New York City. Courtesy, White House Collection.

LANNUIER, CHARLES-HONORÉ

That the French-born ebeniste Charles-Honoré Lannuier (1779–1819) is one of the best-known American cabinetmakers is due not only to the high quality of his work but also to the fact that he regularly marked or labeled it. Indeed, over fifty pieces so identified are now known. These include an array of beds, tables, wardrobes, chests of drawers, and chairs in styles ranging from a modified version of the French Louis XVI through American Federal and Empire modes. Much of this work is impressed

H. LANNUIER/NEW.YORK

However, Lannuier also used three different labels, two printed, one engraved. The last, which features a classic surround and some most unusual spelling, reads,

Hre Lannuier,/Cabinet Maker from Paris/
Kips is Whare house of/new fashion furniture/Broad Street No.60/New-York./
Hre Lannuier,/Ebeniste de Paris, Tient
Fabrique &/Magasin de Meubles/
les plus a la mode,/New-York.

A second and simpler printed version of the

Paper label of Charles-Honoré Lannuier on the Classical mahogany sofa table. Courtesy, White House Collection.

same message, with the proprietor's name misspelled, reads as follows:

HONORÉ LANNIUER/CABINET MAKER,/(FROM PARIS)/Keeps his Warehouse and Manufactory/AND CABINET WARE OF THE/NEWEST FASHION,/AT No.60 BROAD STREET./HONORÉ LANNIUER/EBENISTE/(DE PARIS)/LIENT SON MAGASIN/DE MEUBLES, LES PLUS/A-LA-MODE,/BROAD-STREET No. 60/NEW-YORK

A third, shorter, printed version, which from its use of the archaic *f* for *s* may be the earliest, simply states that

HONORÉ LANNUIER,/French Cabinet-Maker,/From Paris,/KEEPS his Warehouse and/Manufactory of CABINET WARE,/of the neweft fafhion, at No. 60 Broad-Street. NEW-YORK.

Finally, there is a mahogany wardrobe at the New-York Historical Society that is inscribed in longhand

H. Lannuier/New York

Lannuier arrived in New York City in 1803 and by the following year had taken a shop at 60 Broad Street, where he worked until his death. Marked examples of his work may be seen in many museums, including Winterthur, the Metropolitan Museum of Art, and the New York State Museum. Refs.: Cooper; Montgomery; *Antiques,* May 1933, January 1962.

LASSELLES, J.

A mahogany and bird's-eye maple two-drawer work stand at the Henry Ford Museum is twice inscribed within the top drawer

J. LASSELLES/MAKER

The piece dates c. 1825–1835 and is attributed to New York City, but nothing is known of the maker.

LAWS, JAMES M.

A c. 1810–1830 double step-down rod-back Windsor side chair at the Shelburne Museum is labeled on the underside of the seat
James M. Laws, Milford, New Hampshire
This may be the name of a maker, dealer, or owner. Ref.: Kenney.

LAWTON, F.

A New England or New York mixed-woods brace-back continuous-arm chair, dating

c. 1790–1800, is branded beneath the seat

F. LAWTON

which may be the name of a previously undocumented Windsor chair maker.

LAWTON, ROBERT, JR.

The Newport, Rhode Island, cabinetmaker Robert Lawton, Jr., is known for two marked pieces: one a mahogany drop-leaf breakfast table, the other an inlaid mahogany Pembroke table. The breakfast table is labeled Robert Lawton,/JUNIOR,/CABINET-

Brand, F. LAWTON, on the underside of the Windsor continuous-arm chair.

Private collection.

MAKER, carries on faid/bufinefs, in its various Branches, in/Spring Street, Alfo has on Hand, the/new-invented Spring, Crimping, Prefs and/Crimping Boards—with feveral Kinds of/portable Writing Defks./No.33/Newport, 4 of 10 mon. 1798 The Pembroke table bears an identical label except for the fact that it is listed as "No. 7" and is dated "20 of 5 mon. 1794," and, most important, Lawton's address is given as "Broad Street," indicating that during the period 1794–1798 he occupied two separate locations in Newport. Ref.: Bjerkoe.

New York or New England braced Windsor continuous-arm chair of mixed woods, c. 1790–1800, branded beneath the seat by the unknown maker F. Lawton.

Private collection.

LEARNARD, ELISHA

The cabinetmaker Elisha Learnard (1765–1827) worked on Back Street in Boston from 1796 until 1821, and thereafter at 13 Lynn Street and on Foster Street. His printed paper label, found on a Classical mahogany card table and mirrored bureau, reads,

ELISHA LEARNARD,/No. 60 BACK-STREET BOSTON,/KEEPS CONSTANTLY ON HAND, ALL KINDS OF MAHOGANY FURNITURE:/CHEAP AS CAN BE PURCHASED IN TOWN,/FOR CASH OR CREDIT./ALL ORDERS STRICTLY ATTENDED TO.

Refs.: Bjerkoe; *Antiques,* February 1962, May 1975.

LEDYARD

Santore lists a sack-back armchair, c. 1790–1810, which he attributes to a Massachusetts maker and which is branded

Detail of the paper label of Elisha Learnard on the Classical card table. Learnard's shop was at 60 Back Street, Boston, from 1796 to 1821. Courtesy, H. & R. Sandor, Inc., New Hope, Pa.

LEDYARD

Nothing further is known of this individual. Ref.: Santore II.

LEE, CHARLES

The Manchester, Massachusetts, cabinet-maker Charles Lee (1817–1889) specialized in bedsteads, producing large numbers for sale in the South, particularly to the New Orleans market, during the period 1856–1868. These half- and full-tester beds, in the Renais-

Classical mahogany card table, c. 1810–1820, with the label of Elisha Learnard (1765–1827). Learnard worked in Boston from 1796 until his death. Courtesy, H. & R. Sandor, Inc., New Hope, Pa.

sance Revival mode, were made primarily of mahogany or rosewood and branded

C. LEE

An example may be seen at Stanton Hall in Natchez, Mississippi. Ref.: *MAD,* April 1994.

LEE-FRICKER

A birdcage Windsor side chair with medallion back, c. 1805–1815, illustrated in *Antiques Collecting* for March 1978, is branded beneath the seat

LEE-FRICKER

Although the chair is attributed to Philadelphia, nothing is known of the individual (or individuals) whose name appears on it.

LEIGH, JOHN E.

The turner John E. Leigh of Trenton, New Jersey, is known for a relatively crude Windsor continuous-arm chair with writing board, which is said to have been labeled

**John E. Leigh/Cabinet-maker/
107 Factory Street/Trenton, N.J.**

The piece has been dated c. 1785. Refs.: Bjerkoe; *Antiques,* September 1955.

LEMON, CHARLES & JOHN

The brothers Charles and John Lemon were cabinetmakers working on Court Street in Salem, Massachusetts, c. 1795–1800. They are known for a Sheraton mahogany sofa with bulbous, reeded legs, which is inscribed on the frame in chalk

C and J Lemon/Salem

John Lemon was still working, on Bridge Street, Salem, in 1806. Ref.: Bjerkoe.

LEONARD

A Federal inlaid mahogany lady's desk, attributed to Salem, Massachusetts, c. 1780–1790, illustrated in the *Bee* for December 3, 1993, is signed on the back in chalk

Leonard

It is not known if this is the maker's or an owner's name.

LETCHWORTH, JOHN

The highly productive Philadelphia turner John Letchworth (1759–1843) produced a wide variety of Windsors from his shops on Third and Fourth streets during the period 1784–1807. He then moved to Chester County and pursued a career as an itinerant Quaker preacher. Letchworth's chairs were branded

I. LETCHWORTH

and included settees; bow-back, rod-back, and comb-back side chairs; and high chairs. Arms, where present, were often of mahogany. Refs.: Fairbanks and Bates; Hornor.

LEWIS, C.

A braced comb-back Windsor armchair, c. 1780–1790, illustrated in *Antiques* for November 1974, is branded beneath the seat

C. LEWIS

Santore lists the same mark as appearing on a rod-back chair. Nothing further is known of the maker (or owner) of these chairs. Ref.: Santore II.

LEWIS, H.

A c. 1790–1810 mahogany Pembroke table with figural inlay and reeded legs that was sold at auction on July 6, 1994, was signed

Photograph of Charles P. Limbert
(1854–1923), founder of the Charles P.
Limbert Furniture Company. Courtesy, the
Henry Ford Museum, Dearborn, Mich.

H. Lewis

It is attributed to the Portsmouth area. It is not
known if this is a cabinetmaker's mark, although at least one cabinetmaker named Lewis
was working in New Hampshire during this
period. Ref.: *Bee*, July 6, 1994.

Oak Arts and Crafts side chair marked by
the Charles P. Limbert Company, Grand
Rapids and Holland, Michigan,
c. 1902–1922. Private collection.

LIBBY, FRANKLIN

The Shaker brother Franklin Libby (1870–
1899), of the Alfred, Maine, community,
is known for a mahogany sewing chest inscribed

**Bilt by Brother Frank Libby/
Alfred, Maine/1894**

Refs.: Rieman and Burks; *MAD*, September
1994.

LIBBY, WILLIAM

An early-nineteenth-century cherry tilt-top
table, illustrated in *MAD* for March
1976, is stamped three times

WL

It is attributed to William Libby, who was listed as a cabinetmaker in the Shaker community at Canterbury, New Hampshire. Ref.: Edward Deming Andrews and Faith Andrews, *Shaker Furniture* (New Haven: Yale University Press, 1937).

LIMBERT, CHARLES P., COMPANY

The Charles P. Limbert Company, active in Grand Rapids and Holland, Michigan, c. 1902–1922, produced a vast quantity of furniture, not only in the Arts and Crafts style for which they are widely known but also in various traditional or colonial revival modes. Their oak Arts and Crafts or "Mission" furniture is branded with a figure of a man planing a piece of wood and the words

**LIMBERTs/ARTS & CRAFTS/
FURNITURE/MADE IN/GRAND RAPIDS/
AND HOLLAND**

The founder of the firm, Charles P. Limbert (1854–1923), was a furniture salesman, but he went into manufacturing in 1890 and after several false starts established himself in the trade. By 1902 he was employing 200 men. Following his death the firm was continued under the Limbert name until 1944. Ref.: *The Herald* [Dearborn, Mich.: Edison Institute], October 1976.

LINCOLN, THOMAS

Thomas Lincoln (1778–1851), father of President Abraham Lincoln, was a carpenter and cabinetmaker known for a group of blind-door corner cupboards, one of which, in walnut, is incised

T. L./1814

and was made in Hardin County, Kentucky,

before the Lincoln family's move to Indiana in 1816. Refs.: Bjerkoe; *Antiques,* February 1964.

LIND, CONRAD

The Lancaster, Pennsylvania, cabinetmaker Conrad Lind (1753–1834) is known for a c. 1770–1790 Chippendale walnut slant-front desk with shell-carved prospect door, which is signed in pencil within a drawer

Conrad/Lind

There is also a small walnut document box with bracket feet, dated c. 1775–1790, which is inscribed

Conrad Lind

More problematic is a magnificent Chippendale cherry high chest of drawers or highboy, dating c. 1780–1800, which is inscribed in red chalk within a drawer

Lind

This piece has certain stylistic affinities to the signed Conrad Lind pieces but could also be by another of the Lind family cabinetmakers. Refs.: *Antiques,* May 1975, May 1984.

LITTLE, ARTHUR

A c. 1790–1810 Federal mahogany serpentine-front sideboard in a private collection is impressed several times

ARTHUR LITTLE

This is thought to be an owner's brand, as no maker by this name is presently known. Ref.: *Antiques,* January 1968.

LITTLE, WILLIAM

William Little (1775–1848) arrived in North Carolina from England in 1799, settling a year later in Sneedsborough on the Pee Dee River, where he married well and was able to retire from business in 1817. He has left a fair number of pieces in the Chippendale and Federal styles, including an inlaid Federal desk and bookcase or secretary, which is branded

W L

Refs.: Bjerkoe; Fitzgerald.

LIVINGSTON, HORACE

The successful Vermont cabinetmaker Horace Livingston (1798–1877) was active in St. Albans by 1825, continuing there in various partnerships until at least 1860. An 1831 advertisement indicated a wide range of products, including secretaries, bedsteads, chairs, washstands, and a variety of tables. Of all this, the only presently known marked example is a bureau marked

H.Livingston/St.Albans

It is in a private collection. Ref.: Robinson.

LIVINGSTON, JOHN K.

A painted and decorated chest of drawers dated 1874 is said to have borne the signature of the Soap Hollow, Johnstown, Pennsylvania, maker John K. Livingston (1842–1917). Ref.: *Antiques,* May 1983.

LIVINGSTON, TOBIAS

A painted and decorated chest of drawers inscribed

Cherry Hepplewhite chest of drawers with satinwood line and fan inlay signed and dated 1807 by William Lloyd of Springfield, Massachusetts. Courtesy, Maria and Peter Warren Antiques, Inc., Southport, Conn.

1853/Manufactured by T.L.

is attributed to the Soap Hollow, Johnstown, Pennsylvania, carpenter Tobias Livingston (1829–1891). Ref.: *Antiques,* May 1983.

LLOYD, WILLIAM

The Massachusetts cabinetmaker William Lloyd (1779–1845) was in business in Springfield as early as 1802, when he both placed advertisements in a local paper and made for the Carew family two pieces of Federal furniture: an inlaid cherry oval table

Windsor continuous-arm chair in mixed woods labeled by the turner Henry Lock, working in New York City, c. 1790–1795. Private collection.

inscribed

> William Lloyde, cabinetmaker of
> Springfield, January, 1802

and a cherry chest of drawers with French feet, which is similarly signed

> William Lloyde, cabinetmaker of
> Springfield, April, 1802

From the same period is a Federal serpentine-front sideboard, which is inscribed simply

> **William Lloyde**

There is also, in a private collection, a Federal cherry desk and bookcase signed and dated

> **William Lloyde/Luther Bliss/1804**

and a miniature Federal blanket chest over drawers in mahogany and satinwood, which is signed

> **Wm Lloyde/Cabinetmaker/Feb 16/1807**

By 1805, however, Lloyd had a label, a printed oval reading,

> **AT THE/Head of the Ferry,/Springfield, Ms./WILLIAM LLOYDE,/Manufactures all kinds of Cabinet Work./Where may be had—Elegant Clock/Cases, Book-Cases, Desks,/Bureaus, Card-Tables,/ Dining-Tables, &c.**

This uncommon mark may be found on a rectangular-top cherry card table dated 1805 and within a Federal clock case.

In 1811 Lloyd commissioned a much more elaborate engraved label, one that may be found on the majority of the three dozen or so known pieces (including bureaus, tables, sideboards, and clock cases) from his hand. The label form generally found is illustrated with a Federal sideboard, card table, and chest of drawers or bureau and reads,

> William Lloyd,/Cabinetmaker,/
> ACQUAINTS the public and his cus-/tomers,/that he carries on the Cabinet-Making Busi-/ness half a mile north of the Meeting-House/in Springfield, where may be had all kinds of/CHERRY and MAHOGANY WORK,/as low as at any shop in the country. Those who/please to favor him with their custom may de-/pend on having their work done with neatness/and dispatch./Country produce taken in payment, or approv-/ed credit if desired./Springfield Feb. 16, 1811.

While this is the usual form of label found, it is not complete. A lower portion reading,

> **N.B. All Sorts of CHAIRS made as low as/at any shop in town—price from 7 to 9 dol-/lars per set,/Old Chairs mended.**

is usually torn from the whole. It is not known why this is, but it is likely that Lloyd was not a chairmaker. An 1807 ad refers to his having ". . . just received a handsome assortment of dining, fancy and armed CHAIRS. . . ." Perhaps he decided to get out of this line of business. In any case, Lloyd's ads continued in the Springfield papers until 1815, then ceased. Nothing is known of his subsequent career other than that he suffered financial reverses and had to mortgage property. Ref.: *Springfield Furniture, 1700–1850* (Springfield, Mass.: Connecticut Valley Historical Museum, 1990).

LOCK, HENRY

The Manhattan turner Henry Lock is known for a mixed-woods Windsor continuous-arm chair, c. 1790–1795, that is labeled

ALL KINDS OF/WINDSOR CHAIRS & SETTEES,/MADE BY/HENRY LOCK,/ No. 3 CATHERINE-STREET, above the TEA-WATER/PUMP,/NEW YORK, July 1, 1790.

Label of Henry Lock pasted to the underside of the Windsor continuous-arm chair. Private collection.

This example was illustrated in *Antiques* for May 1982.

LOMIS & PELTON

A tall clock case at the Albany Institute of History and Art in Albany, New York, bears the engraved label of the obscure firm of Lansingburgh, New York, cabinetmakers Lomis & Pelton. Featuring illustrations of what appear to be a Federal slant-front desk and a Chippendale secretary-bookcase and drop-leaf dining table, it reads,

ALL KINDS of/CABINET WORK/ neatly and well made by/LOMIS & PEL-TON/LANSINGBURGH

The clock case is dated c. 1795–1800. The Lomis is quite likely Simeon Loomis (1767–

Chippendale mahogany open-arm chair marked by William Long, a Philadelphia craftsman who had a shop on Union Street, c. 1770–1780. Courtesy, Leigh Keno, New York.

1865, see his entry), an East Windsor, Connecticut, cabinetmaker recorded as being in Lansingburgh, c. 1794–1800. Refs.: *New York Furniture Before 1840* (Albany: Albany Institute of History and Art, 1962); *MAD,* January 1994.

LONG, JONATHAN

A walnut chest of drawers inlaid in cherry, in a private collection, is inscribed in red crayon on the backboards

Jonathan 1832

and is attributed to Jonathan Long (1803–1858), who was apprenticed to the Davidson County, North Carolina, cabinetmaker John Swisegood (see his entry) in 1820 and later worked for him as a journeyman as well as possibly having his own shop in Davidson County. Ref.: *The Swisegood School of Cabinetmakers* (Winston-Salem, N.C.: Museum of Early Southern Decorative Arts, 1973).

LONG, WILLIAM

Chippendale mahogany open-arm chair and a side chair, both in private collec-

tions, dating c. 1770-1780, are impressed

Wm LONG

William Long was a Philadelphia craftsman with a shop on Union Street who described himself in advertisements in the *Pennsylvania Packet* as a ". . . Cabinet-Maker and Carver from London. . . ."

LOOMIS, ASA

Though two bureaus of his manufacture, both signed and dated 1816, are in private collections, little is known of the Vermont cabinetmaker Asa Loomis (1793–1868). He was working in Arlington in 1820, but by 1830 he had returned to his native town of Shaftsbury, where he worked into the 1840s. Ref.: Robinson.

LOOMIS, DANIEL

A Federal cherry and maple chest of drawers made by the cabinetmaker Daniel Loomis (1798–1833) is inscribed

Made by Daniel Loomis/Shaftsbury/
In the County of Bennington/
March 18th 1817 A D/Made up on Honor

The phrase "Made up on Honor" would suggest that Loomis, who worked in Shaftsbury, Vermont, c. 1817–1830, sold this piece on credit. There is also a table in a private collection inscribed

R&D LOOMIS & CO./Shaftsbury

indicating a partnership between Daniel (who was a brother of Asa Loomis [see his entry]) and his father, Russell. Ref.: Robinson.

Impressed stamp of William Long on the Chippendale open-arm chair. Courtesy, Leigh Keno, New York.

Federal gilded mirror with eglomise panel made by the looking glass manufacturer Stillman Lothrop, active in Salem, Massachusetts, and, from 1806 through 1831, on Market Street in Boston. Courtesy, Israel Sack, Inc., New York.

LOOMIS, SAMUEL

One of the more important Connecticut cabinetmakers, Samuel Loomis (1748–1814) was born in Colchester and is thought to have apprenticed or worked there with Benjamin Burnham (see his entry). A 1769 Chippendale mahogany block-front slant-front desk from Colchester is signed

Lomis

Sometime after 1800 Loomis moved to Essex, Connecticut, operating a shop there until his death in 1814. Ref.: *Connecticut Historical Society Bulletin,* July 1963.

LOOMIS, SIMEON

The cabinetmaker Simeon Loomis (1767–1865) is known for a c. 1790–1795 Chippendale high chest of drawers or highboy, which is signed on the upper case backboard

Simeon Loomis

Loomis worked in East Windsor, Connecticut, c. 1790–1795 and again after 1800. Ref.: *MAD,* January 1994.

LOOMIS, TIMOTHY, III

Another member of the Loomis family of cabinetmakers, Timothy Loomis III of East Windsor, Connecticut, is credited with a fragmentary Queen Anne high chest of drawers or highboy, which is inscribed on the backboards

T. L./ 1753

Ref.: *MAD,* January 1994.

LORD, ERASTUS A.

Erastus A. Lord (1792–1860) of Litchfield, Connecticut, was a maker of pocket books who, c. 1823, advertised ". . . Ladies & Gentlemens DRESSING CASES—Ladies WORK CASES. . . ." A miniature leather-covered maple and pine chest inscribed in pencil

Made by Erastus A. Lord in/1817

may be one of these. It is quite possible that Lord did not make the chest but only covered it with leather. The chest is owned by the Litchfield Historical Society.

LOTHROP, EDWARD

Ac. 1800–1820 gilded Sheraton looking glass with reverse-painted panel bears a lengthy label reading,
LOOKING-GLASSES CHEAP/EDWARD LOTHROP,/At his Old Stand No. 28 Court-Street,/BOSTON,/. . . Near Concert-Hall . . ./CONTINUES to manufacture Elegant Burnished/GILT LOOK-ING-GLASSES,/Executed in the best

manner, under his immediate in-/spection, which will be found (we need not say) vastly/superior to those that are urged upon the Public every/day at Auction, and by others not acquainted with the/trade. ALSO . . . On Hand at all Times,/A good supply of low-priced Gilt & Mahogany-/framed/GLASSES/Well-suited to the Country Market; which will be sold/extremely Cheap./Traders from the Country, who buy to sell again, have/found and, we trust, will still find it for their interest/to call as above; where they will find good Stock, and/carefully packed up for transportation in the best manner./N.B. Looking-Glasses new Framed, together with Portrait Frames, Needlework, and all sorts of Pictures,/for a reasonable compensation.

It is not known how long Lothrop remained in business in Boston. Ref.: Helen Comstock, *The Looking Glass in America, 1700–1825* (New York: Viking Press, 1964).

LOTHROP, STILLMAN

The gilder and looking glass manufacturer Stillman Lothrop worked in Salem, Massachusetts, before moving in 1806 to Boston, where he had a shop on Market Street until 1831. Although a substantial number of gilded Federal looking glasses bearing the label of

Label of George Dean of Salem, Massachusetts, on the Stillman Lothrop Federal mirror. Dean was a silver and watch dealer. Labels by craftsmen's agents are rare. Courtesy, Israel Sack, Inc., New York.

Lothrop's Salem agent, George Dean (a silver and watch dealer), exist, I know of only one with Lothrop's own (partial) label. It reads,

Looking-Glaffes and Burnifh-Gilding/STILLMAN LOTHROP/RESPECTFULLY informs his friends and the pub-/lic that he has taken a shop in Court-Street nearly oppo/site Concert-Hall, BOSTON, where . . . the seve-/eral . . . Burnish-Gilding . . . Tablet-Paint-/ing . . . Frames, &c. . . . . ./September, 1806

A Federal dressing table bearing Lothrop's label is known, but it is almost certainly by John Doggett (see his entry), who billed Lothrop for toilet tables in 1806, or some other area cabinetmaker. Ref.: *Antiques,* May 1976.

LOVE, BENJAMIN

Santore attributes a Windsor chair branded
B. LOVE
to a turner named Benjamin Love working in Philadelphia, c. 1783–1802. Ref.: Santore II.

LOVE, OSCAR

A walnut and poplar food or pie safe with punched-tin panels bearing a "tree of life" motif, cross of David, and the initials
O Love/1858
is attributed to Oscar Love of Love's Mill, Washington County, Virginia. Love and his father, Leonidas, produced a substantial number of similar pieces during the 1850s and '60s. Ref.: *Antiques,* September 1984.

LOVE, WILLIAM

The Windsor chair maker William Love, working in Philadelphia on North Front and North Second streets, c. 1793–1806, is credited with several Windsors branded beneath the seat
W. LOVE
Ref.: Santore II.

LOW, ALEXANDER

The Scotsman Alexander Low (1741–1836) came to Freehold, New Jersey, in 1744 and established a shop on West Main Street, where he worked for many years producing furniture and clock cases in Chippendale, Federal, and Empire styles. Some examples were initialed
A L
while others were fully signed
Alexander Low
Refs.: *Antiques,* October 1958, September 1960.

LOWERY, WILLIAM

An unusual cherry miniature architectural chest of drawers with molded ogee feet and maple inlay is branded three times
W. LOWERY
It is attributed to the Nelson County, Kentucky, cabinetmaker William Lowery and is dated 1809. Lowery is thought to have worked in Philadelphia around 1800. Ref.: Schiffer.

LUDWIG, LOUI

A Victorian walnut chest of drawers from Texas is inscribed in pencil on the top
Ludwig/Loui C M/Right Side
This appears to be a cabinetmaker's notation, but nothing is known of the craftsman. Ref.: *Antiques,* May 1974.

LUKER, JOHN

A carved and painted pine and maple Masonic Worshipful Master's Chair now at the Museum of Our National Heritage, Lexington, Massachusetts, is inscribed on a stretcher

Manufact'd by JOHN LUKER

It was made, c. 1867–1871, in Swan Township, Vinton County, Ohio, for J. H. M. Houston, master of the local Masonic Lodge at the time. His name also appears on the chair. Nothing is known of John Luker. Refs.: Bishop; Fairbanks and Bates.

LUTZ, IGNATIUS

The Philadelphia cabinetmaker Ignatius Lutz had a shop on Eleventh Street from 1844 until at least 1860. He is described in 1859 as having fifty employees and utilizing lamination in furniture construction. A Victorian Renaissance Revival marble-top sideboard in oak and poplar is stenciled

**FROM/I. LUTZ'/CABINET WARE-
HOUSE/No. 121 S. 11th St./PHIL**

Ref.: *Antiques,* February 1974.

LYELL, FENWICK

The cabinetmaker Fenwick Lyell (1767–1822) was born in Monmouth County, New Jersey but by 1798 was working in New York City at 46 Beaver Street. He remained there at least until 1806. A partial label on a Hepplewhite inlaid mahogany Pembroke table, illustrated in *Antiques* for August 1975, reads,

**FENWICK LYELL,/. . . and
Chair-Maker,/. . . . . Beaver-Street,/
NEW YORK./. . . . . . . ANTED.**

LYON, JULIUS S.

A miniature Sheraton chest of drawers in mahogany with drawer fronts of bird's-eye maple is inscribed within a drawer

Julius S. Lyon/1815 July 12/Sterling, Mass.

The piece is in a private collection, and nothing further has been learned about Lyon. Ref.: *Antiques,* April 1940.

LYON & WEED

The Mount Lebanon, New York, Shaker brothers Benjamin Lyon (1780–1870) and Charles Weed (1831–left the community 1862) collaborated in the construction of a mixed-woods work counter, which is inscribed in pencil

**made Feby 1860 by Benjamin Lyon and
Charles Weed**

Ref.: Rieman and Burks.

M

MACBRIDE, WALTER

The well-known New York City turner Walter MacBride produced a substantial number of Windsors, primarily braced bow-back side chairs and braced continuous-arm chairs, all of which were branded

W. MACBRIDE/N.YORK

He was in business at various locations in Manhattan, c. 1792–1797. Examples of his work are at the Chicago Art Institute and the New York State Museum. Refs.: Scherer; *Antiques,* May 1981.

MACKLE, R.

A c. 1770–1780 Chippendale mahogany commode chair or "necessary," illustrated in *Antiques* for June 1963, is marked

R. MACKLE BALTMORE

Although it seems likely that this is the name of a Baltimore chairmaker, nothing further has been learned of its origin.

MACY, JOSIAH

A Windsor chair branded on the bottom
JOSIAH MACY
is attributed by Santore to a Hudson, New York, turner, working c. 1805–1815. Ref.: Santore II.

MADISON, THOMAS

A country Federal painted and decorated blanket chest over drawers, c. 1820–1850, illustrated in *MAD* for October 1979, is signed

Thomas Madison

a name we cannot presently associate with a known cabinetmaker.

MAERKLIN, HERMANN A. W.

The German-born cabinetmaker and upholsterer Hermann A. W. Maerklin (1826–1921) established himself in Hartford, Connecticut, in 1853, remaining active there until

Windsor braced continuous-arm chair and side chair, both branded by the New York City turner Walter MacBride, active c. 1792–1797. Courtesy, Bernard and S. Dean Levy, Inc., New York.

Detail of the brand of Walter MacBride as it appears on the undersides of the seats of the Windsor arm and side chairs. Courtesy, Bernard and S. Dean Levy, Inc., New York.

he retired in 1911. Primarily an upholsterer, Maerklin usually bought his chair and sofa frames from local cabinetmakers. However, before 1875 he made his own frames, and one of these, for a Victorian Renaissance Revival walnut smoking chair, is signed in black paint

H. Maerklin

Ref.: *Furniture* (Boston: Society for the Preservation of New England Antiquities, 1987).

MAGEE, JOHN

A Federal inlaid walnut slant-front desk with French feet in a private collection is signed on the back of the apron

John Magee 1819

The piece is attributed to John Magee, a cabinetmaker active in Marietta, Ohio, c. 1815–1825.

MAGOWIN, J.

A bamboo-turned, birdcage Windsor side chair, c. 1810–1830, offered at the Bourne Auction in Massachusetts, July 29, 1975, is

Federal inlaid walnut slant-front desk signed and dated by the Marietta, Ohio, cabinetmaker John Magee, working c. 1815–1825. Private collection.

Detail, incised signature of John Magee and the date "1819" on the Federal slant-front desk. Private collection.

stamped beneath the seat
J. MAGOWIN
It is not known if this is the mark of the maker or an owner.

MAHONEY, E. H.

A late Victorian Gothic Revival or "Modern Gothic" folding chair in walnut with textile tapestry seat bears a paper label reading,
Pat. Oct 18, 1875/Mfd. by/E.H. Mahoney/96 Cross Street, Boston
Mahoney is thought to have been in business for a relatively short period of time, and his marked work is uncommon.

Walnut Victorian Modern Gothic folding chair with tapestry seat, c. 1875–1880, with the label of E. H. Mahoney, who worked on Cross Street in Boston. Courtesy, the Smithsonian Institution.

MALLARD, EPHRIAM

A very attractive c. 1790–1800 birch drop-front chest of drawers, inlaid in mahogany and bird's-eye maple, is inscribed
Ephriam Mallard/New Hampshire
and is attributed to the cabinetmaker of that name who worked in Gilmanton, New Hampshire. Mallard is also credited with a c. 1800–1810 Federal apple and birch tall clock case signed
E. Mallard
Refs.: *Antiques,* May 1974, May 1988.

MANNING, GILBERT S.

A Victorian Renaissance Revival walnut work or toilet stand in a private collection bears the printed label

Label of Gilbert S. Manning within the Victorian Renaissance Revival work or toilet stand, showing the 1873 patent date.

Private collection.

LADY'S/Work and Toilet Stand/Patented June 3rd, 1873,/BY G.S. MANNING, DANVILLE, ILLINOIS

Because no maker's name is listed, it is likely that Manning was both the patentee and the manufacturer of this piece.

MAPPS

A New York or New England banister-back armchair, c. 1770–1810, illustrated in *Antiques* for September 1952, is branded

MAPPS

which is thought to be an owner's rather than the maker's mark

Victorian Renaissance Revival walnut work or toilet stand, c. 1873–1875, with the label of Gilbert S. Manning of Danville, Illinois.

Private collection.

MARBLE & SHATTUCK

A set of oak dining chairs (arm and side chairs) with rush seats and slat backs are labeled

The Marble & Shattuck/ Chair Co./Cleveland, O.

The chairs, in a private collection, date c. 1900–1915. Nothing is presently known of the manufacturer.

MARKS A. F. CHAIR COMPANY

A Victorian walnut and iron adjustable invalid's chair in a private collection is stenciled

**M'F'D BY MARKS A.F. CHAIR CO.
LTD./850 Broadway, N.Y./
PAT'D FEB 1st 1876**

while a similar example at the Henry Ford Museum is stenciled

**Sole M'frs./Marks A.F. Chair Co.
Limited/930 B'way/Pat. Feb' 1st 1876**

The chair was patented by Cevedra B. Sheldon of New York City and made by the Marks A. F. Chair Company, c. 1876–1880. As the Marks Adjustable Folding Chair Company, this firm remained in business until 1897. Refs.: Bishop; Scherer.

MARKS, S. H.

P ainted and stencil-decorated c. 1850–1870 Hitchcock-type side chairs bearing the stenciled mark

S.H. MARKS, CANAAN N.Y.

are thought to have been made at a small factory in the Columbia County community. Ref.: Kenney.

MARLEN, WILLIAM

A Federal mahogany and mahogany veneer linen press with a Charleston, South

Victorian walnut and iron adjustable invalid's chair, c. 1876–1880, made and sold by Marks A. F. Chair Company, 850 Broadway, New York City. Courtesy, the Henry Ford Museum, Dearborn, Mich.

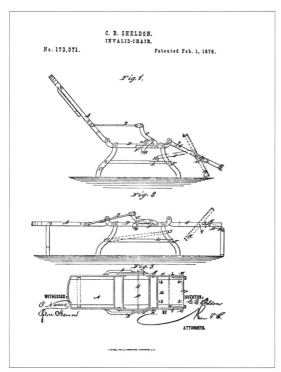

Patent drawing, dated 1876, for the Marks A. F. Chair Company invalid's chair. The inventor, Cevedra B. Sheldon, assigned his rights to the manufacturer. Courtesy, the Henry Ford Museum, Dearborn, Mich.

Carolina, history is inscribed

William Marlen, May 23, 1811

Marlen is listed as a cabinetmaker in the Charleston directories for 1803, 1807, and 1809. Refs.: Bjerkoe; *MAD,* January 1994.

MARLOW, JOHN

A Federal cherry slant-front desk in a private collection, illustrated in *Antiques* for March 1962, is inscribed within a secret drawer

Made by John Marlow this 23 day of Novembir 1822 price is

$ 35./Mountvernon Knox County

Nothing is presently known of this Ohio craftsman.

MARSH, CHARLES

Two bamboo-turned birdcage Windsors, a side chair and an armchair, both c. 1810–1830, illustrated in *Antiques* for May 1930, are labeled

CHARLES MARSH/Windsor Chair Maker/No. 57 John Street, New York

Ref.: Bjerkoe.

MARSHALL, D. N., CO.

A paint-decorated sea chest sold at auction in August 1994 was impressed

D.N. MARSHALL CO./DEER ISLE ME.

This is thought to be an owner's name.

MARTIN, EBENEZER

The Marblehead, Massachusetts, cabinetmaker Ebenezer Martin (1735–1800) is credited with two Chippendale walnut and mahogany chests of drawers. One, illustrated in *Antiques* for May 1984, is inscribed on the bottom board

E.M. 1791

while the other, similar chest, owned by the Connecticut Historical Society, is marked

E.M. 1794

Ref.: Fales, *Essex County Furniture.*

MASER, JACOB

The Mahantango Valley, Pennsylvania, craftsman Jacob Maser (1812–1895) produced highly attractive desks, chests, and cupboards of a late Federal form, which were richly

Inscribed name of William Mason and the date August 24, 1829, beneath the lower shelf of the washstand. Courtesy, the Henry Ford Museum, Dearborn, Mich.

decorated with painted birds, flowers, and geometric forms. Among his known works are a slant-top desk inscribed

Jacob Maser 1834

and two high chests of drawers signed respectively

Jacob Maser 1830

and

Jacob Maser 1834

Ref.: Fales, *American Painted Furniture.*

MASON, THOMAS

The Philadelphia turner Thomas Mason (active 1793–1817) made Windsor chairs

Painted and decorated country pine washstand signed and dated by William Mason of Fryeburg, Maine. Mason was either the maker or the decorator. Courtesy, the Henry Ford Museum, Dearborn, Mich.

at several locations in the city, including Vine, Third, and Callowhill streets. Examples of his work are impressed

T. MASON

Ref.: Santore II.

MASON, THOMAS

A group of eight decorated rod- and arrow-back Windsor side and armchairs, illustrated in *Antiques* for August 1977, were described as labeled

Thomas Mason, 46 Milk St., Boston

The chairs would seem to date c. 1820–1840. It is not known if this is the same Thomas Mason who worked in Philadelphia to 1819.

Mᴀsᴏɴ, Wɪʟʟɪᴀᴍ

A painted country pine washstand embellished with floral decoration is inscribed Wm Mason/Fryeburg August/24th/1829 Mason, from Fryeburg, Maine, was either the maker or the decorator of the piece. Ref.: *Antiques & Arts Weekly,* August 26, 1983.

Mᴀsᴏɴ, Wɪʟʟɪᴀᴍ

A very unusual Chippendale walnut and pine chest of drawers with central prospect door is inscribed in ink

Miss Patsey Hobbses Bureau Made by William Mason February the 30th 1808, and is signed

W. Mason

A William Mason was living in Greensville County, Virginia, at this time, but nothing further is known of this cabinetmaker's career. Ref.: *Antiques,* October 1973.

Mᴀᴛᴛᴇsᴏɴ, J.

A paint-decorated two-drawer blanket chest from southern Vermont is inscribed

By J. Matteson/August 1 A.D. 1803
and is thought to be by an early member of the prolific Matteson family of cabinetmakers and decorators that was centered in the Shaftsbury area.

Mᴀᴛᴛᴇsᴏɴ, Tʜᴏᴍᴀs

Another member of the Matteson family of craftsmen, Thomas, is known for two elaborately painted and decorated pieces. A six-board chest owned by the Henry Ford Museum is inscribed on the back in paint

Thomas G. Matison/South

Shaftsbury/V.t/1824
while a blanket chest over drawers in a private collection is signed on the back, also in black paint

Thomas Matteson/ S. Shaftsbury, Vermont/1824
Ref.: Fales, *American Painted Furniture.*

Mᴀxᴡᴇʟʟ, Jᴀᴍᴇs A.

A Classical large tiger maple desk and bookcase or secretary attributed to New York State, c. 1815–1825, is signed

James A. Maxwell
It is not known if Maxwell was an owner or the cabinetmaker.

Mᴀʏ, Sᴀᴍᴜᴇʟ S.

A nursery rocker in the collection of Old Sturbridge Village is said to bear the branded mark of the chairmaker Samuel S. May (1802–1878) of Sterling, Massachusetts. Ref.: *Antiques,* May 1993.

MᴄAɴᴅʀᴇᴡ, Wɪʟʟɪᴀᴍ

A country Sheraton mahogany and cherry sideboard with bird's-eye maple veneer is inscribed within a drawer

Wm McAndrew/Inez and Lewis/Graham/ . . . ain Run/Jan 15, 1820
It is thought that McAndrew was a cabinetmaker, but nothing else is known of him. Ref.: *Antiques,* May 1973.

MᴄCʟᴇᴀɴ, G. C.

Two Federal mahogany and birch sofas are branded on the seat frames
G.C.MC CLEAN

225

and a mahogany and satinwood Pembroke or breakfast table is branded

G. MC CLEAN

All three date c. 1800–1810 and are thought to have been made in northeastern Massachusetts (possibly Newburyport) or Portsmouth, New Hampshire, by an as yet unknown cabinetmaker of that name.

McCombs & Cornelius

The Nashville, Tennessee, cabinetmaker James W. McCombs had a shop at the corner of Spring and Market streets as early as 1818. He continued in business there with various partners until 1850, when he took as partner William Cornelius. They were still working together in 1853. A Gothic Revival walnut sideboard by them is signed in red joiner's crayon

McCombs/C . . . lious

Ref.: Williams and Harsh.

McCormick, S.

Santore attributes a braced fan-back Windsor side chair, which is stamped beneath the seat

S. McCORMICK

to an unknown, c. 1790–1810, Connecticut turner of that name. Ref.: Santore II.

McCracken, William

The important New Orleans cabinetmaker William McCracken (1808–1872) is known for several pieces of Victorian Rococo and Renaissance Revival rosewood furniture, including armoires, beds, and marble-top center tables. McCracken, who was active in New Orleans, c. 1849–1857, seems to have had both a factory and a store. An armoire is labeled

Federal mahogany tall clock case, c. 1800–1810, bearing the handwritten label of the Duck Creek (Smyrna), Delaware, cabinetmaker James McDowell, active 1785–1836.

Courtesy, Israel Sack, Inc., New York.

Detail of the partial label of James McDowell on the Federal tall clock case.

Courtesy, Israel Sack, Inc., New York.

MANUFACTURED BY WM. McCRACKEN/Corner Custom House & Derbigny Sts./Warerooms, 45, 47 & 49 Royal St./NEW ORLEANS

while an apparently earlier center table is simply labeled

MANUFACTURED/By/ WILLIAM McCRACKEN/No. 45 ROYAL STREET/NEW ORLEANS.

Refs.: *Antiques,* May 1981, July 1984.

McDOWELL, JAMES

The Delaware cabinetmaker James Mc-Dowell (working 1785–1836) of Duck Creek Crossroads (Smyrna) is known for several marked pieces of Federal furniture, including a c. 1800–1810 inlaid mahogany bowfront chest of drawers, now at the Historical Society of

Delaware in Wilmington. It is inscribed in ink

James McDowell/Cabinet Maker/
Duck Creek/Delaware

and a Chippendale mahogany tall clock case, c. 1785–1795, with partial label

. . . . sold by James/. . .
McDowell

A much later Sheraton-Empire transitional mahogany veneer sideboard is signed

James
McDowell/Cabinetmaker/Smyrna/
Dela-ware/May 18th, 1822

Ref.: *Plain and Ornamental.*

McDOWELL, JAMES AND DANIEL

James McDowell (working 1785–1836, see previous entry), the Duck Creek Crossroads (Smyrna), Delaware, cabinetmaker, was in partnership from 1793 to 1803 with a kinsman, Daniel McDowell (working 1793–1830), who later had his own shop in the area. Their association resulted in at least one marked piece, a Chippendale mahogany chest of drawers with paper label inscribed

All Work/Made & Sold by James & Daniel McDowell Duck Creek/X Roads Delaware

Ref.: *Antiques,* May 1985.

McDOWELL, JAMES, & SON

During the period 1822–1829, the Smyrna (formerly Duck Creek Crossroads), Delaware, cabinetmaker James McDowell (see his entry) was in partnership with his son, William, a relationship terminated by the latter's death in 1829. An Empire mahogany veneer chest of drawers in a private collection commemorates this partnership. It is inscribed within the case

James McDowell & Son/
Cabinetmaker/Smyrna/Delaware/
Novr 27th 1824

Ref.: *Antiques,* May 1985.

McDOWELL, R. L.

The Virginia craftsman R. L. McDowell is known for four painted softwood pie or food safes, all dating c. 1825–1830. An example, sold at the Cole auction in Red Hook, New York, in March 1994, is signed

R.L. McDowell

These safes all have punched-tin panels featuring a profile of George Washington. Ref.: *Bee,* March 25, 1994.

McELROY, WILLIAM

William McElroy, a turner known to have been working in Chester Township, Burlington County, New Jersey, c. 1798–1805, is credited with a group of Windsors, including a settee, a bow-back armchair, and a bow-back high chair. All are branded beneath the seat

W. McElroy

There is also a bow-back Windsor side chair impressed

Wm. Mc EL

that was sold at auction in 1994. An example of his work is at Winterthur. Ref.: *MAD,* August 1994.

Federal mahogany sofa, signed and dated by Samuel McIntire, a cabinetmaker working in Philadelphia, c. 1800–1805. Private collection.

McEls, Edward F.

Apartial signature scratched on a drawer of a c. 1800–1820 Sheraton cherry and tiger maple chest of drawers appears to read

Edward F. McEls . . . /1821

The full name is not known, nor can it presently be determined if it is of the cabinetmaker or an owner. Ref.: *Antiques,* October 1974.

McGuffin, Robert

ASheraton mahogany serpentine-front sideboard at the Philadelphia Museum of Art is inscribed on a dust panel

Robert McGuffin/Philadelphia/1806

McGuffin was associated, c. 1806–1809, with the well-known Philadelphia cabinetmaker Henry Connelly (see his entry) at a shop in the South Ward. He continued to be listed in the city through 1811. Ref.: *Antiques,* May 1991.

McHugh, Joseph P., & Co.

Joseph P. McHugh, a New York City interior decorator and furniture manufacturer in business since 1878, introduced, in 1894, the first line of mass-produced oak and ash "Mission" or Arts and Crafts furnishings. His firm continued to produce such pieces—including chairs, desks, settees, and cabinets—until World War I. Many pieces bore an embossed brass tag reading,

THE/McHUGH/(MISSION) FURNITURE:/MADE IN NEW YORK.

Ref.: *Bee,* January 14, 1994.

McIntire, Samuel

ASheraton mahogany sofa in a private collection is inscribed in chalk across the crest rail

Sam.l McIntire 1805

It is attributed, on stylistic grounds, to a cabinetmaker by that name who is listed in the 1803 Philadelphia directory rather than to the well-known Samuel McIntire of Salem, Massachusetts, who, although a carver and builder, is generally thought not to have been a cabinetmaker. Ref.: *Antiques,* September 1972.

McKee, James

AFederal mahogany Pembroke table with serpentine top in a private collection is branded on the apron

McKEE

thought to be the mark of the Manhattan cabinetmaker James McKee, who is listed in the 1797 New York City directory as having a shop at 47 Warren Street. Ref.: *Antiques,* June 1966.

McKeldin, Sinclair

An unusual Empire dressing stand with mirror in mahogany veneer over pine and poplar is signed in pencil

Sinclair McKeldin October 1835 Maker

The c. 1830–1840 piece is thought to have been made in Middle Tennessee by the named cabinetmaker. Ref.: Williams and Harsh.

McKim, Andrew and Robert

The Richmond, Virginia, turners Andrew and Robert McKim, active c. 1790–1819, are credited with several Windsor chairs, including bamboo-turned bow-backs and a square-back writing-arm chair. These bear the printed paper label

ANDw. & ROBt. M'KIM,/Windfor Chair-Makers/NEAR THE POST OFFICE,/RICHMOND.

One such label is also dated in ink "1802." There is also, however, a bow-back Windsor side chair of earlier form (c. 1790–1800) with a partial label reading,

Andrew & Robert McKimm,/makes . . ./ WINDSOR CHAIRS/in the neateft and beft manner at their/Chair Shop near . . ./ RICHMOND

Refs.: Santore II; Robert H. Burroughs, *Southern Antiques* (New York: Bonanza Books, 1981).

McKim, Robert

At some point before 1819, the Richmond, Virginia, chairmaker Robert McKim's partnership with Andrew McKim (see previous entry) apparently was terminated. There is a bow-back Windsor side chair said to bear the label of

ROBERT McKIM/ Windsor Chair Maker/ . . . . Post Office/RICHMOND

Robert McKim is listed alone as a chairmaker in the 1819 Richmond directory. However, I find this label questionable, because the chair bearing it, pictured in *Antiques* for January 1952, appears identical to the one labeled by the McKims that was illustrated in *Antiques* for January 1973, and the form is much earlier than 1819.

McKINNEY BROS. & CO.

A country Victorian walnut plantation desk, dating c. 1850–1860, is stenciled on the back

Mc.K.B.& CO.

and is attributed to James F. McKinney and his brother, J. W. McKinney, who had a furniture outlet at 192 Main Street in Memphis, Tennessee, c. 1850–1860. It is likely that the McKinneys were merchants rather than manufacturers. Ref.: Williams and Harsh.

McKNIGHT, STANLEY

A set of four painted and decorated c. 1830–1850 half-spindle side chairs are inscribed beneath the seats

Stanley McKnight/West Acton, Mass.

This could be the name of an owner or a chair turner. Ref.: *Bee,* August 26, 1994.

McMILLIAN, JAMES

A bombé desk and bookcase or secretary is said to bear the label of James McMillian or McMillan, a Boston cabinetmaker who died in 1769. Refs.: Bjerkoe; *Boston Furniture of the Eighteenth Century* (Boston: Publications of the Colonial Society of Massachusetts, 1974).

McNEMAR, LEVI

The Shaker brother and cabinetmaker Levi McNemar (1793–1866), a member of the Union Village, Ohio, community, is known for a pine and cherry chest of drawers, which is signed in chalk

L. McNemar

and dated in pencil

March 4th 1841

Refs.: Rieman and Burks; Jean M. Burks, *Documented Furniture: An Introduction to the Collections* (Canterbury, N.H.: Canterbury Shaker Village, 1989).

McNIGHT, STANLEY

A c. 1830–1850 painted and decorated half-spindle side chair in a private collection is signed on the underside of the seat

Stanley McNight/West Acton, MA.

No cabinetmaker of this name is currently known. West Acton is a small community near Boston.

MEACHAM, JOSEPH

The Shaker spiritual leader Joseph Meacham (1742–1796), of Enfield, Connecticut, is said to have made and signed a small chest of drawers once owned by Faith Andrews and Edward Deming Andrews and illustrated in *Antiques* for January 1939.

MEADER, DANIEL FITCH

Daniel Fitch Meader (1801–1877) was born in Baltimore and came in 1824 to Cincinnati, Ohio, where, after several other business ventures, he opened in 1847 the Steam Bureau Factory at Front and Smith streets. The firm continued under various names until Meader's death and thereafter into the 1880s under the guidance of his son, Joseph F. Meader. Chairs and tables stenciled

D.F. MEADER & CO./Furniture/

Painted half-spindle side chair c. 1830–1850 signed beneath the seat Stanley McKnight/West Acton, Mass. The form is typical of New England, but at present no turner by this name has been located in West Acton, a community just west of Boston. Courtesy, Curran & Curran, Ltd.

MANUFACTURERS/COR SMITH &/ FRONT ST./CINCINNATTI. O. may be dated c. 1850–1870. Ref.: Sikes.

MEADS, JOHN

The Albany, New York, cabinetmaker John Meads (1777–1859) was born in England, served his apprenticeship (1791–1797) in New York City, and was by 1802 in business in Albany, where he soon opened a shop on Market Street. A Classical mahogany armchair from this early period (c. 1805–1815) is impressed in an oval

J.M./IN A.

which is presumed to stand for "John Meads in Albany." There is also said to be a marked piece reflecting the c. 1802–1808 partnership between Meads and William Randall. From 1827 until 1837, Meads was in partnership with one William Alvord, and a late Sheraton sofa in a private collection is labeled

Made by Meads & Alvord/
Market Street/Albany.

Following Alvord's death, John Meads, Jr., was taken into the firm. After his father's retirement, he continued the business until 1850. Ref.: Randall.

MEADS, JOHN, & CO.

A c. 1835–1845 Empire three-legged mahogany stand at the New York State Museum bears a printed paper label indicating that it is

FROM/MEAD'S/FURNITURE WARE-
HOUSE,/No. 549 Broadway, Albany./
(Near Delavan House.)

After the death in 1837 of his partner William Alvord, John Meads took into partnership his son, John Meads, Jr., and another cabinetmaker, Francis Tows, under the title John Meads & Company. Tows left the firm in 1844, and John Meads, Sr., retired, leaving management of the factory to John Jr. The labeled piece could have been made either during the 1838–1844 partnership or after John Jr. assumed full control in 1844. Refs.: Randall; Scherer.

MEEKS, EDWARD

The Manhattan cabinetmaker Edward Meeks was the brother and business partner, c. 1797–1800, of the well-known Joseph Meeks (see his entry). Presently associated with Edward is a Classical mahogany drop-leaf table,

Stenciled mark of D. F. Meader & Co. of Cincinnati, Ohio, on a c. 1850–1870 chest of drawers. Founded in 1847 by Daniel Fitch Meader (1801–1877), this firm remained in business into the 1880s. Private collection.

which is inscribed in chalk

E. M. 7

The piece has a Meeks family history; however, it appears to date c. 1815–1825, and Edward vanished from the Manhattan directory in 1806. It is also possible that the piece is late enough to be attributed to an Edward J. Meeks (possible son of Edward), who appears as a cabinetmaker in Manhattan directories from 1843 until 1874. This thesis is supported by the existence of an Empire mahogany dining table signed in chalk

E. Meeks

Refs.: *Antiques,* April 1964, July 1966, May 1976.

MEEKS, JOHN AND JOSEPH W.

Before 1836 the Manhattan cabinetmaker Joseph Meeks (1771–1868) turned his prosperous business over to his sons, John (1801–1875) and Joseph W. (1806–1878). An

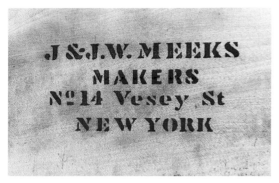

Stenciled mark of John and Joseph W. Meeks on the Classical sofa table. The Meeks brothers were at 14 Vesey Street from 1836 to 1855. Courtesy, Peter Hill, Washington, D.C.

Empire sideboard labeled

**J. & J.W. MEEKS,/CABINETMAKERS/
43 & 45 BROAD STREET,/
NEW-YORK/AND/23 CHARTERS
STREET,/NEW-ORLEANS**

reflects their ascendency to the old Broad Street shop as well as the fact that Joseph had also established a wholesale outlet in New Orleans. Following a disastrous fire in the neighborhood,

the brothers removed their business to Vesey Street and began to use a new label reading,

**J. & J.W. MEEKS,/CABINET
MAKERS,/No.14 VESEY STREET,**
Second door before the/ASTOR HOUSE,/
NEW-YORK/AND 23 CHARTRES
STREET,/NEW-ORLEANS

as well as the stenciled mark

**J. & J.W. MEEKS/MAKERS/
No.14 VESEY ST./NEW YORK**

The firm remained on Vesey Street from 1836 until 1855. Refs.: *Antiques,* April 1964, May 1981.

MEEKS, JOHN, & SON

An Empire mahogany secretary-desk offered at Christie's, October 13, 1984, bears the exceedingly rare stamp of

JOHN MEEKS AND SON/NEW YORK

John Meeks apparently took his son, John Jr. (1835–1889), into the business on Vesey Street around 1855, at which time the partnership between John Sr. and Joseph W. Meeks ceased to appear in the Manhattan directories. John Meeks, Jr., continued the family furniture dynasty until 1868.

MEEKS, JOSEPH, & SONS

Joseph Meeks (1771–1868) had a cabinet shop in Manhattan by 1800, and from 1829 until 1836 he was located at 43–45 Broad Street

Classical mahogany sofa table with the mark of John (1801–1875) and Joseph W. (1806–1878) Meeks, active in New York City, c. 1830–1855. Courtesy, Peter Hill, Washington, D.C.

in partnership with his sons, John (1801–1875) and Joseph W. (1806–1878). An attractive engraved label from this period, featuring a view of the firm's five-story warerooms, reads,

MEEKS & SONS MANUFACTORY/of/CABINET FURNI-TURE/43 & 45 Broad Street/NEW-YORK

Sometime before 1836 Joseph Meeks, who had grown wealthy through his business and real estate investments, retired, leaving the business in his sons' hands. Refs.: *Antiques,* April 1964, July 1966.

MEEKS, JOSEPH W.

Joseph W. Meeks (1806–1878) may have worked alone on Vesey Street in Manhattan (he is listed there in directories from 1838 until 1855) as well as in partnership with his brother, John. An Empire marble-top mahogany bureau with mirror, dating c. 1840–1855, is branded

J.W. MEEKS

The piece is illustrated in *Antiques* for December 1959.

MEISHAHN, C. F., & CO.

A carved mahogany rocking chair in the Chippendale style but dating c. 1875–1885, which is in the collection of the Smithsonian Institution, is labeled

C.F. MEISHAHN & CO., BALTIMORE

It is an example of early Colonial Revival furniture. Ref.: Fitzgerald.

MELLEN, MOSES

The Boston cabinetmaker Moses Mellen was in business at various addresses in the city

Advertisement of Joseph Meeks & Sons, furniture manufacturers on Broad Street in New York City as it appeared in a trade publication from the early 1830s. Private collection.

from 1821 until his retirement in 1853. He has left furniture marked in two ways. A Classical mahogany card table, c. 1820–1830, illustrated in *Antiques* for September 1983, is simply signed

Moses Mellen

while a looking glass, two late Federal chests of drawers, and a sewing table, all in mahogany or mahogany veneer, are stenciled

Bot of MOSES MELLEN/over the City Market, Brattle St./BOSTON

According to local records, Mellen was at this address only during the period 1822–1825. Refs.: *Antiques,* May 1973, May 1976, May 1992.

MERRILL, C. H.

An Empire grain-painted pine bureau or chest of drawers signed on the backboard in pencil

C. H. Merrill, So. Paris

is attributed to a craftsman of that name working in South Paris, Maine, c. 1825–1845. Ref.: *Bee,* August 26, 1983.

MERRILL, W.

A set of six bamboo-turned Windsor side chairs in a private collection bear, beneath their seats, the impressed mark

W. MERRILL

The chairs would date c. 1810–1840, but nothing is known of W. Merrill.

MERRIT, CHARLES

A walnut marble-top chest of drawers in the c. 1850–1880 Victorian Renaissance Revival mode bears beneath the top a paper shipping tag inscribed

Chas. Merrit/Kingston, N.Y.

This is thought to be an owner's name.

MESSINGER, T. H. H.

A Victorian Renaissance Revival walnut lady's desk in a private collection bears an embossed brass nameplate reading,

**MADE BY/T.H.H. MESSINGER/
611 W. FRONT ST./WILMINGTON, DEL.**

The desk would date c. 1860–1880. Nothing is known of the manufacturer.

METCALF, BENJAMIN

The cabinet and musical-instrument maker Benjamin Metcalf (c. 1793–1840) was in business at Woodstock, Vermont, before 1820, continuing there in various partnerships until 1825. His label

**BENJ. METCALF & CO./
Cabinet Makers/Woodstock, Vt.**

(dating to a c. 1820–1823 partnership) appears on two pieces, a washstand and a single-drawer stand, the latter at the Shelburne Museum. Ref.: Robinson.

Victorian Renaissance Revival walnut lady's desk, c. 1860–1880, marked by the maker, T. H. H. Messinger, West Front Street, Wilmington, Delaware. Private collection.

MICHELL, T.

Two pieces of furniture in private collections—a Queen Anne dressing table or lowboy, c. 1740–1770, and a transitional Queen Anne–Chippendale mahogany side chair, c. 1760–1770—are branded

T. MICHELL

It is not known if this is the maker's or an owner's mark. Ref.: *Antiques,* December 1974.

MIDDLETON, JOSEPH

The Annapolis, Maryland, cabinet- and chairmaker Joseph Middleton, active from 1776 until 1794, is known for a c. 1780–1790 Chippendale walnut slant-top desk

bearing an engraved label reading,

JOSEPH MIDDLETON/CABINET & CHAIRMAKER/ANNAPOLIS

Refs.: William Voss Elder III and Lu Bartlett, *John Shaw, Cabinetmaker of Annapolis* (Baltimore: Baltimore Museum of Art, 1983); *Antiques,* February 1977.

MIDDLETON, WILLIAM

A Queen Anne cherry high chest of drawers or highboy with Chippendale features and dating c. 1770–1780 is initialed

W/M

in paint on the upper-case backboard. It is attributed to the Suffield, Connecticut, carpenter and furniture maker William Middleton (d. 1820). Ref.: *Antiques,* June 1960.

MILLER, ———

A late-Victorian walnut and bird's-eye maple writing desk offered at auction in February 1995 was signed

Miller 1888/Monkton, Vt.

Though several Millers worked as cabinetmakers in Vermont, the author of this piece remains unidentified. Ref.: *Bee,* February 3, 1995.

MILLER, GEORGE W.

The Manhattan cabinetmaker George W. Miller is listed in the New York City directories from 1821 until 1831. His earliest location, from 1822 through 1824, was at 5 Division

Victorian Renaissance Revival walnut lift-top work or sewing table marked "I. Miller/October 7, 1865." Private collection.

Street. A Classical mahogany drop-leaf table with rope-turned legs from this period is stamped

GEORGE W. MILLER/
5 Division Street, N.Y.

During the period 1825–1827, he was at 59 Division Street, and a carved mahogany chest of drawers owned by the Marine Historical Association of Mystic, Connecticut, is marked

GEO. W. MILLER,/CABINET MAKER/
-59-/DIVISION ST./N.Y.

From 1828 until 1831 Miller's shop was located on Broad Street. Several pieces of Empire mahogany furniture, including a work-table, side table, and stencil-decorated card table, are stenciled

GEO. W. MILLER,/
Cabinet Chair & Sofa/Ware House/
No. 64 Broad Street/New-York

Refs.: *Antiques,* January 1972, May 1973, November 1973.

MILLER, I.

A Victorian Renaissance Revival walnut lift-top work or sewing table in a private collection is inscribed in pencil on a drawer bottom

I. Miller/October 7, 1865

It is not known if this is the mark of an owner or the maker.

MILLER, IRA

A mixed-woods marquetry-decorated one-drawer stand sold at auction in 1993 is signed

Ira Miller, 1919, New Market, Ohio

It is the work of a skilled carpenter or home craftsman, not a cabinetmaker. Ref.: *MAD,* May 1994.

MILLIGAN, RICHARD ALEXANDER

The Shaker craftsman Richard Alexander Milligan (b. 1849) was a member of the Pleasant Hill, Kentucky, community. He is known for a walnut cupboard mounted on table in the manner of a plantation desk. The piece has pronounced Victorian characteristics and is inscribed in ink within a drawer

Made March 7th/1879/R.A.
Milligan/Pleasant Hill/Mercer
Co./Kentucky/for S.L. Boisseau/East Family

The piece is at Shaker Village of Pleasant Hill, Harrodsburg, Kentucky. There is also, in a private collection, a table marked

Table Made Sept. 28th 1874 R.A. Milligan

Ref.: Rieman and Burks.

MILLS & DEMING

The firm of William Mills and Simeon Deming (1769–1855, see his entry) was in business on Queen (later Pearl) Street in Manhattan from 1793 until 1798. They are best known for a spectacular Federal mahogany sideboard inlaid with swag and tassel decoration, which was made for Gov. Oliver Wolcott of Connecticut. It and a mahogany and bird's-eye maple Federal tambour desk in a private collection are labeled

Mills & Deming,/No. 374 Queen ſtreet,
two doors above the Friends
Meeting,/NEW-YORK/Makes and ſells all
kinds of Cabinet Furni-/ture and Chairs,
after the moſt modern faſhions/. . . on
reasonable terms.

Refs.: Bjerkoe; Fairbanks and Bates.

Stenciled mark of the
Cincinnati, Ohio, chair and
bedstead maker John
Mitchell (1813–1895) on a
c. 1860–1870 low-back or
"firehouse Windsor" arm-
chair. Mitchell had a shop
in Cincinnati, c. 1839–1877.
Private collection.

MILTON

A William and Mary japanned pine dressing table or lowboy, c. 1710–1730, in a private collection is signed

Milton

in several places. This is probably an owner's name. Ref.: Cooper.

MITCHELL, ISAAC

A Windsor chair at the Newark Museum is credited to the turner Isaac Mitchell, who worked in Elizabethtown, New Jersey, and New York City, c. 1789–1810. The chair is stamped

I M

beneath the seat. Ref.: Walter H. Van Hoesen, *Crafts and Craftsmen of New Jersey* (Rutherford: Fairleigh Dickinson University Press, 1973).

MITCHELL, JOHN

John Mitchell (1813–1895), a brother of Robert Mitchell of Mitchell & Rammelsberg (see their entry), was a chair and bedstead manufacturer in Cincinnati, Ohio, c. 1839–1877. A group of midnineteenth-century low-back or "firehouse" Windsor armchairs used as I.O.O.F. lodge chairs are stenciled

JOHN MITCHELL/WHOLESALE
MANUFACTURER OF/CHAIRS/
SO. SECOND BET. JOHN/& SMITH STS./
CINCINNATI, O.

Ref.: Jane E. Sikes, *Furniture Makers of Cincinnati, 1790–1849* (Cincinnati: The Merten Company, 1976).

MITCHELL, ROBERT

See Mitchell & Rammelsberg.

MITCHELL & RAMMELSBERG

One of the major nineteenth-century midwestern furniture manufacturers, the firm of Robert Mitchell (1811–1899) and Frederick Rammelsberg, was established in Cincinnati in 1846. They produced a wide variety of mahogany, walnut, and rosewood furniture in various Victorian styles, stenciling their products

FROM/MITCHELL &

RAMMELSBERG/MANUFACTURERS/OF
/ALL KINDS/OF Furniture,/
23 & 25/SECOND ST./CINCINNATI

During the period 1857–1868, the firm used a different stencil:

MITCHELL & RAMMELSBERG/
MAKERS/99 W. 4th St. N./
Cor. of 2d & John/CINCINATTI, O.

or a variation reading,

MITCHELL & RAMMELSBERG/MAK-
ERS/No. 99 W. 4th St., Cincinnati, O.

Following the death of Rammelsberg in 1863, Mitchell continued the firm until 1883 under the old company name; thereafter, it remained in business under Mitchell's name until 1940. Refs.: Fairbanks and Bates; Fitzgerald.

MONTFRINO, G.

See Paul Cermenati.

MONTGOMERY, BENJAMIN

An Empire mahogany veneer sideboard at Rose Hill near Geneva, New York, is inscribed within a drawer

Benjamin Montgomery/Maker
June 1830/Pittsburgh

Montgomery may have been associated with the firm of "Graham & Montgomery's Fancy Cabinet Ware Room," listed in the 1837 Pittsburgh directory. Ref.: *Antiques,* May 1975.

MOODY, ENOCH, JR.

A Chippendale walnut oxbow chest of drawers with ball-and-claw feet, illustrated in *Antiques* for July 1963, is incised

E. M. 1792

and attributed to Enoch Moody, Jr. (1754–

1804), a Newburyport, Massachusetts, cabinetmaker. Ref.: Bjerkoe.

MOODY, G.

A c. 1820–1850 comb-back Windsor rocking chair at the Henry Ford Museum is stenciled beneath the seat

G-M

and also bears the painted name

G. Moody

Nothing is known of this individual, who could be either the maker or an owner.

MOOER & TIBBETTS

The firm of Mooer & Tibbetts made and sold country pine and maple furniture in Manchester, New Hampshire, c. 1847–1852. A late Sheraton drop-leaf table at the New Hampshire Historical Society is stenciled

FROM/MOOER & TIBBETTS/NO. 8/MER-
RIMACK BLOCK/MANCHESTER, N.H.

Ref.: Brian Cullity, *Plain and Fancy: New England Painted Furniture* (Sandwich, Mass.: Heritage Plantation of Sandwich, 1987).

MOON, SAMUEL

The turner Samuel Moon worked in Philadelphia at 2 Carter's Alley and 66 S. Fourth Street, c. 1800–1802. By 1803 he was in East Caln Township, Chester County, Pennsylvania, where he remained active until around 1810. His bamboo-turned bow-back side and armchairs are branded beneath the seat

Moon

Refs.: Santore II; Schiffer.

MOORE, ALEXANDER

A Queen Anne cherry slant-front desk in a private collection is said to have borne the oval paper label of

Alexander Moore/Cabinetmaker/
Church & Queen Streets/New Brunswick

An Alexander Moore was New Brunswick treasurer in 1730, but this may not be the New Jersey craftsman. Ref.: Walter H. Van Hoesen, *Crafts and Craftsmen of New Jersey* (Rutherford: Fairleigh Dickinson University Press, 1973).

MOORE, FRANCIS

A Chippendale mahogany slant-front desk with ball-and-claw feet at the New York State Museum is inscribed on the bottom

Francis More Made this Desk/
February 25th, 1772

Little is known of Moore, a cabinetmaker active in New York City during the 1770s. Refs.: Scherer; *Antiques,* May 1981.

MOORE, JOSEPH

Joseph Moore was for some years general manager of the Wooten Desk Manufacturing Company of Indianapolis, Indiana, makers of the famous Wooten Patent Desk (see their entry). Upon leaving the firm he patented a very similar desk, which he termed the "Queen of Desks." Moore's pieces are labeled

Chippendale mahogany slant-front desk
with ball-and-claw feet signed and dated
February 25, 1772, by the cabinetmaker
Francis Moore. Courtesy, Bernard and S. Dean
Levy, Inc., New York.

MOORE CABINET DESK/ Indianapolis,
Indiana/Patented January 8, 1878
Ref.: Correspondence, Eileen Dubrow, 1994.

MOORE, THOMAS

A country Federal cherry drop-leaf dining table in a private collection is signed and dated on a leaf support

Thomas Moore 1804

It was made by Thomas Moore, a Paris, Bourbon County, Kentucky, cabinetmaker. Ref.: *Antiques,* August 1980.

MOORE, W. A.

A Federal mahogany butler's desk, dating c. 1810–1825, is stamped on a drawer

W. A. MOORE

and is credited to a cabinetmaker by that name who worked in New Brunswick, New Jersey. Ref.: *Antiques,* April 1981.

Ink signature of Francis Moore with 1772 date and a small (self-?) portrait on the Chippendale slant-front desk. Courtesy, Bernard and S. Dean Levy, Inc., New York.

MOORE, WILLIAM

A Federal inlaid mahogany serpentine-front sideboard, offered at Sotheby's, May 19–20, 1972, is signed on a bottle drawer

William Moore

and is attributed to William Moore, a cabinet-maker working in Baltimore, Maryland, c. 1790–1800.

MOORE, WILLIAM, JR.

The turner William Moore, Jr. (1764–1833), was making fancy chairs at what was later Hitchcocksville, Connecticut, by 1818. For a time he was associated in business with Lambert Hitchcock (see his entry), but was forced to assign his goods for the benefit of creditors in 1830. He moved the same year to Saugerties, New York. Moore's well-made chairs are stenciled across the back seat rail

Wm. MOORE Jr.

Ref.: Kenney.

MOORE & EMMITT

The turners Joseph T. Moore (d. 1854) and William Emmitt worked together in Chillicothe, Ohio, from 1824 until 1827. A set of painted fancy chairs owned by the Ross County, Ohio, Historical Society is signed in paint

M & E

Ref.: *Made in Ohio.*

MORRILL, ADAM

The shipwright Adam Morrill (d. 1807) of Amesbury, Massachusetts, is known for a Chippendale cherry slant-front desk, illustrated in *Antique Collecting* for October 1979, inscribed beneath a drawer

Made by my old hand. A Morrill 1801.

MORRIS, SAMUEL

A Queen Anne walnut chest of drawers on frame in a private collection is inscribed on the back

**Samuel Morris/Joiner of Logtown/
8 mo 5 1793**

Morris, a resident of Kennett Township, Chester County, Pennsylvania, died in 1809. His will described him as a "cabinetmaker." Ref.: Schiffer.

MORRIS, W.

A Chippendale walnut side chair with ball-and-claw feet, c. 1765–1775, offered at Parke Bernet Galleries, April 6, 1977, is branded

W. MORRIS

The chair is attributed to Philadelphia, but it is not known if Morris was the maker or an owner.

MORSE, ELIAS

Morse, Elias

The Maine cabinetmaker Elias Morse is known for a grained and decorated pine chest of drawers at the Henry Ford Museum, which is inscribed in pencil beneath the top

**Made by E. Morse/Livermore/
June 7th 1814**

Before 1830 Morse moved from Livermore to New Portland, Maine, and a decorated blanket chest over drawers at the Maine State Museum is inscribed

Morse/New Portland

Victorian Renaissance Revival walnut patent desk, c. 1878–1880, with the label of Joseph Moore, Indianapolis, Indiana.

Courtesy, Dubrow Collection.

It is dated c. 1825–1840. Refs.: Brian Cullity, *Plain and Fancy: New England Painted Furniture* (Sandwich, Mass.: Heritage Plantation of Sandwich, 1987); Fales, *American Painted Furniture*.

MORSS, JOSHUA

See Moses Bayley.

MOSELEY, WILLIAM

A Queen Anne walnut and yellow pine drop-leaf table, illustrated in *Antiques* for January 1952, is incised on the underside of the top

Willm Moseley His Tabel Sept 4th 1773

The table is attributed to Chesterfield County,

Virginia, but it is not known if Moseley was a cabinetmaker.

MOSS, ALFRED

A Chippendale walnut desk and bookcase or secretary, illustrated in *MAD* for May 1978, is inscribed

July 1797 Made by Alfred Moss, 25 dollars

The piece is attributed to Virginia, but nothing is known of the cabinetmaker.

MOSS, ISAAC AND RICHARD

The Pennsylvania and New Jersey cabinet-makers Isaac Moss (1726-1790) and Richard Moss (b. 1724) are credited with a c.

1750 Queen Anne walnut Spanish-foot high chest of drawers or highboy in a private collection. The piece, thought to have been made in Philadelphia or Germantown, is inscribed on a drawer bottom

**Isaac Mofs/and R/Mofs his hand/
and pen and/if you dont/beleve me you/
may Look Again/Peep for Peep.**

Ref.: *Antiques,* December 1982.

MOTZER, A.

A c. 1790–1810 comb-back writing-arm Windsor chair, illustrated in *Antiques Review* for November 1977, is branded beneath the seat

A. Motzer

Santore lists the chair as possibly from Con-

View of the interior of the Joseph Moore patent desk. Moore's desks were quite similar to those made by his former employer, William S. Wooten. Courtesy, Dubrow Collection.

Hepplewhite mahogany desk and bookcase or secretary made in 1814 by the Lynn, Massachusetts, cabinetmaker Emery Moulton. Moulton was active c. 1770–1815. Courtesy, Israel Sack, Inc., New York.

necticut. It is not known if Motzer was an owner or the manufacturer. Ref.: Santore II.

MOULTON, E. W.

An unusual arrow-back, writing-arm Windsor rocking chair, c. 1830–1850, and a

Arrow-back writing-arm Windsor rocking chair, c. 1830–1850, marked by E. W. Moulton, Cuba, New York. Nothing is known of the maker. Private collection.

country secretary-desk are both branded

E.W. MOULTON CUBA, N.Y.

Although the mark is in appearance that of a maker, the pieces are so dissimilar in appearance that one would doubt they came from the same shop.

MOULTON, EMERY

The cabinetmaker Emery Moulton of Lynn, Massachusetts, is credited with a c. 1770–1790 Chippendale mahogany blocked slant-front desk signed

Moulton

as well as a matching Hepplewhite secretary and card table identified as his by an 1814 bill of sale. Refs.: *Antiques,* September 1957, April 1962.

MOVERS, ABRAHAM

A Hepplewhite cherry slant-front desk, illustrated in the *Bee* for November 19,

Chippendale mahogany fret-carved mirror, c. 1770–1780, labeled by James Musgrove, a looking glass and picture frame manufacturer with a shop on South Second Street, Philadelphia. Courtesy, C. L. Prickett, Yardley, Pa.

1993, is signed

> Abraham Moyers 1823

It is not known if Moyers was a cabinetmaker. However, that he *was* is made more likely by the appearance in 1995 of a second desk, this one signed

> Abraham Moyer, 1825

MULLEN, JOHN

A bamboo-turned bow-back Windsor side chair, c. 1800–1820, illustrated in *Antiques* for April 1969, is branded beneath the seat

> John Mullen

It is not known if this is the mark of the chair-maker or an owner.

MULLIKIN, NATHAN

The Massachusetts clockmaker Nathan Mullikin (1722–1767) opened a clock shop on the present Massachusetts Avenue in Lexington in 1752. A Chippendale mahogany tall case clock of his manufacture, offered at Christie's, October 19, 1991, is signed in chalk on the backboard

> Nathaniel/Mullikin/Clock Case

Mullikin's name is also inscribed on the brass dial.

MUNSON, EPHRAIM

The cabinetmaker Ephraim Munson (1762–1834), of Woodbury and Bethlehem, Connecticut, is credited with a Chippendale cherry slant-front desk, c. 1785–1790, illustrated in *Antiques* for July 1972. The piece is branded

> EPHRAIM MUNSON

Ref.: Bjerkoe.

MURDOCK, JOSHUA

A c. 1815–1825 Federal mahogany desk and bookcase or secretary offered at auction in New York State, August 1994, bears the label of the cabinetmaker, Joshua Murdock. Ref.: *Bee,* August 19, 1994.

MUSGROVE, JAMES

A Philadelphia Chippendale mahogany fret-carved mirror, c. 1770–1780, bears the printed label of the little-known maker James Musgrove:

> JAMES MUSGROVE/CARVER, GILDER,

Label of James Musgrove affixed to the backboard of the Chippendale mirror.

Courtesy, C. L. Prickett, Yardley, Pa.

LOOKING GLASS/AND/PICTURE-FRAME/MANUFACTURER,/No. 111 South 2d. Street,/TWO DOORS BELOW DOCK,/Philadelphia./Takes this opportunity of informing his friends and the public, that he has/commenced the above mentioned bran-/ches of business./All orders will be thankfully received/and punctually executed in the most fashionable and durable manner./Old Frames re-gilt, to appear/as new./

MYRICK, BENJAMIN

A late Federal mahogany card table with rope-twist legs, c. 1815–1825, illustrated in *Antiques* for October 1987, is signed

Myrick

and attributed to the Charlestown, Massachusetts, cabinetmaker Benjamin Myrick.

MYRICK, JOSEPH

The Shaker elder Joseph Myrick (1804–1849) of the Harvard, Massachusetts, community is known for a single piece, a pine chest of drawers, which is inscribed on a drawer bottom

Built by Elder Joseph/Myrick 1844.
Finished March 8.

Ref.: Rieman and Burks.

NATT, THOMAS

The Philadelphia looking glass manufacturer Thomas Natt (working c. 1800–1820) produced a number of marked pieces, including overmantel mirrors and mahogany shaving stands. His more familiar label reads,

THOMAS NATT/LOOKING GLASS MANUFACTURER,/Printseller, and importer of British Plate Glass/Mirrors, &c./No. 164 Market Street,/three doors above Fourth on the south side,/PHILADELPHIA,/Constantly on hand an extensive and elegent assortment/of fancy framed looking glasses, gilt mantel and pier glasses,/mahogany and curled maple do., toilettes, sconces, swings, &c. &c./—Tablet, stained pillar and fluted framed looking glasses/in great variety . . . Plain, fancy and ornamental gilding and resilvering/. . . On hand, looking glass plates, prints and mirrors of

superior quality and late importations.
Natt also used another similar label. This one,
however, was headlined "Cheap! Cheap!
Cheap!/LOOKING-GLASSES," and was illustrated with a group of mirrors and gave his
address as 134 Market Street. We have not been
able to obtain a fully readable copy of this label.
Ref.: *Antiques,* June 1974.

NEEDHAM, THOMAS, II

Thomas Needham II (1755–1787), son of
one Salem, Massachusetts, cabinetmaker
and father of another, is credited with a
Chippendale mahogany serpentine-front, ball-
and-claw-foot chest of drawers, which is
marked on the bottom board
T. N. 1783
Refs.: Cooper; *Antiques,* June 1979.

NEEDHAM, THOMAS, III

Son of Thomas Needham II (see previous
entry), Thomas Needham III (1780–1858)

produced a number of labeled pieces of Federal
furniture, including serpentine-front chests, a
drawing table, bedsteads, a recamier sofa at
Winterthur, and card tables. His paper label reads,
Cabinet Work of all kinds,/
MADE & SOLD BY/Thomas Needham,/
Charter Street, Salem.
He is thought to have opened his shop on
Charter Street in 1802. He retired in 1841.
Refs.: Montgomery; *Antiques,* May 1982.

NEEDLES, JOHN

The Baltimore cabinetmaker John Needles
(1786–1878) established a shop on Hanover Street in 1810, remaining active until
1853. Some two dozen pieces of Federal and
Classical furniture are attributed to him. One, a
Gothic Revival mahogany pier table, is simply
stenciled
J. NEEDLES
More often found are pieces stenciled
John Needles/Cabinet Maker/54 Hanover
St./BALTo.

Federal mahogany sideboard, c. 1810–1815, labeled by the Baltimore cabinetmaker John Needles, who worked on Hanover Street from 1810 until 1853. Courtesy, John S. Walton, Inc., New York.

Label of John Needles on the Federal sideboard. Courtesy, John S. Walton, Inc., New York.

a mark used by Needles, c. 1835–1853. He also employed two paper labels. The earlier, perhaps, is engraved

John Needles/Manufacturer/of/
CABINET FURNITURE,/
54 Hanover Street/Baltimore

while a printed label reads,

JOHN NEEDLES,/MANUFACTURER OF/
Cabinet Furniture,/
54 Hanover STREET,/BALTIMORE

Refs.: Elder and Stokes; *Antiques,* April 1954.

NEES

A group of decorated rod-back Windsor side chairs, c. 1820–1840, from Manheim,

Pennsylvania, illustrated in *Antique Collecting* for July 1979, are signed

Nees

It is not known if this is the name of the maker or an owner.

**Uncommon and perhaps earlier variation of John Needles's label.
Courtesy, John S. Walton, Inc., New York.**

NEFF, ADAM

A pine and poplar sgraffito-decorated six-board chest from Frederick, Maryland, now at the Museum of Early Southern Decorative Arts, is inscribed in paint

ADAM NEFF 1791

Neff could have been owner, maker, or decorator. The piece was illustrated in *Antique Collecting* for December 1978.

NELSON, O.

A sack-back Windsor armchair, attributed to Connecticut, c. 1790–1800, is branded beneath the seat

O. NELSON

It is not known if Nelson was the maker or an owner. Ref.: Santore II.

NETTERVILLE, JOHN W.

A c. 1840–1850 Empire mahogany veneer footstool at the Yale University Art Gallery is labeled

**FROM/J.W. NETTERVILLE'S/
CABINET WARE HOUSE,/
17,19 & 21 Church-st./ALBANY.**

John W. Netterville (active c. 1833–1867) was a cabinetmaker and undertaker in Albany, New York, who advertised in 1867 that he had a ". . . refrigerator for preserving deceased persons"! Ref.: Kane.

NEWBURYPORT CHAIR FACTORY

A number of painted plank-bottom half-spindle side chairs bear the label of the Newburyport (Massachusetts) Chair Factory, located during the 1820s and '30s in a building known as the Market House. The label reads,

**WARRANTED/CHAIRS/Made and Sold at
the/NEWBURYPORT CHAIR FACTORY/
BY/NATHAN HASKELL/
Agent for the Proprietors**

Haskell was probably a businessman, not a craftsman. The "Proprietors" remain unknown. Ref.: Fales, *Essex County Furniture*.

NEWLIN, JOSEPH

A c. 1770–1790 Chippendale walnut desk and bookcase or secretary at the Delaware Historical Society is labeled

**JOSEPH NEWLIN,/CABINET/Maker,
High ftreet/Wilmington.**

A second piece, a Chippendale walnut chest of drawers with a partial label, sold at auction in 1994. Nothing further is known of this Wilmington, Delaware, craftsman. Ref.: *Antiques,* November 1972.

NEWMAN, BENJAMIN

A painted pine and maple Salem rocker at the Essex Institute is branded beneath the seat

BENJn NEWMAN

Benjamin Newman (1781–after 1829) had a chairmaking shop in Gloucester, Massachusetts, c. 1810–1825. Ref.: Fales, *Essex County Furniture*.

NEWTON, R.

A New England fan-back Windsor armchair, c. 1790–1800, at Historic Deerfield is stamped on the underside of the seat

R. Newton

It is not known if this is the maker's or an owner's mark. Ref.: Fales, *Historic Deerfield*.

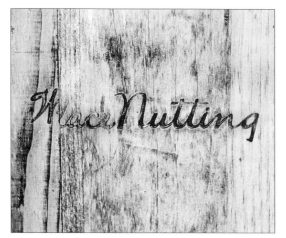

Script brand, "Wallace Nutting," which was used c. 1922–1923 by the individuals to whom Nutting briefly sold his Ashland, Massachusetts, firm. Private collection.

NIMURA & SATO CO.

A c. 1905–1915 pine, poplar, and bamboo Anglo-Japanese dressing chest of drawers at the Brooklyn Museum is labeled,
NIMURA & SATO CO.,/Japanese Bamboo Works/Parlor, Bed Room and Hall Sets/All Kinds of Fancy Work made to order, and/Japanese Crockery and Fancy Goods./Everything Guaranteed to be First Class and of the Latest Style/at Lowest Price./No. 707 Fulton Street,/ BROOKLYN, N.Y.
Ref.: Fairbanks and Bates.

Braced fan-back Windsor side chair labeled by Wallace Nutting, a manufacturer of reproduction furniture, c. 1917–1922 and 1923–1941. Private collection.

NOE, ALBERT E.

The New Jersey cabinetmaker Albert E. Noe worked in Newark c. 1834–1836, then moved to Rahway, where he made a mahogany and pine two-drawer work stand now at the Newark Museum. Noe's only known piece, this is twice stenciled
A.E. Noe./Cabinet & Sofa/Maker./ Rahway N.J.
and is also inscribed in pencil
A.E. Noe/Rahway N J/Aug 30 1845
Ref.: *Antiques,* May 1983.

NOLEN, SPENCER

A Classical mahogany and pine dressing glass at Winterthur is labeled

S. Nolen's/Looking-Glass/and Picture Frame/Manufactory/No. 78, Chesnut Street./Philadelphia./Ornamental Enamelling and/Painting on Glass./Old Frames Re-Gilt—Prints and/Paintings Cleaned.

Spencer Nolen worked in Philadelphia at 78 Chestnut Street from 1828 until 1849.

NOLEN, W. W.

A c. 1790–1800 Federal mahogany and curly maple gentleman's desk, illustrated in *Antiques* for March 1979, is branded on the backboard

W. W. NOLEN

It is not known if this is the maker's or an owner's mark.

NORMAN, M.

A Sheraton mahogany cylinder-top desk in a private collection bears a partial label reading,

M. NORMAN & . . . ./CABINET MAKER/RICHMOND . . .

The piece appears to date c. 1810–1830, and it is thought that Norman was a Richmond, Virginia, craftsman.

NORTHWESTERN PARLOR SUITE COMPANY

A c. 1880–1900 upholstered walnut easy chair with Rococo Revival features, illustrated in *MAD* for April 1990, is labeled

Northwestern Parlor Suite Company/Chicago, IL.

This was a large firm that mass-produced late-nineteenth-century home furnishings.

NOYES, SAMUEL S.

The cabinetmaker Samuel S. Noyes (1785–1832) is known for a dozen labeled pieces of furniture, including a Sheraton mahogany bowfront chest of drawers, a drop-leaf table, and several card tables. His engraved label reads,

HOUSE FURNITURE,/OF THE MOST FASHIONABLE KIND, MADE, SOLD,/ AND EXCHANGED, BY/SAMUEL S. NOYES,/CABINET MAKER,/EAST SUDBURY, NEAR THE CAUSEWAY.

Interestingly enough, some pieces bear a label identical in every respect other than that Noyes's name is misspelled "NOYSE."

Samuel Noyes also appears to have made chairs. Several step-down, rod-back Windsor side chairs branded

S. NOYES

are known. Noyes worked in East Sudbury (now Wayland), Massachusetts, from 1810 until 1832. Refs.: Montgomery; *Antiques,* September 1984.

NUTT, CALEB

The Ohio cabinetmaker and tavern keeper Caleb Nutt (1805–1896) worked in Centerville, Montgomery County, and, after 1850, in Sidney, Shelby County. He is known for an Empire cherry pedestal-base work stand, which is inscribed within a drawer

Made by Cale Nutt/Centerville, Ohio 1847/for Eliza Gregg Springboro/Ohio

Ref.: *Made in Ohio.*

NUTTING, WALLACE

The historian, collector, and ultimately furniture manufacturer Wallace Nutting pro-

Paper label, c. 1917–1922, on the underside of the Wallace Nutting Windsor side chair.

Private collection.

duced a vast quantity of high-quality American furniture reproductions in all seventeenth- to early-nineteenth-century styles. He opened his first factory at Saugus, Massachusetts, in 1917, moving it to Ashland, Massachusetts, in 1920. He sold the business in 1922, bought it back a year later, and continued until his death in 1941. Nutting's reproductions were typically branded

WALLACE NUTTING

or

WALLACE/NUTTING

The branded script signature

Wallace Nutting

was used only during the period 1922–1923, when the business was not in Nutting's hands.

Some of Nutting's earlier pieces bear a paper label reading,

TRADE/WALLACE
NUTTING/MARK/Correct Windsor
Chairs, Settees, Stools,/and all/Windsor
Forms in the hand turnings/Quaint, Early,

Rare Native Wood/Furniture, Court Cupboards, Desks, Tables, Chairs, carved and plain

Although Nutting reproductions were by no means always historically "correct," they have at times been taken for period pieces.

O'CONNOR, MATTHIAS

A c. 1790–1810 gilded Federal looking glass offered at Christie's, June 25, 1991, bears on the backboard the following label:

M. O'CONNOR,/LOOKING-GLASS
MANUFACTURER,/No. 315 PEARL-
STREET,/OPPOSITE PECK SLIP,/NEW-
YORK/Has on hand a general assortment
of Looking-/Glasses—Plain and Convex
Mirrors—Bed and Window/Cornices,
Brackets, &c. of newest fashions./N.B.
Looking-Glass Plates silvered-Prints,
Draw-/ings and Needle-Work/neatly
framed./May 1st, 1811

O'Connor was in business in Manhattan, c. 1811–1855. Ref.: *Antiques,* May 1981.

ODELL, REUBEN

A bamboo-turned rod-back Windsor side chair at Winterthur, illustrated in *Antiques* for April 1969, bears the label of the turner Reuben Odell, who worked at several locations in New York City, c. 1815–1836. Ref.: Santore II.

OGILBY, J.

A c. 1770–1790 sack-back Philadelphia Windsor armchair listed in Santore is

described as being branded beneath the seat
J. OGILBY
It is not known if this is a maker's mark. Ref.: Santore II.

OLD HICKORY CHAIR COMPANY

Best known among the numerous manufacturers of rustic furniture, typically made of unpeeled tree branches, was the Old Hickory Chair Company of Martinsville, Indiana. Established in 1892, the firm remained in business, under various managements, until 1965. Its products were branded
OLD HICKORY CO./MARTINSVILLE/INDIANA
Some later pieces bear identifying paper labels or brass tags. Ref.: Ralph Kylloe, *The Collected Works of Indiana Hickory Furniture Makers* (Nashua, N.H.: Rustic Publications, 1989).

OLDHAM, THOMAS

The Wayne County, Ohio, turner Thomas Oldham was in business at Wooster during the 1830s making "Plain and Fancy" chairs. He sold out to John Jones in December 1838. A rod-back Windsor side chair in a private collection bears his brand:
T. OLDHAM
Ref.: Hageman II.

OTIS, GEORGE W.

A Queen Anne cherry high chest of drawers or highboy with bonnet top, illustrated in *Antiques* for July 1987, bears the label
GEO. W. OTIS,/LYNN, MAFS.
The word "LYNN" has been crossed out in ink and "Boston" substituted, indicating that the cabinetmaker had moved to the latter city. The piece dates c. 1760–1770, but nothing is known of its manufacturer. He may have had some connection to the Boston cabinetmakers Isaac and John Otis listed in Bjerkoe. Ref.: Bjerkoe.

OVERTON, NATHAN

A grain-painted southern pine corner cupboard, illustrated in Fales, *American Painted Furniture,* is described as being signed
Nathan Overton
Overton worked in Randolph County, North Carolina, c. 1821–1850. The cupboard is in the collection of Colonial Williamsburg. Ref.: Fales, *American Painted Furniture.*

PABST, DANIEL

Although many pieces of Victorian Renaissance Revival and Modern Gothic furniture are attributed to the Philadelphia cabinetmaker Daniel Pabst (1827–1910), only a single example, a sewing box dated 1854, is marked with his name. It was in this year that Pabst opened his shop near the corner of Second and Dock streets. He remained in business until his retirement in 1882. Refs.: Comstock, *American Furniture; Antiques,* March 1933.

PADELFORD, JOHN

A Federal mahogany secretary-desk inlaid in satinwood, illustrated in *Antiques* for November 1940, is inscribed on the underside of the writing flap
Robert Dean's Property/Made by John Padelford/1806/Cost 36 Dollars

Nothing is known of Padelford the cabinet-maker, and it is possible that the inscription is that of the owner.

PAINE, S.

Santore records a comb-back Windsor side chair branded under the seat

S. PAINE

which he attributes to a Stephen Paine of Medford and Charlestown, Massachusetts, working c. 1743–1752. There is also a low-back armchair stamped

S.O. PAINE

which he attributes to either Stephen Paine or a later Philadelphia turner. Ref.: Santore II.

PAINE'S FURNITURE COMPANY

An elaborate Victorian Renaissance Revival upholstered swivel or revolving chair in a private collection bears a label reading,

PAINE'S/FURNITURE COMPANY/MAN-UFACTURERS AND IMPORTERS/-OF-/FINE FURNITURE/48 CANAL ST. AND/41 FRIEND ST./BOSTON/MASS/No. 7913

The piece would appear to date c. 1870–1910, but nothing is known of the manufacturer.

PALMER, THEODORE J.

Theodore J. Palmer of New York City was awarded a prize at the Philadelphia Centennial of 1876 for his patent Victorian Eastlake platform rocker in walnut with spring-steel arms. Examples of this rocker bear an embossed metal tag reading,

Palmer's Patent Rocking Chair/ New York/Patented May 3, 1870.

It is likely that this is the Palmer of Palmer & Embury (see their entry). Ref.: *MAD, April 1990.*

PALMER, WILLIAM

An Empire two-drawer mahogany work-table is stenciled within a drawer

Wm. PALMER/CABINET MAKER/ 11/Catherine St./New York

The cabinetmaker and carpenter William Palmer was listed in the New York City directory from 1816 until 1851; however, he was at 11 Catherine Street only during the period 1818–1823, so this piece may be dated to that time. Ref.: *Antiques, September 1964.*

PALMER & COE

A c. 1800–1810 Federal mahogany tall case clock in the collection of the Preservation Society of Newport County bears an engraved label featuring a Federal serpentine-front side-board. It reads,

Palmer & Coe./Cabinet & Chair Maker/ Long Wharf/NEWPORT

While Palmer remains a mystery, the Coe is undoubtedly Adam S. Coe (1782–1862), who was in partnership with Robert Lee on Long Wharf in 1820. Refs.: Bjerkoe; *Antiques, July 1953.*

PALMER & EMBURY

A Victorian Eastlake ebonized and gilded, upholstered platform rocker in a private collection is labeled

PALMER & EMBURY'S/NEW YORK ROCKER./Design Patent Dec. 27th. 1877./Mechanical Patent Jan. 1st. 1878

The rocker dates c. 1875–1885. Nothing is

known of the manufacturers, although it is possible that one is the Theodore J. Palmer discussed in the entry under his name.

PANBAUGH, JOHN

A country Sheraton single-drawer stand in maple and tiger maple, with traces of old blue paint, appears to be signed under the drawer

John Panbaugh 1845/Slaid St/. . . . . . Pa.
Nothing is known of this individual.

PAPE BROTHERS & KUGEMANN

The Cincinnati, Ohio, firm of Edward W. and Theodore Pape and Emil Kugemann was in business from 1871 until 1887, making,

among other things, picture and mirror frames. A Victorian walnut mirror in a private collection bears their stenciled mark:
PAPE BROS./&/KUGEMANN/ CINCINNATI.O.
Ref.: *Made in Ohio.*

PARKER, JOHN, JR.

Several pieces of c. 1800–1810 Federal mahogany furniture, including a worktable and a small sofa, are stenciled

John Parker Jr.
Parker is thought to have been a furniture dealer in Boston, Massachusetts, rather than a manufacturer. Refs.: Montgomery; *Antiques,* May 1991.

PARKER, ROBERT

A mahogany, cherry, and curly maple Sheraton bowfront chest of drawers, c. 1800–1815, offered at Garth's auction house in May 1975, bears the printed paper label of
ROBERT PARKER,/CABINET AND CHAIR MAKER,/BEDFORD, N.H.
Nothing further is known of this manufacturer.

PARKER, THOMAS M.

The turner Thomas M. Parker (1803–1884) was active in Providence, Rhode Island, c. 1828–1838. His printed paper label on an Empire cane-seated saber-leg side chair reads,

Maple and tiger single-drawer stand inscribed, "John Panbaugh 1845/Slaid St/ . . . . . .Pa." Nothing more is known of this Pennsylvania craftsman.
Private collection.

THOMAS M. PARKER./Green-Street,/Providence, R.I./Warranted to do good service, or the money refunded./Chairs made to order./Old Chairs repaired, painted and regilt.

Thomas Parker appears to have been at the Green Street address c. 1832–1836. He also worked on Broad and Westminster streets in Providence. Refs.: Bjerkoe; *Antiques,* October 1966, June 1982.

PARKER, W.

See Matthew Patton.

PARKIN, RICHARD

Bjerkoe mentions a pair of c. 1840 Empire footstools said to have been labeled by Richard Parkin of Philadelphia. Nothing further is known about this individual. Ref.: Bjerkoe.

PARKS, CHARLES

An Empire mahogany and maple chest of drawers at the Connecticut Valley Historical Museum is inscribed within a drawer

Made by C. Parks, State Streete Springfield

Charles Parks had a cabinet shop on State Street in Springfield, Massachusetts, c. 1836–1839. Ref.: *Springfield Furniture, 1700–1850* (Springfield, Mass.: Connecticut Valley Historical Museum, 1990).

PARRISH

A set of three c. 1770–1785 Philadelphia Chippendale mahogany side chairs, illus-

Paper label of Oliver Parsell affixed to the Federal two-drawer stand.

Courtesy, John S. Walton, Inc., New York.

trated in *Antiques* for April 1968, are branded

PARRISH

This is an owner's name, not that of a cabinetmaker.

PARSELL, OLIVER

The cabinetmaker Oliver Parsell (1757–1818), who worked in New York City and Neshanic, New Jersey, before settling in New Brunswick, New Jersey, around 1797, is known for a variety of labeled Federal furniture, including worktables, clock cases, a bureau-desk, and a clothespress. All are labeled

OLIVER PARSELL,/CABINET MAKER,/CHURCH STREET,/ NEW BRUNSWICK.

Ref.: Walter H. Van Hoesen, *Crafts and Craftsmen of New Jersey* (Rutherford: Fairleigh Dickinson University Press, 1973).

PARSONS, THEODOSIUS

A c. 1765–1785 Chippendale cherry tilt-top table owned by the Yale University Art Gallery is labeled

THEODOSIUS (PARSONS)/CHAIR-MAKER AND JOINER/WINDHAM

The Windham, Connecticut, craftsman Theodosius Parsons advertised in local newspapers during the years 1787–1788. He is possibly also the maker of a c. 1800–1810 Hepplewhite mahogany chest of drawers signed

Parsons

Ref.: *Connecticut Furniture: Seventeenth and Eighteenth Centuries* (Hartford: Wadsworth Atheneum, 1967).

PATTON, MATTHEW

A Sheraton cherry chest of drawers or bureau in a private Ohio collection is inscribed

W. Parker/Maker of this Bureau/Made at Mr. Patton Shop/January 7th 1829

Matthew Patton (1778–1856) was a well-known Dayton, Ohio, cabinetmaker, active from 1805 until after 1830. Parker was probably one of his employees, or, possibly, an apprentice. Ref.: Hageman I.

PATTON, WILLIAM

A Hepplewhite secretary or desk and bookcase in cherry wood, which is at the Tennessee State Museum, is signed twice in red joiner's crayon

William/Patton

The piece can be dated c. 1790–1810, and two William Pattons are known to have been residing in Tennessee at that time. There is no evi-

---

Federal inlaid mahogany two-drawer stand labeled by Oliver Parsell (1757–1818), a cabinetmaker working in New Brunswick, New Jersey, c. 1797–1818. Courtesy, John S. Walton, Inc., New York.

dence that either was a cabinetmaker. Ref.: Williams and Harsh.

PAUL, C.

A c. 1760–1780 Chippendale curly maple slant-front desk, illustrated in *MAD* for April 1978, is stamped three times on the back

C. PAUL

It is not known if this is an owner's or the maker's mark.

PEABODY, WILLIAM

A Federal inlaid mahogany bowfront chest of drawers, dating c. 1790–1810, is branded

WM. PEABODY

No cabinetmaker of this name is presently known. The mark is likely that of an owner.

PEARSON & GOODALE

A rocking chair at the Shelburne Museum bears the label

PEARSON & GOODALE,/Chair Manufac-turers/Brookfield, Vt./WARRANTED of Moses Pearson (b.c. 1800) and Normus Goodale (1806–1878), who worked together in Brookfield, Vermont, c. 1830–1860. Ref.: Robinson.

PECK, W. E. AND J. C.

A c. 1850–1860 Victorian Elizabethan Revival cherry bedstead at the New York State Museum is labeled

W.E. & J.C. PECK/Newburgh./Via Fishkill. The brothers William E. and Jonathan C. Peck had a wholesale and retail furniture and carpet business on Water Street in Newburgh as early as 1851. The business was continued under various names into the 1880s. There is no evidence that the Pecks made furniture. Ref.: Scherer.

PENNERY, WALTER

A n Empire maple marble-top dressing bureau at Winterthur is inscribed on a drawer bottom

The year of our lord/one thousand eight hundred/and thirty/Philadelphia June 11th 1830/Walter Pennery. Pennery is believed to have been an apprentice or journeyman cabinetmaker working, c. 1820–1830, for the Philadelphia cabinetmaker John Jamison. Ref.: *Antiques,* May 1994.

PENOYAR, JOHN

A c. 1800–1830 maple ladder-back side chair owned by the Columbia County Historical Society is stamped

JOHN PENOYAR
on the tops of the front posts. Penoyar or

Penoyer (1775–1841) lived and worked in Kinderhook, Columbia County, New York. Ref.: *Antiques,* May 1981.

PENTLAND, JAMES

A fan-back Windsor side chair, illustrated in *Antiques* for July 1965, is branded beneath the seat

I. PENTLAND
for James Pentland, a turner active on North Front Street in Philadelphia from 1791 until 1806. Ref.: Santore II.

PERKINS, A. B.

A t the Shelburne Museum is a painted six-board chest inscribed

A.B. Perkins/Castleton, Vt./1838
It is currently not known if this is the name of a cabinetmaker or an owner of the piece. Ref.: Robinson.

PERRY, SAMUEL

A Federal inlaid cherry chest of drawers owned by the Warren County [Ohio] Historical Society is inscribed within a drawer **Maid by Me Samuel Perry this the 24 Day of February price 65 dolars/Lebanon February the 25, 1811/Maid by me Samuel Perry for Thomas Unphr-es price dolars.** Samuel Perry is believed to have been a Lebanon, Ohio, cabinetmaker. Ref.: *Antiques,* March 1965.

PETTIT, JOHN

A country Federal cherry chest of drawers at the New York State Museum bears the label of John Pettit, a cabinetmaker working in Waterford, Saratoga County, New York, c. 1813–1820. Pettit's label, embellished with engravings of a Federal table and sideboard, reads,

> CABINET FACTORY./THE subscriber continues the Cabinet Factory at/his old stand, two doors east of John House, & Co's./Store, where may be had on the shortest notice, the/following articles, viz./SECRETARIES/DINING TABLES/WRITING do./CARD do./ PEMBROKE do./BEDSTEADS,/CRA-DLES,/BOOK CASES,/CLOCK do./SIDE-BOARDS,/BUREAUS,/CANDLE STAND/WASH STAND do./DESKS./Waterford, Jan 27, 1813.

Ref.: Scherer.

PHELPS, RUSSELL

A c. 1820–1840 inlaid chest of drawers in a private collection is inscribed

> Made by Russell Phelps for
> Harvey Dresser

Phelps is thought to have been a Charlton, Massachusetts, craftsman who worked for the Southbridge, Massachusetts, cabinetmaker Harvey Dresser. Ref.: *Antiques,* May 1993.

PHILLIP, T.

Two very similar Chippendale cherry slant-front desks, c. 1760–1780, are branded on a lid support

> T. PHILLIP

Both have a Pennsylvania history, but no record of a T. Phillip, cabinetmaker, has been found. Refs.: *Antiques,* April 1941, June 1966.

PHIPPEN, STEPHEN

A Queen Anne inlaid walnut and maple high chest of drawers or highboy, offered at Sotheby's, November 16–18, 1972, is signed in chalk within a drawer

> Stephen Phippin

The c. 1840–1860 piece is attributed to Stephen Phippen, a Salem, Massachusetts, cabinetmaker who died in 1774. Ref.: Bjerkoe.

PHOENIX CHAIR COMPANY

An oak bentwood high stool with turned legs and pine seat, dating c. 1880–1910, bears a paper label reading,

> PHOENIX CHAIR CO./
> SHEYBOYGAN, WISCONSIN

The Phoenix Chair Company was one of the many midwestern factories making mass-produced kitchen and utility furniture.

PHYFE, DUNCAN

Although he is one of our best-known craftsmen, Duncan Phyfe (1768–1854) is lamented for his supposed lack of marked or labeled furniture, with the number of such pieces estimated at somewhere between twelve and sixteen. One would suspect, however, that this is inaccurate. One thing is clear: Phyfe used a far greater variety of marks than most of his contemporaries.

Duncan Phyfe was born in Scotland and came to America in 1784, serving his apprenticeship in Albany, where he may also have worked briefly before moving to Manhattan around 1790. By 1792 he had a shop on Broad Street, staying there until 1795, when he established himself on Partition (later Fulton) Street, where

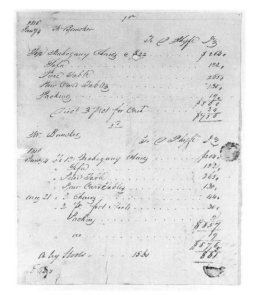

Bill of sale for various pieces of furniture sold by Duncan Phyfe to a member of New York's Livingston family in 1812. Courtesy, John S. Walton, Inc., New York.

he remained throughout his long career. No Broad Street marks are known. However, Partition Street is well represented. A Sheraton mahogany tambour worktable in a private collection is labeled

**D PHYFE'S/CABINET WAREHOUSE,/
No. 35 Partition-street,/
NEW-YORK.**

The New York directory gives this as Phyfe's location during the years 1796–1805. From

Upholstered Federal mahogany armchair, c. 1800–1810, by Duncan Phyfe (1768–1854), who worked in New York City from around 1790 until 1847. Courtesy, White House Collection.

1811 through 1815 he was listed at 33–35 Partition Street, and his label (on a two-drawer worktable at Winterthur) reads,

D. PHYFE./CABINET MAKER,/33 & 35 PARTITION-STREET,/New-York.

In 1816 Partition became Fulton Street. Phyfe's workshops and warerooms now occupied 168–172 Fulton, and his c. 1816–1827 label on a Sheraton mahogany desk and bookcase reflects this:

D. PHYFE'S/ CABINET WAREHOUSE,/No. 170 Fulton-street,/ NEW-YORK./N.B. CURLED HAIR MATTRESSES, CHAIR AND/SOFA CUSHIONS./AUGUST, 1820.

No. 170 was the showroom. The other two buildings were a warehouse and the workshop. There is also, from this period, a mahogany chamber table (at the Chicago Historical

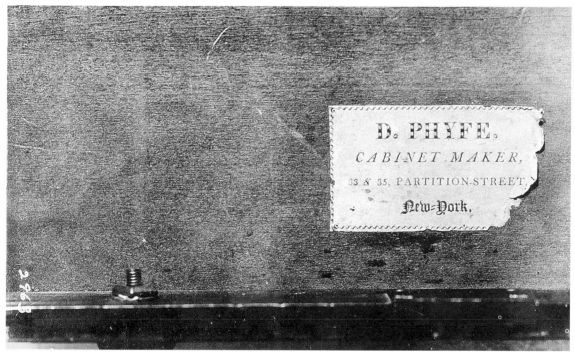

Label of Duncan Phyfe used when his shop was at 33 and 35 Partition Street, New York City, c. 1811–1815. Private collection.

Society) with the rare penciled inscription

D. Phyfe./Shop 170 Fulton St./N. York
1822

A year later Phyfe made a set of rosewood veneer window benches, illustrated in *Antiques* for September 1984, one of which is signed

D. Phyfe

on the webbing. In 1837 Phyfe took two of his sons into partnership, and the firm's label became

Made By D. Phyfe & Sons,/CABINET
WAREHOUSE/NEW YORK/Duncan
Phyfe, James D. Phyfe, William Phyfe.

After the death of one son, the firm became "Duncan Phyfe and Son" in 1840, continuing thus until the master's retirement in 1847. Furniture attributed to Phyfe ranges from Federal through English Regency to Empire in style. Refs.: Bishop; Bjerkoe; Montgomery.

PICKARD, JOHN

An oak Brewster chair at the Smithsonian Institution is inscribed

J.P./1691

and attributed to John Pickard, a joiner from Rowley, Massachusetts. Ref.: Fitzgerald.

PIERCE, RUFUS

A gilded mahogany veneer bureau or chest of drawers, illustrated in *Antiques* for February 1977, is stenciled within an oval

RUFUS PIERCE/Furniture/Ware-

House/No. 17 Market St./BOSTON
and also signed twice

R. Pierce

Other marked pieces by Pierce include a mahogany dressing glass and two sewing tables in the same wood. Rufus Pierce worked at 17 Market Street in Boston from 1827 until at least 1830, sometimes alone, sometimes in partnership. Ref.: *Antiques,* May 1976.

PIMM, JOHN

The Boston cabinetmaker John Pimm (d. 1773) had a shop on Fleet Street, c. 1736–1753. He is known for a Queen Anne japanned high chest of drawers or highboy, which is signed in chalk on each drawer

Pimm

Refs.: Fairbanks and Bates; *Antiques,* May 1929.

PIPPITT, ISAAC

The Philadelphia cabinetmaker Isaac Pippitt worked on Walnut, Dock, and Spruce streets, c. 1820–1833. A Classical carved mahogany card table, offered at Sotheby's, January 28–31, 1994, is labeled

**ISAAC PIPPITT/CABINET & CHAIR
MAKER/No. 71 Walnut St. below
3d.St./On the Nth Side—All Orders
Thankfully/Received and
Punctually Attended To**

Pippitt was at this location c. 1820–1827.

**Classical mahogany three-drawer work-
table, c. 1825–1830, with the stenciled
mark of Rufus Pierce, active on Market
Street in Boston, c. 1827–1830.**

Private collection.

Refs.: *Antiques,* January 1979, May 1994.

PITMAN, MARK

The Salem, Massachusetts, cabinetmaker Mark Pitman (1779–1829) worked, c. 1800–1827, on Essex Street near Cambridge. He is known for several pieces of Federal furniture bearing three different labels. What is thought to be the earliest is one reading,

**Cabinet Work,/OF ALL KINDS,/Made and
Warranted, by/Mark Pitman/ESSEX
STREET, SALEM/Shop nearly oppofite to
Cambridge Street./Orders gratefully
acknowledged, & promptly executed.**

Because Pitman's name is written in ink on a piece of paper glued across the label, he appears to have been using a predecessor's label. Pitman

soon had his own, somewhat similar, oval label reading,

CABINET WORK,/OF ALL
KINDS,/MADE AND
WARRANTED/BY/MARK
PITMAN/ESSEX STREET/NEARLY
OPPOSITE CAMBRIDGE
STREET,/SALEM

A later, also oval, label on a mahogany gentleman's desk in a private collection reads simply,
AT ESSEX STREET/SALEM. MA./Mark
Pitman,/Manufactures
All kinds of/Cabinet Work.

There is also a rare Sheraton mahogany sideboard, which is signed

M. Pitman, Salem, 1804

Refs.: Hewitt, Kane, and Ward; Montgomery.

PLAIN, BARTHOLOMEW

A Chippendale mahogany looking glass by Bartholomew Plain of New York City is illustrated in *Antiques* for March 1930. Plain worked at various addresses in Manhattan from 1803 through 1818, later becoming a merchant. His engraved label, illustrated with an image of a mirror, reads,

LOOKING/GLASSES/Chatham/33/Street/
NEW-YORK/B. Plain,/Manufacturer
of/LOOKING GLASSES, PICTURE
FRAMES/Plain and Ornamental
Gilding/executed in the best
manner/LADIES' NEEDLE WORK
FRAMED & GLAZED/ORDERS FROM
THE COUNTRY/. . . executed on the
most reasonable/terms.

Plain, who was always described in the directories as a "picture-maker," was at 33 Chatham Street from 1815 through 1818.

Gilded Federal mirror, c. 1820–1825, labeled by Isaac L. Platt, a New York City maker of looking glasses and frames who was at that time working at 128 Broadway.

Private collection.

PLATT, ISAAC L.

Isaac L. Platt, working c. 1810–1830, was another of the numerous New York City looking glass and frame makers. Platt's business was on Broadway in Manhattan, and his labels indicate several locations. An ornate c. 1830 gilded pier mirror is labeled

ISAAC L. PLATT,/LOOKING GLASS
MANUFACTURER/AND/IMPORTER./
WAREHOUSE/No. 176 Broadway,/
NEW YORK

while that on a c. 1820 gilded Sheraton architectural mirror reads,

LOOKING-GLASS STORE/ISAAC L.
PLATT/LOOKING-GLASS MANUFAC-
TURER,/& LOOKING-GLASS
SELLER,/Framer of Ladies' Needle Work,
Drawings, &c./No. 128
BROADWAY,/NEARLY OPPOSITE THE
CITY HOTEL, NEW-YORK,/Has for sale,
parlor, ...

the rest of the list being unreadable.

A third label, this on a Chippendale mirror,
reads,

LOOKING GLASS STORE/ISAAC
L.PLATT/Looking Glass Polisher and
Silverer,/Frame and Looking Glass
Seller,/And Framer of Ladies' Needle
Work, Drawings, &c./No. 196
Broadway/NEW-YORK/Has for Sale,
Parlor, Cylinder . . . .

Again, the lower two lines of products cannot
be deciphered.

POFF, JOHN W.

A midnineteenth-century grain-painted
six-board chest on bracket base, illustrated in the *Bee* for October 2, 1992, is signed

Jno. W. Poff, Wrightsville

and is attributed to Wrightsville, York County,
Pennsylvania. It is not known if Poff was the
maker or an owner of the chest.

**Chippendale walnut high chest of drawers
signed on a drawer bottom Pointer/1788
and possibly by William Pointer, active in
Richmond, Virginia, c. 1780–1790. Pointer,
however, has previously been known only
as a maker of Windsor chairs. Courtesy,
William C. Adams Antiques, Richmond, Va.**

POHLE, R. E.

A c. 1870–1890 Victorian Renaissance Revival mahogany center table at the
Chicago Historical Society is labeled

R.E. POHLE/Nos. 313, 315 and
317 South Clinton Street/Chicago, Ill.

It is quite possible that Pohle was a dealer
rather than a manufacturer.

POIGNAND, DAVID

A Chippendale-Hepplewhite transitional
mahogany desk and bookcase or secretary
now at the City Art Museum, St. Louis,

Missouri, bears a lock plate inscribed

DP 1788

for David Poignand, an English cabinetmaker who worked in Boston before migrating c. 1814 to Kentucky and finally to Missouri. Ref.: Bjerkoe.

POINTER, WILLIAM

A fan-back Windsor side chair at the Museum of Early Southern Decorative Arts is labeled

WINDSOR CHAIRS,/Made and Warranted by/WILLIAM POINTER,/In the neateſt manner and may/be had at his shop, between/Crouch's Tavern and the Go-/vernor's House—RICHMOND

William Pointer appears in the 1782 Richmond city directory, and the chair would date c. 1780–1790. He is also the likely author of a Chippendale walnut high chest of drawers signed on a drawer

Pointer/1788.

Refs.: Santore II; Paul S. Burroughs, *Southern Decorative Arts* (New York: Bonanza Books, 1981).

POINTER & CHILDRES

A c. 1780–1790 fan-back Windsor side chair, illustrated in *Antiques* for January 1952, is labeled

WINDSOR CHAIRS/Made and Warranted by/Pointer & Childres/And may be had at their ſhop be-/tween Crouch's Tavern and the/Governor's Houſe, RICHMOND.

While William Pointer is listed in the 1782 Richmond census, nothing is known of his partner. Ref.: Paul H. Burroughs, *Southern Antiques* (New York: Bonanza Books, 1981).

POMEROY, SIMEON

A c. 1760–1780 Queen Anne cherry high chest of drawers or highboy at Historic Deerfield is signed within a drawer

Sim Pomeroy/Northampton

Simeon Pomeroy (1725–1812) was a cabinetmaker who worked in Northampton and Amherst, Massachusetts. Refs.: *Antiques,* March 1985, December 1992.

POMMER, CHARLES

A Classical mahogany desk and bookcase or secretary, c. 1820–1830, illustrated in *Antiques* for December 1974, bears a brass plate inscribed

CHARLES POMMER/Philadelphia

It is not known if Pommer was the maker, the seller, or an owner of the piece.

POOK, C., JR.

A miniature mahogany blind-door secretary in the late Federal (c. 1815–1825) manner, illustrated in *MAD* for March 1975, is signed on the backboards

C. Pook, Jr.

It is not known if Pook was the maker or an owner.

PORTER, LEMUEL

The clock- and cabinetmaker Lemuel Porter was working in Waterbury, Connecticut, as early as 1795. Though listed as a "carpenter" in the 1816 tax rolls, Porter was an able cabinetmaker who made a fine Chippendale-Hepplewhite transitional inlaid cherry desk and bookcase or secretary, illustrated in *Antiques* for March 1979. It is inscribed

Cabinet Work Made/by Lemuel
Porter/price of this Secretary/$$ 26

Porter removed to Tallmadge, Portage County,
Ohio, in 1818. None of his Ohio work has been
identified. Ref.: Hageman II.

PORTER, W.

A c. 1780–1790 Chippendale mahogany
ribbon-back side chair is branded on the
back seat rail

W. PORTER

This may be the mark of William Porter, a
craftsman working in Charlestown, Massa-
chusetts, in the late-eighteenth and early-nine-
teenth centuries. Ref.: Bjerkoe.

POSTAWKA, L., & Co.

A Victorian Renaissance Revival walnut
adjustable curule-form piano stool at
the Stowe-Day Foundation in Hartford,

Connecticut, is labeled

THE X PIANO TABORET/MANUFAC-TURED BY/L. POSTAWKA & Co./FACTORY AT CURRY'S PLANING MILL/STATE STREET CAMBRIDGE-PORT MASS./Patented April 4, 1871

This stool was awarded a prize at the Phila-
delphia Centennial of 1876. Ref.: Fitzgerald.

POTTHAST BROTHERS

A Victorian Modern Gothic wardrobe in
walnut, now at the Peale Museum in
Baltimore, Maryland, is marked

POTTHAST BROS./507 N. Howard Street/Baltimore, Md./1904

Nothing further is presently known of this firm.

POTTIER & STYMUS

T he New York City firm of Pottier &
Stymus, furniture makers and decorators
to the wealthy, including John D. Rockefeller,
produced a variety of elaborate late Victorian
(c. 1875–1895) furniture in several styles. A
Renaissance Revival rosewood cabinet, illus-
trated in *MAD* for August 1993, bears bronze
mounts stamped

P. & S.

the usual identification for Pottier & Stymus
furniture.

Victorian adjustable curule-form walnut
piano stool bearing the label of L. Postawka
& Company, State Street, Cambridgeport,
Massachusetts. This form was patented in
1871 and awarded a prize at the
Philadelphia Centennial, 1876.
Private collection.

Painted and decorated arrow-back Windsor armchair, c. 1820–1840, made and labeled by Joel Pratt, Jr. (1789–1868), of Sterling, Massachusetts. Courtesy, the Henry Ford Museum, Dearborn, Mich.

POWER, JEREMIAH S.

A maple and pine bedstead in a private collection is stenciled on the headboard
**J.S. POWER MAKER/
LA-PORTE OHIO/WARRANTED**
Jeremiah S. Power was born in Kentucky, c. 1810, and moved to LaPorte, Lorain County, Ohio, between 1840 and 1850. He was de-

scribed in the 1850 census as a maker of ". . . Bureaus, Bedsteads and other furniture. . . ." Ref.: *Made in Ohio.*

POWERS, NICHOLAS

A grain-painted country Empire desk and bookcase or secretary, c. 1820–1840, is inscribed
Nicholas Powers
This could be the name of either an owner or the maker. Ref.: *Bee,* June 24, 1994.

PRATT, JOEL, JR.

The turner Joel Pratt, Jr. (1789–1868), of Sterling, Massachusetts, was producing 8,000 chairs per year at the time of the 1820 census. He remained active into the 1840s, making arrow-back side and armchairs, Boston rockers, and half-spindle fancy chairs. Examples are at Old Sturbridge Village and the Henry Ford Museum. His printed paper labels read,
**WARRANTED/CHAIRS/MADE AND
SOLD BY/JOEL PRATT JUN./
STERLING; (MASS.)**
Refs.: Bishop; *Antiques,* May 1993.

PRATT, JOHN D.

The turner John D. Pratt (1792–1863) was probably related to Joel Pratt (see previous entry). He was in Sterling, Massachusetts, in 1823 and moved to Lunenburg, some fifteen miles north, around 1830. There he made rod-back and half-spindle chairs very similar to those produced at Sterling, although his are branded beneath the seat
**J.D. PRATT LUNENBURG MS./
WARRANTED**
Pratt moved to Fitchburg, Massachusetts, in

Federal inlaid mahogany
Pembroke table signed and dated,
1806, by Oliver Prentice, who
worked in Boston, c. 1806–1828.
Courtesy, Nathan Liverant & Son,
Colchester, Conn.

1840, and that probably marked the termination of his chair business. Refs.: Tarrant; *Antiques,* May 1993.

PRATT, LEVI

The turner Levi Pratt (b. 1797) was working in Fitchburg, Massachusetts, by 1816 and was producing 2,000 chairs per year by 1820. The fact that he made painted and decorated chairs similar to those produced by Joel and John Pratt (the latter of whom moved to Fitchburg in 1840) suggests that he, too, was part of this family of chairmakers. A labeled rocking chair by Levi Pratt is at Old Sturbridge Village. Ref.: *Antiques,* May 1993.

PRENTICE, OLIVER

A well-made Federal inlaid mahogany Pembroke table, illustrated in the *Bee* for March 1994, is inscribed in chalk beneath the top

Made by/Oliver/Prentice/AD 1806

Prentice was in business in Boston by this date. He appears to have remained active there until 1828, when the stock of the partnership of William Tibbils and Oliver Prentice was offered for sale at auction. Ref.: Bjerkoe.

PRESCOTT, LEVI

The turner and cabinetmaker Levi Prescott (1777–1823) appears to have made a variety of furnishings. Both a c. 1800–1820 sack-back Windsor armchair at Old Sturbridge Village and a c. 1800–1810 Federal cherry tall clock case bear his label:

LEVI PRESCOTT,/Cabinet &
Chair/MAKER/BOYLSTON./1799.

Prescott had a shop in Boylston, Massachusetts, as early as 1799. Refs.: *Antiques,* July 1936, May 1993.

PRESKUTT, ASA

Ahigh chest of drawers or highboy at the Shelburne Museum is inscribed on a drawer

Asa Preskutt/Auchmuty/Shirley

The piece has Boston characteristics and would date c. 1725–1740, but the names are probably those of owners. Ref.: *Antiques,* November 1974.

PRICE, W. I.

Ac. 1810–1820 Sheraton mahogany card table, illustrated in *MAD* for October 1977, is signed

W.I. Price Salem

No Salem, Massachusetts, cabinetmaker of this name is known, but there may be a connection to Ephraim S. Price, active in Salem c. 1828–1839. Ref.: Bjerkoe.

PRICE, WARWICK

AChippendale mahogany ribbon-back side chair, c. 1770–1780, in a private collection is branded on the back seat rail

W P

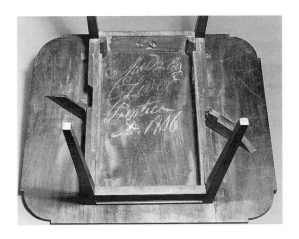

which may be the cipher of Warwick Price, a cabinetmaker working at 45 Bridge Street in Baltimore, Maryland, c. 1790–1810. It may also be an owner's mark. Ref.: Bjerkoe.

PRINCE, SAMUEL

The early Manhattan cabinetmaker Samuel Prince (d. 1778) advertised his wares in New York City newspapers from 1772 through 1776. Two pieces of Chippendale furniture dating from this period—a desk and bookcase or secretary and an unusual "Beau Brummell" that combines the features of desk, dressing table, and chest of drawers—bear Prince's trade card used as a label:

Samuel Prince/JOYNER At the Chest of Draws/In Cart & Horse Street NEW YORK/Makes and Sells all Sorts of JOYNERS/Work on the Lowest Terms

Refs.: Bjerkoe; Downs.

PROCTOR, B.

AMassachusetts Chippendale mahogany side chair, c. 1760–1770, illustrated in *Antiques* for May 1975, is branded on the back seat rail

B. PROCTOR

This is thought to be an owner's name.

Chalk inscription "Made by/Oliver/Prentice/AD 1806" on the underside of the top of the Federal Pembroke table. Courtesy, Nathan Liverant & Son, Colchester, Conn.

PROUD, JOSEPH

A c. 1770–1790 mahogany side table with D-shaped marble top in the Bayou Bend Collection, Houston, is stamped

I P

which may be for Joseph Proud, a cabinet-maker known to have been working in Newport, Rhode Island, during the 1760s. Ref.: Comstock, *American Furniture.*

PROUTY, AMARIAH TAFT

A n elaborate c. 1825–1835 Classical carved mahogany pedestal-base drop-leaf table in a private collection is stenciled

**Amariah T. Prouty/Cabinet Maker/
Glen's Falls N.Y.**

Amariah Taft Prouty (born c. 1802) worked in

Glens Falls, Warren County, New York, during the period 1826–1835. There is also, at the New York State Museum, a simple mahogany veneer two-drawer stand from the same period, which is labeled

**CABINET/WARE,/THE SUBSCRIBER IN-/forms his friends and the public,/that he is constantly manufacturing/all kinds of Cabinet Ware in the/most fashionable style/Bureaus, Sideboards, Secretaries,/Card, Center, Pembroke, Dining and/Tea Tables, Ladies Work and Toilet/Tables, Work and Light Stands, High-/post, Field, French, Low-post, and Cot-/Bedsteads. And various other ar-/ticles can be had on short notice,/which he will sell as cheap as at/any other shop this side of New York./Lumber and most kinds of/country produce will be taken in part payment.—Glen's Falls N.Y./
A.T. PROUTY.**

Refs.: Scherer; *Antiques,* May 1973.

PRUYN, JOHN V. L.

S antore records a bamboo-turned bow-back Windsor child's side chair that is branded beneath the seat

JOHN V L PRUYN.

He suggests it may be of New York origin, c. 1800, but there is no evidence that this is a maker's as opposed to an owner's mark. Ref.: Santore II.

Carved Classical mahogany lift-top work-table, c. 1825–1835, bearing the engraved label of the Philadelphia cabinetmaker Anthony Gabriel Quervelle (1789–1856). Private collection.

PUBLIC WORKS

Largely isolated from the rest of the United States, the Mormon settlers in Utah for some years produced their own furnishings in community-based workshops. One of these made painted Empire chairs, some of which were stenciled

PUBLIC WORKS/1856/G.L.S. CITY

The "G.L.S. CITY" stands, of course, for Salt Lake City, Utah. Under the guidance of turner William Bell, the shop operated c. 1854–1869. Ref.: Fairbanks and Bates.

PUGH, S.

A rod-back Windsor side chair, c. 1820–1840, illustrated in *MAD* for September 1979, is branded several times on the underside of the seat

S. PUGH

It is possible that this is the mark of an as yet unidentified manufacturer.

QUARLES, JAMES OR JOHN B.

A Federal walnut slant-front desk with maple inlay, c. 1810–1815, is signed

J.Q

within the case back. These could be the initials of either James Quarles (d. 1816) or his son, Capt. John B. Quarles (d. 1814). Both appear to have been cabinetmakers, and John B. bought land in 1808 near Statesville, Wilson County, Tennessee, upon which a cabinet shop was erected. Ref.: Williams and Harsh.

Elaborate engraved label of Anthony G. Quervelle on the Classical worktable. Quervelle's shop was on South Second Street from 1825 until 1849.

Private collection.

QUERVELLE, ANTHONY GABRIEL

The famous Philadelphia cabinetmaker Anthony Gabriel Quervelle (1789–1856) was in the city by 1817 and had his own shop, the United States Fashionable Cabinet Ware House, on South Second Street by 1825. In 1849 he moved to Lombard Street, remaining there for the rest of his life. Quervelle was a prolific manufacturer of ornate, high-style furniture, which he marked in several ways. The earliest, perhaps, was an engraved label on a Classical mahogany desk and bookcase or secretary, now at the Philadelphia Museum, which was awarded a silver medal by the Franklin Institute in 1827. This reads,

126/ANTHONY G. QUERVELLE'S/
CABINET AND SOFA
MANUFACTORY,/SOUTH SECOND
STREET A FEW DOORS BELOW
DOCK,/PHILADELPHIA.

From a somewhat later period (c. 1835–1845) is the oval stencil

ANTHONY G. QUERVELLE'S/CABINET
& SOFA/Manufactory/126 So.2d
Street/PHILADA

appearing on an Empire rosewood sofa table in the collection of the St. Louis Art Museum. Best known, however, is an elaborate engraved label reading,

A.G.QUERVELLE./United
States/Fashionable/CABINET WARE-
HOUSE./No. 126./South Second
Street/Below Dock./PHILADELPHIA

Refs.: *Antiques,* September 1964, May 1973, January 1974, March 1974.

❧R❧

RAMSEY, THOMAS

Windsor cradle sold at auction in Ohio is branded

T. RAMSEY

and is thought to be the work of Thomas Ramsey, a chairmaker advertising in Pittsburgh, Pennsylvania, in the 1790s. Ref.: Hageman I.

RAMSEY & DAVIS

A pair of c. 1780–1800 bow-back Windsor side chairs illustrated in Santore are branded beneath the seats

T. RAMSEY/W.DAVIS/PITTSBURGH

and are credited to Thomas Ramsey (see pre-

Chippendale mahogany side chair with strapwork splat and ball-and-claw feet, c. 1760–1775, bearing the label of the Philadelphia cabinetmaker Benjamin Randolph (1737/8–1791). Courtesy, Israel Sack, Inc., New York.

vious entry) and W. Davis of Pittsburgh, Pennsylvania. Ref.: Santore II.

RANDALL, WILLIAM

See John Meads.

RANDLE, WILLIAM

The Boston craftsman William Randle or Randall worked, c. 1715–1749, as both cabinetmaker and japanner. In the former capacity he is known for a c. 1730–1745 maple dressing table or lowboy, which he made in conjunction with the cabinetmaker John Scottow (see his entry). It is signed on the backboard

J. Scottow W. Randlc

and was illustrated in *Antiques* for February 1984. His painted signature

Randl(e)

also appears on the base of a c. 1715–1725 William and Mary japanned high chest of drawers, but it is felt that he decorated this piece rather than made it. Refs.: Bjerkoe; *Antiques,* May 1974.

RANDOLPH, BENJAMIN

Sometimes referred to as "the Chippendale of colonial America," the successful Philadelphia cabinetmaker Benjamin Randolph (1737/8–1791) worked on Chestnut Street from 1755 until 1778. His elaborately carved Chippendale mahogany chairs sometimes were labeled

ALL SORTS of/CABINET-/AND CHAIR-WORK/MADE and SOLD by/BENJN RANDOLPH,/At the Sign of the Golden Ball,/in Cheftnut-Street, PHILADELPHIA There is also a Chippendale walnut Marlboro foot armchair (sold at Sotheby's, February 2, 1985), which is signed beneath the slip seat

B. Randolph/Philadelphia 1762

Refs.: Bjerkoe; John T. Kirk, *American Furniture and the British Tradition to 1830* (New York: Alfred A. Knopf, 1982).

RANK, JOHANNES

The Jonestown, Dauphin County, Pennsylvania, craftsman Johannes Rank (1763–1828) is known for several painted, signed, and dated dower chests decorated with urns of flowers, including a blanket chest over three horizontal drawers inscribed

Johannes Rank 1789

a six-board chest signed and dated

Johannes Ranck 1794

Painted and decorated pine dower chest, dated 1794 and signed by Johannes Rank (1763–1828) of Jonestown, Dauphin County, Pennsylvania. Courtesy, Bernard and S. Dean Levy, Inc., New York.

which is at Winterthur, a blanket chest over three horizontal drawers also inscribed

Johan Rank 1794

a six-board chest signed and dated

Johann/Rank/1796

and an unusual bracket-foot blanket chest over two vertical drawers, which is signed

J. Rank 1797

Refs.: Bjerkoe; *Antiques, April 1927.*

RANK, JOHN PETER, SR.

A probable brother of Johannes Rank (see previous entry), John Peter Rank, Sr. (1765–1851), also of Jonestown, Pennsylvania, worked in a very similar manner. He is credited with a six-board chest with urns of flowers set in panels, which is inscribed

Peter Rank His Hand/1790

the date being uncertain. John Peter Rank is also credited with a blanket chest over three horizontal drawers dated 1796. Refs.: Bjerkoe; *Antiques, April 1927.*

RANK, PETER, JR.

Thought to be a son of John Peter Rank or a grandson of Johannes Rank (see their entries), this Jonestown, Pennsylvania, craftsman worked in the manner of his forebears. An urn-decorated six-board chest signed

Peter. 1807

is attributed to him. Refs.: Bjerkoe; *Antiques, April 1927.*

RAWSON, JOSEPH

Son of the Providence, Rhode Island, cabinetmaker Grindall Rawson (1719–1803), Joseph Rawson (c. 1765–1835) was trained in his father's shop on Long Wharf. From around 1790

until 1808, he worked alone on the "west side of the bridge" in Sugar Lane. A Federal inlaid mahogany card table (at Winterthur) and a Chippendale-Federal transitional mahogany chest of drawers bear his label from this period:

MADE/BY/Joseph Rawfon,/PROVIDENCE

There is also a Hepplewhite inlaid mahogany serpentine-front chest of drawers, which is signed

Josp Rawfon/1806/May 12

In 1808 Joseph Rawson took his son Samuel (1756–1852) into a partnership that lasted through 1828 (see next entry). Refs.: Bjerkoe; Montgomery; *Antiques, July 1980.*

RAWSON, JOSEPH, & SON

In 1808 Joseph Rawson took into partnership in the cabinetmaking trade his son Samuel (1756–1852). They worked together until at least 1828, first "near the Theatre," later at Westminster Street, and, finally, on Broad Street. Their earliest label, c. 1808–1815 (on a Federal mahogany card table at the Yale University Art Gallery), reads,

**JOSEPH RAWSON & SON,/Cabinet
and Chair Makers,/NEAR THE THEATRE
. . . . . SUGAR-LANE,
PROVIDENCE/Rhode-Island**

During the period 1815–1828, they employed a slightly different label, reading,

**Joseph Rawson and Son's/CABINET FUR-
NITURE/MANUFACTORY,/NEAR THE
THEATRE,/PROVIDENCE/All kinds of
Cabinet Furniture executed in the neweft
Fafhions.**

Refs.: Bjerkoe; *Antiques, July 1980.*

RAWSON, SAMUEL AND JOSEPH, JR.

Another of Joseph Rawson's sons, Joseph Jr. (1788–1870), entered the family firm in 1824, and by 1828 he had taken his father's place in the business. An Empire mahogany washstand at the Museum of the China Trade, Milton, Massachusetts, bears the brothers' label:

S. & J. RAWSON, JR./CABINET MAKERS/ No. 68 Broad Street,/GRATE-FUL to their friends and the public for past/favors, and relying on the superior quality of/their work, for fashion and durability,/take this method to inform them that they/have constantly on hand, and/are continually making,/CABINET FURNITURE,/IN ALL ITS VARIETY,/Of all descriptions, faithfully made of the best mate-/rials,/Which they will dispose of as cheap as any regular/Cabinet-Maker in this town./Knowing that deception in work made for/auction,/we trust that if people

Sheraton mahogany and bird's-eye maple sideboard, c. 1815–1820, bearing the label of Joseph Rawson (c. 1765–1835) and his son, Samuel (1756–1852), Rhode Island cabinetmakers working together in Providence, c. 1808–1828. Courtesy, David Stockwell, Inc., Wilmington, Del.

would examine for/themselves, and compare the work and prices, that/business so destructive to all good work, and de-/ceptive to the public, would have an end./ALL ORDERS FAITH-FULLY EXECUTED, AND PUNCTUALLY ATTENDED TO./Providence, May 1, 1828.

Sometime after 1830 the brothers Rawson began to employ yet another printed paper label, this one reading,

Furniture Warehouse/S. & J. RAWSON, JR./No. 68 BROAD STREET, PROVIDENCE,/HAVE CONSTANTLY ON HAND OF THEIR OWN MANUFACTURE, AND WILL MAKE TO ORDER,/ALL KINDS OF/CABINET FURNITURE,/SUCH AS/SIDEBOARDS, SECRETARIES AND BOOK-CASES, SOFAS, &C./Which they will dispose of as cheap as any regular Cabinet Maker in town./ALSO/PIER TABLES, a very superior article;/Pillar, Claw, Card and Dining TABLES/WARDROBES; BUREAUS;/Mahogany and Birch

BEDSTEADS/All orders from a distance will be thankfully received and punctually attended to.

Refs.: Bjerkoe; *Antiques,* July 1980.

RAWSON, WILLIAM

A son of Joseph Rawson of Providence, Rhode Island (see his entry), William Rawson, cabinetmaker, was listed in the 1819 Charleston, South Carolina, directory and is remembered for a late Sheraton mahogany mirrored bureau bearing a partial label reading,

. . . . RAWSON/. . . . . An ELEGANT . . . . . FURNITURE,/ CABINET WAREHOUSE,/No. 86 MEETING STREET/CHARLESTON, S.C.

It is unlikely that William Rawson actually made furniture in Charleston. He was probably an agent for the Providence firm. Refs.: Paul H. Burroughs, *Southern Antiques* (New York: Bonanza Books, 1981); *Antiques,* July 1980.

RAYMOND, J.

Several Salem-type armed rocking chairs with stenciled decoration are branded beneath the seat

J. RAYMOND

They are thought to date c. 1825–1835 and are attributed to an as yet unknown Essex County, Massachusetts, turner. Ref.: Fales, *American Painted Furniture.*

RAYNES, JONATHAN

The furniture manufacturer Jonathan Raynes of Lewiston Falls, Maine, working c. 1840–1860, produced a variety of inexpensive painted pine furnishings, including a dressing table at Old Sturbridge Village, which is stenciled

**JONA RAYNES/Manufacturer/
Lewiston Falls/ME**

READ, J. H.

A c. 1860–1880 walnut Victorian marbletop wash stand in the Renaissance Revival mode was signed beneath the top

J.H. Read/Morristown, N.J.

Read could have been the owner, the maker, or a merchant who sold the piece. Ref.: *MAD,* December 1994.

READ, JOSHUA

A Queen Anne high chest of drawers or highboy from the Norwich area of Connecticut is inscribed

Made by Joshua Read in the year 1752

Read was listed in Norwich records as late as 1774.

READSBORO CHAIR COMPANY

The Readsboro Chair Company of Readsboro, Vermont, is known for such diverse objects as folding camp stools and a child's "shoo-fly"–type rocking toy. Dating c. 1880–1910, these pieces are labeled

**READSBORO CHAIR
COMPANY/READSBORO, VT**

REED, SAMUEL

The Cincinnati, Ohio, craftsman Samuel Reed (active c. 1829–1834) is known for late Federal and Empire mirrors, some gilded, others with reverse glass painted panels, labeled

**Samuel Reed/Looking Glass,/PICTURE
FRAME,/AND/VENITIAN
BLIND/Manufacturer/MAIN/No.105/
STREET/CINCINNATI/Wholesale and
Retail/ Old Looking Glasses Refitted.**

Ref.: *Made in Ohio.*

REED, THOMAS D.

An upholstered armchair at historic Cherry Hill in Albany, New York, is marked

REED

and attributed to the Albany cabinetmaker Thomas D. Reed, working c. 1835–1845. Ref.: *Antiques,* May 1981.

REES & GAVIN

An unusual c. 1840–1860 rod-back Windsor armchair fitted with a headrest for use as a barber's chair is stamped beneath the seat

REES & GAVIN

possibly the makers' name. The piece was found in Pennsylvania.

Detail of the unusual inlay on the lid or top of the Reese Chippendale desk. Courtesy, Israel Sack, Inc., New York.

REESE

A Lancaster, Pennsylvania, Chippendale walnut slant-top desk with geometric inlay and the inlaid date "1771" is branded
REESE
It is not known if this is the maker's or an owner's mark.

REGESTER, BELL & CO.

A Victorian Renaissance Revival walnut marble-top end table at the William Penn Memorial Museum is marked
Regester, Bell & Co.,/526 Callowhill St., Phila. Pa.
The piece would date c. 1855–1885, but noth-

Lancaster, Pennsylvania, Chippendale walnut inlaid slant-front desk, dated 1771 and branded REESE. It is not known if this is a cabinetmaker's name. Courtesy, Israel Sack, Inc., New York.

ing is known of the manufacturer. Ref.: Fairbanks and Bates.

RENSHAW & BARNHART

An elaborate Federal painted and decorated settee at the Baltimore Museum of Art is inscribed
THOs RENSHAW No. 37 S. Gay St. Balte/John Barnhart Ornamentor.
Thomas S. Renshaw (born c. 1780), a noted Baltimore, Maryland, cabinetmaker, is thought to have worked in the city from 1811 until 1816, when he moved to Ohio. He was listed at 37 Gay Street only during the period 1814–1815. The decorator John Barnhart was listed in city directories off and on from 1822 through 1829. Ref.: Elder and Stokes.

REVERE

A c. 1780–1790 fan-back Windsor armchair, sold at Sotheby's auction of April

Elaborately carved Jacobean oak wainscot armchair dated 1695 and having the initials of the Freehold, New Jersey, joiner Robert Rhea and his wife, Jennett. Courtesy, Monmouth County (N.J.) Historical Association.

27–30, 1977, was branded beneath the seat
REVERE
The piece is attributed to Pennsylvania, but the mark is more likely that of an owner than of the maker.

REYNOLDS, JAMES, JR., AND HENRY

The brothers James Jr. (b. 1772) and Henry (b. 1774) Reynolds were carvers and look-ing glass manufacturers, active on Market Street in Philadelphia, c. 1795–1800. A Chippendale mahogany mirror from this period at Win-terthur is labeled

JAMES & HENRY REYNOLDS,/CARVERS AND GILDERS,/At their LOOKING-GLASS Store, No. 56 Market Street,/PHILADEL-PHIA/EXECUTE all their various Branches in the newest and genteelest Taste/and likewise Sell all kinds of LOOKING-GLASSES in Carved and Gold, Cuya/and White or Carved Mahogany Frames, Ditto in Pediment, Mock Pediment, Raffled or Ornamental Frames; Mahogany and Gold, Walnut and Gold, or/Plain ditto Swinging and Dressing Glasses: Also Brackets for Patent Lamps/in Gold, White and Gold, or plain White of various Patterns./PICTURE FRAMES, in Burnished or Oil Gold, White and Gold,/Black and Gold, or Plain Black, &c. in great variety/N.B. Frames repaired, and old Looking Glasses new Silvered.

Refs.: Downs; *Antiques,* May 1984.

RHEA, ROBERT

A large Jacobean oaken wainscot armchair in the collection of the Monmouth County (New Jersey) Historical Association bears on the back the carved inscription
16/R/95/RI
for the Freehold, New Jersey, joiner and car-penter Robert Rhea and his wife, Jennett Rhea. Robert Rhea was living in Freehold as early as 1685. Refs.: Bjerkoe; Benno M. Forman, *American Seating Furniture, 1630–1730* (New York: W. W. Norton, 1988).

RIBBER, JONATHAN

A c. 1790–1810 Federal mahogany square-back side chair in a private collection is stamped on the front seat rail

JNO. RIBBER

It is not known if Ribber was an owner or the maker.

RICHARDS, A. C.

A c. 1865–1885 Victorian Renaissance Revival sideboard in walnut with a marble top, which was sold at auction in 1995, was inscribed

A.C. Richards/Maker/
No. 12 East Fourth St./Cincinnati O.

Richards was in business in Cincinnati during the second half of the nineteenth century. Ref.: *MAD*, March 1995.

RICHARDS, JASON

A n attractive Hepplewhite inlaid mahogany tall clock case, illustrated in *Antiques* for August 1989, is signed within the case

Jason Richards

for the cabinetmaker Jason Richards, active in Woburn, Massachusetts, c. 1790–1810.

Hepplewhite inlaid mahogany tall clock case signed on the interior "Jason Richards" for a cabinetmaker by that name who worked in Woburn, Massachusetts, c. 1790–1810. Courtesy, Israel Sack, Inc., New York.

RIDDELL, CRAWFORD

T he cabinetmaker Crawford Riddell (d. 1849), active c. 1835–1849, was both a craftsman and, from 1837 through 1844, agent for Philadelphia's Society for Journeymen Cabinet Makers. His stenciled mark:

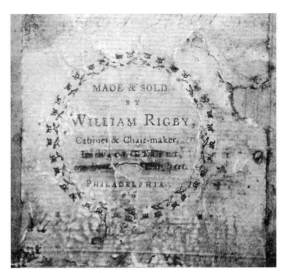

Label of the Philadelphia cabinetmaker William Rigby (d. 1796) on a Chippendale mahogany bracket-foot chest of drawers (dating c. 1785–1795). Rigby worked at the corner of Race and North Front streets from 1785 until his death. Private collection.

CRAWFORD RIDDELL'S/JOURNEYMEN CABINET MAKERS/FURNITURE WARE-HOUSE./48./S.FIFTH St./PHILAD
was applied both to his own work and to that produced by the journeymen. Ref.: *Antiques*, May 1976.

RIGBY, HENRY

A Philadelphia Federal walnut card table sold at Parke Bernet Galleries in New York, January 30–February 1, 1975, bears within its drawer a partial paper label handwritten

Henry Rigby Cabinet Maker/on Front Street one door above the/. . . . . . .

Rigby, son of the North Front Street, Philadel-phia, cabinetmaker William Rigby (see next entry), was in business c. 1780–1790. Ref.: *Antiques*, May 1947.

RIGBY, WILLIAM

The Philadelphia cabinetmaker William Rigby (d. 1796), father of Henry Rigby (see previous entry), worked on Race and North Front streets as early as 1785 and as late as 1796. He is credited with a card table and a bracket-foot chest of drawers, both mahogany and in the Chippendale manner. Rigby's circular printed paper label reads,

MADE & SOLD/BY/WILLIAM RIGBY,/Cabinet & Chair-maker,/ IN RACE STREET,/one door from Front Street/PHILADELPHIA.

Ref.: *Antiques*, June 1966.

RILEY, RICHARD

A small Chippendale walnut spice chest with bracket feet is inscribed

Made by Richd Riley—/Goshen

A similar Chippendale walnut spice chest is signed

Made by Rich Riley 1773

Richard Riley (1735–1820) was listed as a joiner in Chichester Township, Chester County, Pennsylvania, in 1773. He died in 1820. Refs.: Schiffer; Lee Ellen Griffith, *The Pennsylvania Spice Box* (Westchester, Pa.: Chester County Historical Society, 1986).

ROADS, JOHN H.

A folky paint-decorated country Victorian one-drawer stand in a private collection is inscribed

John H. Roads/June 5, 1845/New Castle, PA.

It is likely that this piece was made by an amateur or home craftsman for the family member whose initials, H R, are inlaid in the drawer front.

ROBERTS, ELY

A c. 1790–1800 Chippendale cherry high chest of drawers or highboy in a private collection is signed on a drawer back

Ely Roberts/Windsor

Ely Roberts (b. 1767) was listed as a cabinetmaker in East Hartford, Connecticut, in the 1790s and is thought to have worked in nearby Windsor during the same period. Ref.: *MAD,* March 1993.

ROBERTS, JOHN

The Connecticut cabinetmaker John Roberts (1744–1837) advertised his services in a 1778 Hartford newspaper. He appears to have been in business some years previously, because there is a c. 1765–1775 Queen Anne cherry flattop high chest or highboy, which is signed

John Roberts

Ref.: *MAD,* March 1993.

ROBERTS, L.

A c. 1830–1850 cane-seated slat-back side chair in the Hitchcock style, which is part of the Hitchcock Chair Company collection, is stenciled

L. ROBERTS

It is probably a product of the Roberts family chair shop at Colebrook, Connecticut. Ref.: Kenney.

Hepplewhite mahogany inlaid tall clock case labeled by the Concord, New Hampshire, cabinetmaker George W. Rogers, active c. 1801-1819. Courtesy, Israel Sack, Inc., New York.

ROBERTS, S.

A Sheraton bamboo-turned fancy chair exhibited at the New Jersey State Museum in 1953 is branded beneath the seat

S. ROBERTS/New Mills

It was made by a turner of that name in New Mills, Burlington County, New Jersey, c. 1815–1820. Ref.: *Early Furniture Made in New Jersey, 1690–1870* (Newark: Newark Museum Association, 1958).

ROBERTS, SAMUEL

See Holmes & Roberts.

ROBERTSON, GEORGE, & Co.

The Savannah, Georgia, cabinetmaker George Robertson is known for a Hepplewhite mahogany and yellow pine chest of drawers signed in chalk beneath a drawer

Geo. Robertson & Co

The piece would appear to date c. 1800–1810, but nothing further is known of George Robertson. Ref.: *Antiques,* September 1976.

ROBINSON, CHARLES

The furniture maker Charles Robinson was in business in Rochester, New York, by 1834 and continued active until 1878. Among the most often seen examples from his shop are painted ladder-back side chairs impressed (usually on the back of the top slat)

C. ROBINSON/ROCHESTER, N.Y.

Refs.: Scherer; *Antiques,* May 1981.

Label of George W. Rogers within the Hepplewhite tall clock case. Courtesy, Israel Sack, Inc., New York.

ROBINSON, CHARLES N.

A pair of small Federal gilded girandole mirrors offered at Christie's, June 17, 1992, are labeled

C.N. ROBINSON,/CARVER AND GILDER,/LOOKING-GLASS/AND/ PICTURE-FRAME/MANUFACTURER,/ No. 56, south Second-Street,/OFFERS FOR SALE,/An assortment Girandoles,/ Brackets, Cornices, &c. &c./Also a great variety of/profile frames./N.B. Old glasses/resilvered.

Charles N. Robinson was active in Philadelphia, c. 1811–1857. He was on South Second Street from 1813 through 1822. Ref.: *Antiques,* April 1976.

ROBINSON, JAMES

A late Federal mahogany and walnut fall-front butler's desk in a private collection is inscribed on the underside of the top

James Robinson/Washington Agust 28th 1817/B.M. Belt Shop/Washington City D C
Robinson was probably an apprentice or journeyman employed by Benjamin Middleton Belt, who had a cabinet shop in Washington, D.C., c. 1808–1829. Ref.: *Antiques,* May 1975.

ROCH (ROSCH)

A c. 1825–1835 carved and upholstered mahogany "Grecian Couch" at Winterthur is branded

ROCH

and incised

R. Rosch CR

on the bottom of the frame. It is not known if this is the mark of an owner or the maker. Refs.: Fairbanks and Bates; Montgomery.

ROCKFORD CHAIR & FURNITURE CO.

A Victorian Eastlake oak desk and bookcase or secretary in a private collection is labeled

Manufactured by,/Rock-ford Standard Furniture Company/Rockford, Illinois
The piece dates c. 1900–1910, but nothing further is known of the manufacturer.

ROGERS, EBENEZER

A fine Hepplewhite satinwood, mahogany, and curly maple card table, illustrated in *Antiques* for April 1987, bears beneath the top the signature

Rogers

and is attributed to Ebenezer Rogers (1783–1866), the Newburyport, Massachusetts, cabinetmaker. The table would date c. 1800–1810. Refs.: Bjerkoe; *Antiques,* April 1987.

ROGERS, GEORGE W.

T wo Hepplewhite birch tall clock cases, c. 1800–1815, bear the label of the Concord, New Hampshire, cabinetmaker George W.

Federal mahogany and satinwood card table, c. 1810–1818, with the label of Ebenezer Rogers (1783–1866) and Thomas Atwood (1782–1818), who had a shop on Merrimack Street in Newburyport, Massachusetts. Following Atwood's death, Rogers continued the business until 1854. Courtesy, Bernard and S. Dean Levy, Inc., New York.

Partial label of Rogers & Atwood on the Federal card table. Courtesy, Bernard and S. Dean Levy, Inc., New York.

Rogers (active c. 1801–1819). It reads,
Warranted/Cabinet Work & Chairs,/OF ALL KINDS,/Made in the neatest manner and latest/fashions,/BY GEORGE W. ROGERS,/Opposite the Court-House, Concord, N.H./Orders for any work executed on/the shortest notice and lowest terms. Refs.: *The Decorative Arts of New Hampshire, 1725–1825* (Manchester: Currier Gallery of Art, 1964); *Antiques,* July 1968.

ROGERS & ATWOOD

The Newburyport, Massachusetts, partnership of Ebenezer Rogers (see his entry) (1783–1866) and Thomas Atwood (1782–1818) is known for a c. 1810–1818 mahogany and satinwood card table, which bears an engraved label featuring a tea table and slant-front desk and reading,
ROGERS & ATWOOD/CABINETMAKERS/On MERRIMACK STREET/NEWBURYPORT
Nothing further is known of Atwood, but Rogers was listed as a cabinetmaker at the Mer-

rimack Street address as late as 1854. Refs.: Bjerkoe; Hewitt, Kane, and Ward; *Antiques,* May 1982.

ROHLFS, CHARLES

One of the few American furniture makers to work in the Art Nouveau mode, Charles Rohlfs (1853–1936) was in business in Buffalo, New York, c. 1900–1925, producing a variety of highly eclectic oak furnishings. His work gained great favor and was featured at numerous international expositions. Many of Rohlfs's pieces are marked
R
within the outline of a wood-saw frame. Refs.: Fitzgerald; *New York–Pennsylvania Collector,* September 1983.

ROLLINS, B. F.

Two unusual country painted pine two-drawer stands with shaped tops bear the signature of B. F. Rollins, thought to be a Camden, Maine, craftsman. One at Old Sturbridge Village is inscribed
Made by B.F. Rollins, March, 1818
The other, which sold at auction in 1993, is signed
Made by B.F. Rollins, February, 18——
Nothing further is known of Rollins. Ref.: John T. Kirk, *Early American Furniture: How to Recognize, Buy and Care for the Most Beautiful Pieces—High Style, Country, Primitive and Rustic* (New York: Alfred A. Knopf, 1970).

ROSE VALLEY SHOPS

A product of the turn of the century Arts and Crafts movement, the Rose Valley Community at Moylan, Pennsylvania, was inspired and largely funded by the Philadelphia architect William L. Price (1861–1916). Although the community lasted but a few decades (roughly 1900–1920), its workshops produced a variety of materials, including oak chairs designed by Price and branded

ROSE VALLEY SHOPS

Most of these date c. 1901–1909.

Label of Abraham Rosett and Abraham M.

Mulford, on the Federal tall clock case.

Courtesy, Bernard and S. Dean Levy, Inc.,

New York.

ROSETT, ABRAHAM

A Sheraton mahogany reeded-leg Pembroke table, c. 1790–1810, owned by the New Jersey Historical Society is labeled

Made & Sold By/ABRAHAM ROSETT/Elizabeth Town, N.J.

Abraham Rosett or Rousett (1780–1815) served an apprenticeship in New York City before opening his own cabinet shop "near the stone bridge" in Elizabethtown, New Jersey, in 1803. During the period 1807 1808, he was

Federal inlaid mahogany tall clock case

with the label of Abraham Rosett

(1780–1815) and Abraham M. Mulford, who

worked together in Elizabethtown, New

Jersey, 1807–1808. Courtesy, Bernard and

S. Dean Levy, Inc., New York.

in partnership with Abraham Mulford (see next entry), and following dissolution of this firm he continued in business until he sold his stock in March 1810. Ref.: Walter H. Van Hoesen, *Crafts and Craftsmen of New Jersey* (Rutherford: Fairleigh Dickinson University, 1973).

ROSETT & MULFORD

During their partnership of one year (1807–1808), the cabinetmakers Abraham Rosett or Rousett (1780–1815, see previous entry) and Abraham Marsh Mulford produced at least one marked piece, a Federal inlaid mahogany tall case clock labeled

ELIZABETH-TOWN/Cabinet/Ware-house/Rosett & Mulford, CABINET-MAKERS near the stone/Bridge in Elizabeth-Town intend keeping for Sale a hand-/fome variety of FASHIONABLE FURNITURE, which they/are determined to fell low for Cafh or Produce.—They intend/that their work fhall be compofed of the beft materials; and having at/prefent in their employ, fome of the beft workmen from the City of New-/York, they can, with fome degree of affurance requeft a moderate fhare/of public patronage, which they will make it their ftudy to merit./ABRAHAM ROSETT,/ABRAHAM M. MULFORD,/March 27, 1807./Mahogany for Fale. Apply as above.

Refs.: Walter H. Van Hoesen, *Crafts and Craftsmen of New Jersey* (Rutherford: Fairleigh Dickinson University Press, 1973); *Antiques,* March 1931.

ROSI, JOHN E.

An Empire mahogany sideboard with carved feet in a private collection is inscribed

Made January 29, 1828 in Philadelphia by John E. Rosi

Nothing further is known of this cabinetmaker. Refs.: Bjerkoe; *Antiques,* January 1930.

ROSS, BENJAMIN

The Boston cabinetmaker Benjamin Ross is credited with a c. 1760–1770 Chippendale mahogany architectural chest on chest, which is signed in chalk on the top board

Mr Rofs Joiner

ROSS, J. S.

A Hepplewhite inlaid mahogany bowfront chest of drawers in a private collection is signed

J.S. Ross/September 1812

Ross was a cabinetmaker working in Salisbury, New Hampshire, c. 1810–1815.

ROUX, ALEXANDER

The Manhattan cabinetmaker Alexander Roux (1813–1886) worked in New York City from 1836 until his retirement in 1881. His son, Alexander J., continued the firm through 1898. Specializing in Victorian furnishings from the Gothic to Rococo Revival, he employed a variety of marks during his long career. The earliest of these, a stencil reading

FROM/ALEXANDER ROUX/ 478 B.Way/N.Y.

dates to the period 1843–1847, when Roux occupied a single building at 478 Broadway. A rosewood sofa table with this mark was illustrated in *Antiques* for July 1976. During the years 1847–1849, Roux was joined in the business by his brother, Frederick. Their stenciled mark was From/A. & F. ROUX/479 Broadway/N.Y.

Elaborate engraved label of Alexander Roux on the Rococo Revival dressing table. It is thought that this label was used c. 1850–1857. Courtesy, Peter Hill, Washington, D.C.

A Gothic side chair at the Museum of Fine Arts, Boston, is so marked. Following Frederick's return to Paris, Alexander Roux adopted another stencil, reflecting his leasing of a second building, at 481 Broadway. This stencil, used from 1850 until 1857, reads,

---

Victorian Rococo Revival marble-top dressing table, c. 1850–1857, with the label of the New York City cabinetmaker Alexander Roux (1813–1886). Courtesy, Peter Hill, Washington, D.C.

FROM/A. ROUX/FRENCH/CABINET MAKER/Nos. 479 & 481 BROADWAY/ NEW YORK

It may also have been during this period that Roux employed an elaborate engraved label illustrating his workshop and warehouse, numbered 479 and 481 respectively, and worded simply

A. ROUX/Cabinet Maker/ 481 Broadway/NEW-YORK

A Renaissance Revival sofa table at the St. Louis Art Museum is identified in this manner. From 1857 through 1860 Roux appears to have entered into a business partnership reflected in a rare partial printed label on a Renaissance Revival sideboard, which reads,

A. ROUX & CO./479 Broadway,/43 & 46 MERCER ST./CABINET-MAKERS . . . . .

. . . .

Photograph of Elbert Hubbard (1856–1915), founder of the Roycroft community at East Aurora, New York, makers of Arts and Crafts furniture, c. 1903–1937. Courtesy, the Henry Ford Museum, Dearborn, Mich.

By 1860, though, he had returned to a single proprietorship employing the following label:
**FROM/ALEXANDER ROUX,/
479 BROADWAY,/43 & 46 MERCER
ST./NEW-YORK/FRENCH CABINET
MAKER,/AND IMPORTER OF/
FANCY BUHL/AND/MOSAIC
FURNITURE/ESTABLISHED 1836.**
By 1867 the city directory listed a new Broadway address, which was reflected in a new label:
**From/ALEXANDER ROUX/827 & 829
Broadway,/NEW-YORK/French Cabinet
Maker,/and importer of/Fancy & Mosaic**

Furniture/Established 1836.
In 1870 Alexander's son, Alexander J. Roux, entered the business, which again became Roux & Co. A paper label on an upholstered side chair at the Smithsonian Institution from this period reads,
**FROM/ROUX & CO./COR. 5th AVENUE
AND 20th STREET/NEW YORK./. . . .**
reflecting a change not only in the proprietors but also in location, to 133 Fifth Avenue. This label appears to have been used until the business came to an end in 1898. It should be noted that there are a few vagrant marks as well: the script signature
ROUX
beneath the marble top of a c. 1855–1865 Rococo Revival center table and the brand
A. ROUX
on a c. 1850–1860 Renaissance Revival walnut sideboard. Refs.: Fairbanks and Bates; Scherer.

ROWE, GEORGE W.

Bjerkoe refers to a labeled c. 1780 Hepplewhite secretary by the cabinetmaker George W. Rowe of Portsmouth, New Hampshire. Ref.: Bjerkoe.

ROWLAND, M.

A c. 1780–1800 Windsor bow-back high chair, illustrated in *Antiques & Arts Weekly* for October 28, 1977, is signed
M. ROWLAND
It is not known if this is the maker's or an owner's mark.

ROYCROFT

The Roycroft community at East Aurora, New York, was established by Elbert Hubbard (1856–1915) in 1897 and remained viable until 1937. Furniture in the Arts and Crafts mode, largely handmade, was produced from 1903 on. The marks employed were the word

Roycroft

or the letter

R

within an orb. Both were stamped into the wood. Refs.: Cathers; Scherer; *Antiques,* October 1983.

RUGGLES, LEVI

The Boston cabinetmaker Levi Ruggles (working c. 1810–1855) is known for a Sheraton mahogany bowfront chest of drawers or bureau at Winterthur, which is labeled

LEVI RUGGLES/CABINET MAKER
No. 2 WINTER STREET—BOSTON

Because Ruggles worked at this address only from 1813 to 1816, the piece may be dated accordingly. His shop was later located on Charles and, finally, on Marlborough Street. Refs.: Montgomery; *Antiques,* February 1962.

RUGGLES, NATHAN

The Hartford, Connecticut, looking glass manufacturer Nathan Ruggles (1774–1835) was in business on Main Street from 1803 until his death. His Chippendale and Federal mirrors as well as some picture frames are typically marked by an engraved label featuring a fret-cut mirror frame, within which appears

Nathan Ruggles,/LOOKING-GLASS/Man-
ufacturer,/Main-Street, Hartford;/Con-
necticut./Embroidery &
Pictures/-Framed-/Glass-Silvered, Let-
tered, &c./Looking Glass Plates. Silvered.

In 1994 another label appeared at a Connecticut

auction. This one, on the reverse of a late Chippendale mahogany and gilt mirror, features an engraving of a large eagle and the words

RUGGLES/EAGLE LOOKING
GLASS/MANUFACTORY HARTFORD,
CON./WARRANTED/ 18 . . . 2

the date being probably 1822, because Ruggles's Eagle Looking-Glass Manufactory is listed in the Hartford directory for the period 1819–1828. Refs.: Comstock, *The Looking Glass in America*; Montgomery.

RUGGLES & DUNBAR

During the period 1804–1806, the Hartford, Connecticut, craftsman Nathan Ruggles (working 1803–1835, see previous entry) was in partnership with one Azell Dunbar. A framed mourning picture at the Connecticut Historical Society bears their rare label, the words set within an engraved Chippendale mirror:

Ruggles & Dunbar,/LOOKING-
GLASS/Manufacturers./Main-Street,
Hartford,/Connecticut./Embroidery & Pic-
tures/-Framed-/Glass-Silvered, Lettered,
&c./Looking Glass Plates. Silvered.

Ref.: Montgomery.

RUST, HENRY

The obscure Salem, Massachusetts, cabinetmaker Henry Rust (1737–1812, working c. 1773–1800) is known only for a Chippendale mahogany blocked slant-front desk, illustrated in *Antiques* for May 1977, which bears on its bottom the incised signature

H x Rust

Because Rust was working in Boston as early as 1762, it is possible the desk was made there. Family provenance, however, would indicate a

c. 1765–1775 Salem origin. Ref.: *Boston Furniture of the Eighteenth Century* (Boston: Publications of the Colonial Society of Massachusetts, 1974).

RUSTIC HICKORY FURNITURE COMPANY

The Rustic Hickory Furniture Company of La Porte, Indiana, was in business from 1902 until 1933, making not only chairs and tables of unpeeled hickory but simple case pieces as well. Their products were similar to those produced by the rival Old Hickory Chair Company of Martinsville, Indiana (see their entry). However, Rustic Hickory products were always marked with either a paper label or a brand that read,

RUSTIC HICKORY FURNITURE CO.
LAPORTE, INDIANA

Ref.: Ralph Kylloe, *The Collected Works of Indiana Hickory Furniture Makers* (Nashua, N.H.: Rustic Publications, 1989).

RYNOR & SMITH

A Victorian Gothic mahogany sewing table offered at Sotheby's, April 3, 1982, is labeled

Rynor & Smith/Cabinet, Chair and Sofa
Manufactory/Washington, Street,
BOSTON

The table would date c. 1840–1850, but nothing further is known of the manufacturers.

Grain-painted lift-top box, signed and dated "Feb 28 1842/Walter Safer/. . . Ny" Courtesy, the Henry Ford Museum, Dearborn, Mich.

SACKRITER, DAVID

A pair of rare cylindrical mahogany knife boxes or urns are attributed to the Philadelphia cabinetmaker David Sackriter, active at various addresses in the city from 1807 through 1845. One of these Classical boxes is signed in pencil

David Sackriter/Jan. 12, 1814

at which time Sackriter's shop was at the corner of Bedford and Seventh streets. No other signed Sackriter piece is known. Ref.: Catalog of the Philadelphia University Hospital Antiques Show, 1974.

SAFER, WALTER

A grain-painted lift-top box at the Henry Ford Museum is inscribed in paint on the back

Feb 28 1842/Walter Safer/. . . Ny

It is not known if Safer was the maker, the decorator, or an owner of this box.

Signature and date scratched in wet paint on the back of the lift-top box. Safer could have been maker, decorator, or owner. Courtesy, the Henry Ford Museum, Dearborn, Mich.

SAILOR, JOHN

The Philadelphia cabinetmaker John Sailor (active 1813–1833) is known for two mahogany worktables. The earlier, a Sheraton three-drawer, astragal-end piece, is inscribed in pencil on a removable interior tray

John Sailor/Maker/Phila July 11, 1813

while the second, a Classical carved two-drawer pedestal-base table, is signed

John Sailor/Cabinet Maker/
No. 57 N. 8th St.

Sailor worked at this address in 1822 and 1823. Refs.: Montgomery; *Antiques,* May 1994.

SALA, JOHN

Several pieces of decorated furniture bear the mark of John Sala (1819–1882), a cabinetmaker from the Soap Hollow area of Johnstown, Pennsylvania. There is at the Henry Ford Museum a country Sheraton painted poplar chest of drawers stenciled

MANUFACTURED BY
JOHN SALA/RW/1850

A nearly identical chest of drawers in a private collection is marked

Manufactured.by.John Sala/GW/1852

There is also said to be a flat wall cupboard signed by Sala and dated 1845. Refs.: Fales, *American Painted Furniture; Antiques,* May 1983.

SALMON, BIRDSALL

Birdsall Salmon, an apprentice or employee of Hugh Spier, a Newburgh, New York, cabinetmaker, is known for a Hepplewhite inlaid chest of drawers inscribed in pencil on the bottom

April 4/Newburgh 1809/Made by
Birdsall Salmon/at shop of Hugh Spier

Salmon left Newburgh before 1820, when he was living in Groton, near Ithaca, New York. He worked at various places in western New York through 1850. Ref.: *Antiques,* May 1991.

SALTER, JOHN

A c. 1760–1780 Chippendale armchair, illustrated in *Antiques* for March 1966, was described as branded on the front seat rail

JOHN SALTER

There is no record of a cabinetmaker of this name.

SAMLER, I.

A c. 1780–1800 brace-back continuous-arm chair, illustrated in *Antiques & Arts Weekly* for April 4, 1975, is branded beneath the seat

I SAMLER/N-YORK

The mark appears to be that of a turner, but nothing has been learned of him. Ref.: Santore II.

SANBORN, REUBEN

T he Boston turner Reuben Sanborn, active on Doane Street, c. 1789–1800, is known

for a pair of bamboo-turned rod-back Windsor side chairs branded beneath the seat

BOSTON/SANBORN

Also attributed to Sanborn is a Windsor bow-back armed rocker with comb from the same period, which bears on the underside of the seat the name

Sanborn

written in chalk. Refs.: Bjerkoe; Santore II.

SANBORN, REUBEN

A Reuben Sanborn (1823–1901), turner, who worked at Union, Wakefield Township, New Hampshire, c. 1845–1891, may have been a descendant of the Reuben Sanborn of Boston. The New Hampshire Sanborn made splint-seated ladder-back side chairs, which bear a paper label reading,

Reuben Sanborn/Manufacturer of/Basket Bottomed/Chairs of all kinds,/ UNION, N.H.

Examples are at the New Hampshire Historical Society. Ref.: New Hampshire Historical Society Accession Record, June 5, 1991.

SANDERSON, ELIJAH

T he Salem, Massachusetts, cabinetmaker Elijah Sanderson (1752–1825), working c. 1779–1820, had a shop on Federal Street,

Painted and stenciled country Sheraton poplar chest of drawers, stencil-signed and dated 1850 by John Sala (1819–1882), a Soap Hollow, Johnstown, Pennsylvania, craftsman. Courtesy, the Henry Ford Museum, Dearborn, Mich.

where, with his brother, Jacob (see next two entries), he produced Federal furnishings for the so-called venture trade, shipping as far as South America and India. Many of his pieces, including a Sheraton card table and a Hepplewhite commode, both of mahogany and in private collections, are branded

E S

In fact, Elijah Sanderson noted on an 1803 venture invoice that ". . . my furniture is all marked with a brand ES on the back of each piece. . . ." Refs.: Bivins; Bjerkoe; Fales, *Essex County Furniture.*

SANDERSON, JACOB

Brother and partner of Elijah Sanderson (see previous entry and next entry), Jacob Sanderson (1758–1810) worked at their shop on Federal Street in Salem, Massachusetts, from around 1779 until his death. He is known for a c. 1780–1790 Chippendale mahogany desk and bookcase or secretary, illustrated in *Antiques* for December 1957, which is signed

Jacob Sanderson

Also attributed to him is a c. 1790–1800 Federal mahogany and birch card table, which bears the painted initials

I + S

Ref.: Bjerkoe.

SANDERSON, ELIJAH AND JACOB

During the period of their partnership, c. 1779–1810, Elijah and Jacob Sanderson (see previous entries) of Federal Street, Salem, Massachusetts, produced a quantity of fine Chippendale and Federal furniture, some of which bore their paper label reading,

MADE BY/E. & J. Sanderfon,/CABINET AND CHAIR-MAKERS,/In Federal-Street,/SALEM,/MASSACHUSETTS

Among pieces so distinguished is a Federal Pembroke table, now at Winterthur. Refs.: Bjerkoe; Montgomery.

SANFORD, DAVID

A banister-back armchair with the so-called heart-and-crown crest is labeled on the lower back rail

Made by David Sa{nford} . . . Milford, X 1742

and is attributed to the Milford, Connecticut, turner David Sanford (1709-1751). Refs.: Fairbanks and Bates; *Antiques,* September 1981.

SANFORD, ICHABOD

An inlaid mahogany tall clock case, illustrated in *Antiques* for November 1959, is inscribed on the back

Luther Metcalf, clock case made by Ichabod Sanford, 1796, clock made by Caleb Wheaton, Providence.

Ichabod Sanford worked in Luther Metcalf's cabinet- and chairmaking shop at Medway, Massachusetts, until 1798.

SARGEANT, JOSEPH

An Empire mahogany dressing mirror in a private collection is stenciled on a drawer bottom

J. SARGEANT,/Looking Glass/MANU-FACTURER,/Superior St./Cleveland, Ohio

Joseph Sargeant (born c. 1800) made mirrors at his shop on Superior Street in Cleveland, Ohio, from around 1837 until 1863. Ref.: *Made in Ohio.*

SARGENT, JAMES

A country Federal desk and bookcase or secretary in old red paint is inscribed within the document drawer

James Sargent Candia

The piece is attributed to New Hampshire, c. 1810–1830, but it is not known if Sargent was a cabinetmaker. Ref.: *MAD,* July 1994.

SASS, EDWARD GEORGE

Two Federal inlaid mahogany card tables, illustrated in *Antiques* for September 1986, are signed in pencil

E. G. Sass/October 10, 1811

They are attributed to Charleston, South Carolina, cabinetmaker Edward George Sass (1788–1849), son of Jacob Sass (see next entry). Edward George worked with his father on Queen Street, Charleston, as early as 1811. Ref.: Bjerkoe.

SASS, JACOB

The Charleston, South Carolina, cabinetmaker Jacob Sass (1750–1836) worked in the community for over fifty years after his arrival in 1773, much of the time in partnership with his son, Edward George (see previous entry), at their shop on Queen Street. He retired in 1828.

However, the only signed piece of his known is a Chippendale mahogany desk and bookcase or secretary, which is inscribed,

Made by Jacob Sass/October 1794

Refs.: Bjerkoe; E. Milby Burton, *Charleston Furniture, 1700–1725* (Charleston, S.C.: Charleston Museum, 1955).

SAULS, HENRY

The obscure Northampton County, North Carolina, cabinetmaker Henry Sauls (d. 1832) is known only for a Chippendale walnut slant-front desk, which is inscribed on a drawer back

July 3 1805 Henry Sauls

Sauls is thought to have been working at his craft as early as 1798 and, presumably, continued until his death. Ref.: Bivins.

SAUNDERS, PHILIP H.

An elaborately grained and painted Country Federal two-drawer drop-leaf pine

C. 1820–1840 country Federal grain-painted pine drop-leaf two-drawer work stand signed by the cabinetmaker Philip H. Saunders of Danvers, Massachusetts. Courtesy, the Henry Ford Museum, Dearborn, Mich.

Incised signature of Philip H. Saunders, Danvers, Massachusetts, on a drawer bottom of the country Federal work stand.

Courtesy, the Henry Ford Museum, Dearborn, Mich.

work stand at the Henry Ford Museum is inscribed on a drawer bottom

P. H. Saunders/Mill St Danders

The c. 1820–1840 piece is attributed to a Philip H. Saunders, cabinetmaker, working in Danvers, near Salem, Massachusetts. Ref.: John T.

Chippendale mahogany chest of drawers, c. 1760–1770, labeled by the Philadelphia cabinetmaker William Savery (1721/2–1787), active on Second Street, c. 1750–1780.

Courtesy, Diplomatic Reception Rooms, U.S. Department of State.

Kirk, *Early American Furniture: How to Recognize, Buy and Care for the Most Beautiful Pieces—High Style, Country, Primitive and Rustic* (New York: Alfred A. Knopf, 1970).

SAUTELL, S.

A bow-back Windsor armchair, c. 1780–1800, at the Shelburne Museum is signed in script beneath the bottom

S. Sautell

It is not known if Sautell was the maker or an owner.

SAVERY, WILLIAM

The Philadelphia Quaker chair- and cabinetmaker William Savery (1721/2–1787) completed his apprenticeship around 1741 and by 1750 was already established as a "chairmaker" at a shop on Second Street, where he remained throughout his career. Although there is in a private collection a c. 1745–1755

Extremely rare, c. 1745–1755, chalk signature of William Savery on a Queen Anne walnut trifid-foot side chair. Courtesy, Israel Sack, Inc., New York.

Queen Anne walnut trifid-foot side chair signed in chalk

Savery

the craftsman labeled most of his work, utilizing several marks. Perhaps the earliest of these is an oblong piece of paper printed

WILLIAM SAVERY

without address or advertising material. This has been found on a Chippendale walnut dower chest and a Chippendale mahogany serpentine-front chest of drawers, both c. 1760–1770. Another early form is the rare label advertising

ALL SORTS OF RUSH-BOTTOM/CHAIRS/Made and Sold By/William Savery/At the Sign of the Chair/a little below the Market, in/Second-ftreet/PHILADELPHIA

A somewhat more expansive view of his work is taken in a slightly later label, found on a Chippendale mahogany dressing table. It reads,

All Sorts of Chairs and/Joiners Work/Made and Sold by/William Savery,/At the Sign of the/Chair, a little be-/low the Market, in/Second Street./PHILADELPHIA.

A variation of this label has Savery's name in capitals. At some point the chair trade sign that hung over Savery's shop was replaced by one featuring a chair, a chest of drawers, and a coffin. His label was changed accordingly:

All Sorts of/CHAIRS and JOINER'S/WORK Made and fold by

Label of William Savery on the Chippendale chest of drawers. Courtesy, Diplomatic Reception Rooms, U.S. Department of State.

William Savery,/At the Sign of the Cheft of Drawers, Coffin and Chair,/a little below the Market, in/Second-ftreet,/ PHILADELPHIA

Refs.: Bjerkoe; Downs; Hummel.

SAWYER & BROWN

A c. 1840–1860 Hitchcock-type stencil-decorated half-spindle side chair, illustrated in *MAD* for April 1993, is stamped

SAWYER & BROWN

While this appears to be a maker's mark, nothing has been learned of the manufacturers.

SCHAFFER, MICHAEL

A six-board dower chest with three decorated panels, attributed to Dauphin County, Pennsylvania, and illustrated in *Antique Collecting* for December 1978, is inscribed

Michael Schaffer 1808

It is not known if Schaffer was cabinetmaker, decorator, or the one for whom the chest was made.

SCHAFNER, CHARLES

A Chippendale walnut slant-top chest of drawers, illustrated in *MAD* for December 1993, is inscribed

Charles Schafner, 1787

It is not known if Schafner was the owner or the maker of the desk.

SCHANTZ, MINGES, SHALE & CO.

A Victorian Renaissance Revival walnut marble-top center table at the Margaret Woodbury Strong Museum, Rochester, New York, bears a shipping tag of the Rochester firm of

SCHANTZ, MINGES, SHALE & CO./Manufacturers and Wholesale Dealers in/CABINET WARE/Office & Warerooms, 15, 17 & 19 North Water St./Manufactory, 131 to 134 North Water St./ROCHESTER. N.Y.

which was in business c. 1873–1877.

SCHEAFE, J. B., JR.

A c. 1785–1795 Federal mahogany bow-front chest of drawers, credited to Portsmouth, New Hampshire, is marked on the backboard

J.B. Scheafe, Jr.

It is not known if this is the mark of the maker or an owner.

SCHMEIG & KOTZIAN

A matching pair of marquetry-top inlaid demilune tables, sold at auction in 1994, was labeled

Schmeig & Kotzian/Cabinetmakers/ 72nd St.NY

These reproductions of an eighteenth-century French style would appear to date to the early twentieth century.

SCHOLZE, P. W.

A c. 1780–1800 Hepplewhite mahogany bowfront chest of drawers at the Schuyler Mansion in Albany, New York, is inscribed beneath a drawer

P. W. Scholze/Cabinetmaker/ #7 East Lexington Street/Balto Md.

Nothing further is known of this Baltimore, Maryland, craftsman. Refs.: Bjerkoe; *Antiques,* April 1954.

SCHROEDER, HEINRICH

Ared-stained pine rocking cradle with porcelain blanket fasteners is inscribed

Heinrich Schroeder 1902

Schroeder was a Mennonite craftsman who made this piece at Blumenfeld Village, Alexanderwohl, Kansas. He is also known for other pieces, including bedsteads. Ref.: Reinhild K. Janzen and John M. Janzen, *Mennonite Furniture: A Migrant Tradition, 1766–1910* (Intercourse, Pa.: Good Books, 1991).

SCHUMM, J.

Apair of bamboo-turned rod-back Windsor side chairs, advertised in *Antiques* for July 1985, are branded beneath the seats

J. SCHUMM

They are thought to be the work of a c. 1805–1815 Pennsylvania turner. Ref.: Santore II.

SCOTT, CHARLES

See Webb & Scott.

SCOTT, D.

Ac. 1760–1770 Chippendale mahogany block-front chest of drawers, illustrated in *Antiques* for January 1968, is stamped on the backboard

D. SCOTT

It is not known if this is the mark of the maker or an owner.

SCOTTON

Asouthern Chippendale walnut block-front chest of drawers, c. 1760–1770, is inscribed on the drawers

L.B. Scotton/John W. Scotton/
Spencer Scotton

These are thought to have been owners. Ref.: *Antiques,* January 1952.

SCOTTOW, JOHN

The Boston, Massachusetts, joiner John Scottow is credited with a c. 1725–1735

Japanned William and Mary high chest of drawers or highboy, c. 1725–1735, made and signed by John Scottow of Boston. Courtesy, Israel Sack, Inc., New York.

Signature of John Scottow as it appears in chalk on each drawer of the William and Mary high chest of drawers. Courtesy, Israel Sack, Inc., New York.

William and Mary japanned high chest of drawers or highboy, now at the Richmond (Va.) Museum of Fine Arts. It is signed in chalk
SCOTTOW
throughout the drawers. He is also associated with a c. 1725–1735 Queen Anne dressing table inscribed on the backboard
Scottow W. Randle
and made in conjunction with the Boston cabinetmaker and japanner William Randle. Refs.: Fairbanks and Bates; *MAD,* March 1992.

SCUDDER, JOHN

A Federal mahogany tall clock case, illustrated in *Antiques* for February 1967, is labeled

Unusual mixed-woods bow-back Windsor rocking cradle with the label of the Boston turners William Seaver and James Frost, in business together from 1800 to 1803. Courtesy, Bernard and S. Dean Levy, Inc., New York

MADE AND SOLD BY/JOHN SCUDDER/CABINET-MAKER/WESTFIELD
There is also a clock case with a handwritten label reading,
June the 5th 1793. Made by John Scudder, Jr., a cabinetmaker in Westfield.
John Scudder (b. 1770), who worked in West-

field, New Jersey, c. 1790–1815, made cases for the clockmaker Joakim Hill of Flemington, New Jersey. He moved to Ohio in 1815. Refs.: Bjerkoe; Walter H. Van Hoesen, *Crafts and Craftsmen of New Jersey* (Rutherford: Fairleigh Dickinson University Press, 1973).

SEAL, W.

A c. 1755–1775 Pennsylvania Chippendale walnut tripod-base tea table, illustrated in *Antiques* for December 1972, is marked

W. SEAL

This is thought to be the brand of an owner.

SEATON & MATTHEWS

A c. 1820–1840 bamboo-turned rod-back Windsor side chair in a private collection is labeled

**ALL KINDS OF/WINDSOR
CHAIRS/MADE & SOLD, WAR-
RANTED/BY/SEATON & MATTHEWS/
. . . BELOW/SYCAMORE
STREET,/PETERSBURG.**

Nothing further is known of this Petersburg, Virginia, firm. Ref.: Paul H. Burroughs, *Southern Antiques* (New York: Bonanza Books, 1981).

SEAVER, WILLIAM

The Boston, Massachusetts, chairmaker William Seaver (working 1789–1803) is known for Windsor chairs branded

SEAVER

or

W. SEAVER

as well as others that bear a label reading,
**WARRANTED/Fancy, Bamboo and Wind-
sor/CHAIRS & SETTEES/Of every denomi-
nation, of the newest style/fancy and of a**

**Label of Seaver & Frost on the Windsor
rocking cradle. Courtesy, Bernard and S. Dean
Levy, Inc., New York.**

**superior quality, Made and Sold,/By
WILLIAM SEAVER,/. . . the Golden
Chair, Battery/North-Street/Boston**

A variant of this label, including an address ". . . Near Liberty Square, . . ." is given in Santore. Refs.: Bjerkoe; Santore II; *Antiques,* December 1969.

SEAVER & FROST

The Boston, Massachusetts, turners William Seaver (see previous entry) and James Frost were in partnership from 1800 through 1803, producing a variety of Windsor chairs, including an unusual mixed-woods bow-back Windsor rocking cradle labeled

**WARRANTED/WINDSOR CHAIRS/and
SETTEES/in the newest stile and of a
superior quality/Made and sold
by/SEAVER & FROST/Sign of the WIND-
SOR CHAIR/No. 57 . . . Street BOSTON**

Refs.: Bjerkoe; Ormsbee; *Bee,* November 6, 1981.

SEEM, HENRY

A miniature Victorian mahogany serpentine-front chest of drawers is inscribed,

Built by Henry Seem when an apprentice at Sam Hoagland and Dan Pitinger in Easton—in the year 1856.

The piece, at the Yale University Art Gallery, is attributed to Easton, Pennsylvania, but nothing is known of its maker. Ref.: Schiffer.

SEITZ, OTTO

See George Ackerman.

SELDEN, JOHN

The Norfolk, Virginia, cabinetmaker John Selden (d. 1777) was working in the city by 1768 and may have been apprenticed to a Norfolk cabinetmaker in 1756. Selden is known for a Chippendale walnut chest of drawers signed in chalk

John Selden

and a Chippendale mahogany clothespress inscribed

J. S./1775

Refs.: Bivins; Fitzgerald; Wallace B. Gusler, *Furniture of Williamsburg and Eastern Virginia, 1710–1790.*

SELLEG, D. N.

A c. 1870–1900 Victorian curule-form walnut folding chair in a private collection is labeled

D.N. SELLEG,
Manufacturer of folding chairs

Nothing is known of this company.

SELLEW, T. G.

A c. 1870–1880 Victorian walnut flat-top desk in a private collection is stenciled

T.G. SELLEW/111 Fulton St./N.Y.

It is believed that Sellew was a maker or seller of furniture in New York City during the late nineteenth century.

SELTZER, JOHN

John or Johannes Seltzer (or Selzer, 1774–1845) of Jonestown, Lebanon County, Pennsylvania, learned the craft of chest making and decorating from his father, Christian (see the Selzer, Christian entry), and produced very similar work. His two- and three-panel chests are also decorated with urns of flowers with the

Painted poplar two-panel dower chest signed and dated by Christian Selzer (1749–1831), a Jonestown, Lebanon County, Pennsylvania, craftsman. Courtesy, Bernard and S. Dean Levy, Inc., New York.

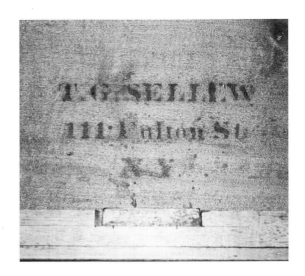

Stenciled mark of T. G. Sellew of New York City on a c. 1870–1880 Victorian walnut desk. Courtesy, Robert Weltz, House of Weltz, Port Chester, N.Y.

maker's signature and a date incised into the wet paint. Among known examples are a two-panel chest inscribed

John/Selzer/1804

another inscribed

John/Selzer/1808

a three-panel chest inscribed

John/Selzer/1792

another inscribed

Johannes Seltzer/1790

another inscribed

John/Selzer/1794

and another inscribed

John/Selzer/1805

In some cases Seltzer would sign one vase on a chest "John Seltzer" and the other, the Germanic "Johannes Seltzer." Seltzer's work may be seen at the Philadelphia Museum of Art and the Baltimore Museum of Art. Refs.: Bjerkoe; Fitzgerald.

SELTZER, JACOB

Jacob Seltzer (b. 1767), a relative of the Jonestown, Lebanon County, Pennsylvania, chest painters Christian and John Seltzer (see preceding and following entries), is known for a single piece, a six-board dower chest decorated with two panels, each containing the typical vase of flowers. The chest is inscribed

Jacob Seltzer/1797

SELZER, CHRISTIAN

Christian Selzer, Selser, or Seltzer (1749–1831) was a Jonestown, Lebanon County, Pennsylvania, craftsman known for painted pine six-board dower chests typically decorated with two or three panels containing vases of flowers. These were often identified by the maker's name and a date scratched into the wet paint over a vase.

One authority describes dated examples ranging from 1771 to 1796. We have located the following: a two-panel chest inscribed

Christian/Selzer/1773

another inscribed

Christian/Selser/1775

another inscribed

Christian/Selzer/1777

another inscribed

Christian/Selzer/1783

another inscribed

Christian/Selzer/1784

another inscribed

Christian/Selzer/1785

another inscribed

Christian/Selzer/1789

a three-panel chest inscribed

Christian/Selzer/1785

and a three-panel chest inscribed

Christian/Selzer/1796

303

Detail of the Christian Selzer dower chest showing Selzer's name and the date "1773" as they were incised into the wet paint over an urn of flowers. Courtesy, Bernard and S. Dean Levy, Inc., New York.

Examples of Selzer's work may be seen at the Museum of Fine Arts, Boston, and the Philadelphia Museum of Art. Refs.: Bjerkoe; Fairbanks and Bates.

SEPTEMBER, S.

A Hepplewhite cherry chest of drawers, c. 1800–1820, in a private collection is signed beneath a drawer

S. September

It is not known if this is the maker's or an owner's name.

SERING, DANIEL

The Shaker cabinetmaker Daniel Sering (1792–1870), of the Union Village, Ohio, community, made a walnut case of drawers or high chest of drawers, which is inscribed in red ink on one drawer

Daniel Sering Maker/November 9th 1827

and on another

Daniel Sering/November 9th 1827

Although Sering served the Ohio communities as carpenter and cabinetmaker for half a century, this is his only signed piece. It is at the Warren County (Ohio) Historical Society Museum. Ref.: Rieman and Burks.

SERR, JOSEPH

A c. 1870–1890 Victorian Rococo Revival upholstered sofa in a private collection is signed on the frame

Jos. Serr Erie, Pa.

This could be the maker's name or that of an upholsterer.

SEYMOUR, HENRY I.

The New York State Museum in Albany has three chairs made at the factory operated in Troy, New York, during the 1860s and '70s by Henry I. Seymour, a relative of the well-known Troy pottery owner Israel Seymour.

These are a walnut side chair branded
MADE BY H.I. SEYMOUR,
TROY, N.Y./PATENTED SEPT. 28, 1862
a cane-seated, bentwood side chair with a paper
label reading,
Manufactured by HENRY I. SEYMOUR
Troy, N.Y./PATENTED MAY 31st, 1870
and a child's rocking chair labeled
MANUFACTURED BY/The Henry I.
Seymour Manufactory, Troy, N.Y./. . . . .
9th 1873
Ref.: Scherer.

SEYMOUR, JOHN

The renowned cabinetmaker John Seymour
(c. 1738–1818) arrived in Portland,
Maine, from County Devon, England, in 1785.
He moved to Boston in 1794 and opened a shop
on Creek Square, where he appears to have
worked until about 1813. Several pieces of
marked furniture have been attributed to him,
including a Federal mahogany tambour-door
sideboard, illustrated in *Antiques* for May 1954,
which is signed
J. Seymour/$15
beneath the marble top, and a Sheraton inlaid
mahogany card table branded
J. S.
on the underside of the apron. A Federal
tambour-front desk with this brand (illustrated in *Antiques* for September 1966) is also
known. There is also a Sheraton mahogany
card table, illustrated in *MAD* for January
1979, that is said to have been inscribed in
chalk on a drawer bottom
John Semour/1814, October
Refs.: Bjerkoe; Montgomery; Michael J. Flanigan, *American Furniture from the Kaufman Collection* (Washington, D.C.: National Gallery of
Art, 1986).

SEYMOUR, THOMAS

Son of the famous John Seymour (see previous entry), Thomas Seymour (1771–1848)
was trained in the craft and worked with his
father until 1804, when he opened his Boston
Furniture Warehouse on Common Street, later
moving to Congress Street and finally to Washington Street, where he remained active until
1843. It is not known if Thomas Seymour made
furniture during this period. There is no doubt,
though, that he sold pieces made by other cabinetmakers. A gilded Federal mirror stamped
by the well-known Stephen Badlam of Boston
(see his entry) also bears Thomas Seymour's rare
label:
BOSTON/Furniture Warehouse,/Bottom of
the Mall./THOMAS SEYMOUR now offers
for sale, as/above an extensive assortment
of/CABINET FURNITURE, LOOKING-
GLASSES,/CHAIRS, BEDS, &c.&c. on the
lowest terms./The above articles are just
received from the most approved/
Manufacturers, and are of the newest fash-
ion./Second-hand Furniture bought or
received for sale.
Refs.: Bjerkoe; Montgomery; Michael J. Flanigan, *American Furniture from the Kaufman Collection* (Washington, D.C.: National Gallery of
Art, 1986).

SEYMOUR & SON

Sometime between 1794 and 1796, the
Boston cabinetmaker John Seymour took
his son, Thomas, into the business (see previous
entries). They worked together on Creek Square
until around 1804, when Thomas established
his own Boston Furniture Warehouse on Common Street. Less than a half dozen pieces of Federal furniture—including two tambour-front

desks and two card tables—are known to bear their printed paper label, which reads,

JOHN SEYMOUR & SON,/CABINET MAKERS,/CREEK SQUARE,/BOSTON

It is generally felt that most furniture made by this partnership was the work of the father. Refs.: Bjerkoe; Montgomery; Michael J. Flanigan, *American Furniture from the Kaufman Collection* (Washington, D.C.: National Gallery of Art, 1986).

SHAKER'S

The Shaker religious communities produced some furniture, primarily chairs and footstools, for sale to outsiders (referred to as "the World"). An early hand stamp reading,

TRADE-MARK/SHAKER'S/MT.LEBANON, N.Y./No.

is known, however, no furniture so marked has been found. Elder Robert M. Wagan (1833–1883) of the Mount Lebanon, New York, community began the mass production of chairs and rockers in the 1870s. He also introduced the use of a gold decal featuring a slat-back

rocking chair and reading,

SHAKER'S/No /TRADE/MARK MT. LEBANON, N.Y.

Various numbers from 0 to 7 were used to indicate standard chair sizes. Large numbers of chairs so marked exist today.

There is also a Shaker-made maple picture frame at the New York State Museum, which bears a circular paper label:

GENUINE/SHAKER/WORK/ MT./LEBANON/N.Y.

It is believed that this label was used primarily for small goods, such as baskets and boxes, rather than for furniture. Refs.: Scherer; Robert F. W. Meader, *Illustrated Guide to Shaker Furniture* (New York: Dover, 1972).

SHARP, CURLEY

A Chippendale walnut side chair, illustrated in *Antiques* for January 1952, bears a paper label on the seat rail reading,

John Carter owner/Curley Sharp maker 1793

This turner is unknown, and the label was probably placed there by an owner.

SHARP, JAMES

The Boston and Watertown, Massachusetts, furniture maker and decorator James Sharp (1790–1873) was active from the 1820s until 1869, producing a range of decorated fur-

Turned pine and maple Shaker footstool, c. 1870–1920, with decal mark of the Mount Lebanon, New York, community. Courtesy, the Henry Ford Museum, Dearborn, Mich.

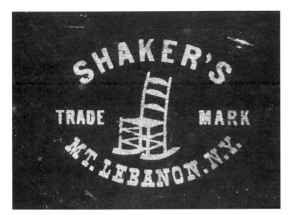

Decal label of the Mount Lebanon, New York, Shaker community on the footstool. Courtesy, the Henry Ford Museum, Dearborn, Mich.

nishings from Federal fancy chairs to Victorian painted cottage furniture. He is known for a set of bedroom furniture bearing the stenciled mark

J. SHARP 1841

a tilt-top table inscribed

J. Sharp 1868

a bedroom set of painted cottage pine, which is signed

J. Sharp 1869

and several floral paintings. Refs.: Fairbanks and Bates; Monkhouse and Michie.

SHARPLESS, ABRAHAM

The Chester County, Pennsylvania, turner Benjamin Sharpless (1748–1833) is known only for a child's bamboo-turned rod-back Windsor armchair inscribed beneath the seat

From Abrm Sharpless/To Isaac Sharpless/1800/Take care of this.

Ref.: Schiffer.

SHARROCK, GEORGE

George Sharrock, a Northampton and Franklin County, North Carolina, cabinetmaker (active until at least 1814), is known for a Chippendale walnut chest of drawers in a private collection, which is inscribed in ink on a drawer back

Maid by George Sharrock May 21th/in the year of/Our Lord one thousand Seven/ hundred and Eighty Seven

Ref.: Bivins.

SHAW, ALEXANDER

The Philadelphia, Pennsylvania, cabinetmaker Alexander Shaw was active in the city c. 1801–1815. He is known for a Federal mahogany card table with the fragmentary label

ALEXANDER SHAW/. . . . .— CHAIR—/. . . . .

and a Sheraton mahogany bowfront chest of drawers at the Philadelphia Museum of Art, which is labeled

ALEXANDER SHAW/CABINET AND CABINETMAKER/HAS REMOVED TO No. 63, South Front Street,/ PHILADELPHIA.

Refs.: Bjerkoe; Hewitt, Kane, and Ward.

SHAW, F.

A c. 1750–1770 Queen Anne mahogany tray-top tea table and a c. 1770–1790 Chippendale slant-front desk of the same wood are both branded

F. SHAW

Nothing is known of this cabinetmaker. Refs.: Bjerkoe; *Antiques,* April 1938, May 1940.

SHAW, JOHN

The skilled and prolific cabinetmaker John Shaw (1745–1829) arrived in Annapolis, Maryland, in 1763 and was established as a cabinetmaker on Church Street by 1770. He remained active, sometimes in partnership, until at least 1816 and possibly 1828. Over fifty pieces of fine Chippendale and Federal mahogany furniture bear his label. Examples may be seen at the Baltimore Museum of Art. Despite his long career, Shaw employed only a single individual label, an oblong piece of paper

Label of John Shaw as it appears on the Chippendale secretary. It is dated in ink "1797." Courtesy, White House Collection.

with a decorative border incorporating thirteen stars for the states of the new union and reading, **JOHN SHAW,/CABINET-MAKER,/ANNAPOLIS.**

There is also a variant of this from another printing with minor differences in the border but no changes in text. Also, many of these labels are dated—"1791," "1796," "1797," "1801," and so on—to reflect the year a piece was made or sold. Refs.: William Voss Elder III

Chippendale mahogany desk and bookcase or secretary, 1797, labeled by John Shaw (1745–1829), active in Annapolis, Maryland, from 1770 until 1816 or later. Courtesy, White House Collection.

and Lu Bartlett, *John Shaw, Cabinetmaker of Annapolis* (Baltimore: Baltimore Museum of Art, 1983); *Antiques,* February 1977.

SHAW & CHISHOLM

During the period 1772–1776 and again c. 1783–1784, the cabinetmaker John Shaw of Annapolis, Maryland (see previous entry), was in partnership with the cabinetmaker and musical instrument maker Archibald Chisholm. Their wares were labeled

> SHAW AND CHISHOLM,/Cabinet and
> Chair Makers,/ANNAPOLIS

with an engraved decorative border of which there are two variants. Little is known of Chisholm other than that he was in partnership in Annapolis in 1793 with a craftsman named Waters. Refs.: Bjerkoe; Montgomery.

SHEARER, JOHN

John Shearer (c. 1765–1810), master of an eccentric cabinetmaking style that incorpo-

Label of Shaw & Chisholm as found on the Chippendale card tables. Courtesy, private collection, Anne Arundel County, Md./ Rafael Osona Auctioneer, Nantucket, Mass.

rated Chippendale and Federal elements and often involved the vertical rather than horizontal placement of drawer pulls, was born in Scotland and worked in Martinsburg, West Virginia, c. 1790–1810. His earliest marked piece is a Chippendale walnut and cherry desk and bookcase or secretary (offered at Sotheby's February 1–4, 1978), which is variously inscribed

> made by Shearer Aug.1801/God Save
> the King 1801/made by me, John
> Shearer . . . . . from Edinburough 1779
> made in Martinsburgh/Down with
> the . . . of Ireland/Shearer joiner/Shearer
> joiner 1801/Shearer from Edin.

As may be seen from this, John Shearer had a

Pair of matching c. 1772–1776 Chippendale mahogany card tables, each of which bears the label of Shaw & Chisholm, Annapolis, Maryland. Courtesy, private collection, Anne Arundel County, Md. /Rafael Osona Auctioneer, Nantucket, Mass.

penchant for signing his pieces (as well as expressing his strong and generally unpopular political views). Indeed, most of his known work is signed more than once. Other examples include a walnut chest of drawers with central tambour door that is signed numerous times

Shearer 1804/ finished by Shearer 1804/ the bureau by Shearer

and, on the interior,

From a Tory/Vive Le Roy/1804/God Save the King/by me John Shearer

There is also a pair of walnut serpentine-front chests of drawers, both dated 1809 and signed numerous times

John Shearer

Perhaps Shearer's final piece is a Chippendale walnut serpentine slant-front desk dated "1810" four times and signed eleven times

John Shearer

Refs.: Fitzgerald; *MAD,* April 1994.

SHEDD, JAMES P.

An Empire tiger maple chest of drawers with splash back, c. 1840–1850, was signed on the backboard

James P. Shedd

Shedd (1816–1894) was a rural cabinetmaker working in Norway, Maine, north of Portland. Ref.: *MAD,* November 1978.

SHEPARD & CO.

A simple c. 1845–1855 rod-back side chair at the Henry Ford Museum is stenciled under the seat

SHEPARD & CO./Manufacturer/ CLEVELAND, OHIO

The chairmaker Daniel A. Shepard first advertised in Cleveland in 1835, at which time he was on Superior Street. From 1836 until at least 1853, he was at several locations on Water Street. Advertisements indicate that he assumed the name Shepard & Co. in 1848. Ref.: Hageman II.

SHEPPARD, C.

Santore records a Philadelphia-type rod-back Windsor armchair, c. 1810, which is branded beneath the seat

C. SHEPPARD

It is not known if this is the maker's or an owner's mark. Ref.: Santore II.

SHERMER, JAMES

A gilded Federal frame, c. 1805–1815, illustrated in *Antiques* for September 1926, bears the label of the Philadelphia looking glass and frame maker James Shermer. The partially legible label reads, below an elaborate representation of the American eagle,

LOOKING GLASS/AND/PICTURE FRAME/MANUFACTORY./JAMES SHERMER/Respectfully informs his friends and the public, that he carries/on the above business at/. . . . . ./ PHILADELPHIA./N.B. Ladies Needle Work framed and glazed in the neatest/ manner—Bed and Window Cornices made or re-gilt—old Look-/ing Glasses re-gilt or repaired and all other Fancy Gilding done/with neatness and dispatch.

The street address seems to have been scratched out, perhaps indicating a move from one shop location to another.

SHIELDS, ROBERT

A c. 1800–1820 Federal walnut desk and bookcase or secretary at the Cumberland County Historical Society, Carlisle, Pennsylvania, is signed on the bottom in chalk

Robert Shields/James

The cabinetmaker Robert Shields is recorded as working at Big Spring or Springfield, Pennsylvania, from 1817 through 1829. A tall clock case from his hand is also known. The significance of the word "James" is not known. Ref.: *Antiques,* May 1983.

SHIPLEY, GEORGE

G eorge Shipley (d. 1801) was a Manhattan cabinetmaker and seller of other craftsmen's furniture who worked at various addresses on Water Street, c. 1791–1801. His two marked pieces bear different labels. That on a Federal mahogany card table reads,

A large assortment of/CABINET FURNI-TURE/of the newest fashion at/G. Shipley's Manufact'/No. 161 Water Street/NEW YORK/Mahogany for Sale.

while a Federal inlaid mahogany sideboard bears an engraved label featuring an illustration of a Federal desk and bookcase and reading,

Mahogany ready Saw'd up for Staircases & other purposes for Sale/ELEGANT MAH-OGy. FURNITURE/of the newest Fashion, at/SHIPLEY's/Manufactory/No. 161 Water Street,/N. YORK.

Both pieces may be dated to 1791–1795, the period when Shipley's warerooms were at 161 Water Street. Refs.: Hewitt, Kane, and Ward; *Antiques,* April 1961.

SHIPMAN, HENRY T.

T he turner Henry T. Shipman of Coxsackie, New York, is known for two Windsor chairs: a comb-back armchair illustrated in *MAD* for April 1975 and a rod-back side chair at the New York State Museum. Both date c. 1790–1805 and are stenciled beneath the seat

H.T. SHIPMAN/COXSACKIE

Shipman, a Connecticut craftsman, resided in Coxsackie, Greene County, before moving to Binghamton in 1805. Ref.: Scherer.

SHIVELY, JOHN D.

A late-nineteenth-century pine bench in a private collection is signed on the seat bottom in blue paint

John D. Shively maker

Though listed in the census as a farmer, Shively (born c. 1862) was the grandson of a cabinetmaker. Ref.: *Made in Ohio.*

SHOEMAKER, JONATHAN

A Chippendale walnut chest on chest in a private collection is signed

Jonathan/Shoemaker

and attributed to the Philadelphia cabinetmaker Jonathan Shoemaker (1726–1793), working c. 1757–1793. Refs.: Bjerkoe; *Antiques,* May 1985.

SHORT, CHARLES

A late Federal mahogany and birch card table in a private collection is branded

CHARLES SHORT

Short (1792–after 1872) was a Massachusetts cabinetmaker who worked in Newburyport, Haverhill, Andover, and Salem, primarily as an employee of others. Ref.: Hewitt, Kane, and Ward.

SHORT, ISAAC

Son of the well-known Joseph Short (see next entry), Isaac Short (1803–1847), a chair and cabinetmaker active in Newburyport, Massachusetts, before 1827, is known for a Chippendale-Federal transitional maple ribbon-back side chair with a pencil-written paper label reading,

Isaac Short/Newburyport, Mass.

Ref.: John T. Kirk, *Early American Furniture: How to Recognize, Buy and Care for the Most Beautiful Pieces—High Style, Country, Primitive and Rustic* (New York: Alfred A. Knopf, 1970).

SHORT, JOSEPH

The Newburyport, Massachusetts, cabinet-maker Joseph Short (1771–1819) produced a variety of fine Federal mahogany furniture in his shop on Merrimack Street. A substantial number of pieces are labeled

WARRANTED/CABINET WORK/OF ALL KINDS, MADE AND SOLD BY, JOSEPH SHORT,/At his shop, Merrimack-Street, between/Market-Square and Brown's Wharf,/NEWBURYPORT./ ALL orders for Work will be gratefully/received and punctually executed.

A variation of this label adds the phrase **". . . also makes Martha Washington Chairs."**

There is also a Federal mahogany open armchair, c. 1795–1805, which is branded

J. S.

and attributed to Joseph Short. An example of Short's marked work may be seen at Winterthur. Refs.: Bjerkoe; Hewitt, Kane, and Ward.

SHOVE, LYND ABRAHAM

A c. 1800–1810 Federal New England desk and bookcase or secretary in cherry, adver-

---

Federal inlaid mahogany and satinwood butler's desk, labeled WILLIAM SINCLAIR/Cabinet Maker./FLOWER-TOWN/1803. Sinclair was in Flowertown, Montgomery County, Pennsylvania, until 1819, when he moved to Philadelphia. Courtesy, Leigh Keno, New York.

tised in *Antiques* for June 1969, is signed

Lynd Abraham Shove

This is thought to be an owner's mark.

SHOVE, THEOPHILUS

A Chippendale curly maple chest of drawers, c. 1760–1780, offered at Sotheby's, September 30–October 1, 1978, is branded

T*SHOVE/BLRKLEY

for Theophilus Shove, who is known to have opened a joiner's shop in Boston, Massachusetts, in 1739. Ref.: Bjerkoe.

SHUMWAY, W. D.

A cherry and maple blanket chest over drawers, which sold at auction in August 1994, was marked

Built by W. D. Shumway 1835
when he was 18 years old

Shumway (w. 1841–18/5), though not a member of the order, was often employed by the Shakers at Mount Lebanon, New York. Ref.: Rieman and Burks.

SIEVERS, JACOB

A c. 1810–1830 country Sheraton pine and maple cupboard over drawers, said to be from Old Winston Salem, North Carolina, is signed

Jacob Sievers

It is not known if Sievers was the cabinetmaker or an owner.

SIMMS, ISAAC P.

A c. 1790–1800 bow-back Windsor side chair is branded beneath the seat

ISAAC P. SIMMS

This is thought to be the mark of an as yet unknown turner. Ref.: Bjerkoe.

SINCLAIR, FRANCIS A.

Several sets of splint-seated ladder-back side chairs, c. 1860–1880, are branded

F. A. SINCLAIR/MOTTVILLE, N.Y.

Francis A. Sinclair (b. 1834) opened a shop in Mottville, Onondaga County, New York, in 1859. His firm, known as the Union Chair Company, remained in his hands until 1905. Other owners maintained the business until 1938. Ref.: Scherer.

SINCLAIR, WILLIAM

A Federal inlaid mahogany and satinwood butler's desk, illustrated in *Antiques* for June 1988, bears the oval label

WILLIAM SINCLAIR/Cabinet
Maker./FLOWERTOWN/1803

The cabinetmaker William Sinclair worked in Flowertown, near Chestnut Hill, Montgomery County, Pennsylvania, until 1819, when he moved to Philadelphia, where he had shops at several locations through 1837. Ref.: *Antiques,* October 1929.

SINGLETON, WILLIAM

A Federal mahogany shield-back side chair (one of a set of eight) with eagle inlay in the Diplomatic Reception Rooms of the Department of State, Washington, D.C., is branded

W.S.

for William Singleton, a cabinetmaker working in Baltimore, Maryland, c. 1796–1802. Refs.: Bjerkoe; *Antiques,* May 1974.

Pair of Federal inlaid
mahogany shield-back side
chairs branded "W.S." for
William Singleton, a Baltimore, Maryland, cabinet-
maker, active
c. 1796–1802. Courtesy,
Diplomatic Reception Rooms,
U.S. Department of State.

SIPERLY, F.

A small painted pine six-board chest, illustrated in *Antiques* for March 1968, is
inscribed on the underside of the lid

F. Siperly was born/September the 21.

1765 and made this chest November the
17./1835 for/G. Spencer.
Nothing further is known of Siperly.

SKELLORN, GEORGE W.

Several in a set of c. 1800–1820 rod-back
Windsor side and armchairs are labeled
GEORGE W. SKELLORN,/FANCY AND
WINDSOR CHAIR-MAKER, No. 356,
PEARL STREET, NEW-YORK./N.B. All
orders thankfully received and executed
with neatnefs and difpatch & at the
fhortefh notice.
Skellorn made Windsors and Sheraton fancy
chairs in Manhattan, c. 1798–1827. He was at

Cherry Hepplewhite chest of drawers with
inlay bearing the signature of cabinetmaker
William Slayer and the date 1809. Courtesy,
Bradford Galleries, Ltd.

356 Pearl Street from 1800 until 1819. Ref.: Scherer.

SLACK, JOSEPH R.

A child's bamboo-turned rod-back Windsor side chair at the New Jersey State Museum, Trenton, is branded beneath the seat
J. R. SLACK
It is attributed to Joseph R. Slack, a turner working in Franklin Township, Hunterdon County, New Jersey, c. 1830–1850. Ref.: *Furniture and Furnishings from the Collection of the New Jersey State Museum* (Trenton: New Jersey State Museum, 1970).

SLADE, FREDERICK

A braced fan-back Windsor armchair, c. 1780–1800, illustrated in *Antiques* for July 1976, is marked beneath the seat
MADE BY FREDERICK SLADE IN NANTUCKET 1799
Nothing further is known of Slade.

SLAYER, WILLIAM

A Hepplewhite cherry chest of drawers with fan inlay, sold at auction in 1994, was signed
William Slayer cabinet maker . . . 1809
The piece is attributed to Connecticut, but nothing is presently known of the maker.

Hepplewhite inlaid mahogany tall clock case bearing the label of Abraham A. Slover, active c. 1792–1805, and Kortright, who were associated on Cortland Street in New York City. Courtesy, Bernard and S. Dean Levy, Inc., New York.

SLOVER & KORTRIGHT

The brief partnership of cabinetmakers Abraham A. Slover and Kortright, 1795–1796, produced two Hepplewhite inlaid mahogany tall clock cases, both labeled
Slover and Kortright/CABINET-MAKERS,/No. 30 Cortland STREET/ NEW-YORK.

Paper label of Slover & Kortright on the Federal tall clock case. They worked together only during the period 1795–1796.

Courtesy, Bernard and S. Dean Levy, Inc., New York.

Although nothing is known of Kortright, Slover worked at various addresses in Manhattan from 1792 until 1805. During the period 1805–1809, he was listed in the city directory as a grocer.

SLOVER & TAYLOR

Several in a set of Sheraton mahogany square-back side chairs, described in *Antiques* for October 1961, bear partial labels reading,

SLOVER & TAYLOR,/CABINET-
MAKERS,/No. 94 Broad Street/
NEW-YORK

Federal inlaid bowfront chest of drawers labeled by Abraham A. Slover and a man named Taylor. They worked on Broad Street in New York City from 1802 to 1804.

Courtesy, Bernard and S. Dean Levy, Inc., New York.

Abraham A. Slover (working c. 1792–1805), a Manhattan cabinetmaker, was in partnership at 94 Broad Street from 1802 through 1804 with one Taylor, first name and history unknown. Refs.: *Antiques,* November 1923, October 1961.

SMART, M. P.

A pine and maple country tap table, c. 1800–1830, is signed

M.P. Smart, So. Parkman

South Parkman is a small Maine community, but nothing is known of M. P. Smart. The name is likely that of an owner.

SMITH, BENJAMIN F. H.

The Canterbury, New Hampshire, Shaker brother and cabinetmaker Benjamin F. H. Smith (1829–1899) signed a cherry and butternut double sewing desk in pencil

B.H. Smith 1862, NF 1862

and another, similar desk, in pine and maple, in red ink

B.F.H. SMITH Sept 1861

The latter is at Canterbury Shaker Village, Canterbury, New Hampshire. Ref.: Rieman and Burks.

SMITH, CHARLES B. F.

The Wilmington, Delaware, carpenter Charles B. F. Smith (born c. 1814) made a miniature mahogany veneer on tulipwood chest of drawers, which is inscribed

This minature Bureau/was built by/Charles B.F. Smith/at Harlan Hollingsworth Car shop/in February 1837

Smith was listed in the Wilmington directories as a carpenter from 1845 through 1882. Ref.: *Plain and Ornamental.*

SMITH, GEORGE AND JACOB

The Boston cabinetmakers George and Jacob Smith, active c. 1822–1829 at Orange and, later, Washington streets, are known for several marked pieces, including Sheraton mahogany dressing tables. Their stencil reads,

G. & J. SMITH/Cabinet & Chair/Manufacturer/No. 12 Orange St./BOSTON

Their shop was at 12 Orange Street from 1822 through 1826. Ref.: *Antiques,* May 1976.

SMITH, JACOB

A c. 1780–1800 Queen Anne vase-back side chair at the New York State Museum is stamped

IACOB/SMITH

across the tops of the front legs. Jacob Smith

Partial label of the New York cabinetmakers Slover & Taylor. Courtesy, Bernard and S. Dean Levy, Inc., New York.

(active c. 1787–1812) was a well-known New York City turner and cabinetmaker who, in 1788, led a group of rush-seat chairmakers in the parade to honor ratification of the U.S. Constitution. Smith, who worked at 13 Beekman Street, is also credited with chairs branded

J S

Refs.: Scherer; *Antiques,* May 1981.

SMITH, JACOB C.

A handwritten label within a late Federal cherry and walnut tall clock case reads,
The works in this clock/were made by Gideon Roberts/Bristol Conn in the year/1780/This clock case was made/by Jacob C. Smith in Jef-/ferson County Tenn in the year/1826
Nothing further is known of Smith, and it seems likely that the inscription was made by a later owner of the clock.

SMITH, JAMES X.

The Shaker cabinetmaker James X. Smith (1806–1888) of Mount Lebanon, New York, made a cherry and maple sewing case of drawers at the Metropolitan Museum of Art stamped

**JAS. X. SMITH NEW LEBANON
N.Y./1843**

and a child's potty-chair impressed

JAS. X. SMITH/NEW-LEBANON/N.Y.
Ref.: Rieman and Burks.

SMITH, JOHN

A c. 1790–1810 inlaid mahogany and birch desk and bookcase or secretary with a Portsmouth history, illustrated in *MAD* for June 1994, is signed in pencil

Made by John Smith in 1807

Nothing is known of Smith. However, Bjerkoe mentions a John Smith, cabinetmaker, advertising in Boston in 1804. Ref.: Bjerkoe.

SMITH, JONATHAN, JR.

A nineteenth-century chest on chest, acquired by Historic Deerfield in 1991, bears the label of the Conway, Massachusetts, cabinetmaker Jonathan Smith, Jr.

SMITH, LEVI

The label within a c. 1830–1840 shelf clock at the Henry Ford Museum reads,

**IMPROVED TIME-PIECE./Made
by/SILAS HOADLEY,/PLYMOUTH,
Conn./Cased and sold by L. SMITH/
WARRANTED MOVEMENT.**

Levi Smith, a Bristol, Connecticut, cabinetmaker, frequently made cases for Hoadley clock movements. Ref.: *Antiques,* July 1972.

SMITH, MICHAEL

Two New York–type side chairs now at the Metropolitan Museum of Art that are similar to those made by Jacob Smith (see his entry on page 317) are impressed in the same manner with

MICHAEL SMITH

They are thought to have been made, c. 1770–1780, by a brother or father of the Manhattan turner. Ref.: *Antiques,* May 1981.

SMITH, W.

A pair of painted ladder-back side chairs sold at auction in 1994 are marked

W. SMITH/CATSKILL, N.Y.

It is not known if this is the mark of the maker or an owner. Ref.: *Bee,* April 15, 1994.

SMITH & HITCHINGS

An exceedingly rare Federal mahogany card table at the Yale University Art Gallery bears the partial label

**SMITH &
HITCHINGS/Cabinetmakers,/At
STORE No. 40 MIDDLE-STREET,/. . . . .
BOSTON/. . . . MAKING . . . . A
General . . . CABINET-WORK/. . . . .
CHAIRS . . . . . .**

John Smith and Samuel Hitchings were in business together in Boston, Massachusetts, only during the period 1803–1804. Ref.: Hewitt, Kane, and Ward.

SMITH & NORTON

A c. 1815–1825 gilded Federal mirror bears the engraved label of its manufacturers:
SMITH AND NORTON/LOOKING-

GLASS/MANUFACTURERS/OPPOSITE THE/Court Houfe Northamp-/ton./Embroidery and Pictures/Framed./Old Looking-Glafs/PLATES FRAMED, OR/REPAIRED/Warranted Copal Varn.,/AND JAPAN/Gold and Silver Leaf,/&c. &c. &c.

Ref.: Fales, *Historic Deerfield.*

SOPER FURNITURE COMPANY

A c. 1860–1890 oak rod-back armchair, illustrated in *Antiques* for March 1965, is inscribed in paint beneath the seat

S & S Oshkosh

thought to stand for members of the Soper Furniture Company of Oshkosh, Wisconsin.

SPENCER & GILMAN

T he looking-glass and frame-making partnership of Stephen Spencer and Eli Gilman, active on Main Street in Hartford, Connecticut, from 1808 through 1825, is known for two engraved labels. The earlier, perhaps, reads,

SPENCER/&/GILMAN/LOOKING-GLASS/MANUFACTURERS/Main-street, Hartford,/Keep constantly for/sale, Looking-Glasses,/Looking-Glass plates,/Profile Frames, Picture/Glass, &c. Embroide-/ry, and Pictures of all/kinds framed; Old Glasses, Pictures, &c./repaired on short no-/tice.

within a representation of a gilded Federal mirror. The second label, a copy of which is dated in ink "1812," features an engraved eagle holding a banner saying,

LOOKING GLASSES

and reads,

SPENCER & GILMAN,/Looking-Glass Manufacturers,/Main Street, Hartford—/KEEP CONSTANTLY FOR SALE/LOOKING GLASSES,/LOOKING GLASS PLATES,/PROFILE FRAMES, &c./Pictures of all kinds Framed in elegant style./Repairing done on short notice.

Ref.: Montgomery.

SPICER, ABEL

A c. 1775–1785 fan-back Windsor side chair at Historic Deerfield is stamped

A S

on the seat back and attributed to the turner Abel Spicer (1736–1784) of Groton, Connecticut. Ref.: Fales, *Historic Deerfield.*

SPIER, HUGH

S ee Birdsall Salmon.

SPOONER, ALDEN

T he cabinetmaker Alden Spooner (1784–1877) had for many years a shop on Main Street in Athol, Massachusetts. A number of pieces of Federal furniture, including a mahogany card table at the Yale University Art Gallery and an inlaid mahogany sofa, illustrated in *Antiques* for June 1971, bear his stamp:

SPOONER/ATHOL

There are also inscribed pieces, including a cherry bowfront chest of drawers at Old Sturbridge Village signed in ink

Alden Spooner/Athol/July 1807

and another with turned Sheraton legs, which is inscribed

Alden Spooner/Athol/. . .

Spooner was still in business in 1850. Refs.: Hewitt, Kane, and Ward; *Antiques,* October 1979, May 1982, December 1992.

SPOONER, GROVER

Apainted pine dressing table bears a penciled inscription indicating that it was sold in October 1835 by Grover Spooner of Barre, Massachusetts. Because Spooner listed himself as a "fancy and sign painter," it is more likely that he decorated than that he made the piece.

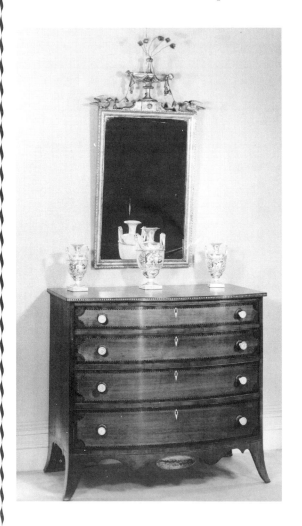

SPOONER & FITTS

During the period 1808–1813, Alden Spooner (see his entry) was in partnership with George Fitts (1785–1866) at his shop, Main Street, Athol, Massachusetts, producing Federal furniture and Windsor chairs. A Hepplewhite inlaid cherry bowfront chest of drawers of their manufacture, offered at Sotheby's, May 23–25, 1980, is branded

SPOONER & FITTS ATHOL

A similar stamp was used on their Windsor chairs. A rod-back armchair is branded

SPOONER & FITTS/ATHOL

while a rod-back side chair from the same period is impressed

SPOONER/&/FITTS/ATHOL

Refs.: Fales, *Historic Deerfield; Antiques,* October 1979, March 1985.

SPOONER & THAYER

For some period after 1813, the Athol, Massachusetts, cabinet- and chairmaker Alden Spooner (see his entry) was in partnership with one Jesse Thayer. A chair stamped

SPOONER & THAYER

is said to be in a private collection. Ref.: *Antiques,* May 1993.

Hepplewhite inlaid cherry bowfront chest of drawers branded SPOONER & FITTS/ATHOL by the cabinetmakers Alden Spooner (1784–1877) and George Fitts (1785–1866), associated on Main Street in Athol, Massachusetts, 1808–1813. Courtesy, Bernard and S. Dean Levy, Inc., New York.

SPOONER & TRASK

From 1825 until 1828 the cabinetmakers Sherlock Spooner (working c. 1825–1835) and George Trask (working c. 1825–1830) were in business together on Washington Street in Boston, Massachusetts. A set of Classical side chairs at the Art Institute of Chicago bears their stenciled mark:

SPOONER & TRASK/No. 663

The rest of the address is missing. Ref.: *Antiques,* May 1992.

SPRAGE, D.

See Frothingham & Sprage.

SPRING & HASKELL

A set of c. 1830–1850 decorated half-spindle side chairs sold at auction on August 29, 1994, were branded beneath the seats

SPRING & HASKEL, HIRAM

They are attributed to a shop located at Hiram, Maine. Ref.: *MAD,* November 1994.

SPRINGER, JOSEPH W.

Joseph W. Springer advertised wares from his ". . . Cheap Furniture Rooms . . ." in Wilmington, Delaware, between 1850 and 1853, offering mahogany and native hardwood washstands, worktables, and "chamber furniture" stenciled

**From/J. W. SPRINGER/Furniture/
WAREROOMS/N.W. COR./
2d & Shipley Sts./WIL. DEL.**

A washstand with this mark is at Winterthur. Refs.: *Plain and Ornamental; Antiques,* May 1985.

SPRINGER, ROBERT M.

The New Garden Township, Chester County, Pennsylvania, cabinetmaker Robert M. Springer (c. 1813–1853) is known for a country Sheraton mahogany veneer desktop chest of drawers in a private collection, which is inscribed

Robert M. Springer/May 3rd 1838

Springer worked in New Garden Township, c. 1838–1850. Ref.: Schiffer.

SPRINGMEYER BROTHERS

Following the death of John Henry Belter (see his entry) in 1863, his then partners, the Springmeyer Brothers—J.H., Fred, and William—took over the firm, operating it with diminishing success until 1867. Their rare stenciled mark:

**Springmeyer Brothers/
Successors to J.H. Belter**

appears on a Victorian Renaissance Revival walnut kneehole writing desk. Ref.: Marvin D. Schwartz, Edward J. Stanek, and Douglas K. True, *The Furniture of John Henry Belter and the Rococo Revival* (New York: E. P. Dutton, 1981).

SPROSEN, JOHN

The turner John Sprosen, active in Philadelphia, c. 1783–1788, and New York City, 1789–1798, is known for Windsor chairs branded beneath the seat

I. SPROSEN

Among these are braced bow-back side chairs and a braced continuous-arm chair. Ref.: Santore II.

STACEY, ALFRED E.

Alfred E. Stacey of Elbridge, Onondaga County, New York, manufactured a variety of c. 1865–1885 Victorian Eastlake-style rocking chairs, including folding examples, which are labeled

East Lake and Bamboo/ROCKING CHAIRS,/MANUFACTURED BY/ALFRED E. STACEY,/ELBRIDGE, ONONDAGA COUNTY, N.Y.

These typically have turned members and woven fabric seats and backs.

STAHL, JEREMIAH H.

A c. 1850–1860 painted and stencil-decorated poplar flat-wall cupboard with glazed doors in the upper section, which was sold at Skinner's auction gallery, June 10, 1989, is stenciled

MANUFACTURED BY JEREMIAH H. STAHL

The Somerset County, Pennsylvania, cabinetmaker Jeremiah H. Stahl (1830–1907) worked in Soap Hollow until 1880, when he moved to Kent County, Michigan. Ref.: *Antiques,* May 1983.

STANYON, J.

A small bamboo-turned Windsor stool, which was offered at Christie's, June 17, 1992, is branded on the underside of the top

J. STANYON

The piece is attributed to Pennsylvania, c. 1790–1820, but it is not known if the mark is that of the maker or an owner. Ref.: Santore II.

STARKEY, NATHAN

A mahogany portable or "lap" desk in a private collection is dated "1842" and bears the label

N. STARKEY,/Manufacturer of Portable Desks./Dressing Cases, Medicine Chests,

Painted and stencil-decorated c. 1850–1860 poplar flat-wall cupboard with the stenciled name of the Soap Hollow, Somerset County, Pennsylvania, cabinetmaker Jeremiah H. Stahl (1830–1907). Courtesy, Skinner, Inc., Bolton, Mass.

and/Ladies' Work Boxes,/137 WALNUT STREET,/6 doors before Fifth St./PHILADELPHIA./Cabinet Furniture of Every Description.

Nathan Starkey is listed in the Philadelphia directories at various addresses from 1831 until 1865. He was at 137 Walnut Street only in 1841 and 1842. A variant of this label, listing Starkey also as the maker of ". . . Medical Saddle Bags . . ." and giving a South Fourth Street address, is also known. Ref.: *Antiques,* September 1955.

STEDMAN, GEORGE

An unusual c. 1815–1825 Federal cherry and mahogany chest of drawers with bombé front is signed in pencil on a drawer

Made by/G. Stedman/Norwich Vermont

The piece, now at Winterthur, is attributed to George Stedman (b. 1795), a cabinetmaker advertising in nearby Chester, Vermont, in 1816. He may have worked briefly in Norwich, Windsor County, before moving to New York and on to Ohio. Refs.: Montgomery; *Old Time New England Furniture* (Boston: Society for the Preservation of New England Antiquities, 1987).

STEEL, ANTHONY

The turner Anthony Steel worked at various addresses in Philadelphia from 1791 through 1817. A variety of Windsor chairs—including a low-back writing armchair, a bamboo-turned rod-back settee, and several rod-back side and armchairs—are branded beneath their seats

A. STEEL

Refs.: Monkhouse and Michie; Santore II.

STEEL, E. B.

A Hepplewhite inlaid mahogany and maple desk and bookcase or secretary, c. 1790–1800, is signed

E.B. Steel

which may be the maker's or an owner's mark.

STEEN, JOHN

A late Federal mahogany dressing glass at the New York State Museum bears an oval printed paper label reading,

CARVING/GILDING/LOOKING GLASS MANUFACTORY/JOHN STEEN/ Fulton/161/Street/NEW-YORK./ PRINTS AND NEEDLEWORK NEATLY FRAMED.

Steen worked alone on Fulton Street in Manhattan as a carver and cabinetmaker from 1812 until 1816. From 1817 through 1828 he ran a looking glass store. Ref.: Scherer.

STEPHENS, N. R.

A stencil-decorated pine six-board chest at the Henry Ford Museum is stenciled on the underside of the lid

N.R. STEPHENS/CHAIR./ FACTORY/1832:

The N. R. Stephens Chair Factory was located in Cooperstown, New York, c. 1830–1840. Ref.: Fales, *American Painted Furniture.*

STEPHENS & SATLER CO.

A Federal mahogany shield-back side chair, c. 1790–1810, is inscribed on a piece of fabric beneath the seat

Chas. Burling Stevenson/Stephens & Satler Co./Providence 1810.

This could be the mark of the maker or the upholsterer. More likely, it is that of an owner. Ref.: Montgomery.

STEPHENSON, E.

A c. 1750–1760 Queen Anne mahogany side chair from Massachusetts or Rhode Island, illustrated in *MAD* for August 1978, is signed on the inside of a chair rail

E. Stephenson

It is not known if this is the mark of the maker or an owner.

STEPILTON, JOSEPH

A c. 1830–1840 Empire cherry chest of drawers with unusual reeded legs is signed on the back by Joseph Stepilton,

Signature of Edward Steves on the underside of the lid of the countinghouse or schoolmaster's desk. Private collection.

Stoutsville, Fairfield County, Ohio. Ref.: Hageman I.

STEVENS, STEPHEN F.

T hough usually described in the census as a farmer, his surviving account books show that Stephen F. Stevens (1795–1857) of Monkton, Vermont, was an active cabinetmaker from at least 1830 until 1856. A tall chest of drawers from his hand is inscribed

Manufactured by S.F. Stevens/ Monkton, 7th Mo. 1826

Several signed pieces are at the Rokeby Museum. Ref.: Robinson.

Cypress slant-top countinghouse or schoolmaster's desk with the inscribed signature and date "1858" of the Cypress Creek, Texas, craftsman Edward Steves (1829–1880). Private collection.

STEVENSON, THOMAS

The Smyrna, Delaware, cabinetmaker Thomas Stevenson (1787–1865) is known for a Hepplewhite inlaid mahogany chest of drawers at Winterthur, which is inscribed twice in chalk on drawers

Thomas Stevenson

and in pencil on a third drawer

Thos. McDowell/March 18, 1808/
Jany 20 1804

Stevenson was apprenticed to the Smyrna, Delaware, cabinetmaker Thomas McDowell, following which he established his own shop in Dover, Delaware, where he worked on State Street until after 1840. Ref.: *Plain and Ornamental.*

STEVES, EDWARD

A cypress slant-top countinghouse or schoolmaster's desk in a private Texas collection is inscribed on the underside of the lid

Ed Steves/Cypress Creek/Made out of his
own/cut Cypress trees/and made by
himself/1858

Steves (1829–1880), a lumberman, came to Texas from Germany in 1848. Ref.: *Antiques,* May 1974.

STEWART, AMOS

The Shaker brother and cabinetmaker Amos Stewart (1802–1884) of Mount Lebanon, New York, produced several pieces of marked furniture, including a c. 1870 butternut sewing desk pencil signed

Amos Stewart

a cherry and pine counter with drawers inscribed on the rear panels

AS 1873

an ash fall-front desk and cupboard at the New York State Museum inscribed

Made 1873 by Amos Stewart

a pine and ash washstand signed in pencil on the top drawer

Amos Stewart March 1878

and a butternut kneehole desk having the following pencil-written note on a drawer bottom:

made in 1877 by Amos Stewart with
one hand age 74

an ironic commentary on the fact that Stewart, some months previously, had lost his left hand in a shop accident. Ref.: Rieman and Burks.

STEWART, DANIEL

A painted step-down rod-back Windsor side chair, illustrated in *MAD* for August 1983, bears the label of

DANIEL STEWART,/Chair-Maker &
Painter,/Farmington, Me.

Stewart worked in Farmington from 1812 through 1827. There is also a c. 1825–1835 Empire mahogany card table, illustrated in *MAD* for April 1994, said to be signed in chalk

Daniel Stewart

However, this high-style piece seems inappropriate for a rural chairmaker. Ref.: Santore II.

STICKLEY, GUSTAV

The innovative furniture maker Gustav Stickley (1857–1942), of Eastwood, Onondaga County, New York, produced, during the period 1898–1915, a variety of primarily oak furniture in the Arts and Crafts mode. Much of this was marked with several different brands and labels. His earliest pieces, made in conjunction with the Tobey Furniture Company of Chicago (see their entry), do not bear his name. However, in 1901 he introduced his well-known brand or decal, featuring a joiner's

compass and the words

Als Ik Kan

("as well as I can"). Over the next fourteen years this mark was periodically altered as follows:

In 1901 it was a brand with the initials "GS" within the compass and "Als Ik Kan" in a rectangular box below, followed by

**Gustave Stickley/Cabinet Maker/
Syracuse/N.Y/**

During the years 1902–1903 the mark was a red decal with "Als Ik Kan" within the compass and "Stickley" in a rectangular box below.

During the period 1902–1904 the brand was a similar red decal but with the entire mark enclosed within a bordering rectangle.

The 1904–1912 version, the most common, lacks the bordering rectangle, and for the first time the signature is "Gustav Stickley" rather than just "Stickley." Although usually a red decal was used, some c. 1910–1912 pieces are stamped in black.

From 1912 through 1915 Stickley's mark was a black brand consisting only of the joiner's compass and the word "Stickley."

Stickley also employed several printed paper labels, usually in conjunction with decals or brands. The first of these, used from 1905 through 1907, reads,

**TRADE/MARK/THE CRAFTSMAN
WORKSHOPS/GUSTAV
STICKLEY/DESIGNED AND MADE
BY/Gustav Stickley/EASTWOOD, N.Y.**

and incorporated a representation of the joiner's compass. From 1907 to 1912 the label, also illustrating the compass and Als Ik Kan motif, reads,

**The name "CRAFTSMAN" is our/registered TRADE MARK and/identifies all
our Furniture—/CRAFTSMAN/Made by
Gustav Stickley in the/CRAFTSMAN
WORKSHOPS/Eastwood New York/NEW
YORK CITY SHOWROOMS/29 West**

Arts and Crafts oak sideboard, c. 1912–1915, with the mark and label of Gustav Stickley (1857–1942) of Eastwood, New York. Courtesy, University of Nebraska, Lincoln, Nebr.

Decal and brand of Gustav Stickley on the oak sideboard. This mark was used c. 1912–1915. Courtesy, University of Nebraska, Lincoln, Nebr.

Thirty Fourth Street

Finally, from 1912 through 1916, Stickley products carried a lengthy and "preachy" label that reads,

CRAFTSMAN/TRADE/MARKS/REG'D/ IN U.S./PATENT/OFFICE/Stickley/THIS PASTER TOGETHER WITH MY DE-/ VICE AND SIGNATURE (BRANDED) ON A/PIECE OF FURNITURE STANDS AS MY/GUARANTEE TO THE PUR-/ CHASER THAT/THE PIECE IS MADE WITH THE SAME/CARE AND EARNESTNESS THAT HAS/CHARAC-/ TERIZED ALL MY EFFORTS/FROM THE BEGINNING AND IS MEANT THAT I WOULD HOLD MYSELF RE-/SPONSI-/ BLE FOR ANY DEFECTS IN MATE-/

Gustav Stickley's paper label, used c. 1912–1916, on the oak sideboard. Courtesy, University of Nebraska, Lincoln, Nebr.

RIAL WORKMANSHIP OR FINISH THAT/MAY BE DISCOVERED BY THE PUR-/CHASER EVEN AFTER THE PIECE HAS/BEEN IN USE FOR A REASON-ABLE/LENGTH OF TIME. AND THAT I WILL EITHER MAKE GOOD ANY DEFECTS OR/TAKE BACK THE PIECE AND REFUND/THE PURCHASE PRICE./THIS PIECE WAS MADE IN MY/CABINETSHOPS AT EASTWOOD, N.Y./GUSTAV STICKLEY

Ref.: David M. Cathers, *Furniture of the American Arts and Crafts Movement: Stickley and Roycroft Mission Oak* (New York: New American Library, 1981).

STICKLEY, LEOPOLD AND J. GEORGE

Leopold and J. George Stickley, brothers of Gustav Stickley (see previous entry), set up

shop in Fayetteville, Onondaga County, New York, not far from Gustav's factory, in 1902. Two years later they were selling their line of oak "Hand-Craft" furnishings closely resembling his wares. The brothers' products initially bore a decal reading,

The Onondaga Shops/L. & J. G. STICK-LEY/FAYETTEVILLE, N.Y.

This was used only from 1904 until 1906. In the latter year the firm adopted a new mark, featuring a woodworker's clamp upon which was printed,

L. & J.G. STICKLEY/HANDCRAFT/TRADE MARK

In the form of a red decal or a brand, this continued to be used until 1912. In that year another mark was chosen, a red and yellow decal within a rectangular reserve and reading,

THE WORK OF/L. & J.G. STICKLEY

This mark, too, is sometimes found branded upon a piece of furniture. The last Arts and Crafts furniture mark employed by the Stickley Brothers was introduced in 1918, following termination of Gustav Stickley's firm. This featured conjoined woodworker's clamp and joiner's compass, reflecting that the brothers now owned a controlling interest in Gustav's factory. The new red-and-yellow circular decal reads,

STICKLEY/HANDCRAFT CRAFTS-MAN/SYRACUSE & FAYETTEVILLE, N.Y.

Ref.: David M. Cathers, *Furniture of the American Arts and Crafts Movement: Stickley and Roycraft Mission Oak* (New York: New American Library, 1981).

Yet two other of Gustav Stickley's brothers (see his entry), George and Albert, set up their own furniture factory in Grand Rapids, Michigan, in 1892. This firm remained in business until 1954, producing a wide variety of furnishings, including Arts and Crafts pieces, Colonial Revival, and adaptations of period styles. Their products are labeled,

MADE BY/STICKLEY BROS.CO./ GRAND RAPIDS, MICH.

Ref.: *Antiques,* May 1993.

Chippendale mahogany serpentine-front chest of drawers labeled by William Stone and Samuel or William Alexander, active together at Prince and Back streets in Boston, c. 1792–1796. Private collection.

STITCHER & CLEMMENS

A Federal inlaid fall-front desk and book-case or secretary, c. 1795–1805, at the Baltimore Museum of Art is labeled

Stitcher & Clemmens,/CABINET AND CHAIR-MAKERS, Corner of South and Water-Streets,/BALTIMORE./Orders from the city or country attended/to with punc-tuality./They have St. DOMINGO MAHOGANY/of the best quality for sale.

The firm of Stitcher & Clemmens is listed on South Street in the city directory for 1804. Refs.: Bjerkoe; Paul H. Burroughs, *Southern Antiques* (New York: Bonanza Books, 1981).

STODDARD, MOSES

A Chippendale cherry desk and bookcase or secretary in a private collection bears the mark of the Litchfield, Connecticut, cabinet-maker Moses Stoddard (1741–1831). The circular paper label on an interior drawer reads,

M. Stoddard,/Litchfield

while the date, "1770," is handwritten in ink. Ref.: *Antiques,* July 1969.

STOKES, C. M. AND W. H.

A c. 1790–1810 Chippendale mahogany mirror, illustrated in *Antiques* for May 1974, was described as being labeled by the firm of C. M. and W. H. Stokes of Philadelphia. Nothing further is known of this firm. A James Stokes of Philadelphia, c. 1791–1811, sold but did not make looking glasses.

STONE, DANIEL

*T*he cabinetmaker Daniel Stone (married 1803) was active in Dracut, Massachu-setts, c. 1800–1810. He is known for a Chip-pendale maple chest of drawers inscribed within the back

Daniel Stone,/Dracutt 1807/Daniel Stone cabinetmaker,/October 6th 1807.

Ref.: *Antiques,* October 1979.

STONE, ISAAC

A c. 1790–1810 Hepplewhite mahogany desk and bookcase or secretary, illustrated in *Antiques* for January 1985, is branded

I. STONE

for Isaac Stone, a cabinetmaker who is listed as working on Essex Street in Salem, Massachu-setts, in 1809. Ref.: Bjerkoe.

STONE, SAMUEL

A c. 1795–1805 Federal mahogany inlaid bowfront chest of drawers, offered at Sotheby's, May 15–17, 1975, is signed

S. Stone

on a drawer bottom. Samuel Stone (b. 1760) was a Boston cabinetmaker who advertised in the *Massachusetts Gazette* in 1794 and was work-ing on Pitts Lane in 1796. Ref.: Bjerkoe.

STONE & ALEXANDER

*T*he cabinetmaking partners William Stone and Samuel or William Alexander worked together c. 1792–1796 in Boston at Prince and Back streets. A pair of Federal mahogany side chairs at Winterthur bear their early round paper label:

Stone &/Alexander/BOSTON/179

A "2" written in ink after the "179" occurs on one example. A later label, on a Chippendale mahogany serpentine-front chest of drawers, reads,

Stone and Alexander,/Cabinet and Chair-Makers,/Makes Tables of all kinds,/in the neweft Fafhion/Cornices, Defks, Book Cafes, Mahogany Chairs,/Sofas, Lolling and eafy Chairs, &c.

Refs.: Montgomery; *Antiques,* April 1948.

STOUT, C.

Bamboo-turned bow-back Windsor side chairs, c. 1790–1800, which are branded on the underside of the seat

C. STOUTs

are attributed to the Reading, Pennsylvania, area. Nothing is known of the maker. Ref.: Santore II.

STOW, JOHN

The Philadelphia turner John Stow is known for a c. 1780–1800 fan-back Windsor side chair branded under the seat

J. STOW/PHILA. fecit

Nothing further is known of Stow's career in Philadelphia. Ref.: Santore II.

STOWERS, JOSEPH

Joseph Stowers (1801–1851) made looking glasses and picture frames in his shop at 296 Essex Street, Salem, Massachusetts, from 1824 until his death in 1851. An Empire gilded mirror and a gilded white pine frame at the Essex Institute bear his label:

JOSEPH STOWERS/GILDER/ESSEX STREET,/SALEM LOOKING GLASSES, PORTRAITS, PICTURES/AND NEEDLE-

Smoke-grained c. 1840–1850 Windsor footstool with the stenciled mark beneath the top of W. Stripe, Canton, Ohio. Courtesy, the Henry Ford Museum, Dearborn, Mich.

WORK/. . . . . GILT FRAMED LOOK-ING-GLASSES./. . . . .
. . . .

STRIPE, W.

A c. 1840–1850 smoke-grained Windsor footstool in red, yellow, and green, illustrated in *Antiques* for March 1965, is stenciled under the top

MANUFACTURED By/W. STRIPE/ CANTON, O.

Nothing further is known of Stripe's career.

STRUBLE, F.

A c. 1860–1880 Victorian desk and bookcase or secretary in a private collection is signed

F. Struble/De Graff Ohio

It is likely that this is the name of an owner.

STUART, L.

Each chair in a set of six decorated bamboo-turned rod-back Windsor side chairs, c. 1830–1850, offered at Skinner's Auction Gallery, October 29–30, 1981, is branded beneath the seat

L. STUART WARRANTED

Nothing further is known of this chairmaker.

SWAN, E. B.

A bow-back Windsor side chair and a continuous-arm chair converted to a rocker are both branded beneath their seats

E. B. SWAN

The chairs would date c. 1790–1810, but nothing is known of Swan. It seems likely, though, that this is a maker's mark.

SWAN, OLIVER

[A] pine blanket chest over three drawers at the New York State Historical Association, Cooperstown, is marked in paint on the front

1808/W.P.

and bears the label of Oliver Swan, an Otsego, New York, cabinetmaker:

CABINET WORK,/&/WINDSOR CHAIRS,/BY/OLIVER SWAN,/OTSEGO.

The museum has two other pieces of Swan's work with the same label. Ref.: *Antiques & Arts Weekly,* April 30, 1993.

SWEENEY, JOHN

[A] late Sheraton mahogany looking glass with reverse-painted panel, illustrated in *Antiques* for May 1972, is labeled,

Looking Glass/MANUFACTORY,/321

Pearl-Street, New York./JOHN SWEENEY/Respectfully informs his friends and the public,/that he has commenced Business in the above/line, and has on hand an elegant assortment of/GILT AND MAHOGANY FRAMED/LOOKING GLASSES,/of the newest and most fashionable patterns;/and having the entire Stock manufactured by/himself, which he warrants to be of the best/workmanship, is enabled to sell them on the/most reasonable terms./Country Merchants and Dealers will find it/to their advantage to call and give a preference./Pictures, Needlework . . . framed.

Sweeney was listed as a carpenter in New York City directories until 1824, when he appeared as a looking glass maker. He continued in this field until 1832. He was located at 321 Pearl Street only from 1824 through 1828. Ref.: *Antiques,* May 1972.

SWETT, JONATHAN

A Chippendale mahogany slant-front desk in a private collection, illustrated in *Antiques* for July 1955, bears an ivory label inscribed

**Made by Jonathan Swett in/
Newport Rhode Island 1753**

Swett (active c. 1753–1774) is known to have worked in Newport in the 1750s. Ref.: *Old Time New England Furniture* (Boston: Society for the Preservation of New England Antiquities, 1987).

SWIFT, REUBEN

A c. 1800–1815 Federal inlaid mahogany tambour desk at the Metropolitan Museum of Art is labeled

CABINET FURNITURE,/IN ALL ITS

VARIOUS BRANCHES,/MANUFAC-
TURED WITH NEATNESS AND
DISPATCH, BY/REUBEN SWIFT,/
HEAD OF ACUSHNET-RIVER,/
NEW BEDFORD, (MASS.)

Reuben Swift (1780–1843) was advertising his wares in the local *Columbian Courier and Weekly Miscellany* by December 1802, continuing intermittently until December 1808. It should be noted that Santore attributes a writing-arm, fan-back Windsor armchair branded

SWIFT

and another Windsor branded

R. W. SWIFT

to Reuben Swift or Reuben and his younger brother, William (b. 1790). I have, however, been able to find no evidence that Reuben Swift made Windsor chairs. Refs.: Santore II; *Antiques,* October 1977.

SWISEGOOD, JOHN I.

Two nearly identical Federal walnut and cherry slant-top desks bear the signature of John I. Swisegood (1796–1874), a Davidson County, North Carolina, cabinetmaker. The earlier is inscribed

**I John Swisegood/his hand and pen
this/8th d of March in the year 1817**

while the inscription on the other reads,

**John Swisegood March the 26
1820/George Fultz's Desk/Jno./
John Swisegood/George Fultz/Jonathan**

The "Jonathan" was Jonathan Long, an apprentice to Swisegood. John Swisegood worked in Davidson County until 1848, when he migrated to Illinois. Two other signed pieces are known, as well as over forty attributions. Ref.: *The Swisegood School of Cabinetmakers* (Winston-Salem, N.C.: Museum of Early Southern Decorative Arts, 1973).

SYPHER & CO.

The New York City firm of Sypher & Company (active c. 1880–1910) both sold antiques and made high-quality reproductions labeled

**Sypher & Co./Successors To
T.Masley/Antiques & Articles of Vertu/
739 & 741 Broadway, N. York**

T

TANNER, B.

A c. 1780–1790 Chippendale mahogany desk and bookcase or secretary, illustrated in *Antiques* for January 1974, is signed

B. Tanner

The piece has a Petersburg, Virginia, history, but it is not known if Tanner was an owner or the maker.

TARIN, CRUZ

A pine ladder-back side chair in a private collection is inscribed beneath the seat

**Hoy 10 de Marzo de 1903/
Manos de Cruz Tarin/ Lorenzo Ramirez**

which translates to

**Today, the 10th of March 1903/
Hands of Cruz Tarin/Lorenzo Ramirez**

The chair was made in southern New Mexico, but nothing is known of the *carpintero,* or maker. Ref.: Lonn Taylor and Dessa Bokides, *New Mexican Furniture, 1640–1900* (Santa Fe: Museum of New Mexico Press, 1987).

TARR, LEVIN

The Baltimore, Maryland, cabinetmaker Levin Tarr (1772–1821) was in the city by 1794. He advertised his shop on Light Street from 1800 until 1815. Two marked pieces exist: a half-round pier table inscribed

Levin Tarr May 2, 1799

and a mahogany Pembroke table on which appears

Made by/Levin S. Tarr No. 28/Light Street Baltimore/January 10, 1806

Ref.: Michael J. Flanigan, *American Furniture from the Kaufman Collection* (Washington, D.C.: National Gallery of Art, 1986).

TARR, WESLEY

Classical painted and decorated poplar four-tier étagère with single drawer, which was offered at Sotheby's, January 23–25, 1992, is signed on the drawer

Wesley Tarr

Tarr was listed as a cabinetmaker during the 1830s in Baltimore, part of the time at a shop on Gay Street. It is likely that he was a relative, possibly a son, of Levin Tarr (see previous entry).

TAYLOR, JAMES S.

A Federal mahogany sofa, illustrated in *Antiques* for November 1977, is signed on the top rail

J. S. TAYLOR

James S. Taylor was a cabinetmaker listed in the directories as working in New York City from 1804 through 1815.

TAYLOR, JOHN B.

The Stafford County, Virginia, cabinetmaker John B. Taylor is known for a Federal southern pine chest of drawers with a handwritten paper label reading,

Made and Sold—/by—/John B. Taylor/—At His—/Cabinet Manufactury/Stafford County/July—/Virginia—/1816

This is thought to be the same John B. Taylor listed by Bjerkoe as working in Alexandria, Virginia, in 1804. Refs.: Bjerkoe; *Antiques,* January 1952.

TAYLOR, ROBERT

The Philadelphia turner Robert Taylor (d. 1817) was working in the city as early as 1792. Over the next quarter century he occupied shops at several addresses, much of the time on South Front Street. Taylor's printed paper label, found on bamboo-turned rod-back side chairs with medallion crests, reads,

Windsor and Fancy Chairs & Settees,/WHOLESALE & RETAIL/ROBERT TAYLOR,/WINDSOR & FANCY CHAIR-MAKER,/informs his friends and the public that he continues to carry on the Windsor and Fancy Chair-making business in all its various branches, and upon the most reasonable terms./At No. 99 South-Front Street (near Walnut Street)/where he has constantly on hand the most fashionable plain, gilt and orna/mental chairs./Orders from masters of vessels, and others who may favour him with their/custom, shall be attended to with accuracy and dispatch./Cabinet Ware may be had at the same place.

Taylor occupied the 99 South Front Street shop only during the 1802–1806 period. Ref.: Hornor.

TAYLOR, SAMUEL

The document drawer of a Chippendale mahogany slant-front desk is inscribed

Newburyport Samuel Taylor 1779

The piece is from Newburyport, Massachusetts, and the name is believed to be that of an owner. Ref.: *Antiques,* July 1994.

TAYLOR & KING

During the brief period 1799–1800, the Philadelphia Windsor chair maker Robert Taylor was in partnership with one Daniel King on South Front Street. They produced a number of Windsors, including bowbacks, which either were branded

TAYLOR & KING

or bore a printed paper label, a partial copy of which reads,

TAYLOR & KING/FANCY & WINDSOR
CHAIR-MAKERS/Respectfully inform
their friends and the public that . . . . . .
. . . ./PHILADELPHIA

Ref.: Hornor.

TERRY, I. F.

A sack-back Windsor armchair, c. 1790–1800, illustrated in the *Bee* for February 11, 1977, is branded four times beneath the seat

I. F. TERRY

This appears to be a maker's mark, although nothing further is known.

THAXTER & ROUSE

A c. 1780–1800 Federal cherry and curly maple tambour desk, illustrated in *Antiques* for June 1955, bears the printed label

THAXTER & ROUSE/Cabinet and Chair Makers/Ann Street/Three Doors South of the Draw Bridge/BOSTON

Ref.: Bjerkoe.

THAYER, A.

Two Windsor chairs—a fan-back side chair illustrated in *MAD* for June 1975, and a low-back writing armchair illustrated in Santore II—bear the brand

A. THAYER

This is thought to be the c. 1800–1820 mark of a New Jersey manufacturer. Ref.: Santore II.

THAYER, JESSE

See Spooner & Thayer.

THOMAS, ELI

The Norwalk, Huron County, Ohio, cabinetmaker Eli Thomas advertised in Norwalk and Fairfield, Ohio, c. 1837–1847. He is known for a country Empire table signed

Eli Thomas

Ref.: Hageman II.

THOMAS, ELIAS

A Sheraton mahogany mirror bearing a partial label of Elias Thomas, who worked at 354 Pearl Street, Manhattan, c. 1818–1825, reads,

LOOKING-GLASSES/ELIAS
THOMAS/No. 354 PEARL
STREET,/NEAR THE . . . . BANK/. . . .
. . . and for sale/an assortment of/Mantel,
Pier and Toilet/LOOKING-GLASSES/Old
glasses . . . ./Store keepers supplied
with gilt frames as usual.

The label is dated October 1818, but an accompanying receipt indicates that the mirror was sold in 1820. Ref.: *Antiques,* July 1937.

THOMAS, ISAAC

Although the Willistown Township, Chester County, Pennsylvania, craftsman Isaac Thomas (1721–1802) was called a joiner in tax lists from 1764 until 1779, he was also listed as a clockmaker from 1796 through 1799. And the only known pieces from his hand are clocks, including a walnut tall case clock and a dwarf tall case clock in the same wood (at the Chester County Historical Society), both of which are signed
Isaac Thomas Willis Town
A slight variant is another Chippendale walnut tall case clock, which is inscribed
Isaac Thomas WILLIS TOWN
Both pieces are late Chippendale, dating c. 1780–1800. Ref.: Schiffer.

THOMAS, JOHN W.

A mahogany astragal-end worktable at the Historical Society of Delaware, Wilmington, is inscribed on a drawer back
. . . . . Oct 16/th 1813—/John W.
Thom/mas No 30 South/fifth St
The Philadelphia, Pennsylvania, cabinetmaker John W. Thomas was active c. 1809–1814. He is listed at 30 South Fifth Street from 1811 through 1814. Ref.: *Antiques,* May 1991.

THOMAS, LAMBERT

A Federal inlaid mahogany five-leg card table, c. 1805–1815, is signed on the frame

L. Thomas

for Lambert Thomas, a cabinetmaker working on High Street in Baltimore, Maryland, c. 1810–1833. Ref.: Bjerkoe.

THOMAS, MORDECAI

The Willistown Township, Chester County, Pennsylvania, cabinetmaker and clockmaker Mordecai Thomas (1767–1837), son of Isaac Thomas (see earlier entry), is, like his father, known primarily for clock cases. A Federal walnut tall case clock at the Chester County Historical Society is inscribed
MORDECAI THOMAS WILLIS TOWN
Chester County
Mordecai Thomas appeared in local tax lists as cabinetmaker and joiner from 1796 until 1801. Ref.: Schiffer.

THOMAS, PETER K.

The Soap Hollow, Johnstown, Pennsylvania, cabinetmaker Peter K. Thomas is known for at least two pieces of painted and decorated furniture, a chest of drawers with turned Sheraton legs and shaped splash back, which is stenciled
MANUFACTURED BY
PETER K. THOMAS/E T/1861
and a decorated six-board chest with bracket feet, which is stenciled
M.F. by P.K.T./S.T. 1861
Both pieces are decorated with stenciled floral motifs, including wreaths and vases of flowers. Another similar chest is known. Ref.: *Antiques,* May 1983.

THOMAS, WILLIAM J.

An Empire mahogany dressing mirror at the New York State Museum is stenciled within a drawer

**W. J. THOMAS/FULTON ST./
BROOKLYN**

The cabinetmaker and furniture dealer William J. Thomas worked in Manhattan from 1829 until 1848, when he relocated to Fulton Street in Brooklyn, remaining there through 1855. Ref.: Scherer.

THOMPSON, JOHN H.

An Empire mahogany mirror, c. 1830–1840, offered at Christie's, October 13, 1984, is described as being labeled

John H. Thompson, Rochester

Thompson, of Rochester, New York, may have been a dealer in mirrors rather than a manufacturer.

THOMPSON & WEEKS

A c. 1825–1835 Classical mahogany sofa with brass inlay, sold at Weschler's Auction Gallery, January 15, 1994, is inscribed,

Thompson & Weeks/New York

Archibald Thompson and William Weeks were working together in New York City in 1830. Ref.: *MAD,* March 1994.

Painted and stencil-decorated country Federal chest of drawers with the stenciled mark of Peter K. Thomas, a cabinetmaker from Soap Hollow, Johnstown, Pennsylvania, and the date "1861." Private collection.

THORNTON, D.

A c. 1770–1780 Philadelphia comb-back Windsor armchair, illustrated in *Antiques* for August 1982, is branded beneath the seat

D. THORNTON

It is not known if this is the maker's or an owner's mark.

THWAITES, WILLIAM G.

A c. 1860–1870 walnut flat wall cupboard fitted out as a desk and showing characteristics of the Victorian Elizabethan and Renaissance Revival styles is stamped on a drawer

**W. G. THWAITES/
85/Hudson St./BOSTON**

The cabinetmaker, William G. Thwaites, was listed on Hudson Street in Boston from 1859 through 1871, in 1873, and finally from 1875 until 1880. The piece is in a private collection.

TIFFANY STUDIOS

During the period 1890–1905, the Tiffany Glass and Decorating Company of New York City made some furniture in European and American Revival styles. A Federal-style mahogany and satinwood sideboard, offered by Sotheby's, December 3–4, 1976, bears an impressed brass plaque reading,

TIFFANY STUDIOS/NEW YORK

and an identical label was found on an Art

Nouveau bronze and oak side table. Ref.: Bishop.

TILLMAN, JAMES W.

A c. 1840–1860 mahogany oval tilt-top pedestal-base table at the Henry Ford Museum is stenciled twice

**J. W. TILLMAN/Furnishing/
WAREHOUSE/DETROIT.**

James W. Tillman (d. 1867) established a furniture warehouse and manufactory on Jefferson Avenue in Detroit in 1836; it remained active through at least 1868.

TILLMAN & BENJAMIN

An Empire carved mahogany bureau with mirror or chest of drawers at the New York State Museum bears a printed paper label reading,

**MANUFACTURED AND
SOLD/BY/TILLMAN & BENJAMIN/
No. 41, GENESEE STREET,/UTICA**

Eli F. Benjamin, a cabinetmaker who had been in business in Cooperstown, New York, since 1810, moved to Utica, New York, in 1822 to open a "Mahogany Chair Manufactory" with William Tillman. They remained in business together, on Genesee Street, until Tillman left for Geneva, New York, in 1833. Their shop was at 41 Genesee Street from 1822 until 1829. Refs.: Scherer; *Antiques,* May 1973, May 1981.

**Victorian walnut, c. 1860–1870, flat wall cupboard with desk fittings bearing the stamped mark of the Hudson Street, Boston, cabinetmaker William G. Thwaites.
Courtesy, Joan Pearlman.**

TILLOU, PETER

An arrow-back Federal fancy chair from New York City, now at Winterthur, is branded on the top of the front posts

PETER/TILLOU

The chair dates c. 1800–1815. A Peter Tilyou was listed as a chairmaker in the 1791–1798 New York directories. Ref.: *Antiques,* May 1981.

TILLOU, VINCENT

A Queen Anne vase-back side chair, c. 1780–1800, is stamped on the back splat

V. TILYOU

Vincent Tillou or Tilyou was listed as a chairmaker or turner in the New York City directories from 1787 through 1799. He appears to have retired in 1800. Ref.: *Antiques,* May 1981.

TIMPSON, THOMAS

A sack-back Windsor armchair, illustrated in the *Bee* for March 18, 1994, is branded

T.TIMPSON/N.YORK

The turner, Thomas Timpson, was listed in the Manhattan directories for the period 1801–1805. A marked chair from his hand is at the Metropolitan Museum of Art. Ref.: *Antiques,* May 1981.

Braced mixed-woods Windsor continuous-arm chair, c. 1801–1805, bearing the mark of Thomas Timpson of New York City. Courtesy, Bernard and S. Dean Levy, Inc., New York.

TITCOMB, EDMUND

The joiner Edmund Titcomb (d. 1723) of Newbury, Massachusetts, is known for a c. 1700 William and Mary pine and maple chest on frame, which bears his signature. It is at the Historic Winslow House, Marshfield, Massachusetts. Ref.: Fairbanks and Bates.

TOBEY & BISHOP

Santore cites a c. 1805–1815 Windsor chair, which is branded beneath the seat

D TOBEY/G BISHOP

as possibly the work of the Maine turners Daniel Tobey and George Bishop. Ref.: Santore II.

Brand of the turner Thomas Timpson beneath the seat of the braced continuous-arm Windsor.

Courtesy, Bernard and S. Dean Levy, Inc., New York.

TOBEY FURNITURE COMPANY

During the period 1898–1901, Gustav Stickley (see his entry) sold his first Arts and Crafts furnishings through the Tobey Furniture Company of Chicago, Illinois. Such pieces would possibly have borne the round paper label that reads,

> The.Tobey.Furniture.Company.Chicago/
> THE/NEW/FURNI-/TURE

or a brass plaque reading,

> THE TOBEY FURNITURE CO./
> CHICAGO.

An oak tall-case clock illustrated in *MAD* for August 1994 bore a different mark,

> Tobey, Chicago, 1856.

Ref.: David M. Cathers, *Furniture of the Arts and Crafts Movement: Stickley and Roycroft Mission Oak* (New York: New American Library, 1981).

TODD, JAMES

The prolific looking glass manufacturer James Todd (1794–1866) produced a surprising number of labeled Federal and Empire mirrors during his long career (c. 1820–1860) on Exchange Street in Portland, Maine. Two labels are known. The first, engraved with an American eagle and shield, reads,

> PORTLAND/LOOKING-GLASS MANU-
> FACTORY,/AT THE SIGN OF THE
> LOOKING-GLASS—EXCHANGE-
> STREET./JAMES TODD,/Keeps constantly
> for sale, an elegant assortment of GILT
> AND MAHOGANY FRAMED/LOOK-
> ING-GLASSES,/TOILET DO., PROFILE
> FRAMES; CLOCK GLASSES, GOLD LEAF,
> &c./Ladies Needle Work, Prints, &c.
> Framed to any pattern.—Looking-Glass
> Plates set in/Old Frames/N.B. Old Look-
> ing-Glasses new Gilt and repaired. Glass

339

Federal gilded pine mirror with reverse-painted panel, c. 1805–1815, and the label of the Portland, Maine, looking glass manufacturer James Todd (1794–1866), which appears on its backboard. Courtesy, Bernard and S. Dean Levy, Inc., New York.

cut to order./WHOLESALE AND RETAIL. A second label features an engraving of an Empire mirror and reads,

EXCHANGE-STREET./JAMES TODD/Keeps constantly/for/sale an elegant assort-/ment of Gilt and Mahogany/framed/LOOKING-GLASSES,/Toilet Glasses, &c. Embroi-/dery; Portrait, Prints, &c./framed to any pattern. Looking-Glass plates set in/old frames. N.B. Old Looking-/Glasses new gilt and re-/paired.

This label makes no reference to a manufactory, raising the possibility that at this point Todd was only selling other makers' mirrors. Todd may have worked in Boston before moving to Portland. There is a painted wooden trade sign in the form of a Chippendale mirror (ex–Israel Sack) that is inscribed

"J. Todd/MANUFACTURER OF/ LOOKING-GLASSES/Plain and Ornamental/GILDING/Wholesale and Retail/No. 42 CORNHILL" (Boston).

TODD, TITUS B.

An Empire mahogany chest of drawers in a private collection is inscribed on a drawer

**Made by Titus Briant Todd./Big Flat
February 15th 1832**

also in a balloon issuing from the mouth of a small figure

**this bureau was made for Eleazor Owens,
Big Flat by Titus Bryunt Todd Feb 1832**

and under the top

Titus Briant Todd $ 30

Big Flats is a community near Corning, New York. Eleazer Owens (Owen) was an early settler, but nothing is known of the cabinetmaker, Titus Todd. Ref.: Big Flats Historical Society, *Salute to a Proud Past* (Painted Post, N.Y.: Painted Post Press, 1972).

TODD, WILLIAM

See Adams & Todd.

TOLEDO CHAIR FACTORY

A set of four child's spindle-back, plank-seat side chairs at the Miami Purchase Association for Historic Preservation in Cincinnati, Ohio, is stenciled

The SOLID Toledo Chair

The Toledo Chair Factory, Toledo, Ohio, was owned from 1879 through 1894 by Harry Y. and Frank R. Williams. Ref.: *Made in Ohio.*

TOOKER, C. J.

A Sheraton mahogany Pembroke table is labeled

MANUFACTURED BY/C.J.

TOOKER,/FAYETTEVILLE, N.C.

The cabinetmaker C. J. Tooker, who claimed in ads to have learned his trade ". . . in the first shops of the North . . . ," was in business in Fayetteville, North Carolina, from 1819 until 1824, when he left for Raleigh, North Carolina. Ref.: Bivins.

TOPPAN, ABNER

The Newburyport, Massachusetts, cabinetmaker Abner Toppan (1764–1836) is known for an unusual inlaid mahogany marble-top sideboard table, which is branded on the back

TOPPAN

The piece would date c. 1790–1800. An unsigned desk, chest on chest, and desk and bookcase, all made in 1795, are also known. The Toppan family home was on High Street in Newburyport. Refs.: Bjerkoe; *Antiques,* April 1945, March 1968.

TORREY, PURLEY

The Worcester, Massachusetts, cabinetmaker Purley Torrey is known for a labeled late Federal mahogany two-drawer work stand, now at Old Sturbridge Village. He is listed as working in Worcester from 1825 to 1828. Ref.: *Antiques,* May 1993.

TOV, P. S.

Santore lists a Philadelphia rod-back side chair, c. 1800–1820, which is branded beneath the seat

P. S. TOV

or possibly "TOY." It is not known if this is the mark of the maker or an owner. Ref.: Santore II.

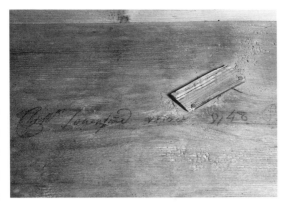

Pencil signature of Christopher Townsend within the case of the Queen Anne highboy.
Private collection.

TOWNSEND, CHRISTOPHER

A Queen Anne mahogany flat-top high chest of drawers or highboy offered at Sotheby's, June 26–27, 1991, is inscribed in pencil within the upper case

Christr. Townsend Made 1748

The cabinetmaker Christopher Townsend (1701–1773) of Easton's Point, Newport, Rhode Island, was the brother of Job Townsend and father of John Townsend, both renowned craftsmen (see later entries). He was working in Newport as early as 1738. Refs.: Bjerkoe; *Old Time New England Furniture* (Boston: Society for the Preservation of New England Antiquities, 1987).

Queen Anne mahogany flat-top high chest of drawers or highboy made, signed, and dated "1748" by the Newport, Rhode Island, cabinetmaker Christopher Townsend (1701–1773). Private collection.

TOWNSEND, EDMUND

Edmund Townsend (1736–1811), a Newport, Rhode Island, cabinetmaker and son of Job Townsend (see next entry), is known for a single piece of furniture, a Chippendale mahogany bureau table or kneehole desk, dating c. 1765–1775 and bearing within a drawer a handwritten paper label reading,

Made by/Edmund Townsend/
In/Newport, Rhode Island

This piece is now at the Museum of Fine Arts, Boston. Edmund was working with his father on Easton's Point as early as 1767. Refs.: Bjerkoe; Fairbanks and Bates.

TOWNSEND, JOB

The Easton's Point, Newport, Rhode Island, cabinetmaker Job Townsend (1699–1765), brother of Christopher Townsend and father of Edmund (see previous entries), is known for a c. 1750–1765 Chippendale mahogany blind-door desk and bookcase or secretary bearing within the prospect door a handwritten paper label reading,

Made/by/Job Townsend/in Newport

A c. 1750–1760 Chippendale maple slant-lid desk, illustrated in *Antiques* for December 1961, and signed in script within a drawer

Job Townfend

has also been attributed to him, as has a c. 1730–1750 Queen Anne drop-leaf table inscribed under the frame

C.J.T. MA 31

which was illustrated in the *Bee* for May 4, 1994. Refs.: Bjerkoe; *Antiques,* May 1975.

TOWNSEND, JOHN

During his long and productive career, extending from 1764 until 1809, the cabinetmaker John Townsend (1732–1809), of Easton's Point, Newport, Rhode Island, used a variety of written and printed marks. The earliest, probably employed while he was still at his father, Christopher's, shop (see earlier entry), are simply signatures on the wood. These

---

Federal mahogany shield-back side chair with handwritten paper label reading, "Made by John Townsend/Newport 1800." The Newport, Rhode Island, cabinetmaker John Townsend (1732–1809) used a variety of marks. Private collection.

include a Chippendale mahogany dining table inscribed

John Townsend 1756

a Chippendale block- and shell-carved mahogany document cabinet pencil-signed

John Townsend Newport

a Chippendale mahogany card table signed in script on a gate

John Townsend/Newport/1762

and a second time on the frame

John Townsend/1762

and a Chippendale mahogany slant-front desk, which is initialed

I T

At some point, possibly after he established an independent business c. 1764, John Townsend began to use a handwritten paper label. The general form of this was

Printed paper label, dated in ink "1793," of John Townsend on the Federal banquet table. Courtesy, Israel Sack, Inc., New York.

Made by/John Townsend/Rhode Island followed by a date (1760, 1765, 1791, and 1792 are known). The form may vary, however. A Federal mahogany shield-back side chair is labeled

Made by John Townsend/Newport 1800

and the label on a Chippendale mahogany shell-carved block-front chest of drawers reads,

Made by John Townsend/
Newport R.I./August 1783

No doubt even a thrifty Quaker eventually recognized the value of a printed label. The first

Federal inlaid mahogany three-piece banquet table bearing the printed paper label of John Townsend. Courtesy, Israel Sack, Inc., New York.

employed by John Townsend consisted merely of the words

MADE BY/JOHN TOWNSEND

to which he found it necessary to add more information, such as the phrase "Newport Rhode Island 1789" on a tall clock case at the Metropolitan Museum of Art. The final product was a completely printed label, which reads,

MADE BY/JOHN TOWNSEND/ NEWPORT

Townsend seems to have customarily added to this label a handwritten date, presumably the year in which the labeled piece was made or sold. Known dates include 1786, 1792, 1793, 1794, 1796, 1797, and 1800. Refs.: Bjerkoe; Downs; Montgomery.

TRACY, EBENEZER

Arguably the best-known maker of American Windsor chairs, Ebenezer Tracy (1744–1803), working in Lisbon, Connecticut, c. 1764–1803, was also a competent cabinetmaker. His brand:

E. B.: TRACY

is found on a variety of Windsors, including sack-back and continuous-arm chairs, writing-arm fan-backs and low-backs, and fan-back side chairs. However, it is also on a painted pine blanket chest over drawer illustrated in *Antiques* for February 1971. Moreover, an inventory of Tracy's estate reveals that he had on hand at the time of his death such things as Pembroke tables, tall clock cases, and candle stands. Refs.: Bjerkoe; Santore II; *Antiques,* December 1936.

TRACY, ELIJAH

Elijah Tracy (1766–1807), of Lisbon and Scotland, Connecticut, son of the chairmaker Ebenezer Tracy (see previous entry), was also a turner. A number of fan-back and bow-back side chairs as well as braced continuous-arm and sack-back armchairs, all branded

E. TRACY

and dating c. 1790–1800, are attributed to him by some. Others, however, say the maker was another son, Ebenezer Tracy, Jr. (1780–1822), of Lisbon. Ref.: Santore II.

Mixed-woods low-back writing-arm Windsor with comb, branded E. B.: TRACY for the Lisbon, Connecticut, turner Ebenezer Tracy, active c. 1764–1803. Courtesy, Israel Sack, Inc., New York.

TRACY, STEPHEN

Stephen Tracy (1782–1866), a nephew of Ebenezer Tracy (see earlier entry), took over Ebenezer's shop in Lisbon, Connecticut, in 1803. He is credited with c. 1800–1815 Windsor chairs branded beneath the seat

S. TRACY

A pair of continuous-arm chairs so marked was illustrated in *Antiques* for April 1986. Fan- and bow-back side chairs are also known. Like Ebenezer, Stephen Tracy was a cabinetmaker as well as turner, and there is a Federal cherry slant-front desk that bears the same brand he used on chairs. Ref.: Santore II; *Antiques,* April 1971.

TREADWELL, NATHANIEL

A Chippendale mahogany chest on chest, c. 1780–1800, at the Yale University Art Gallery is branded five times within the case

TREADWELL

It is attributed to Nathaniel Treadwell of Beverly, Massachusetts, listed as working in the city in 1799.

TROYER, MOSES K.

The cabinetmaker and carpenter Moses K. Troyer (1838–1923) is known for two poplar blanket chests, one inscribed on the lid

M K Troyer Maker

and the other

NT/MT

Sack-back Windsor armchair, c. 1790–1805, of mixed woods, branded by the Battery March Street, Boston, turner Samuel J. Tucke. Private collection.

The latter was made in 1865 for his wife, Nancy. Moses Troyer worked in Walnut Creek, Holmes County, Ohio. Ref.: *Made in Ohio.*

TRUMBLE, FRANCIS

The Philadelphia turner Francis Trumble (c. 1716–1798) worked at various addresses on Front and Second streets from around 1740 until 1798. He is known for fan-back side chairs and sack-back armchairs impressed beneath the seat

F. TRUMBLE

or

F. T.

One of his marked armchairs is at Independence National Historical Park, Philadelphia. Ref.: Santore II.

Brand of Samuel J. Tucke, active in Boston c. 1790–1805, beneath the seat of the sack-back Windsor armchair. Private collection.

TRYON, ISAAC

The Glastonbury, Connecticut, cabinet-maker Isaac Tryon (1741–1823) was the maker of a Queen Anne cherry high chest of drawers or highboy, which is inscribed in chalk on a drawer bottom

Glastonbury october 26th 1772/then this Case of Draws/Was made by me/ Isaac Tryon

Refs.: Bjerkoe; *Antiques,* August 1931.

TUBBS, W. F., CO.

Unusual bentwood and leather furniture, including tables and chairs, based on the design of snowshoes, was produced during the 1920s and 1930s by a Maine firm that labeled its products

W.F. Tubbs, Co./Trade Mark/Sno-Shu Chair/Norway, Maine, U.S.A.

Norway is a small community some 30 miles north of Portland.

TUCK, MADISON

A painted, stencil-decorated pine dressing table, illustrated in *Antiques* for October 1983, and now at the Maine State Museum, bears two paper labels. One, beneath a drawer, reads,

Madison Tuck/Cabinet Maker/Hallowell

while the other, on the back, reads,

MANUFACTURED BY/MADISON TUCK,/FOOT OF WINTHROP-STREET,—HALLOWELL/M.T. KEEPS CONSTANTLY ON HAND/A GOOD ASSORTMENT OF/

Cabinet Furniture and Chairs.

The maker, Madison Tuck (1809–1894), was a turner and cabinetmaker of Hallowell, Maine. Ref.: *MAD,* January 13, 1979.

TUCKE, SAMUEL JONES

The Boston chairmaker Samuel Jones Tucke, who worked on Battery March Street, c. 1790–1805, is known for bow- and fan-back side chairs and bow- and sack-back armchairs branded beneath their seats

S. J. TUCKE

A marked example of his work is at Colonial Williamsburg. Refs.: Brian Cullity, *Plain and Fancy: New England Painted Furniture* (Sandwich, Mass.: Heritage Plantation of Sandwich, 1987); Santore II.

TUCKER, ELISHA

The Boston cabinetmaker Elisha Tucker (d. 1827) worked on Middle Street and on Williams Court, c. 1809–1827. He is known for two Federal inlaid mahogany card tables, c. 1800–1810, and a Chippendale mahogany mirror, all labeled

ELISHA TUCKER,/CABINET AND CHAIR/MANUFACTURER,/RESPECT-FULLY informs his friends and the Pub-lick that/he Manufactures and offers for Sale at reasonable terms, at No./40, MIDDLE STREET . . Boston, a general assortment of/CABINET FURNITURE AND CHAIRS./Mahogany Looking-Glass Frames/of all sizes, executed in the neatest manner and at the shortest notice./N.B. No exertions shall be spared which will serve to render/satisfaction to those who may please to favor him with their com-/mands.

A labeled Tucker card table is at Winterthur. Ref.: Montgomery.

TUFFT, THOMAS

The Philadelphia cabinetmaker Thomas Tufft (c. 1740–1788) was working in the city as early as 1768. In 1773 he took over the cabinetmaker James Gillingham's old shop on Second Street (see his entry), and it is this address that appears on his printed paper labels:

MADE and SOLD by/THOMAS TUFFT,/Cabinet and Chair-Maker, FOUR Doors from the Corner of/Walnut-Street in Second/Street, Philadelphia

It should be noted that a variation of this label with an engraved border and differences in the placement of words and capitalization, but not in the wording, appears on an ordinary pine six-board chest illustrated in *Antiques* for August 1940. The ornate label seems com-pletely out of place on this mundane piece.

Among labeled Tufft pieces in institutions there is a c. 1770–1780 Chippendale mahogany dressing table or lowboy at the Philadelphia Museum of Art and a Chippen-dale side chair of the same material and period at Winterthur. Tufft continued to work until 1787, when he moved to the Lancaster, Penn-sylvania, area. Refs.: Bishop; Fairbanks and Bates.

TUFTS, URIAH

Santore credits a c. 1780–1800 Rhode Island Windsor fan-back side chair branded

U. TUFTS

to Uriah Tufts, working c. 1780–1790. The piece seems too early for the cabinetmaker by that name whom Bjerkoe lists as working c. 1834–1837 in Lowell, Massachusetts. Ref.: Santore II.

Federal inlaid mahogany card table, c. 1800–1810, labeled by Elisha Tucker (d. 1827), who worked in Boston c. 1809–1827. Courtesy, Honolulu Academy of Arts, Gift of Mrs. Edward Harrison, in memory of her mother, Mrs. Lamora Sauvinet Gary.

TURNER, GEORGE

A pair of painted and decorated half-spindle Hitchcock-type side chairs, illustrated in *Antiques* for April 1978, bear labels reading,

GEORGE TURNER/ Fancy and Windsor Chair Manufacturer,/No. 108 North Front Street/Corner of Drinkers Alley/ PHILADELPHIA.

The chairs should date c. 1840–1860, but nothing is known of the manufacturer.

TURNER, SAMUEL

The New Lebanon, New York, Shaker brother Samuel Turner (1775–1842) is known for a cherry and butternut tray-top pedestal-base stand, which is stamped

SAMUEL. TURNER. TO./ RUTH JOHNSON 1837

Turner worked as a cabinetmaker at New Lebanon from 1836 until his death. Refs.: Ricman and Burks; Sprigg.

TUTTLE, JAMES CHAPMAN

Several Windsor chairs, including bow-back, fan-back, and birdcage rod-back side chairs bear beneath their seats the impressed mark

I. C. TUTTLE

for James Chapman Tuttle (c. 1772–1849), a

Fan-back Windsor side chair in mixed woods, c. 1795–1805, branded by the Salem, Massachusetts, turner James C. Tuttle (c. 1772–1849). Courtesy, Israel Sack, Inc., New York.

turner and cabinetmaker who worked in Salem, Massachusetts, c. 1795–1815. His shop was on Federal Street in 1796. A Chippendale-Federal transitional slant-front desk, illustrated in *Antiques* for December 1987, which is inscribed

January 1793, J.C.T.

has also been attributed to him. Refs.: Bjerkoe; Fales, *Essex County Furniture.*

TUTTLE, PETER

A Federal cherry chest of drawers, c. 1810–1820, illustrated in *Antiques* for April 1974, is signed

Peter Tuttle

The Virginia-born cabinetmaker Peter Tuttle

Brand of James C. Tuttle
beneath the seat of a
Windsor chair. Tuttle
worked on Federal Street,
Salem, c. 1795–1815.
Courtesy, Mrs. Dean A.
Fales, Jr.

(1782–1859) worked in Mason, Fleming, and Nicholas counties in Kentucky between 1810 and 1830. He later moved to Missouri. The chest was probably made in Mason County.

TWEIDDEN, JERIMIAH

A c. 1820–1840 pine chest of drawers with splash back, illustrated in *MAD* for September 1979, is signed

Jerimiah Tweidden

It is not known if this is the maker's or an owner's signature.

TYGART, WILLIAM

A country Sheraton cherry dressing table or washstand at the Western Reserve Historical Society is inscribed on a drawer

W. Tygart

William Tygart was an itinerant cabinetmaker who was employed by a North Bloomfield, Trumbull County, Ohio, merchant c. 1829–1832. Refs.: *Made in Ohio; Antiques,* May 1972.

TYSON, JONATHAN

The Philadelphia turner and spinning wheel manufacturer Jonathan Tyson was listed in city directories as active on North Front Street from 1809 through 1814. He used a paper label reading,

JONATHAN TYSON/Spinning-Wheel & Chair-Maker,/No. 150 North Front Street,/Between Race and Vine Streets, corner/of Ferris Court, Philadelphia./ N.B. All kinds of Work in the above line of/. . . . made to order . . . .

Ref.: *Antiques,* May 1991.

U

UNION CHAIR CO.

A variety of painted and stencil-decorated midnineteenth-century chairs—including Boston rockers, vase or fiddle-back side chairs with cane seats, and rod-back side chairs—are stenciled

UNION CHAIR CO./

WEST WINSTEAD/CONN

or

UNION CHAIR Co./WEST WINSTEAD, ct.

The Union Chair Company was operated at West Winstead or Robertsville, Connecticut, from 1849 until 1882 by Moses, Paul, and Caleb Camp, who were merchants rather than turners. Refs.: Kenney; *Antiques,* September 1925.

UPHAM, N.

A country Chippendale maple side chair, c. 1780–1810, illustrated in *Antiques* for August 1968, is signed

N. Upham

It is not known if this is the maker's or an owner's mark.

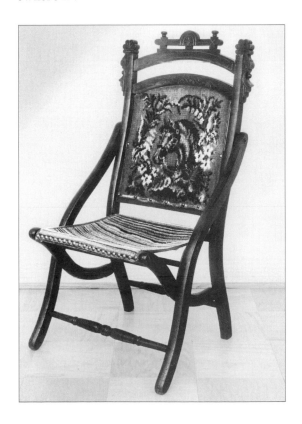

V

VAIL, JOSEPH

A Chippendale mahogany slant-top desk, illustrated in *Antiques* for February 1944, bears an engraved label illustrated with a chest on chest flanked by two side chairs and reading,

Joseph Vail/CABINET AND CHAIR MAKER/. . . . . . No. 32 Beekman Street/At the sign of the Chair/
NEW YORK/Where he carries on the bufinefs/in all its various branches

Joseph Vail was listed variously as a cabinet-maker and chairmaker in Manhattan directories from 1790 through 1806. Ref.: Bjerkoe.

VAILL, E. W.

Several Victorian walnut folding chairs with carpet seats and backs bear rectangular labels reading,

E.W. VAILL,/Patentee and Manufacturer,/WORCESTER, MASS./Patented Oct. 6, 1868/Reissued 5

A label, otherwise identical in wording, reads, "Patented July 18, 1876." On the basis of patent dates, it would appear that Vaill was in business at least from 1868 through 1876. A labeled Vaill chair is at the Margaret Woodbury Strong Museum, Rochester, New York. Ref.: Bishop.

Victorian walnut folding chair, c. 1868–1876, with the label of the patent holder and manufacturer E. W. Vaill of Worcester, Massachusetts.
Courtesy, E. J. Canton.

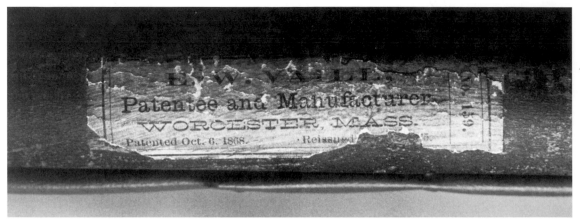

Printed paper label of E. W. Vaill on the Victorian folding chair. The chair was patented in 1868. Courtesy, E. J. Canton.

VAILL, SETH

The Guilford, Connecticut, cabinetmaker Seth Vaill (active c. 1800–1810) is known for a Federal cherry chest of drawers in a private collection, which is incised behind a drawer pull

MADE/by/SETH/VAILL/1806

VAN AHM

A set of painted and decorated c. 1830–1850 rod-back, plank-seat side chairs, illustrated in *MAD* for January 1976, is marked

Van Ahm/Manchester, Vt.

It is not known if this is the mark of the maker or an owner.

VAN BOSKERCK, JOHN

A Classical mahogany desk and bookcase or secretary, illustrated in *Antiques* for September 1964, is stenciled

JOHN VAN BOSKERCK/CABINET

MAKER,/No. 58/Broad Street/New York Van Boskerck is listed at various numbers on Broad Street in Manhattan from 1817 through 1828 and, again, in 1839 and 1840. He was at 58 Broad only from 1824 through 1827 and in 1840. The secretary would appear to date from the 1824–1827 period. Ref.: *Antiques,* September 1964.

VAN DOORN, ANTHONY

The country cabinetmaker Anthony Van Doorn (1792–1871), active in Brattleboro, Vermont, c. 1815–1852, is known for over a dozen marked pieces of pine and maple furniture, including washstands and side tables. Examples are at the Bennington (Vermont) Museum and Historic Deerfield. Van Doorn's engraved label c. 1836–1847 features a Classical side chair, sofa, and desk and reads,

CABINET MAKING/BY/A. VAN DOORN./BRATTLEBORO VT./All Kinds of/Furniture, Chairs, Looking-Glasses, Feathers, Coffins and Grave Stones/ on the best terms.

To my knowledge, this offering of "Grave Stones" is unique among cabinetmakers. Refs.: *Antiques,* May 1974, August 1993.

VANNEVAR, GEORGE

A Sheraton mahogany sideboard, c. 1805–1825, illustrated in *Antiques* for August 1932, is inscribed in pencil within a drawer

George Vannevar/The Maker

The Boston, Massachusetts, cabinetmaker George Vannevar advertised in a local paper in 1823. Ref.: Bjerkoe.

VIGIL, MARIANO

A c. 1855–1865 pine almario or cabinet with doors at the School of American Research, Santa Fe, New Mexico, is inscribed in pencil within a door

Mariano Vigil/Valencia, N.M.

Mariano Vigil is thought to have been a *carpintero* from Valencia, a community in southern New Mexico. Ref.: *Antiques,* September 1989.

Incised signature of Seth Vaill and date on the front of the chest of drawers beneath brass pull. Vaill worked in Guilford c. 1800–1810. Private collection.

VOSBURGH, HERMAN

A braced-back Windsor continuous armchair offered at Sotheby's sale of April 27–30, 1977, was branded on the underside of the seat

H. VOSBURGH/N. YORK

This is the extremely rare mark of Herman Vosburgh, listed as working in Manhattan c. 1785–1800. Ref.: Santore II.

VOSE, ISAAC, & SON

The cabinetmakers Isaac Vose (1767–1823) and his son, Isaac Jr. (1794–1872), were in

Federal cherry chest of drawers, signed and dated "1806" by the Guilford, Connecticut, cabinetmaker Seth Vaill. Private collection.

business together on Washington Street in Boston, Massachusetts, from 1819 until 1823, with the son continuing alone under the same name through 1825. They produced a great quantity of mahogany and rosewood furniture in the Sheraton, Classical, and Empire styles. However, only about a half dozen pieces bearing their stenciled mark:

Isaac Vose & Son/Cabinet, Chair &/Furniture Warehouse/Washington St./BOSTON are known. These include a mahogany secrétaire à abattant at the Smithsonian Institution and an Empire mahogany card table at the St. Louis Art Museum. Refs.: Cooper; *Antiques,* May 1982, May 1992.

VOSE & COATES

From 1805 until 1816, the cabinetmakers Isaac Vose and Joshua Coates (d. 1819) were in partnership on Washington Street in Boston, Massachusetts. They are best known for a charming Federal canted-corner worktable with laminated legs and stretchers and elaborate painted decoration. It is signed on the tray bottom

Vose & Coates

This piece is now at Winterthur. Refs.: Fales, *American Painted Furniture;* Montgomery; *Antiques,* May 1992.

Queen Anne walnut block-front desk, c. 1730–1740, pencil-signed on the interior "Made By Rich Walker" for the Boston cabinetmaker Richard Walker (d. 1761), active c. 1730–1750. Courtesy, Bernard and S. Dean Levy, Inc., New York.

W

WAIN, JACOB

A c. 1785–1790 Chippendale walnut tall clock case in a private collection is signed in chalk within the case

J. Wain

Jacob Wain (1766–1814) was a joiner working in Lancaster, Pennsylvania, until around 1792, when he moved to nearby Harrisburg, where he remained in business until his death. Ref.: *Antiques,* May 1984.

WALE, WILLIAM

William Wale is one of the very few pianomakers to have made his own

cases. He is known for a Classical c. 1815–1825 mahogany pianoforte that is marked

WILLIAM WALE/MAKER/
82 Murray Street/NEW-YORK

Wale was listed in the 1806 Manhattan directory as a carpenter, in that of 1810 as a cabinetmaker, and, finally, in 1817 as a musical instrument maker. He was not listed as a pianoforte maker until 1827. He continued active until 1842. Ref.: *Antiques,* January 1946.

WALKER, RICHARD

An important c. 1735–1745 Queen Anne walnut block-front, slant-front desk is inscribed on a hidden drawer

Made by Rich Walter

The Boston cabinetmaker and shipwright Richard Walker (d. 1761) was in the city by 1720 and had his own cabinet shop from a decade later until 1750. He is among the earliest known makers of American block-front furniture. Refs.: Conversation with Bernard Levy, August 31, 1994; *Antiques,* March 1995.

WALKER, ROBERT

The Charleston, South Carolina, cabinetmaker Robert Walker (1772–1833) was established in the city by 1799 and had his own shop on Broad Street two years later. He occupied shops at various Charleston addresses throughout the remainder of his career. One of his few marked pieces is a Hepplewhite mahogany clothespress at the Charleston Museum, which is labeled

ROBERT WALKER/(LATE WATTS AND
WALKER)/CABINET MAKER,/No. 39,
CHURCH-STREET, CHARLESTON;/Has,
at all times, on hand, a large and hand-
fome/Affortment of every Article in his
Line./Orders from the Country speedily
and carefully/executed in the
neateft manner.

A kidney-shaped chest of drawers at the museum bears the same label. Walker was at 39 Church Street c. 1806–1810. Another piece, a late Federal satinwood desk and bookcase or secretary, bears a similar label. However, this one reads,

ROBERT WALKER/CABINET
MAKER/No. 53 CHURCH-STREET,
CHARLESTON

Walker had his shop at this address only during the years 1813–1819. Refs.: E. Milby Burton, *Charleston Furniture, 1700–1825* (Charleston, S.C.: Charleston Museum, 1955); *Antiques,* June 1970, March 1980.

WALKER, SAMUEL

An Empire birch and maple chest of drawers or bureau now at the Grafton (Vermont) Historical Society is signed

**Made by Samuel Walker/Grafton/
Nov. 15th 1834**

Walker was one of many rural cabinetmakers active in New England in the first half of the nineteenth century.

WALSH & EGERTON

The obscure New York City firm of Walsh & Egerton is known for at least three pieces of marked furniture: a pair of c. 1820–1840 Classical mahogany window seats, illustrated in *MAD* for March 1994, which are labeled

**WALSH & EGERTON/
Cabinet, Chair and Sopha Manufacturers/
No. 46 Broad-Street, N.Y.**

and a Sheraton mahogany server, c. 1810–

Stenciled mark of Walter & Meader on the Empire chest of drawers. Their shop was on Main Street in Cincinnati. Private collection.

1820, having a printed paper label reading,

WALSH & EGERTON'S/CABINET WAREHOUSE/No. 47 Broad-Street,/NEW-YORK./Where all orders will be executed in the Best and most/Fashionable manner.

The New Jersey cabinetmaker Matthew Egerton, Jr. (see his entry), had two sons in the trade. It is possible that one of them was the Egerton in this partnership.

WALTER & MEADER

An Empire pine chest of drawers or bureau in a private collection is stenciled

**WALTER & MEADER/
BUREAU/Manufacturers/
CINCINNATI/WARRANTED GOOD**

Empire pine chest of drawers or bureau, c. 1848–1850, stenciled by the Cincinnati, Ohio, furniture manufacturers Joseph Walter and Daniel Meader.
Private collection.

A pair of Chippendale mahogany Marlborough-leg side chairs, c. 1770–1780, each signed in chalk on the seat frame "Walton" for the Philadelphia cabinetmaker Samuel Walton, working c. 1763–1786. Courtesy, Israel Sack, Inc., New York.

The Pennsylvania cabinetmaker Joseph Walter came to Cincinnati, Ohio, in 1831. He was in business on Main Street until 1850, when his partnership with Daniel Meader (see his entry) was dissolved. This relationship (and the bureau) appears to have dated c. 1848–1850.

WALTON, GEORGE

One of a pair of late Federal satinwood trick-leg card tables illustrated in the *Bee* for November 19, 1993, is inscribed

G ggw 1813

and attributed to the early-nineteenth-century Philadelphia cabinetmaker George Walton.

WALTON, SAMUEL

Two c. 1770–1780 Chippendale mahogany side chairs with Marlborough legs are signed in chalk on the seat frames

Walton

They are attributed to the Philadelphia cabinetmaker Samuel Walton, working c. 1763–1786. Refs.: Bjerkoe; Hornor.

WARD, E.

A Hepplewhite cherry and mahogany chest of drawers with French feet, c. 1785–1795, illustrated in *Antiques* for October 1983, is signed

E. Ward

This is possibly the Salem, Massachusetts, cabinetmaker Ebenezer Ward (1710–1791). Ref.: Bjerkoe.

WARD, JOHN

A Queen Anne mahogany bonnet-top high chest of drawers or highboy, c. 1730–1750, which is inscribed in red chalk

within a drawer

J. W.

was attributed, when offered by Skinner's, March 30, 1984, to the Salem, Massachusetts, cabinetmaker John Ward (1738–1789). The piece seems early for Ward, who would have been quite young when it was made. Ref.: Bjerkoe.

WARE, GEORGE W., & CO.

The Boston firm of George W. Ware & Co. was in business at two locations, 12 Cornhill and 26 Washington Street, from 1862 through 1875. They both manufactured furniture and sold a wide range of dry goods. A c. 1865–1875 walnut étagère in the collection of the Virginia Museum is labeled

GEO. W. WARE & CO./Manufacturers and dealers in/FURNITURE,/Looking-Glasses

and Upholstery Goods,/PLUSHES, DAMASKS & BROCATELLES,/No. 12 Cornhill, and 26 Washington Street,/BOSTON.

A footstool at the Yale University Art Gallery is marked in the same manner. Refs.: Fitzgerald; Kane.

WARNER, ELISHA

The Lexington, Kentucky, cabinetmaker Elisha Warner (d. 1829) arrived in the city soon after 1810. He was listed in the 1818 directory as both cabinet- and clockmaker and left a large estate. However, his only known marked piece is a c. 1810–1820 Hepplewhite cherry chest of drawers, which is inscribed twice in ink

Made by Elisha Warner

It is at the Anglo-American Art Museum, Baton Rouge, Louisiana. Ref.: *Antiques*, April 1974.

WARNER, G.

A well-carved c. 1790–1800 Federal mahogany one-drawer stand with cookie corners owned by the National Society of Colonial Dames is branded within a drawer

G. WARNER

The piece is from New England, possibly the Salem, Massachusetts, area, but nothing is known of Warner.

Federal carved mahogany one-drawer stand, c. 1790–1800, with the mark within the drawer of G. Warner. Courtesy, Cincinnati Art Museum.

WARNER, JOHN

A Chippendale walnut slant-front desk in a private collection is inscribed

**John Warner his hand/And Pen
April the 7 1799**

John Warner (working c. 1799–1814) was listed as a joiner in Goshen Township, Chester County, Pennsylvania, from 1807 through 1811. He appeared in the same capacity in West Whiteland Township in 1814. Ref.: Schiffer.

WARREN, HASTINGS

The Middlebury, Addison County, Vermont, cabinetmaker Hastings Warren (1780–1845) is known for a massive cherry and mahogany Empire–Gothic Revival desk and bookcase or secretary, c. 1820–1830, at the Sheldon Museum, Middlebury, which is signed in pencil beneath the base

H. Warren

Warren was apprenticed to the Middlebury cabinetmaker William Young, became his partner around 1801, and after marrying Young's daughter succeeded to the business in 1805. After 1818 Warren employed a manager for the shop while devoting himself to other business activities. He finally shut down the firm in 1834. Refs.: Robinson; *Antiques,* June 1972.

WARREN, N. E.

An Empire cherry chest of drawers in a private Ohio collection is inscribed in pencil on the back

**Made by N.E. Warren, Geneseo Livingston
County, N.Y., A.S. Gardiner's Shop,
June 1835**

N. E. Warren was apparently a journeyman employed by the cabinetmaker Samuel Gar-

Detail of the drawer of the Federal stand, showing the brand of G. Warner, thought to have been a cabinetmaker from the Salem, Massachusetts, area. Courtesy, Cincinnati Art Museum.

diner (see his entry). Ref.: Scherer.

WARREN, THOMAS E.

An upholstered Victorian iron armchair with centripetal spring mechanism (enabling it to turn and rock) at the New York State Museum is labeled

Thomas E. Warren/Troy, N.Y.

Warren, of Troy, patented the chair in 1849. It was manufactured by the American Chair Company, active on River Street in Troy, c. 1829–1858. The chair received favorable mention at London's Crystal Palace Exhibition of 1851. Refs.: Scherer; *Antiques,* March 1985.

WATERBURY, SAMUEL

A c. 1840–1860 transitional Empire-Victorian mahogany server with marble top pictured in the *Bee* for February 3, 1995, bore the label

Sam'l Waterbery's/Beekman Street,
N.Y.,N.Y.

It seems likely that Waterbery was a furniture dealer rather than a manufacturer.

WATROUS, M.

A miniature Empire chest of drawers, c. 1840–1850, in mahogany, cherry, and pine, at the Connecticut Historical Society, is stenciled on the backboards

Manufactured By/M. Watrous,/
Andover, Conn.

Another miniature by Watrous, a cherry desk and bookcase or secretary in an Empire-Gothic mode, is in a private collection. It dates from the same period.

WATSON, LUMEN

An Empire mahogany hollow-column mantel clock in a private collection bears a label within the case that reads,

IMPROVED MANTEL CLOCKS./MADE
BY L. WATSON,/CINCINNATI, OHIO

Lumen Watson (1790–1834) came to Cincinnati before 1809, establishing a firm that made clock cases. By 1820 he was employing men to make clock movements as well, and later in the decade he began to make organs. By the time of his death he was employing twenty-five men and making thousands of clocks each year. Ref.: *Made in Ohio*.

WATTRING, L. H.

A c. 1840–1850 country Sheraton linen press in cherry is inscribed on the back

L. H. Wattring/Marion/
Marion County Ohio

Although Wattring is presumed to have been a cabinetmaker, nothing seems to be known of his history. Ref.: Hageman II.

WAYNE, CALEB P.

B oth an ornate gilded Empire mirror, c. 1825–1835, and a small c. 1810–1820 Federal mahogany dressing or shaving stand bear the lengthy label of

C. P. WAYNE/ At the South-west corner
of Fourth and Market Streets.

There is, however, nothing in this ad to indicate that Wayne of Philadelphia made these objects. He appears to have been a merchant selling everything from mirrors to Britannia Ware and andirons.

WAYNE & BIDDLE

A substantial number of mirrors bear the label of the Philadelphia firm of Caleb P. Wayne and Charles Biddle, Jr. (active 1811–1822). However, as noted in the previous entry, they were sellers rather than manufacturers of mirrors.

WEAVER, HOLMES

T he cabinet- and chairmaker Holmes Weaver (1769–1848) opened a shop on Meeting Street in Newport, Rhode Island, in 1799 and remained there until at least 1806. During this period he produced a Federal mahogany chest of drawers featuring an engraved label illustrated with a Federal serpentine-front sideboard and reading,

Holmes Weaver,/CABINET AND CHAIR MAKER/Meeting Street/NEWPORT.

While this piece is in a private collection, other labeled Weaver pieces may be seen at the Henry Ford Museum and the Museum of Fine Arts, Boston. The piece in Boston, a c. 1790–1800 Federal inlaid mahogany card table, bears a plainer and perhaps earlier label, which reads,

HOLMES WEAVER/Cabinet & Chair Maker/NEWPORT

Far different are the plain c. 1820–1840 arrow-back Windsor side chairs branded simply

HOLMES WEAVER

A set of six were offered at Sotheby's, November 18–20, 1976. Refs.: Bjerkoe; *Antiques,* February 1942.

WEAVER, ISAAC

The Pennsylvania cabinetmaker Isaac Weaver (d. 1863) was listed in the Westchester borough, Chester County, tax assessments from 1806 until 1813 and again in 1842. He is known for a Federal walnut chest of drawers branded within the drawers

I. WEAVER

as well as another, similar bureau, mahogany veneered and inlaid, which is labeled

ALL KINDS OF/Cabinet Ware/MADE AND SOLD BY/ISAAC WEAVER/WEST-CHESTER

This latter piece is in the collection of the Chester County Historical Society. Refs.: Bjerkoe; Schiffer.

WEBB, D., JR.

A c. 1780–1800 Federal serpentine-base cherry desk and bookcase or secretary,

illustrated in *Antiques* for May 1974, is incised within the case

D Webb Jr

This is possibly the name of an owner, Daniel Webb (1800–1840). Refs.: Bjerkoe; *Antiques,* May 1985.

WEBB, W., II

A c. 1760–1770 Chippendale mahogany side chair, illustrated in *Antiques* for December 1967, is impressed within the seat rail and on the slip-seat frame

W. WEBB II

This is likely to be the mark of the cabinet- and chairmaker William Webb II, of Salem, Massachusetts. His son, William Webb III, was a cabinetmaker in Salem from 1837 until 1849. Ref.: Bjerkoe.

WEBB & SCOTT

Bjerkoe cites a Federal cherry desk and bookcase or secretary, c. 1790–1820, which bears a label reading,

WEBB & SCOTT, Cabinet & Chair Makers,/BENEFIT-STREET,/ PROVIDENCE, Rhode-Island.

The Providence cabinetmaker Adrian Webb (1790–1840), active c. 1816–1828, was listed at 80 Benefit Street in 1828; his partner, Charles Scott (1795–1851), was in business on South Main Street from 1819 until 1830. Their partnership would probably have been in effect c. 1816–1822. Refs.: Bjerkoe; *Antiques,* October 1966.

WELLS, FREEGIFT

The Shaker brother and chairmaker Freegift Wells (1785–1871) of the Watervliet,

New York, community is known for several ladder-back rockers and side chairs stamped

F W

on the front posts and an unusual commode chair, illustrated in *Antiques & Arts Weekly* for May 13, 1994, which is signed in paint on the bottom

F. W./1861

Ref.: Rieman and Burks.

WELLS, JOHN I.

A Chippendale birch oxbow-front chest of drawers owned by the Connecticut Historical Society is branded within the case

J. WELLS

for the Hartford, Connecticut, cabinet- and chairmaker John I. Wells (1769–1832), working c. 1798–1812, who had a shop "south of the bridge." Other marked Wells pieces include a mahogany lolling chair, offered at Sotheby's, January 30–31, 1986, and a one-

drawer stand, also at the Connecticut Historical Society. Refs.: Bjerkoe; *Connecticut Furniture: Seventeenth and Eighteenth Centuries* (Hartford: Wadsworth Atheneum, 1967).

WELLS, THOMAS J.

An unusual cherry and maple desk with fold-out writing surface above graduated drawers is stamped on a drawer rim

T.J. WELLS. WATERVLIET.
APRIL 7. 1839

The Shaker brother and cabinetmaker Thomas J. Wells (b. 1819) was a nephew and apprentice of the well-known Freegift Wells (see earlier entry). He worked at the Watervliet community from around 1830 until 1843, when he went into the "world." A signed clock case from his hand is also known. Ref.: Rieman and Burks.

WERNER, T. J.

A Victorian Rococo Revival mahogany or rosewood upholstered side chair, illustrated in *Antiques* for August 1935, bears a damaged label, which appeared to read,

T. J. Werner/Fashionable/Cabinet
Warehouse/148 Fulton St. New York

The piece would date c. 1850–1870, but nothing further has been learned of Werner. He may have been a dealer rather than a manufacturer.

Cherry and maple desk with fold-out writing surface marked and dated "1839" by the Shaker cabinetmaker Thomas J. Wells (b. 1819) of Watervliet, New York.

Courtesy, Leigh Keno, New York.

WERREY, JACOB

A grain-painted, stencil-decorated six-board poplar blanket chest with turned feet is inscribed on the bottom board in blue pencil

German Township/ Fulton Co./February the 11th 1880/Made by Jacob Werrey

The Fulton County, Ohio, cabinetmaker Jacob Werrey (1838–1893) is known for several signed pieces, the earliest of which is dated 1863. Ref.: *Made in Ohio.*

WETHERBEE, ABIJAH

A rod-back Windsor rocker with comb, illustrated in *Antiques* for April 1958, is among the products of Abijah Wetherbee (1781–1835) of New Ipswich, New Hampshire. Active c. 1813–1835, Wetherbee branded his chairs beneath the seat

A. WETHERBEE/WARRANTED

Ref.: Santore II.

WHEELER, EBENEZER

Little is known of the Vermont cabinetmaker Ebenezer Wheeler. He is listed in the 1820 and 1830 census for Rockingham in the eastern part of the state, and a Federal bureau pictured in *MAD* for December 1982 was said to have been inscribed

Ebenezer Wheeler/Saxton's River/1819

Saxton's River is a community some five miles south of Rockingham. Ref.: Robinson.

WHITE

A c. 1790–1800 inlaid mahogany tea table, offered by Sotheby's, November 16–18, 1978, bears a label described as "White, Charleston." No further information has been obtained on this maker.

WHITE, CHARLES HAIGHT

The Philadelphia cabinetmaker Charles Haight White (1796–1876) was working in the city by 1818, continuing active at various addresses into the 1860s. During his lengthy career White made both Empire and Victorian furniture. An Empire walnut pedestal-base two-drawer worktable at the Philadelphia Museum of Art bears an engraved label featuring a Classical washstand, side chair, and plant stand and reading,

CHARLES H. WHITE/CABINET AND CHAIR MANUFACTURER/No. 109/ WALNUT STREET/PHILADELPHIA

A less ornate label on a Classical mahogany sofa at Winterthur reads simply,

**Charles H. White/Cabinet/
WAREROOMS/No. 109 Walnut St.**

Both labels and the furniture they mark date between 1824 and 1830, the period during which White occupied a shop at 109 Walnut Street. During the years 1828–1851, Charles White was in partnership with his brother John Ferris White (see following entry). After this Charles worked alone again on Chestnut Street. A c. 1850–1860 Victorian Rococo Revival carved rosewood armchair in the Ebenezer Maxwell Mansion, Philadelphia, bears his mark from this period:

**Chas. H. White/
No. 250/Chestnut St/Philada.**

Refs.: *Antiques,* May 1994; *New York–Pennsylvania Collector,* December 1984.

WHITE, CHARLES HAIGHT AND JOHN FERRIS

From 1828 until 1851 the Philadelphia cabinetmakers and brothers Charles Haight White (see previous entry) and John Ferris White (1807–1852) worked together on Walnut Street in Philadelphia. A Classical mahogany butler's desk-sideboard from this period bears their stencil:

**C.H. & J.F. WHITE/CABINET WARE-
HOUSE/No. 107 & 109 Walnut St./
PHILADA.**

as does a Classical mahogany fall-front secrétaire offered at Sotheby's, May 10–11, 1974. Ref.: *Antiques,* May 1994.

WHITE, E.

A Federal inlaid mahogany serpentine-front card table, attributed to Baltimore, Maryland, c. 1790–1800, is signed beneath the top

E. White

It is not known if this is the maker's or an owner's mark.

WHITE, J. D., CO.

A c. 1870–1900 oak platform rocker in a private collection bears a paper label reading,

**J. D. WHITE CO./Furniture and
Undertaking/Picture Frames and
Mouldings/Galien, MICH.**

White may have been only a seller, but the fact that the firm also offered undertaking, a trade that went well with cabinetmaking, makes it likely that he was also a manufacturer.

WHITE, JOHN

A Chippendale mahogany chest of drawers or bureau in a private collection bears the printed paper label of the Wilmington, Delaware, Quaker cabinetmaker John White (1762–1829). It reads,

**JOHN WHITE/JOINER/Respectfully
informs his Friends and the Public/That
he continues to carry on Business in the
Shop lately occupied by White & Byrnes,
and opposite John Moore's/WHERE HE
MAKES/MAHOGANY, CHERRY
& . . . . . /FURNITURE/In a neat
Manner and on reasonable terms./
Wilmington, 5th mo.6. 1791**

White was in business in Wilmington as early as 1789. In 1798 he took over his deceased brother Joseph's apothecary shop and, apparently, ceased to make furniture. Refs.: *Plain and Ornamental; Antiques,* May 1985.

WHITE, LEMUEL

A Federal maple bowfront chest of drawers, offered at Christie's, June 17, 1992, is signed on a drawer bottom

Lemuel White 1815

Although it seems likely that White was a cabinetmaker, nothing further is known of him.

WHITE, SAMUEL K.

Two chairs—a c. 1840–1850 rod-back Windsor side chair, pictured in *MAD* for November 1978, and a Salem rocker from the same period, illustrated in the *Bee* for August 26, 1983—bear the following printed paper label:

WARRANTED/CHAIRS/MADE BY/SAMUEL K. WHITE,/Exeter, Me.

The turner Samuel K. White worked in Exeter, west of Bangor, c. 1840–1849.

WHITE, W. M.

A c. 1790–1800 Windsor fan-back side chair offered at auction in Hampton, New Hampshire, April 20, 1994, is branded beneath the seat

W M WHITE

It is not known if this is the maker's or an owner's mark. However, Santore mentions a William White, Windsor chair maker, active in Boston, c. 1800. Ref.: Santore II.

WHITE, WALTER

A Federal cherry stand with unusual cloverleaf form in the collection of the Storrs Museum is signed

Walter White

White, of Longmeadow, Massachusetts, made this table c. 1800 and gave it to his daughter as a wedding present in 1819. The sophisticated design would indicate that White was a cabinetmaker. Ref.: *Springfield Furniture, 1700–1850* (Springfield, Mass.: Connecticut Valley Historical Museum, 1990).

WHITEHEAD, WILLIAM

Two Federal mahogany sideboards, one with a matching set of knife boxes, bear the label of the Manhattan cabinetmaker William Whitehead:

William Whitehead/CABINET & CHAIR

Federal inlaid mahogany serpentine-front sideboard labeled by William Whitehead, a New York City cabinetmaker, working c. 1792–1799. Courtesy, Israel Sack, Inc., New York.

Partial label of William Whitehead on the Federal sideboard. Whitehead worked at 75 Pearl Street, the address on this label when complete, from 1794 through 1799. Courtesy, Israel Sack, Inc., New York.

MAKER/No. 75/Pearl Street/New York Whitehead was first listed in the New York City directory in 1792. He was working at 75 Pearl Street from 1794 until 1799. Little is known of his later career. One of the sideboards is at the High Museum, Atlanta. Refs.: Cooper; *Antiques,* June 1979.

WHITELOCK, GEORGE

George Whitelock (1780–1833) was a chair- and cabinetmaker with a shop at 137 Market Street in Wilmington, Delaware. His printed paper label reading,
GEORGE WHITELOCK,/CABINET and CHAIR-MAKER,/Next door above the Town-Hall, Market-Street, Wilmington,/Respectfully informs his friends and the public, that he carries on the above busi-/nesses in all their branches. As he is determined to employ only the best workmen, and make use of the best materials, he has no doubt of giving fatisfaction/to those who may favor him with their cuftom./He intends keeping a stock of ready made FURNITURE on hand, so that per-/sons wishing articles in his line may be supplied on the shorteft notice.
has been found on a Hepplewhite inlaid mahogany tall clock case, illustrated in *Antiques* for July 1948, and a Federal mahogany sideboard at the Historical Society of Delaware. Whitelock was active in Wilmington, c. 1802–1822. Refs.: Bjerkoe; Charles G. Dorman, *Delaware Cabinetmakers and Allied Artisons: 1655–1855* (Wilmington: Historical Society of Delaware, n.d.).

WHITMORE, GILBERT D.

The chair- and cabinetmaker Gilbert D. Whitmore was active in Boston, Massachusetts, c. 1843–1865. A child's walnut side chair in a private collection bears a damaged label, reading in part,
GILBERT D. WHITEMORE/MANUFAC-TURER OF/FASHIONABLE FURNI-TURE,/IN ANCIENT AND MODERN STYLE/346 WASHINGTON STREET, CORNER OF HAYWARD/. . . . .
. . . .
Whitmore was in business at 346 Washington Street only from 1843 to 1847. Refs.: Fairbanks and Bates; *Antiques,* May 1982.

WHITNEY, J.

A pair of c. 1830–1850 thumb-back Windsor side chairs advertised in the *Bee,* June 3, 1994, are impressed beneath the seats
J. WHITNEY
It is not known if this is the mark of the maker or an owner.

WHITREY, GEORGE O., & CO.

A c. 1860–1870 Victorian Rococo Revival marble top serpentine front bureau or chest of drawers in a private collection is stenciled within a drawer

**FROM/GEO O. WHITREY & CO./
MANUFACTURERS/& IMPORTERS/
FINE FURNITURE/AND/UPHOLSTERY
GOODS/NOS. 319 & 324 PINE ST./
SAN FRANCISCO**

Nothing further seems to be known of this California firm. Ref.: *Antiques,* June 1966.

WHITWELL, WILLIAM

A c. 1765–1775 Chippendale mahogany block-front kneehole desk, illustrated in *Antiques* for January 1971, and a c. 1780–1800 three-part Federal dining table are branded

W. WHITWELL

The latter was attributed to William Whitwell of Boston, whose labeled mirrors make it rather evident that he was a hardware dealer. Whitwell may have owned these pieces, but it seems highly unlikely that he made them.

WICKERSHAM, GEORGE

The Shaker brother and cabinetmaker George Wickersham (1806–1891) of Mount Lebanon, New York, is known for a pine lap or table desk inscribed on the bottom drawer

**Made by George Wickersham 1841
North Family Phebe Ann Jones**

Ref.: Rieman and Burks.

WIDDIFIELD, WILLIAM

The turner William Widdifield (c. 1768–1822) worked at various addresses in Philadelphia, c. 1790 1816. A sack back armchair in a private collection is stamped beneath the seat

W. WIDDIFIELD

Widdifield also used a printed paper label reading,

All Sorts of WINDSOR and Rufh Bottom Chairs,/MADE and SOLD by,/WILLIAM WIDDEFIELD,/In Spruce-Street, below the Drawbridge, and two/Doors above JONATHAN WAINRIGHTS, PHILADELPHIA.

Though not appearing in the directory, Widdifield appears to have been at the Spruce Street address before 1800. Ref.: Santore II.

WIGGERS, H. H.

A Victorian Gothic Wooten-type desk in a private collection is marked

**H.H. Wiggers, Cincinnati, Ohio
Feb 6, 1877**

Nothing is known of this individual.

WIGGIN, J.

A Portsmouth, New Hampshire, Hepplewhite bowfront chest of drawers in mahogany and bird's-eye maple, dating c. 1780–1800, is branded

J. Wiggin

The piece was illustrated in *Antiques* for June 1987. It is not known if the mark is that of an owner or the maker.

WILDER, ISAIAH

A c. 1800–1820 Sheraton mahogany card table in the collection of the New Hampshire Historical Society is twice branded

I. WILDER J

for Isaiah Wilder (1782–1867), who worked in Hingham, Massachusetts, until 1821 and thereafter in Surrey and Keene, New Hamp-

shire. The *J* stands for Jr., a term Wilder dropped once he moved to New Hampshire. Ref.: Hewitt, Kane, and Ward.

WILDER, JOSEPH

A c. 1820–1840 rod-back Windsor side chair at the New Hampshire Historical Society retains the partial paper label of Joseph Wilder, a member of the Wilder family of turners active in New Hampshire during the early nineteenth century. Ref.: Brian Cullity, *Plain and Fancy: New England Painted Furniture* (Sandwich, Mass.: Heritage Plantation of Sandwich, 1987).

WILDER, JOSHUA

A c. 1790–1800 Hepplewhite mahogany half-height or "grandmother" clock in a private collection is signed

JOSHUA. WILDER, HINGHAM

It is not known if Joshua Wilder of Hingham, Massachusetts, made this case or only the clockworks.

WILDER, JOSIAH PRESCOTT

T he New Ipswich, New Hampshire, turner Josiah Prescott Wilder (working 1787–1825) is known for a variety of c. 1810–1825

Hepplewhite mahogany half-height or "grandmother" clock, c. 1790–1800, case signed JOSHUA. WILDER, HINGHAM. Wilder, from Hingham, Massachusetts, was either a cabinetmaker or a clockmaker. Courtesy, Israel Sack, Inc., New York.

step-down rod-back Windsor side chairs and comb-back and Boston rockers. While most of these are branded

J. WILDER

a pair of simple rod-back, plank-seat side chairs observed at a show in 1994 are impressed

J.P. WILDER/WARRANTED

and a set of six painted and decorated step-down rod-backs in the Abby Aldrich Rockefeller Art Collection are simply branded

WILDER

Ref.: Santore II.

WILEY, JOHN

A plain pine six-board chest illustrated in *MAD* for August 1975 is signed

John Wiley, 1845

This could be the mark of the maker or, more likely, an owner.

WILEY, SETH

A small Federal cherry chest of drawers with line inlay is inscribed in chalk

Made by Seth Wiley for Stephen Mellish

The piece dates c. 1790–1810, but nothing is known of Wiley.

WILKIN, GODFREY

An elaborate Chippendale walnut dower chest, with three drawers below a false box front, which opens down to reveal a group of small drawers, ogee bracket feet, and hearts inlay in sulfur and ivory, is inscribed across the front,

READ THES UP/MARCH./.1 JACOB WILKIN HIS CHEAST A.D 1801/AND READ THES DOWN/GODFREY WILKIN HARDY COUNTY AND STATE OF VIRGINIA

The Hardy County, Virginia (now West Virginia), cabinetmaker and gunsmith Godfrey Wilkin is known for this piece, made for a relative. It is at the Henry Ford Museum. Refs.: Robert Bishop, *How to Know American Antique Furniture* (New York: E. P. Dutton, 1973); Fitzgerald.

WILL, JOHN

A country Empire cherry and walnut desk and bookcase of the type often referred to as a plantation desk is inscribed in pencil within a drawer

**John Will Cabined Maker/
74 years old/No. 1/1863**

John Will (1789–c. 1870) of Amanda Township, Fairfield County, Ohio, was active in Fairfield County as early as 1850. Though listed in the census as a "carpenter," he appears to have been a competent cabinetmaker. Ref.: *Made in Ohio*.

WILLARD, HENRY

Henry Willard (1802–1887), another son of the clockmaker Aaron Willard, was apprenticed to the cabinetmaker William Fish and, after serving his time, made clock cases for his father and brother as well as other manufacturers. A Federal inlaid mahogany tall case clock with works by Aaron Willard, Jr., is stenciled

HENRY WILLARD, Clock Case/Manufacturer/No. 843, Washington St./ BOSTON

Refs.: Chris Bailey, *Two Hundred Years of American Clocks and Watches* (Englewood Cliffs, N.J.: Prentice-Hall, 1975); *Antiques,* October 1974.

WILLARD, O. A.

A pair of late-nineteenth-century oak armchairs at the Shelburne Museum are labeled

Gilded Federal mirror with carved eagle finial and reverse-painted panel, c. 1790–1800, bearing the label of John H. Williams, a looking glass manufacturer who worked on Pearl Street in New York City, c. 1790–1825. Courtesy, Bernard and S. Dean Levy, Inc., New York.

Common sense chair/ Manufactured by/
O. A. Willard, Cavendish, VT./
Patent applied for.
Nothing is known of the manufacturer.

WILLARD AND NOLAN

From 1804 until 1806, Aaron Willard, Jr. (1783–1864), son of the clockmaker Aaron Willard (and himself a clockmaker) was in partnership in Boston with Spencer Nolan making clock dials. They apparently also made mirrors. A carved and gilded Federal looking glass with reverse-painted panel is signed on the back

Willard and Nolen, Boston

This mirror was sold at the auction of the Flayderman Collection, April 1931. Ref.: Chris Bailey, *Two Hundred Years of American Clocks and Watches* (Englewood Cliffs, N.J.: Prentice-Hall, 1975).

WILLETT, MARINUS

A Chippendale mahogany serpentine-front card table, c. 1770–1775, with ball-and-claw feet is signed in chalk on the inner rear rail

Willett

and attributed to the Manhattan cabinetmaker Marinus Willett (1740–1830). Willett was working in New York City as early as 1765. He was a notable Revolutionary War commander and mayor of New York City in 1807. Ref.: Bjerkoe.

WILLEY, CALVIN

A Chippendale cherry desk and bookcase or secretary, illustrated in *Antiques* for November 1964, is signed on two drawers

Calvin Willey

It was made in 1794 for Judge William Walker of Lenox, Massachusetts. Willey was born in 1769 in East Haddam, Connecticut, and was working in Lenox when he made this piece. He later lived in North Haven, Vermont, dying there after 1830.

WILLIAMS, EBENEZER

The cabinet- and chairmaker Ebenezer Williams (1767–1844) worked with Eliphalet Chapin (see his entry) at his shop in East Windsor, Connecticut, c. 1790–1811. He moved to Painesville, Ohio, in 1811. He is known for a birdcage Windsor rod-back side chair in a private collection, which is branded

E. WILLIAMS

and for a Federal cherry chest of drawers, which is inscribed in chalk beneath the top

Decr. 12th 1803/E. Williams E. Winfsor

Refs.: Hageman II; *Antiques,* May 1986.

WILLIAMS, ELAM

A Federal astragal-form mahogany worktable with simulated tambour front, illustrated in *MAD* for October 1974, was said to have been labeled by the New York City cabinetmaker Elam Williams. Nothing further is known of this cabinetmaker.

WILLIAMS, ICHABOD

At least two Federal cherry tall clock cases and a Pembroke table with perforated *X* stretcher, at the New Jersey State Museum, bear the printed paper label of Ichabod Williams:

MADE & SOLD/By Ichabod Williams, CABINET-MAKER/ELIZABETH-TOWN

Williams was active in Elizabeth, New Jersey, c. 1780–1800. Ref.: *Furniture and Furnishings from the Collection of the New Jersey State Museum* (Trenton: New Jersey State Museum, 1970).

WILLIAMS, JACOB

A Federal kidney-shaped inlaid mahogany sideboard, c. 1800–1810, illustrated in *Antiques* for April 1982, is signed beneath the top

J. Williams

The piece is attributed to the Baltimore, Maryland, cabinetmaker Jacob Williams, who appeared in the city directory from 1800 until 1810. Ref.: Bjerkoe.

WILLIAMS, JESSE SCOGGINS

The cabinetmaker Jesse Scoggins Williams (1821–1883) worked in Sparta, White County, Tennessee, c. 1840–1855. He is known for an Empire cherry bureau or chest of drawers, which is pencil-signed

Made By/J.S. Williams/ Sparta Tennessee/1855

Ref.: Williams and Harsh.

WILLIAMS, JOHN

A painted, stencil-decorated Maine dressing table is inscribed

John Williams/February 1832

Ref.: *Bee,* January 28, 1994.

WILLIAMS, JOHN H.

An elaborate carved and gilded c. 1790–1800 Sheraton mirror, illustrated in *Antiques* for March 1987, bears a partial engraved label with eagle grasping arms and reading,

John H. Williams/LOOKING-GLASS/MANUFACTURER/PEARL/315/ STREET/ Opposite/Peck's Slip/New York/Prints, Drawings & Needlework.

A later gilded c. 1815–1825 Federal mirror with reverse-painted panel bears a printed label that suggests Williams no longer made his own mirrors.

Partial printed paper label of John H. Williams on the Federal mirror. Courtesy, Bernard and S. Dean Levy, Inc., New York.

Looking Glass Warehouse,/JOHN H. WILLIAMS,/No. 315 PEARL-STREET,/Opposite Peck's Slip/OFFERS FOR SALE A GENERAL ASSORTMENT OF/LOOKING GLASSES,/In the newest patterns of/Gilt and Mahogany Frames, warranted the best quality at the/lowest

Factory prices./PRINTS, DRAWINGS AND NEEDLE-WORK NEATLY FRAMED./Looking Glass Plates re-silvered and framed at the shortest notice./
. . . . as usual.
Refs.: *Antiques,* May 1981, March 1987.

WILLIAMS, THOMAS RUSSELL

The Salem, Massachusetts, cabinetmaker Thomas Russell Williams (born c. 1783) is known for a Federal inlaid mahogany tambour-front lady's desk and bookcase or secretary, c. 1795–1815, which is twice labeled

CABINET WORK/OF ALL KINDS/MADE AND WARRANTED, BY/THOMAS R. WILLIAMS/BROWN STREET SALEM/North Side of Washington Square/Orders gratefully acknowledged & promptly executed.

Williams was in partnership with the cabinetmaker Nehemiah Adams (see his entry) during the period 1804–1813. Refs.: Bjerkoe; *Antiques,* April 1962.

WILLIAMS, W. R.

A Victorian Renaissance Revival walnut marble-top mirrored bureau, c. 1850–1870, which is in a private collection, is signed in paint

W.R. Williams/Warwick/N.Y.

This is probably an owner's rather than the maker's name.

WILLIAMS & DAWSON

The Manhattan cabinetmakers Thomas Williams and Jacob H. Dawson were in

business together on Broad Street from 1824 until 1832. Dawson continued alone in the same shop through 1835. They are known for a carved Empire marble-top pier table bearing the stenciled mark
WILLIAMS & DAWSON/Cabinet, Chair & Sofa Manufactory, No. 65 Broad Street, NEW YORK
Ref.: Elder and Stokes.

WILLIAMS & EVERETT

A c. 1810–1820 gilded Federal mirror with reverse-painted panel, offered at the April 1931 Flayderman Sale, is labeled,
WILLIAMS & EVERETT/Manufacturers of Looking-Glasses and Picture Frames/. . . . No. 234 Washington Street/BOSTON
Nothing further is known of this firm.

WILLIS, JOHN H.

John H. Willis, probably a journeyman cabinetmaker at the Chapin shop in Hartford, Connecticut, is known for a Federal inlaid mahogany sideboard inscribed beneath the top
Made by John H. Willis Hartford March the 24th 1804 at Mr. Aaron Chapin's Shop. Cabinet Maker Main Street. And intends going in the fall to New Orleans where you will find the maker if not dead. And if not in New Orleans inquire somewhere else—
This piece is also twice signed
John H. Willis
Also attributed by some to Willis is an early Chippendale walnut side chair with trifid feet and dating c. 1760–1770. It is signed on the seat frame
Willis
but appears too early for John H. Willis.

WILLISON, AMOS

A miniature six-board chest decorated with stencils and brass tacks bears the stenciled mark
A. WILLISON Beallsville, O.
Amos Willison was living in Beallsville, Monroe County, Ohio, by 1830. His six-board chest is thought to date c. 1830–1850. Ref.: *Ohio Furniture, 1788–1888* (Columbus: Columbus Museum of Art, 1984).

WILMERDING, WILLIAM

The Manhattan looking glass manufacturer William Wilmerding (1762–1832) has left a substantial number of elaborate Chippendale mirrors bearing his engraved label illustrated with period mirrors and an American eagle and reading,
LOOKING GLASSES/A large and Elegant/ASSORTMENT/BY/Willm. Wilmerding/Maiden 31 Lane/New York.
While it is not certain that Wilmerding, active c. 1789–1794, actually made mirrors as opposed to selling them, the phrase "by Willm. Wilmerding" in his label strongly suggests that. Labeled examples of his work may be found at the Museum of the City of New York and Winterthur. Refs.: Comstock, *The Looking Glass in America; Antiques,* May 1946, June 1964, May 1981.

WILMOT, WILLIAM

A country Sheraton cherry and bird's-eye maple serving table at the New York State Museum is stenciled on a drawer bottom
Wm. Wilmot/cabinetmaker/Unadilla, N.Y.
William Wilmot (1790–1849) was the first cabinetmaker in Unadilla, Otsego County,

active as early as 1810. His son, Daniel, continued the business past 1850. Refs.: Scherer; *Antiques,* May 1981.

WILSON, J.

A Federal cherry card table, c. 1790–1810, from Perry County, Ohio, illustrated in Hageman I is branded
J. WILSON
It is not known if this is the maker's or an owner's mark. Ref.: Hageman I.

WILSON, JOHN R. AND WILLIAM

The turners John R. and William Wilson had a shop on South Market Street in Wooster, Wayne County, Ohio, from 1837 until 1847. A decorated half arrow-back fancy chair of their make in a private collection is labeled
J.R. & W. WILSON,/WINDSOR AND FANCY CHAIR MAKERS,/WOOSTER, O./ALL WORK WARRANTED
Ref.: Hageman II.

WINCHESTER, ZIBA

The Shaker brother and cabinetmaker Ziba Winchester (1800–left 1838) of the Harvard, Massachusetts, community is known for a rare glazed bookcase signed
Ziba Winchester, 1836
which was offered at Skinner's Auction Gallery in June 1994, and a pine blanket box over drawer, which is inscribed in pencil
. . . . . . Winchester Aged 24
1824/Ziba Winchester of Harvard
This piece is at Hancock Shaker Village. Refs.: Rieman and Burks; Sprigg.

WINEBRENNER, EDWARD

A midnineteenth-century grain-painted pine blanket chest advertised in *MAD* for March 1995 was inscribed
Edward Winebrenner/Frederick, Md.
This is thought to be an owner's mark.

WING, SAMUEL

The cabinet- and chairmaker Samuel Wing (1774–1854) of Sandwich, Massachusetts, was active c. 1800–1854, producing a variety of furnishings, including some chairs branded
WING
which are at Old Sturbridge Village. Ref.: Santore II.

WINSTON, ALANSON

Alanson Winston (c. 1794–1862) sold and, presumably, made clocks and cabinet furniture in Lynchburg, Virginia, from 1816 until he went bankrupt in 1856. A clock at the Lynchburg Museum bears a label reading,
A. WINSTON,/CLOCK MANUFACTURER,/LYNCHBURG, Va./DIRECTIONS TO PUT IN MOTION . . . ./CABINET FURNITURE./On hand a general assortment of CABINET FURNITURE consisting of almost every article in the line, of/materials and workmanship equal to any manufactured in the United States, and will be furnished as low as can/be bought in Northern markets. Those in want are solicited to call and examine. A.WINSTON./CHAIRS! CHAIRS!!/WINSTON & CALWELL have a complete assortment of Windsor and Cane-seat Fancy CHAIRS, of/their own manufacture, which for

finish and durability they will warrant to give satisfaction. Ware Room im-/mediately opposite the Franklin Hotel./LYNCHBURG, VA., AUGUST 31, 1841. It is also clear from this label that Winston made chairs. Nothing is known of his erstwhile partner, Calwell. Ref.: Piorkowski.

WIRE, JOHN

The Philadelphia turner John Wire worked on Front and Water streets during the years 1791–1813. A sack-back Windsor armchair of his manufacture, branded beneath the seat

I. WIRE

was offered at Sotheby's, November 16–18, 1972. Ref.: Santore II.

WOLTZ, GEORGE

The Hagerstown, Maryland, cabinetmaker George Woltz (1744–1812) was active c. 1783–1812. He is known for a Queen Anne walnut corner chair, offered at Sotheby's June 21–23, 1979, which is inscribed

G——Woltz Hagers Md

and a c. 1790–1800 Federal mahogany tall clock case, the dial of which is inscribed in paint

GEORGE WOLTZ/HAGER'S TOWN

Another clock, more in the Chippendale mode, is signed

1783, George Woltz Hagers Town

Refs.: Bjerkoe; *Antiques,* March 1939.

WOLTZ, JESSE

A nephew of the Hagerstown, Maryland, cabinetmaker George Woltz (see previous entry), Jesse Woltz (1792–1837) was in Lancaster, Fairfield County, Ohio, by 1815. He

continued to work as a cabinetmaker there throughout his life. Among his marked pieces are a country Sheraton cherry drop-leaf table impressed beneath the top

J. WOLTZ/LANCASTER/OHIO/1824

and an Empire side chair stamped

J. WOLTZ

Refs.: Hageman I; *Made in Ohio.*

WOOD, A. H. AND W. R.

An arrow-back Windsor side chair, owned by the Colonial Dames of America in Tennessee, bears the label of the Wood brothers, working in Nashville, c. 1817–1820. The only pre-1850 Tennessee furniture label known, it reads,

WINDSOR CHAIRS/MANUFACTURED & WARRANTED/BY/AH & WR WOOD/ . . . . . Street, Nashville.

Ref.: Williams and Harsh.

WOOD, LANSFORD

A labeled looking glass by the Worcester, Massachusetts, cabinet- and looking glass maker Lansford Wood (1806–1844), active 1831–1844, is at Old Sturbridge Village. Ref.: *Antiques,* May 1993.

WOOD & TAYLOR

Robert Wood and James S. Taylor were New York City cabinetmakers who, during one of the city's periodic smallpox epidemics, c. 1810–1815, moved to the tiny town of Florida in Orange County, New York. Here they produced a Federal inlaid one-drawer stand in cherry, now at the New York State Museum, which is branded on the drawer

WOOD TAYLOR

and a Federal mahogany inlaid tall case clock bearing a handwritten paper label reading,

Wood & Taylor/Cabinet Makers/Florida

Refs.: Scherer; *Antiques,* May 1981.

WOODBURY, F. B.

A c. 1880–1910 oak armchair with turned spindles in a private collection is inscribed **M.L. Flarety/Bradford, Penn./From/F.B. Woodbury/Chair Manufacturer/ Orwell, New York**

Nothing is known of this manufacturer.

WOODBURY, LUTHER

A c. 1780–1800 gilded Federal mahogany mirror in a private collection is inscribed on the back

Luther Woodbury of Beverly/
30 leaves 12 horns

The mirror is credited to the Beverly, Massachusetts, area, but nothing is known of Woodbury. The reference to quantity of gilding materials suggests that he was a gilder.

WOODRUFF, GEORGE

A Sheraton mahogany Pembroke table at Winterthur appears to be the only known piece bearing the mark of the Manhattan cabinetmaker George Woodruff. It has an engraved label featuring a Federal sideboard and reading, **GEORGE WOODRUFF,/CABINET MAKER,/No. 54 JOHN-STREET,/Informs his friends and the public that he has commenced his busi-/ness at the above place, where all orders in the city or from**

Walnut Superior-grade Wooten "Patent Secretary," made and marked at the factory of William S. Wooten, Indianapolis, Indiana, c. 1874–1880.
Courtesy, Dubrow Collection.

the country,/will be thankfully received and punctually attended to, both with respect/ to workmanship and dispatch./New York May, 1808.

Woodruff's shop was at 54 John Street only from 1808 until 1810. He was at other locations in Manhattan through 1816. Ref.: Montgomery.

WOODRUFF, GOODRICH

Ac. 1800–1820 Sheraton cherry slant-front desk, illustrated in *Antiques* for March 1950, was described as being signed by the maker

Goodrich Woodruff

Nothing further seems to be known of this manufacturer.

WOODS, TITUS, & CO.

Ac. 1840–1850 Empire walnut fall-front desk at the Tennessee State Museum is signed on a drawer back

Titus Woods & Co./Memphis

Titus Woods & Company were commission merchants in Memphis, Tennessee. They are not believed to have manufactured furniture. Ref.: Williams and Harsh.

WOODWARD, ABISHAI

The Preston and New London, Connecticut, cabinetmaker Abishai Woodward (1752–1809) is known for two mahogany tall clock cases, one at the Detroit Art Institute. On the dial of each appears his signature

Abishai Woodward

Woodward lived in Preston at the time, c. 1773–1788, he made these clocks. Ref.: *Antiques,* June 1965.

WOOTEN DESK COMPANY

The Indiana minister turned furniture maker William S. Wooten is known for a group of elaborate walnut folding patent desks in the Victorian Eastlake mode. These were essentially miniature offices and came in four grades: "Ordinary," "Standard," "Extra," and "Superior." Marks were a paper label reading,

WOOTEN Desk Manf. Co., Indianapolis, Ind./W.S. Wooten's Patent, Oct. 6, 1874

and a brass plate embossed

WOOTEN DESK CO./ INDIANAPOLIS, IND.

Wooten established his business in Indianapolis in 1870, patented his famous desk in 1874, and remained active at various addresses in the city until 1893. Ref.: J. Camille Showalter and Janice Driesbach, *Wooten Patent Desks: A Place for Everything and Everything in Its Place* (Indianapolis: Indiana State Museum, 1983).

WRIGHT, BENJAMIN N.

Acountry Sheraton pine chest of drawers, c. 1840–1850, which was exhibited at the San Antonio Museum in 1973, is initialed in pencil on a drawer bottom

B N W

and attributed to the Walker County, Texas, craftsman Benjamin N. Wright.

WRIGHT, ISAAC, & CO.

The Hartford, Connecticut, cabinetmaker Isaac Wright is known for a substantial number of painted and decorated pine washstands and chairs bearing the stenciled mark

ISAAC WRIGHT & Co./CABINET/CHAIR/& UPHOLSTERY/WAREHOUSE/HARTFORD/CON

Examples are at the Connecticut Historical Society. Wright was active in Hartford from 1828 until his death in 1838. Refs.: Fales, *American Painted Furniture; Antiques,* October 1969.

WRIGHT & DAMON

The Shaker cabinetmakers Grove Wright (1789–1861) and Thomas Damon (1819–1880), of the Hancock, Massachusetts, community, are credited with a butternut and pine case of drawers containing a paper label that reads,

This case of Drawers were made by/Elder Grove and Brother Thomas and/placed

here thursday, January 13th 1853./It was the day our Ministry expected to/return to the City of Peace, but were detained/on account of the snow storm which/occured on that day.

Refs.: Rieman and Burks; Sprigg; *Antiques,* May 1979.

WRIGHTINGTON

A c. 1790–1810 bow-back Windsor side chair, illustrated in the *Bee* for April 15, 1994, is marked beneath the seat

Wrightington

It is presumed that this is an owner's name.

YENDELL, S.

A c. 1810–1820 bamboo-turned birdcage rod-back Windsor side chair in a private collection is branded beneath the seat

S. YENDELL

It is not known if this is the mark of the maker or an owner.

YODER, N.

A c. 1840–1850 Empire cherry and curly maple chest of drawers in a private collection is inscribed on the backboards

N. Yoder, Bellfontaine, O.

Birdcage rod-back Windsor side chair of mixed woods, c. 1810–1820, branded several times beneath the seat S. YENDELL. Private collection.

Bellfontaine is in Logan County, Ohio. It is not known if Yoder was a cabinetmaker rather than an owner. Ref.: Hageman II.

YOEMAN, C. N.

An elaborate c. 1825–1835 mahogany two-drawer stand with inlay and carved animal form legs and feet is signed

C. N. Yoemans

It is thought that this is an owner's name.

YORK, JOHN

A Connecticut Federal inlaid mahogany chest of drawers with French feet is inscribed

New Haven John York made in the year 1803

This is the first marked example from the hand of this Connecticut craftsman. Ref.: *MAD,* September 1994.

YOUNG, DAVID

The Hopkinton, New Hampshire, cabinet-maker David Young, active c. 1797–1815, is known for several tall clock cases bearing his label:

MADE/BY/David Young,/JOINER, /Hopkinton,/Newhamp-/shire.

These are usually constructed of mixed hardwoods: cherry, birch, maple, and so on. Refs.: *Antiques,* July 1968, October 1974, May 1979.

YOUNG, G. H., SONS

A group of Arts and Crafts leather-upholstered oak armchairs, c. 1910–1930, illustrated in *MAD* for August 1993, bear an oval paper label reading,

G.H. Young's Sons/Chair Manufacturers/Canton New York

Nothing further is known of this firm.

YOUNG, GEORGE

The Wilmington, Delaware, turner George Young, active c. 1798–1803, produced bamboo-turned, birdcage rod-back Windsor side chairs branded beneath their seats

G. YOUNG

An example is at the Hagley Museum. Ref.: *Plain and Ornamental.*

YOUNG, JAMES

A c. 1790–1810 Federal inlaid mahogany serpentine-front sideboard, offered at Sotheby's, February 1–4, 1978, is signed in chalk within the case

James Young

The Manhattan cabinetmaker James Young was listed as working at No. 6 Reed Street from 1801 until 1820. Refs.: Bjerkoe; *American Collector,* January 1938.

YOUNG, JOHN

A Federal single-drawer worktable in curly maple, illustrated in *Antiques* for June 1986, is inscribed

This desk/made by/
John Young/Boston/May, 1811

Young is listed in Boston directories as a sometime partner of the cabinetmaker Thomas Emmons, Jr.

YOUNG, STEPHEN AND MOSES

Only two labeled pieces by the Manhattan brothers and cabinetmakers Stephen and Moses Young are known. The earlier is a Sheraton mahogany Pembroke table found in a Connecticut consignment shop by the author and now at the New York State Museum. It is labeled

STEPHEN/AND/MOSES YOUNG'S/
Cabinet & Chair Ware-House,/
BROAD STREET,/73/New York.

Sheraton mahogany Pembroke table, c. 1804–1810, with the label of the brothers and cabinetmakers Stephen and Moses Young, active during this period at 73 Broad Street, New York City. New York State Museum. Ex-Author's Collection.

Carved Classical mahogany breakfast table with the label of Stephen and Moses Young of New York City, the address altered in ink to reflect their c. 1810–1818 location, 79 Broad Street. Courtesy, Diplomatic Reception Rooms, U.S. Department of State.

The piece would date to the period 1804–1810, when the Young brothers were located at 73 Broad Street. Their address c. 1810–1818 was 79 Broad Street, and a carved Classical mahogany breakfast table in the Diplomatic Reception Rooms of the U.S. Department of State reflects this. On it, the "73" on the above label form has been crossed out in ink and replaced by "79." Refs.: Bjerkoe; *American Collector,* January 1938.

##

ZABRISKIE, HENRY

Ac. 1840–1850 child's ladder-back rocking chair in the collection of the Newark Museum is stamped

H Z

for the turner Henry Zabriskie of Hawthorne, New Jersey. Ref.: *Antiques,* March 1934.

ZUMBRAGER, C.

Agroup of c. 1870–1890 Victorian Eastlake cane-seated chairs with a St. Louis, Missouri, history are impressed beneath their seats

C. ZUMBRAGER

It is not known if Zumbrager was the maker or an owner of the chairs.

ZUTPHEN, W.

Ac. 1810–1830 Windsor armchair at Colonial Williamsburg is branded beneath the seat

W. ZUTPHEN

The piece is attributed to an unknown New England maker, but the mark could be that of an owner. Ref.: Santore II.

APPENDIX A: INITIALS AS MARKS

Although the great majority of cabinetmakers who marked their work did so with their full names, a few used initials, as did many owners. Because this book is arranged by cabinetmakers' last names, even though in a given case the craftsman may have used initials rather than a full name as a mark, we have included this list of makers' initials.

AB	Amos Bishop
AG	Abner Guild
AS	Abel Spicer
AL	Alexander Low
B	Boyer
BNW	Benjamin N. Wright
CJT	Job Townsend
DE	David Evans
DP	David Poignard
EB	Erastus Blakely
EE	Edmund Edes
EM	Ebenezer Martin
EM	Enoch Moody, Jr.
ES	Elijah Sanborn
FT	Francis Trumble
FW	Freegift Wells
Gggw	George Walton
GM	G. Moody
HZ	Henry Zabriskie
IB	John or Joseph Bright
IH	Joshua Hempstead
IM	Isaac Mitchell
IP	Joseph Proud
IT	John Townsend
I+S	Jacob Sanderson
JAA	Job A. Allen
JJ	Johan Jahn
JK	Jacob Knagy
JM	John Meads
JP	John Pickard
JQ	John Quarles
JS	John Selden
JS	John Seymour
JS	Joseph Short
JW	John Ward
ME	Moses Eastwood
MT	Moses Troyer
M&E	Moore & Emmitt
PKT	Peter K. Thomas
P&S	Pottier & Stymus
R	Robert Rhea
R	Charles Rohlfs
R	Roycroft Shops
RC	Robert Crossman
RC	Robert Cushman
SI	Silas Ingalls
S&S	Soper & Soper
TL	Thomas Lincoln
TL	Timothy Loomis
TL	Tobias Livingston
TN	Thomas Needham
WA	William Axson, Jr.
WL	William Libby
WL	William Little
WM	William Middleton
WP	Warwick Price
WS	William Sinclair
WS	William Singleton

The vast majority of initials found on American furniture were placed there by owners rather than makers. Nevertheless, among these there are always a few makers' marks. We have, accordingly, listed here unidentified initials encountered in the course of this study in the hope that they may, at some future time, be identified.

AG	sausage-turned ladder-back side chair
AS	banister-back side chair
AW/1830	Shaker work counter
BF	Queen Anne highboy
BH	Queen Anne bedstead
BK	Hepplewhite chest of drawers
DA	Queen Anne side chair
DR	Seventeenth-century blanket chest
ER	Federal tall case clock
GH	turned side chair
HY	Shaker washstand
IP	several pieces of Chippendale furniture
IW	vase-back side chair
JB	Classical mahogany games table
JNR	low-back Windsor armchair
JSP	Federal tall case clock
JT	ladder-back chair
MH	Federal blanket chest
MW	arrow-back rocking chair
MW	Hadley chest
PNW	continuous-arm Windsor
RD	late Classical pedestal-base table
RLG	William and Mary highboy
SB&SON	Empire chair
SH	Chippendale highboy
SI	William and Mary highboy
TH	Chippendale easy chair
WA	bow-back Windsor side chair
WCB	child's rocker
WH	Federal demilune card table
WH	Hepplewhite card table

SOURCES

The books and periodicals listed here are those cited as references following the entries in this book. They will provide further information on the careers of the listed craftsmen. In order to avoid needless prolixity, books that are frequently cited are referred to by the author's last name alone, or, in the absence of an author, by short title. For example, Robert Bishop's *Centuries and Styles of the American Chair, 1640–1970,* is listed as "Bishop." In the infrequent instances where more than one book by an author is referred to, a short title is added to the author's last name, as "Fales, *American Painted Furniture.*"

Periodicals are referred to by their popular names. The *Maine Antiques Digest,* for example, is known to all as *MAD* and *The Magazine Antiques* as *Antiques.* References within these periodicals may be to advertisements, auction reports, or articles. Because of limitations on space, it is not possible to list the article titles and authors of the numerous valuable studies that have appeared, particularly in *The Magazine Antiques.* However, we wish to acknowledge our gratitude to the many students of American furniture who have authored these often important contributions to the history of the field.

BOOKS

Bishop, Robert. *Centuries and Styles of the American Chair, 1640–1970.* New York: E. P. Dutton, 1972.

Bivins, John, Jr. *The Furniture of Coastal North Carolina, 1700–1850.* Winston-Salem, N.C.: Museum of Early Southern Decorative Arts, 1988.

Bjerkoe, Ethel Hall. *The Cabinetmakers of America: Their Lives and Works.* Garden City, N.Y.: Doubleday, 1957.

Comstock, Helen. *American Furniture.* New York: Bonanza Books, 1962.

———. *The Looking Glass in America, 1700–1825.* New York: Viking Press, 1964.

Cooper, Wendy A. *In Praise of America: American Decorative Arts, 1650–1830.* New York: Alfred A. Knopf, 1980.

Currier Gallery of Art. *The Decorative Arts of New Hampshire, 1725–1825.* Manchester, N.H., 1964.

Downs, Joseph. *American Furniture: Queen Anne and Chippendale Periods.* New York: Bonanza Books, 1952.

Elder, William Voss, III, and Jayne E. Stokes. *American Furniture 1680–1880 from the Collection of the Baltimore Museum of Art.* Baltimore, Md.: Baltimore Museum of Art, 1987.

Fairbanks, Jonathan L., and Elizabeth Bidwell Bates. *American Furniture 1620 to the Present.* New York: Richard Marek, 1981.

Fales, Dean A. *Essex County Furniture: Documented Treasures from Local Collections, 1660–1860.* Salem, Mass.: Essex Institute, 1965.

———. *American Painted Furniture, 1660–1880.* New York: Bonanza Books, 1986.

Fales, Dean A. *The Furniture of Historic Deerfield.* New York: E. P. Dutton, 1976.

Fitzgerald, Oscar P. *Three Centuries of American Furniture.* New York: Gramercy, 1982.

Gusler, Wallace B. *Furniture of Williamsburg and Eastern Virginia, 1710–1790.* Richmond: Virginia Museum, 1979.

Hageman, Jane Sikes. *Ohio Furniture Makers, 1790 to 1845,* Vol. I. Privately published, 1984.

———. *Ohio Furniture Makers, 1790 to 1860,* Vol. II. Privately published, 1989.

Heckscher, Morrison H. *American Furniture in the Metropolitan Museum of Art, II: Late Colonial Period, The Queen Anne and Chippendale Styles.* New York: Random House, 1985.

Hewitt, Benjamin H., Patricia E. Kane, and Gerald W. R. Ward. *The Work of Many Hands: Federal Card Tables, 1790–1820.* New Haven, Conn.: Yale University Art Gallery, 1982.

Hinckley, F. Lewis. *A Dictionary of Antique Furniture.* New York: Bonanza Books, 1953.

Hornor, William MacPherson, Jr. *Hornor's Blue Book of American Furniture.* Washington, D.C.: Highland House, 1935, 1977.

Hummel, Charles F. *A Winterthur Guide to American Chippendale Furniture: Middle Atlantic and Southern Colonies.* New York: Rutledge Books/Crown, 1976.

Jobe, Brock, and Myrna Kaye. *New England Furniture: The Colonial Era.* Boston: Houghton Mifflin, 1984.

Kanc, Patricia E. *300 Years of American Seating Furniture.* Boston: New York Graphic Society, 1976.

Kenney, John Tarrant. *The Hitchcock Chair.* New York: Clarkson N. Potter, 1971.

Lovell, Margaretta M. *Boston Blockfront Furniture.* In Vol. 48, Publications of the Colonial Society of Massachusetts, Boston, 1974.

Made in Ohio: Furniture, 1788–1888. Columbus: Columbus Museum of Art, 1984.

Monkhouse, Christopher, and Thomas E. Michie. *American Furniture in Pendleton House.* Providence: Museum of Art, Rhode Island School of Design, 1986.

Montgomery, Charles F. *American Furniture, The Federal Period, 1785–1825.* New York: Viking Press, 1966.

Ormsbee, Thomas H. *The Windsor Chair.* New York: Deerfield Books, Harthside Press, 1962.

Piorkowski, Patricia A. *Piedmont Virginia Furniture: Product of Provincial Cabinetmakers.* Lynchburg, Va.: Lynchburg Fine Arts Center, 1982.

Plain and Ornamental: Delaware Furniture, 1740–1890. Wilmington: Historical Society of Delaware, 1984.

Randall, Richard H., Jr. *American Furniture in the Museum of Fine Arts, Boston.* Boston: Museum of Fine Arts, 1965.

Rieman, Timothy D., and Jean M. Burks. *The Complete Book of Shaker Furniture.* New York: Harry N. Abrams, 1993.

Robinson, Charles A. *Vermont Cabinetmakers Before 1855: A Checklist.* Shelburne, Vt.: Shelburne Museum, 1994.

Santore, Charles. *The Windsor Style in America, 1730–1830.* Philadelphia: Running Press, 1981.

Santore, Charles. *The Windsor Style in America, 1730–1840.* Vol. II. Philadelphia: Running Press, 1987.

Scherer, John L. *New York Furniture at the New York State Museum.* Alexandria, Va.: Highland House, 1984.

Schiffer, Margaret. *Furniture and Its Makers of Chester County, Pennsylvania.* Exton, Pa.: Schiffer, 1966.

Sikes, Jane E. *The Furniture Makers of Cincinnati, 1790–1849.* Cincinnati: The Merten Company, 1976.

Sprigg, June. *Shaker Design.* New York: W. W. Norton, 1986.

Tracy, Barry B. *Federal Furniture and Decorative Arts at Boscobel.* New York: Harry N. Abrams, 1981.

Williams, Derita Coleman, and Nathan Harsh. *The Art and Mystery of Tennessee Furniture and Its Makers Through 1850.* Nashville: Tennessee Historical Society, 1988.

PERIODICALS

American Collector
American Antiques Review (Ohio Antiques Review)
Antiques & The Arts Weekly (The Bee)
Antiques Collecting
Christie's Auction Gallery catalogs
The Magazine Antiques (Antiques)
Maine Antiques Digest (MAD)
New York–Pennsylvania Collector
Skinner Auction Gallery catalogs
Sotheby's Auction Gallery catalogs

ACKNOWLEDGMENTS

This book has been more than twenty years in preparation, and many people have contributed to the project. Dr. Robert Bishop conceived it and he, along with Katherine B. Hagler, did the initial research. I wish to thank the following institutions that so generously provided them with photographs and information:

The Brooklyn Museum, the Cincinnati Art Museum, Colonial Williamsburg, Cooper Union, the Diplomatic Reception Rooms, the Henry Ford Museum, the Honolulu Academy of Arts, the Metropolitan Museum of Art, the Monmouth County Historical Association, the Munson, Williams Proctor Institute, the Newark Museum, the Smithsonian Institution, the United States Department of State, the University of Nebraska, and the White House Collection.

Among the many individuals and dealers who have contributed images, we wish to particularly thank the premier American firms of Bernard and S. Dean Levy, Inc., and Israel Sack, Inc., both of which have provided me with photographic material and consultation. Other contributors include the magazine *Antiques;* Bider's Auction Gallery; Bradford Galleries; E. T. Canton; Curran & Curran, Inc.; Gary Davenport; Jacqueline and Frank Donegan; the Dubrow Collection; James E. Elliott Antiques; Estate Antiques; Mrs. Dean A. Fales, Jr.; Donald L. Fennimore; Peter Hill; the Hitchcock Chair Company; Richard W. Howland; Index of American Design; Leigh Keno; Nathan Liverant & Son; George Michael; Neal Auction Company; Osona Auctioneers; C. L. Prickett; Frank and Barbara Pollock; H. & R. Sandor, Inc.; Skinner, Inc.; David Stockwell; and John S. Walton, Inc.

The Museum of American Folk Art staff and Director Gerard C. Wertkin have been supportive in every way; and I particularly want to thank the following graduate students in the Folk Art Institute Program who have devoted many hours to the research and the seeking out of images for use in this book: Joan Bloom, Jennifer Brody, William Brooks, Suzanne Demish, Dodie Doheney, Juliette V. Ibelli, Linda Moore, Joan Pearlman, and Patricia Wells. Their help is greatly appreciated.

INDEX

Italicized page numbers indicate illustrations that appear on a page different from their citation in the text.

A